D1084740

ISLAM AND THE ABOLITION OF SLAVERY

Dedicated to the memory of my father
Jack Clarence Smith

'Does man not have hard service on earth? Are not his days like those of a hired man, or a slave longing for the evening shadows?' (Job 7:1–2)

William Gervase Clarence-Smith

Islam and the Abolition of Slavery

OXFORD

UNIVERSITY PRESS

2006

OXFORD
UNIVERSITY PRESS

Oxford University Press, Inc., publishes works that further
Oxford University's objective of excellence
in research, scholarship, and education.

Oxford   New York
Auckland   Cape Town   Dar es Salaam   Hong Kong   Karachi
Kuala Lumpur   Madrid   Melbourne   Mexico City   Nairobi
New Delhi   Shanghai   Taipei   Toronto

With offices in
Argentina   Austria   Brazil   Chile   Czech Republic   France   Greece
Guatemala   Hungary   Italy   Japan   Poland   Portugal   Singapore
South Korea   Switzerland   Thailand   Turkey   Ukraine   Vietnam

Published by Oxford University Press, Inc.
198 Madison Avenue, New York, New York 10016
www.oup.com

Oxford is a registered trademark of Oxford University Press

Library of Congress cataloging-in-publication data is available

ISBN 13: 978-0-19-522151-0
ISBN 10: 0-19-522151-6

1 3 5 7 9 8 6 4 2

Printed in India on acid-free paper

CONTENTS

v

MAPS

PREFACE AND ACKNOWLEDGEMENTS

Various streams of experience flowed together in the making of this book. In personal terms, I often found myself close to the historical frontiers of the abode of Islam, through my birth in Gujarat, as a child in Eritrea, as a youth in Cameroun, in my first teaching job in Zambia, and carrying out research in Sumatra and the Moluccas. These were areas where countless multitudes passed into servitude over the centuries. In the course of my academic career, I gradually taught more about Islam, initially focusing on Africa and the Near East, and later exploring Southeast, East and Inner Asia. Research on the Hadhrami diaspora brought Arabia and South Asia into the frame.

Attending a landmark conference in Nantes, organised by the late Serge Daget in 1985, stimulated a shift in my existing interest in slavery, from Christendom to Islamdom. Scholars are increasingly integrating Islam into the immense body of writings on world slavery, throwing up intriguing problems of comparison. Controversies rage regarding the place of women in Islam, raising the issue of the distinctiveness of servile experiences. Fierce polemics between faiths seize repeatedly upon the emotive issue of slavery, in a context of competition for converts, bloody communal clashes, and the spectre of global religious conflict.

All this gelled when Gwyn Campbell invited me to comment on papers treating the Islamic factor in Indian Ocean and Asian slavery, at an Avignon conference in 2000. I was studying Muslim reformers in Southeast Asia for a new undergraduate course at the time, and the potential connections with abolition struck me forcefully. My focus widened to the entire Islamic world for an inaugural lecture in January 2002, to mark my promotion to a personal chair in the economic history of Asia and Africa. Revising that lecture for publication, I collected so much material that I decided to attempt a more substantial publication.

Primary research on this topic would require a knowledge of a forbidding multitude of tongues, not to mention several lifetimes of study. Fortunately, scholars have made their detailed regional findings increasingly accessible over the years. Many of them, including the readers of my first draft, have generously provided me with further information. I crave pardon from anybody whom I have inadvertently failed to mention below, and stress my responsibility for all remaining errors and omissions. These are bound to be numerous, for I am acutely aware of my temerity in trying to cover 14 centuries of global history.

Among general historians of servitude, Sue Miers presented me with a copy of her book, and discussed aspects of twentieth-century slavery. Olivier Pétré-Grenouilleau let me see the draft of his forthcoming book in electronic format, and commented on a summary of my inaugural lecture. David Eltis and Stan Engerman sent me their draft introduction for a forthcoming volume of the Cambridge History of Slavery series. Joe Miller commented on my attempts at quantification.

In attempting to understand slavery in Islam, I benefited from discussions with Michael Brett, Ulrike Freitag, and Peter Riddell. Amal Ghazal allowed me to cite an unpublished paper, commented on one of mine, summarised fatwas, and helped me to clarify my ideas. Laila Moustafa provided me with documents. Ehud Toledano warned me against attempting so ambitious a project, and pointed out a daunting number of pitfalls. Further help came from Ben Braude, Faisal Devji, Dahlia Gubara, Muhammad Masud, Ruud Peters, Olivier Roy, and Elizabeth Sirriyeh.

For the Arab world, Gerald Hawting made suggestions on the early Islamic phase. Martin Kramer sent me some crucial documents, and pointed me to a web site. Ismael Musah Montana let me quote his unpublished paper on Tunisia, and Kristina Richardson did likewise for Iraq. Mona Abaza provided an issue of *al-Manar*, translated for me by Ashraf ul-Hoque. Riad Nourallah summarised passages from 'Abduh's commentary on the Quran. Youssef Choueiri gave me the gist of a passage from Sayyid Qutb, and Bernard Haykel expounded on aspects of Zaydi law. I gleaned further elements from Sebastian Balfour, Jamila Bargach, Michael Cook, Paul Dresch, Daniel Duran, Mike Feener, Hala Fattah, Bernard Freamon, David Gutelius, Jane Hathaway, Shamil Jeppie, Albertine Jwaideh, John King, Keiko Kiyotaki, Joshua Teitelbaum, Bob Tignor, and Mahmoud Yazbak.

Marie Miran made many suggestions for Sub-Saharan Africa, and Roger Botte plied me with materials. Zekeria Ould Ahmed Salem allowed me to cite his forthcoming article on Mauritania, and Mark

Smith sent a transcript of Northern Nigerian assembly debates. Taj Hargey allowed me to quote from his thesis on the Sudan, and Jonathan Miran sent me a copy of his thesis on Massawa, together with Italian materials. Richard Gray supplied a chapter from a forthcoming edited collection, and David Robinson did likewise for a recent book. Succour also came from Anne Bang, Cedric Barnes, Ismaël Barry, Odile Goerg, Abdulrazak Gurnah, Christine Hardung, Constance Hilliard, Jan Hogendorn, Martin Klein, Roman Loimeier, Xavier Luffin, Ghislaine Lydon, Abdullahi an-Na'im, Beatrice Nicolini, Arye Oded, Lamin Sanneh, Shobana Shankar, and Farouk Topan.

My forays into the Caucasus and the Turkic world were steered by conversations with Ben Fortna. Adeeb Khalid gave me the gist of an Uzbek text, Ahmet Kanlidere translated selections from Tatar originals, and Scott Levi provided me with his article on West Turkistan. For Turkey, Deniz Kandiyoti and Ferhunde Özbay sent me their articles, Yucel Yanikdag photocopied a document for me, and Gulay Yarikkaya allowed me to cite an unpublished paper. Anna Zelkina and Michael Kemper instructed me on the Caucasus, while Nathalie Clayer suggested materials for the Balkans. I also obtained advice from Virginia Aksan, Ali Akyildiz, Palmira Brummett, Hakan Erdem, Caroline Finkel, Alan Fisher, Allen Frank, Colin Imber, Hasan Kayali, Leslie Peirce, Kevin Reinhart, Florian Riedler, Stanford Shaw, Vahram Shemmassian, Derin Terzioglu, Brian Williams, and Galina Yemelianova.

For Iran, Ina Baghdiantz McCabe sent me the typescript of a forthcoming major study on Safavid élite slavery, with the permission of her co-authors, Susan Babaie, Kathryn Babayan, and Massumeh Farhad. Behnaz Mirzai permitted me to cite her unpublished paper, and scrutinised a draft chapter. Vanessa Martin passed on some archival materials, and discussed the issue at length. More assistance came from Willem Floor.

I consulted Avril Powell on South Asian matters from an early date, and borrowed readings from her. She allowed me to refer to a chapter in her forthcoming book, so that I profited from the work of S. J. Qadri, her collaborator in translating Urdu texts. Claudia Preckel filled me in on matters South Asian and literalist, and provided me with a fatwa. Alan Guenther, Shireen Moosvi, and Jan-Peter Hartung sent me various materials. I was further aided by Jamal Elias, Marc Gaborieau, Siobhan Lambert-Hurley, Jamal Malik, Barbara Metcalf, Margrit Pernau, Francis Robinson, and Shabnum Tejani.

For Southeast Asia, Albert Dekker transcribed materials, and helped with bibliography and internet sites. Nur Ichwan and Howard Federspiel sent extracts from Indonesian publications, and Mike Laffan checked works in Leiden. Mason Hoadley allowed me cite an unpublished paper on Java, while Heather Sutherland shared her long experience of the topic. Help also came from Barbara Andaya, Martin van Bruinessen, Joep à Campo, Peter Carey, Erwiza Erman, Greg Fealy, John Gullick, Muhammad Hisyam, Virginia Hooker, Tony Johns, Nico Kaptein, Johan Meuleman, Laurent Metzger, Tony Reid, Michael Salman, Karel Steenbrink, and Esther Velthoen.

In an East Asian context, Laura Newby guided me through the complexities of East Turkistan, commented on a preliminary draft, and summarised an article in Chinese. Further assistance was forthcoming from Jackie Armijo-Hussein, David Atwill, Michael Dillon, Raphael Israeli, Jonathan Lipman, Jianping Wang, Jake Whittaker, and Sean Yom.

In regard to Islam in the West, Eric Germain alerted me to the Woking connection in England, and sent me writings by Western Muslims. Paul Lovejoy steered me towards internet resources, and made available proofs of an edited collection. Manolo Florentino, João Reis, and Tufy Cairus succoured me in matters Brazilian. Munawar Karim, Nancy Naro, and Robert Slenes provided me with other elements.

From a comparative religion perspective, I learned much on Judaism from Daniel Schroeter and Jonathan Schorsch. Claude Prudhomme filled gaps on the Catholic side, while David Appleyard and Yoseph Mengistu searched for materials pertaining to the Ethiopian Orthodox Church. Daniel Fields, Daniel Brouwer, Richard Hellie, and Geoffrey Hosking oriented me for the Russian Orthodox Church, while Hans-Heinrich Nolte advised me on Old Believers. Victor van Bijlert, Indrani Chatterjee, Gyan Prakash, and Sheldon Pollock helped with Hinduism. Murari Kumar Jha covered both Hindus and Jains, while Lars Laamann piloted me through Confucian complexities.

I owe a particular debt to librarians. This book is largely a product of materials held by my own institution, the School of Oriental and African Studies. I turned to Peter Colvin for Islam and the Middle East, Barbara Turfan for Africa, Nick Martland for South and Southeast Asia, and Sue Small for China. Annabel Gallop, of the British Library, looked out for Indonesian materials, and the personnel of the Woking Mosque gave me the opportunity to glance through their collection. I further thank the library staff of the London School of Economics and Political Science, the Institute of Historical Research, Senate House, University of London, and the University of California at Irvine.

Special appreciation is reserved for authors who have prepared a decent index, or had one compiled for them. This has proved vital to the extensive browsing necessary for a broad synthesis of this type. Indexes, when present at all, are often perfunctory, limited to proper names, or set out in separate lists. It is thus a real joy to come across a good one.

My thanks are further due to those who helped with my inaugural lecture. Patrick O'Brien, my mentor in global history for many years, introduced me with kind words. Colin Bundy presided magisterially, and Mary O'Shea worked her usual magic behind the scenes. It was gratifying to see many colleagues and students, former and actual, together with loyal family and friends. Among the latter was my late father, already in poor health, to whom this book is dedicated.

Andrew Osmond and Michael Dwyer encouraged me to turn the lecture into a book. Kazuko Tanaka lent a helping hand at crucial moments, and Sarah and Keiko put up cheerfully with the strains of writing. Keiko also made valuable suggestions on redrafting the introduction.

London, June 2005   W.G.C.-S.

ABBREVIATIONS, DATES, SPELLINGS, GLOSSARY, SCRIPTURAL REFERENCES

Abbreviations

b. = bin [son of; Ibn if used as the first part of a name]
c. = circa [about]
d. = died
ed. = edited
edn = edition
n.d. = no date
n.p. = no place
n. pub. = no publisher
pl. = plural
r. = ruled
tr. = translated

Dates

Common Era (CE) dates are used throughout. For correspondence between CE and Islamic (AH) dates, see Hodgson 1974: I, 20–2.

Spellings and translations

Islamic expressions considered to have entered the English language are not italicised, although they are explained in the glossary below. They are given English plurals, except for ulama, a plural noun.

Ayn (') and *hamza (')*, rasp and stop, are both represented by the appropriate curved apostrophe. Other diacritics are generally omitted.

Turkish s-cedilla is written sh, as are words in Indian languages pronounced like the English sh.

Pinyin romanisation is used for Chinese whenever possible.

English translations from other languages are my own.

Glossary

'alim	expert in the holy law (pl. ulama)
ayatollah	spiritual leader of Shi'i Islam, literally 'sign of God'

caliph (*khalifa*)	supreme religious and political leader
Dalit	pariah, untouchable, scheduled or Harijan castes
devshirme	tax in slave youths
emir (*amir*)	ruler; governor; military commander
fatwa (pl. *fatawa*)	opinion on an aspect of the holy law
Hadith	sayings or deeds of the Prophet and his Companions
harem (*harim*)	secluded quarters for women of a household
Imam	supreme religious and political leader, Shi'i and Khariji
jahiliyya	state of ignorance, prior to Islam or among the infidel
jihad	striving in the path of God; holy war
khan	ruler; governor; military commander
madrasa	educational establishment at secondary or tertiary level
Mahdi	millenarian leader
mamluk	military slave
muezzin	person who calls the faithful to prayer
mufti	person who delivers opinions on aspects of the holy law
mujtahid	interpreter of the holy law, usually Shi'i
polygyny	marrying more than one wife
qadi	judge in a sharia court
Quran (*Qur'an*)	Revelations of God to the Prophet Muhammad
Sayyid	descendant of the Prophet through Husayn
scriptuaries	Christians, Jews, and other 'people of the book'
sharia (*shari'a*)	the holy law of Islam
Sharif	descendant of the Prophet through Hasan
shaykh	mystical or tribal leader
Shaykh al-Islam	chief mufti of a state
Sufi	Islamic mystic
ulama, see *'alim.*	

Scriptural references

For the Quran, all quotes are from J. Arberry, *The Koran interpreted*, Toronto: Macmillan. 1969. Verse numbers follow <http://cwis.usc. edu/dept/MSA/quran/>

For the Bible, Old and New Testament, all quotes are from *The Holy Bible, New International Version*, 1991, London: Hodder and Stoughton, 1991.

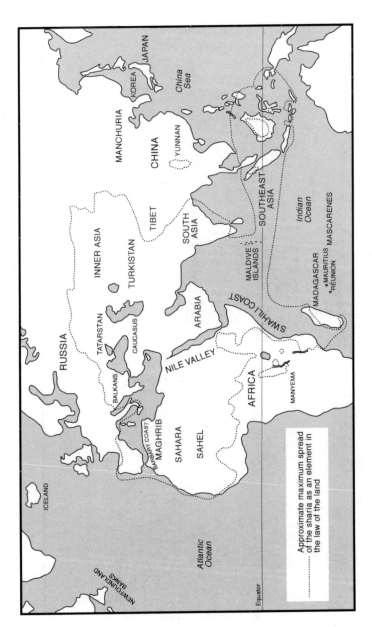

The 'Abode of Islam'

The Western Mediterranean

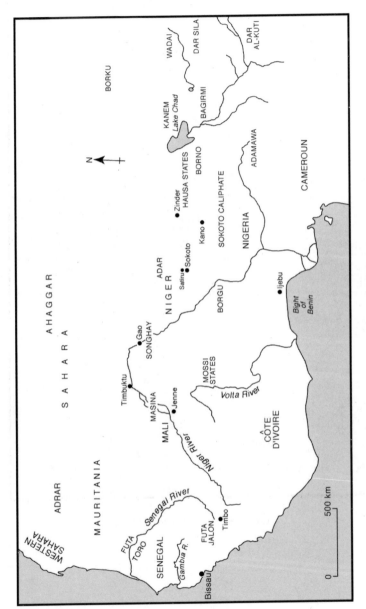

West Africa and the Sahara

xix

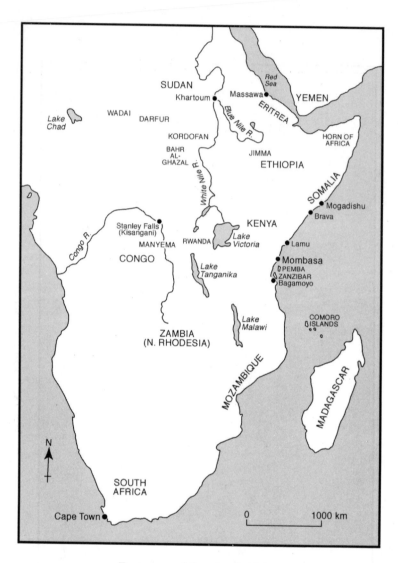

Eastern and Southern Africa

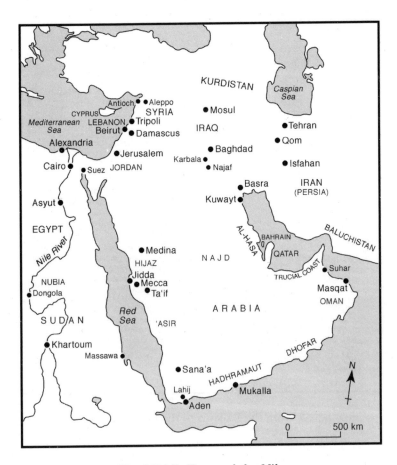

The Middle East and the Nile

From the Balkans to the Caucasus

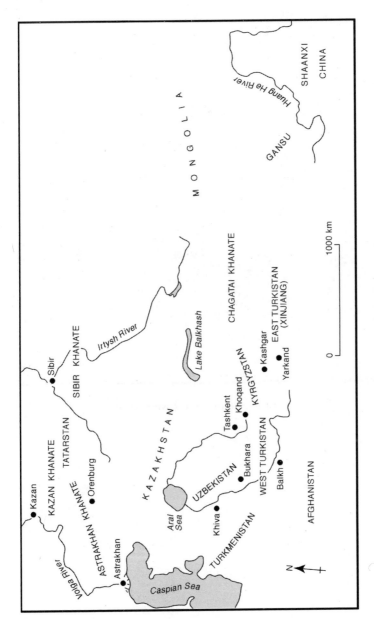

Turkistan, Tatarstan and Northwest China

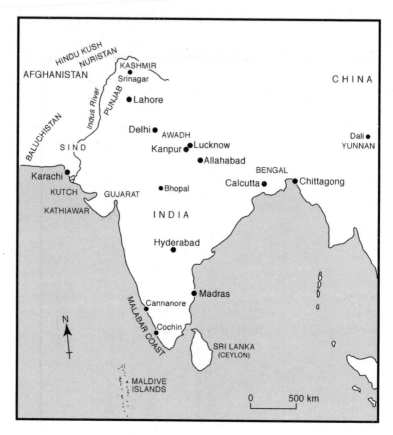

South Asia and Southwest China

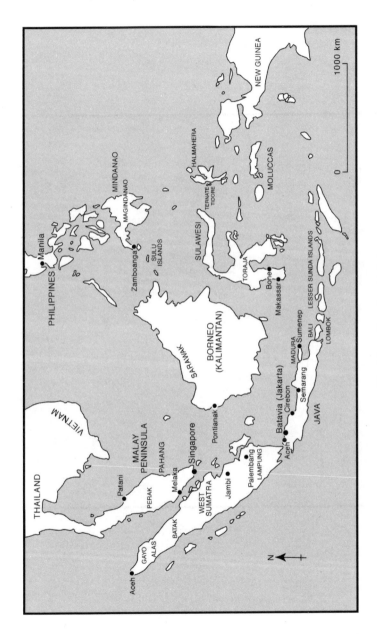

Maritime Southeast Asia

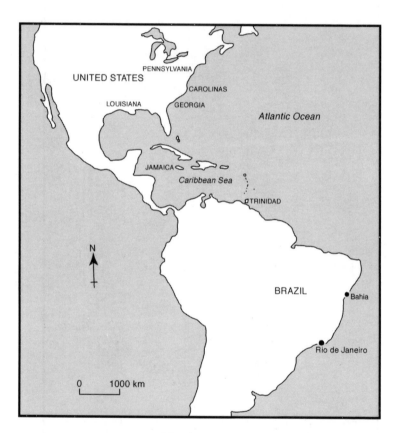

The Americas

1

INTRODUCTION

THE EMBARRASSING INSTITUTION

Slavery is a topic that all too often encourages silence, for, as Orlando Patterson acutely observes, it is not so much 'the peculiar institution' as 'the embarrassing institution'.[1] Echoing this notion in the title of his book, Michael Salman adds that accusations of slavery are 'a lasting source of anxiety' for all civilisations.[2] Mortified that slavery should have persisted in mediaeval Christendom, some European writers have blamed Islamic influences.[3] Muslim writers, for their part, often display intense unease that Islam accepted slavery for so long, without any mass movement emerging to advocate abolition.[4] Intellectual paralysis springs from a contradictory desire to condemn slavery and spare Islam.[5] Learned authors expatiate at length on political emancipation, free will, and 'slavery to God', without breathing a word about the social realities of servitude.

Another way to avoid the problem is to treat slavery as 'the modern world's trope for impermissible forms of domination'.[6] Hamdan b. 'Uthman Khoja declared in 1833 that he could see 'the English government make its glory immortal by the emancipation of the Negroes', at the very time that Algeria was being enslaved by 'free France'. He did not mention Christian slaves in Algiers, used as a justification for the French invasion.[7] Similarly, delegates from 33 countries at the sixth World Muslim Congress, meeting in Moga-

---

[1] Patterson 1982: ix.
[2] Salman 2001: 14.
[3] Heers 1981: 10–14.
[4] Hassan 2000: 244; an-Na'im 1998.
[5] Erdem 1996: xvii–xix; Hamel 2002: 29–30; Hunwick and Powell 2002: ix–x; Gordon 1989: xi.
[6] Salman 2001: 266.
[7] Holsinger 1994: 11.

1

dishu in 1964–5, agreed that, 'as followers of Islam, they could have no truck with any kind of colonialism, imperialism or slavery, for according to Islam all these are crimes against humanity'. However, they apparently failed to consider slavery in Islam.[8] Such myopia, equally manifest in the nineteenth-century Ottoman élite, had close parallels in the West. Thomas Jefferson, the American 'apostle of liberty', himself owned slaves.[9]

To understand how slavery ended in Islam, its fundamental characteristics first need to be grasped. An analysis of types of slavery, together with modes of acquiring people, points to many characteristics shared with servitude in other civilisations, despite some marked peculiarities. A preliminary and tentative stab at quantification further shows that slavery in Islam was on a grand scale. Conjectures as to how abolition came about are mixed, and the central suggestion made here is that Islam played a neglected role in the process.

The nature of slavery in Islam

Problems of definition in the Islamic world mainly arose where customary law was strong, generating complex and conflicting gradations of servitude.[10] In contrast, wherever the sharia, the holy law of Islam, predominated, the definition of slavery was simple and precise. Slaves were chattels, similar to livestock in many respects, and yet they possessed certain carefully circumscribed rights, arising from their undeniable humanity. They were not slaves because they were 'outsiders', although many happened to be in that category, but because they were born as slaves, or had been rightfully enslaved.[11]

Despite this clear legal definition, slaves were allocated a bewildering variety of social roles, from emirs to outcasts. This has hindered both scholarly generalisation and common feeling between former slaves and their descendants, who have rarely coalesced into combative associations.[12] Rulers relied on military and administrative slaves to such a degree that they sometimes seized power.[13] Eunuchs were trusted as officials and harem guards because their genitals had been partially or entirely removed, so that they could

[8] Khan 1965.
[9] Toledano 1998: 128.
[10] Fisher 2001: 54–9; Sy 2000: 46–7; Lombard 1990: II, 144–50; Reid 1993: 67; Matheson and Hooker 1983.
[11] Brunschvig 1960.
[12] Toledano 1998: 158.
[13] Miura and Philips 2000; Pipes 1981.

have no heirs.[14] Singing-girls also exerted considerable sway, even over caliphs.[15] If a concubine bore a son for a mighty man, she could wield immense influence, especially after her master's death.[16] Indeed, the early-seventeenth-century Ottoman Turkish empire was called the 'sultanate of the women', or the 'sultanate of the African eunuchs'.[17]

The brilliant careers of élite slaves have fascinated historians and novelists for centuries, but they obscure the experience of the vast majority. Youths for military duties were subjected to forced transportation, made to forget their homelands, and sometimes denied a family life. The lives of many common soldiers were nasty, brutish, and short.[18] Some were 'virtually cannon fodder'.[19] For every successful eunuch, many others died from castration, and survivors endured complex physical and mental consequences.[20] Singing-girls were as much prostitutes as courtesans.[21] Enforced sexual continence was the lot of discarded and neglected sexual partners in large harems, while the bondmaiden who attended to them faced both celibacy and drudgery.[22]

'Domestic slavery' is repeatedly said to have dominated servitude in Islam, but this misleading term conceals a range of productive tasks. These were already impressive in ninth-century Iraq.[23] Slaves of Inner Asian Turkmens had to 'watch the flocks, prepare the food, make felts, and weave carpets'.[24] Those belonging to South Asian Muslims performed a variety of outdoor tasks.[25] In Islamic Southeast Asia, slaves filled 'almost every conceivable function'.[26] A Malay master around 1900 expected slaves to 'plant his fields, weed and tend his crops, to wash and guard his kine [cattle], ... to punt his boat, to attend to him upon his journeys, to cook his rice, and to serve in his house'.[27] Similar lists of duties were recorded for East

---

[14] Juynboll 1912; Meinardus 1969; Hambly 1974; Marmon 1995.
[15] Jahiz 1980; Richardson 2004; Gordon 2001: 94, 134.
[16] Peirce 1993; Babaie *et al.* 2004
[17] Toledano 1998: 44.
[18] Gordon 2001: 74, 79, 143–4, 148–9; Pipes 1981: 90–2, 97–9; Crone 1980: 79.
[19] Risso 1995: 16.
[20] Hogendorn 2000; Millant 1908.
[21] Richardson 2004.
[22] Peirce 1993: 138, 141–2; Elbashir 1983: 127; Gervaise 1971: 83–5; Montesquieu 1960: 241.
[23] Beg 1975: 110–17.
[24] Cumming 1977: 68.
[25] Adam 1840; Sarkar 1985: 101–3, 123; Nicolini 2002: 125; Burton 1973: 242, 253–4; Banaji 1933: 201; Hjejle 1967: 83–4.
[26] Reid 1993: 68.
[27] Clifford 1913: 123–4.

Africa.[28] Servile labour was common on medium and even small properties, and slaves were widely employed in irrigation, pastoralism, mining, transport, public works, proto-industry, and construction.[29]

It is particularly hazardous to generalise about treatment, because the voices of slaves have nearly always been obliterated from the historical record.[30] Islamic law strictly prohibited the molestation of dependants, but subordination in the protected sphere of the household made it hard to police transgressions.[31] A Hadith of the Prophet allowed for corporal punishment, and a widely quoted Arab proverb declared that 'slaves are beaten with a stick'.[32] Abu al-Faraj b. al-Jawzi (d. 1201) held that, 'it is incumbent upon a woman to endure her husband's mistreatment as a slave should'.[33]

While some sources depicted placid relations, others told much more sombre stories.[34] Of Istanbul in 1870, one observer noted that slaves 'pass through the hands of ten or twenty masters, who make them lead the life of cab-horses, beat them at intervals, and at last sell them'.[35] Unusually, quite a few slaves in the Barbary states of North Africa wrote down their experiences, leading historians to make comparisons with the Communist Gulag.[36] To take an extreme example, the ulama prohibited mutilating slaves or filing their teeth, on pain of severe penalties for owners and emancipation for slaves.[37] However, in the sixteenth-century, Barbary corsairs branded slaves on the soles of their feet, while Crimean Tatars marked their foreheads.[38] Nineteenth-century Egyptian owners marked the faces of slaves to deter fugitives, while Libyan Sufis burned the word 'Allah' on to their slaves.[39] Born slaves in northern Nigeria received facial scars of servitude as late as the 1950s.[40]

---

[28] Harries 1965: 207–8; Mirza and Strobel 1989: 30–9.
[29] Talbi 1981; Renault 1989.
[30] Heers 2003: 178–243.
[31] Hodgson 1974: I, 344.
[32] Awde 2000: 102; Rosenthal 1960: 95.
[33] Abou El Fadl 2001: 213.
[34] Adam 1840: 188, 192–3; Garnett 1891: II, 412–13; Maugham 1961: 167–71; Elbashir 1983: 127; Christelow 1985b: 67–70; Christelow 1994: 117–92; Hunwick and Powell 2002: 199–206.
[35] Hunwick and Powell 2002: 124.
[36] Davis 2003: 134.
[37] Meinardus 1969: 50–1; Letourneau 1897: 285; Brunschvig 1960: 27, 31; Hunwick and Powell 2002: 27–8; Salman 2001: 91.
[38] Clissold 1977: 1; Fisher 1972: 585.
[39] Elbashir 1983: 122; Triaud 1995: I, 224.
[40] Stilwell 1999: 174; Lovejoy 1981: 223.

The institution of slavery further depended on brutal raids, pathetic sales of destitute people, traumatic forced marches, dangerous sea journeys, and the demeaning routines of the slave market. There might be a temptation to dismiss eloquent nineteenth-century European denunciations as imperialist propaganda.[41] However, Islamic sources describe the same horrors and suffering. Ibn Battuta, the great Moroccan globe-trotter of the fourteenth-century, noted in a chilling passage that Hindu Kush 'means slayer of Indians, because the slave boys and girls who are brought from India die there in large numbers as a result of the extreme cold and the quantity of snow'.[42] Five centuries later, an African survivor graphically narrated different torments endured in crossing the Sahara.[43]

Slaves delivered their own verdict by engaging in rebellion, murder, sabotage and flight.[44] Rahaina, taken by the Prophet from the defeated Jewish Qurayza tribe, may have tried to poison her illustrious master, and in 644 a Persian slave assassinated 'Umar b. al-Khattab, one of the rightly-guided caliphs.[45] The Zanj rebellion in ninth-century Iraq was among the most impressive servile insurrections in world history.[46] Numbers of runaways were high, especially in harsh occupations such as diving for pearls in the Gulf.[47] In Turkey, badly treated slaves 'have often been known to set fire to the wooden houses of Stamboul'.[48]

The most striking indictment came as governments hesitated on the brink of ending the institution. From Senegal to the Philippines, a tidal wave of servile humanity simply headed for home, or for any kind of refuge. Contrary to the sage prognostications of experts, the exodus was joined by many concubines and household slaves born into servitude.[49] Several hundred thousand people decamped in French West Africa in 1905–6, making this 'one of the most significant slave revolts in history'.[50]

In short, this was recognisably the same institution as in other civilisations. Servitude sprang from coercion or destitution, turned

[41] Daniel 1966: 307–8.
[42] Battuta 1983: 178.
[43] Hunwick and Powell 2002: 199–206.
[44] Brunschvig 1960: 33; O'Shea 1947: 176; Inalcik 1997: 285.
[45] Gunasekara n.d.: 14; Ruthven 2000: 72, 293; Netton 1992: 252.
[46] Popovic 1976.
[47] Brunschvig 1960: 33.
[48] Hunwick and Powell 2002: 124.
[49] Baldé 1975: 212–13; Cooper 1980: 49–50, 179–80; Christelow 1985a: 120; Erdem 1996: 160–73; Panikkar 1989: 52; Bigalke 1983: 347; Salman 2001: 53, 74–84.
[50] Lovejoy 1983: 266–7.

human beings into things, and was often repressive and degrading. Some victims found kind owners, occupied tolerable social niches, or were manumitted at an age when they could still enjoy their freedom. A tiny handful of slaves reached dizzy social and political heights. Unless they could secure a meaningful form of liberation, however, their good fortune remained vulnerable to the whims of the free.

Rhythms of expansion and contraction

A libertarian whiff accompanied the birth of the new faith in early-seventh-century Arabia, but the legitimacy of slavery was only ever contested by scattered sects. The breathtaking scope and speed of early conquests generated a flood of cheap captives, from Iberia to Sind. Under the Abbasid dynasty from 750, Byzantine, Ethiopian, and Indian resistance hardened. Over-extended Arab armies also turned back from France, the Caucasus and the marches of China and Tibet.[51] However, the Abbasids obtained floods of European, Turkic, Indian, and African slaves through purchase and tribute, for 'everywhere in Islam the increase of commerce and monetization went together with an enormous increase in the trade and use of slaves'.[52] Advances in Sicily, Sardinia, Corsica and southern Italy also yielded fresh captives, notably after the sack of Rome in 827.[53]

In turn, the products of servile hands reached the far corners of the known world.[54] Estates existed in places, growing sugar, among other crops. This was despite traumas caused by slave uprisings, and despite respect for the land rights of smallholders who had submitted to the new rulers.[55] Moreover, servile labour was quite common on medium and small rural properties, notably in the western Mediterranean and in oasis cultivation.[56] In part, the ubiquity of slavery reflected the inadmissibility of serfdom and forced labour, which violated the rights of free believers and submissive infidels.[57]

The middle period of Islam, roughly from 1000 to 1500, witnessed a consolidation of slavery, as 'the stifling acceptance of the divi-

---

[51] Heers 2003; Hodgson 1974: I.
[52] Wink 1999: I, 98.
[53] Musca and Colafemmina 1989: 287, 290.
[54] Renault 1989: 43–8; Renault and Daget 1985: 62–5.
[55] Davis 1984: 7, 28; Hunwick 1992: 20–1; Inalcik 1979: 25, 30–4; Heers 2003: 219–43.
[56] Talbi 1981; Moroney 2003; Clissold 1977: 11; Verlinden 1955: 188–9; Brett 2001: 70.
[57] Pipes 1981: 98; Rosenthal 1960: 77–80.

sion of society into free men and unfree men made itself always felt'.[58] Marshall Hodgson suggested the paradox that, 'an egalitarian and socially mobile society seemed to require ... such a class to set off those who momentarily had risen to the top'.[59] Elite slavery became a menace to the integrity of public life, with concubines a parallel threat in the private sphere.[60] Productive slavery was embedded in enterprises of varying sizes, both urban and rural.[61] Among tasks routinely allocated to thirteenth-century slaves were 'the cultivation of estates' and 'the grazing of flocks'.[62] The attractions of servile labour grew in the thirteenth and fourteenth centuries, when Eurasian populations contracted owing to the Mongol fury and the Black Death.[63]

Despite hammer blows from the steppe, Islam enlarged its frontiers in this middle period. Animist Turkic tribes formed the initial threat, but they generally converted to Islam on crossing the pale, stimulating fresh bouts of conquest in Anatolia and northern India. The Mongols damaged Islamic prestige more severely in the mid-thirteenth-century, and only went over to Islam slowly and selectively. Nevertheless, the Golden Horde in the Volga basin embraced Islam in the early fourteenth-century, and exacted a heavy tribute in people and commodities from Russia and the Ukraine. Other western Mongols also opted for Islam, and helped to propel Muslim Turks into Anatolia and northern India.[64] Although the eastern Mongols plumped for Tibetan Buddhism, they employed numerous Muslim officials in China, giving rise to influential Islamic communities.[65]

Muslims failed to have it all their own way, however. Europeans went onto the offensive, reconquering Sicily in the eleventh-century and pressing down the Iberian peninsula. By the thirteenth-century, they had shifted the balance of war captives in their favour.[66] Iberians obtained footholds in the Maghrib from 1415, completed the occupation of Andalusia in 1492, and confronted Muslims with the unpalatable choice between conversion and expulsion.[67] The most

---

[58] Rosenthal 1960: 122.
[59] Hodgson 1974: II, 355.
[60] Crone and Cook 1977: 148.
[61] Lal 1994; Inalcik 1979; Inalcik 1997: 284–5; Fisher 1972: 584–5.
[62] Tusi 1964: 183.
[63] Hodgson 1974: II, 373; Furió: 19, 32.
[64] Hodgson 1974: II, 39–57, 532–74.
[65] Lipman 1997.
[66] Constable 1994: 234–5; Koningsveld 1995: 5, 15.
[67] Dozy 1913.

western Tatars came under a milder form of infidel rule, following Lithuania's conversion to Christianity and union with Poland in 1386.[68] Oyrat (Kalmyk) Mongols began to roll back the insecure Islamic frontier in the northern Chagatai khanate from the early fifteenth-century.[69] The advent of the Ming dynasty in China, in 1368, signalled the end of the Muslims' privileged position.[70]

Compensation for these reverses came from expansion in Southeast Asia and Africa. A mixture of peaceful conversion and local holy wars generated further throngs of slaves from the thirteenth-century, many of them locally employed. The spread of Islam under such conditions undermined the chances of restoring a single caliphate, promoted new languages of learning, and brought additional local customs into competition with the holy law. Muslims and non-believers intermingled in a complex mosaic, fostering the emergence of syncretic religious tendencies.[71]

'Gunpowder empires' renewed Islamic power on a more stable basis from the sixteenth-century, and extracted infidel captives on a grandiose scale.[72] Ensconced in Maghribi ports under Moroccan or Ottoman suzerainty, Barbary corsairs culled people from as far as the Newfoundland Banks and Iceland.[73] A Moroccan army crossed the Sahara in 1590–1, returning with many slaves, and Moroccan sugar plantations seemed poised to rival those of the West.[74] Muslim hosts nearly submerged Christian Ethiopia, and an Omani sea-borne empire took shape in the northwestern Indian Ocean.[75] The Ottomans took the Balkans and penetrated into Central Europe, only being checked at the gates of Vienna in 1529, and again in 1683.[76] Crimean Tatars, Ottoman vassals, sacked Moscow outside the Kremlin walls in 1571, and assiduously 'harvested' Christians.[77] Iranian Shi'i armies garnered more Christians from the Caucasus, while importing Africans and Indians.[78] The Mughals pressed further down into southern India than any preceding Muslim dynasty, flooding Inner Asia with Hindu captives.[79]

---

[68] Bohdanowicz 1942: 164–9.
[69] Golden 1992: 313–15.
[70] Israeli 1980: 82–3.
[71] Lovejoy 1983: 28–35; Ricklefs 1993: 3–21.
[72] Heers 2003: 21–3.
[73] Davis 2003; Monlaü 1964.
[74] Renault and Daget 1985: 30–2.
[75] Trimingham 1965: 77–96; Risso 1986.
[76] Inalcik 1997: 307–8.
[77] Williams 2001: 49–51; Hellie 1993: 290–1, 297; Inalcik 1997: 284–5.
[78] Babaie *et al.* 2004.
[79] Levi 2002.

These impressive achievements concealed structural weaknesses. Digesting new conquests proved unexpectedly difficult, as Christians and Hindus refused to convert.[80] The Mediterranean balance of power shifted further in favour of Europeans, whose bridgeheads in West Africa exported Muslim slaves to the Americas from around 1650.[81] Ethiopia reversed the tide of conquest in the late sixteenth-century, with some help from the Portuguese. The latter seized East Africa's Muslim city states, established Christian naval hegemony in the Indian Ocean, and contained the Omani challenge.[82] Moscow annexed the Tatar khanates of Kazan, Astrakhan, and Sibir between 1552 and 1598.[83] Combative Cossacks were settled on Islamic frontiers, and Tatars under Russian rule could no longer own Christian slaves after 1628.[84] Oyrat Mongols migrated westwards from 1608, displacing Muslim Tatars as far as the lower Volga.[85]

Unhappiness with slavery emerged in gunpowder empires, although the role of Islam in this process remains uncertain. Monarchs ruling over large and restive Hindu and Christian populations restricted methods of enslavement to prevent rebellions.[86] Military servitude decayed, as centralising rulers sought to end military usurpation and create modern armies. The training of free artisans undermined urban bondage, and some rural slaves blended into a free peasantry.[87] However, Ottoman probate records reveal a persistent pattern of middling rural properties with a few slaves.[88]

Falling behind Europe technologically in the eighteenth-century, gunpowder empires contracted or collapsed, causing the first significant crisis in the long history of slavery in Islam. Russian and Austrian armies advanced on the Black Sea, the former seizing the Crimea in 1783, while Manchu hosts encroached on East Turkistan from 1697. Maratha and British forces seized wide swathes of India, and Hindu Balinese and Protestant Dutchmen contested Muslim power in Java.[89] Economic decay hampered purchases, and high mortality, low fertility, and extensive manumission eroded existing stocks of slave.[90]

---

[80] Hodgson 1974: III, 59–133.
[81] Valensi 1969: 62–8; Colley 2002: 45; Lovejoy 2004: 15.
[82] Heers 2003: 33–7; Risso 1986.
[83] Golden 1992: 321–2, 329.
[84] Barrett 1999: 1–55; Hellie 1982: 73–4, 82.
[85] Golden 1992: 327.
[86] Ruthven 2000: 272; Erdem 1996: 19–20, 23, 30.
[87] Lal 1994: 96–104; Inalcik 1979: 41–2; Inalcik 1997: 125–6, 156, 284–5.
[88] Fisher 1980a: 32–40.
[89] Hodgson 1974: III, 134–61.
[90] Inalcik 1997: 284–5.

A dramatic nineteenth-century resurgence of slavery was driven by the production of export commodities, drawing Islam closer to New World models of servitude. On the supply side, holy wars from Senegal to Yunnan glutted markets with cheap captives. On the demand side, voracious capitalist requirements for raw materials pushed up commodity prices from the 1840s. Slaves of Muslim owners thus produced sugar, cotton, cloves, dates, sesame, coconuts, coffee, millet, wheat, and other cash crops, as well as pearls, gold, tin, copper, and salt. Slaves also grew foodstuffs, wove cloth, carried goods, crewed ships, and served in households.[91]

Small and medium proprietors acquired more slaves, anchoring the institution firmly in Muslim societies. During the Egyptian cotton boom of the 1860s and 1870s, triggered by the Civil War in the United States, even modest Egyptian peasants bought slaves. Apart from field work, they performed domestic tasks or corvée for the state, while Circassian concubines became status symbols.[92] Anatolian agrarian prosperity rested to some extent on Black and Circassian field slaves, and there was scarcely an Iraqi family or middling Muslim household in India without a slave.[93]

'Smallholder slavery' was generally most intense on the Islamic frontier. The upsurge in exports of pepper from North Sumatra depended on a mix of slaves and other workers.[94] Many Oromo in the Ethiopian kingdom of Jimma owned 'one or two' slaves, freeing owners to market coffee.[95] In the Gambia in 1869, where groundnut exports were expanding, 'as soon as each has been able to purchase a horse and a gun, [he] considers himself a warrior, lives by plunder and works his fields by the slaves he captures in his expeditions, and thinks it beneath his dignity to perform any work whatsoever, which is left to women and slaves'.[96]

The significance of this type of slavery reflected local modes of cultivation.[97] Datu Mandi of the southern Philippines explained in 1901 that it was women's agricultural skills that accounted for their high price, not their role as concubines.[98] A Dutch report of 1878

[91] Lovejoy 1983; Savage 1992; Mowafi 1981; Larguèche 2003; Clarence-Smith 1989; Carrère d'Encausse 1966; Warren 1981.
[92] Baer 1969: 163–6; Mowafi 1981: 13–14, 23–4; Beachey 1976a: 130–1; Cooper 1968: 8.
[93] Toledano 1993: 44; Erdem 1996: 53, 63–4; Douin 1936–41: III/2, 662; Sarkar 1985: 101–3, 123.
[94] Snouck Hurgronje 1906: I, 19–23.
[95] Lewis 1965: 66.
[96] Klein 1968: 68–9, 99.
[97] Binger 1891: 23–4.
[98] Salman 2001: 90–1.

described agricultural slaves growing rice in South Sulawesi as mere 'work animals'.[99] Fulbe (Fulani) notables in Futa Jalon, West Africa, declared that, 'God imposed work on our father Adam, but he made pagans, with thick skulls and strong arms, good only for working the land, and clearly destined to serve believers'.[100]

Productive servitude suddenly declined again in the Islamic world from the 1880s. The cost of coerced labour rose, just as free labour became more readily available and commodity prices stagnated or fell. Colonial regimes and independent Muslim states repressed slave raiding and trading, urged on by Western liberals and fledgling Islamic abolitionist movements. Holy wars ground to a halt, and slaves deserted en masse when officials ceased to return fugitives.[101]

Eradicating slavery completely proved harder, despite the steady growth of Islamic abolitionist sentiment. Several Muslim governments refused to endorse international agreements against slavery, co-ordinated by the League of Nations from 1926. The same problem arose with the United Nations' 1948 Universal Declaration of Human Rights, and its Supplementary Anti-Slavery Convention of 1956.[102] Even though slavery had become formally illegal everywhere in Islam by the early 1980s, the institution persisted clandestinely into the new millennium.[103]

Slave numbers

Patricia Risso's suggestion, that military slaves ran 'into the tens of millions', is perhaps more properly applicable to all slaves in the course of Islamic history.[104] Fragmentary and problematic figures, often based on informed guesses, can only suggest an order of magnitude, and a more thorough trawl would undoubtedly uncover additional information, even in secondary materials. The scope of the task is awesome, however, as the Muslim yoke, at one time or another, fell on almost every people in the Old World, from Siberia to South Africa, and from Iceland to New Guinea.

Ralph Austen originally proposed that 17,000,000 Black slaves crossed the Sahara, the Red Sea, and the Indian Ocean.[105] This was

[99] Sutherland 1983: 278–9.
[100] Baldé 1975: 198.
[101] Miers and Roberts 1988; Miers 2003.
[102] Awad 1966.
[103] Segal 2001; Bushell 2002.
[104] Risso 1995: 16.
[105] Austen 1987: 275.

criticised as excessive, and he later abstained from putting forward an overall figure.[106] Paul Lovejoy reworked the data to indicate that over 6,000,000 left between 650 and 1500, about 3,000,000 between 1500 and 1800, and around 2,000,000 in the nineteenth-century. The total came to some 11,500,000 human beings.[107]

Considerable numbers of Black slaves were retained by Muslim owners in and below the Sahara, with Lovejoy's 'East African coastal region' absorbing some 769,000 in the nineteenth-century.[108] Assuming that 10 to 15 per cent of the population were slaves in the nineteenth-century, Patrick Manning suggested that there were over three million in the 'Savanna and Horn', and nearly one and a half million on the 'Eastern Coast', both regions where Muslim owners were numerous.[109] His assumption seems conservative, however. A French census of 1904 reported servility rates of 30 to 50 per cent in Islamic West Africa, while an Italian census of 1903 classified about a quarter of the population of Somali towns as slaves.[110]

Turks, spanning a racial continuum from Mongoloid to Caucasoid, were probably roughly as numerous as Africans in the central lands of Islam from the ninth to the fourteenth-century, when supplies from the steppe dried up.[111] If this impression is at all accurate, several million Turks were imported, including a number of Iranian and Mongol peoples classified as such. Most Muslim chroniclers accepted that the Turkish military slave corps of the ninth-century caliphate numbered some 70,000, while a modern estimate, informed by archaeology, exceeds 100,000. Sizeable fresh imports were required to compensate for high mortality, many subordinate rulers owned their own soldiers, and steppe peoples were employed for other purposes.[112]

European slaves were also abundant. Egyptians, Syrians, Persians, Berbers, and Iberians were taken through conquest, and others were raided or purchased thereafter, so that they were only slightly less common than Africans and Turks up to 1500.[113] For later centuries, up to 1,250,000 Christian captives entered the Maghrib from 1530 to 1780, of whom under five per cent escaped or were

[106] Sheriff 1987: 33–41; Austen 1989; Austen 1992.
[107] Lovejoy 2000: 26, 47, 62, 142, 156. (Exports to the Mascarenes are excluded.)
[108] Lovejoy 2000: 156; Sheriff 1987: 60; Cooper 1977: 56.
[109] Manning 1990: 78, 81. See also Lovejoy 1983: 265.
[110] Lovejoy 2000: 192; Cassanelli 1988: 312.
[111] Lewis 1990: 55; Hodgson 1974: III, 32–3.
[112] Gordon 2001: 72–4.
[113] Sourdel 1985: 120; Lewis 1990: 55; Pipes 1981: 124, 142; Verlinden 1955: 201–2.

ransomed.[114] From 1520 to 1830, Algeria alone imported about 625,000.[115] The *devshirme* system of levies netted some 200,000 Balkan youths for the Ottomans between 1400 and 1650.[116] To this should be added an unknown tally of captives taken in Anatolian, Balkan, and Central European campaigns. The Ottomans allegedly seized 80,000 in 1683 alone, when attempting to take Vienna.[117] Russian captives long abounded in Turkistan and the Muslim North Caucasus.[118]

Lands to the north of the Black Sea probably yielded the most slaves to the Ottomans from 1450. A compilation of estimates indicates that Crimean Tartars seized about 1,750,000 Ukrainians, Poles, and Russians from 1468 to 1694.[119] Patchy sixteenth- and seventeenth-century Crimean export statistics indicate that around 10,000 slaves a year, including some Circassians, went to the Ottomans, suggesting a total of around 2,500,000 for 1450 to 1700.[120] Crimean Tatars took fewer slaves from 1694 to the Russian conquest of 1783, but their last raid was in 1774. The population of the khanate itself, around 400,000 at this time, included a high proportion of slaves.[121]

The densely populated Caucasus was a major source of White slaves for the Middle East. Circassians were superficially Christianised Animists, only converted to Islam between 1717 and the 1830s. Circassian military slaves dominated Egypt from 1382, and about 100 a year were still exported there in the late eighteenth-century, when the trade was long past its peak.[122] Persians relied heavily on Caucasus slaves, capturing 15,000 Georgians in a single campaign in 1795.[123] From 1800 to 1909, the Ottomans imported some 200,000 slaves from the Caucasus, mainly Circassians, with another 100,000 or so arriving with their Circassian masters in the 1850s and 1860s.[124] In a last gasp, up to 200,000 Armenian women and children may

---

[114] Davis 2003: 21, 23.
[115] Wolf 1979: 151.
[116] Sugar 1977: 56.
[117] Erdem 1996: 30.
[118] Burton 1998; Barrett 1999.
[119] Fisher 1972: 577–83, 592–3.
[120] Inalcik 1997: 285; Fisher 1972: 583–4.
[121] Williams 2001: 69–72.
[122] Jaimoukha 2001: 57, 149–52.
[123] Baghdiantz McCabe 1999: 38–46; Hambly 1991b: 583; Lang 1957: 218.
[124] Toledano 1982, 82, 90; Toledano 1993: 44; Erdem 1996: 118; Jaimoukha 2001: 69.

have been enslaved from 1915, as millions were driven from their homelands to perish in the Arabian deserts.[125]

Persian 'heretics' themselves were abundant in the Ottoman empire after 1500, and formed the majority in Turkistan by the nineteenth-century.[126] In the early 1840s, the Uzbek states of Bukhara and Khiva contained an estimated 900,000 slaves.[127] The total probably rose well above one million if the khanate of Khoqand was included, for slave numbers were expanding rapidly at the time.[128] In addition, Turkmen and Kazakh pastoralists owned many slaves.[129]

South Asian slaves were significant at an earlier date in Inner Asia and Persia. The conquest of Sind in 712–13 yielded 60,000, and the Ghaznavids of eleventh-century Afghanistan drove hundreds of thousands home.[130] The servile population of West Turkistan included many South Asians from at least 1326, and Indian slaves were routinely exchanged for Inner Asian horses.[131] In the late fourteenth-century, Timur the Lame killed a hundred thousand Indians captured before reaching Delhi, but still brought thousands back to West Turkistan.[132] As many as 200,000 Indian rebels were supposedly taken in 1619–20, for sale in Iran.[133] Indian slaves in East Turkistan raised diplomatic problems in the nineteenth-century.[134]

Slaves were copious in India itself, but distinguishing Muslim from non-Muslim owners is difficult. Sultan Alauddin Khalji (r. 1296–1316) possessed 120,000 personal slaves in North India, while his fourteenth-century successor, Sultan Firoz Tughluq, claimed to have 180,000.[135] Muslims owned many of the estimated 8,000,000 to 9,000,000 bondsmen in 1841, of whom about half were in the Bengal Presidency. However, most of these helots were probably Dalit castes in Hindu hands.[136]

An even smaller proportion of East Asia's teeming slaves belonged to Muslims. Hui, Chinese Muslims, bought several hundred thousand destitute children from the mid-seventeenth-century to

---

[125] Shemmassian 2003: 86, 95.
[126] Erdem 1996: 21; Levi 2002.
[127] Balfour 1885: III, 676.
[128] Scott Levi, personal communication.
[129] Cumming 1977; Olcott 1987.
[130] Lal 1994: 18–20, 23, 121–4.
[131] Levi 2002.
[132] Lal 1994: 56; Levi 2002: 278.
[133] Levi 2002: 283–4; Kolff 1990: 13–14.
[134] Skrine and Nightingale 1973.
[135] Lal 1994: 49–53.
[136] Balfour 1885: III, 676; Levi 2002; Hardinge 1928: 379; Chattopadhyay 1977: 251–2.

the mid-nineteenth-century, acquiring 10,000 as the result of a single famine in Shandong in 1790.[137] A trickle of Chinese captives also reached Turkistan well into the nineteenth-century.[138] Maritime exports of Chinese and Japanese girls grew from the late nineteenth-century, especially to Southeast Asia, for purchase by both Muslims and unbelievers.[139]

The archbishop of Manila claimed in 1637 that Moro raiders from the south had seized an average of 10,000 Catholic Filipinos a year over the previous 30 years. Descriptive materials indicate fairly steady raiding, which might thus have yielded a total booty of some two million slaves in the first two centuries of Spanish rule after 1565.[140] A shipping capacity calculation suggests that between 200,000 and 300,000 captives entered the Sulu sultanate from 1770–1870, lower than contemporary European estimates.[141] However, Spanish and Dutch naval patrols became more effective from the 1840s, leading Moros to seize unquantified numbers of Animists in inland Mindanao.[142]

Elsewhere in Southeast Asia, Muslims enslaved Hindus and Animists, and even fellow Muslims, from the thirteenth-century. Bali exported around 100,000 Hindu slaves from 1620 to 1830, and South Sulawesi exported another 100,000 between 1660 and 1810, mainly Muslims. Quite a few were acquired by Europeans and Chinese.[143] Supplies of Animists from Nias Island to Aceh from 1790 to 1900 may have amounted to around 50,000, while some 12,000 Toraja Animists were obtained in South Sulawesi from 1880 to 1905.[144] There are no figures for similar local trades from Animist uplands to Muslim lowlands, notably in Sumatra, Malaya, and Borneo. The proportion of slaves in nineteenth-century Muslim societies varied widely. Rare in Java in the 1810s, they accounted for 6 per cent in an 1879 census of the Malay sultanate of Perak, about a third in villages on the eastern edge of West Sumatra in the 1860s,

[137] Hartmann 1921: 100; Anderson 1876: 229.
[138] Laura Newby, personal communication.
[139] Miers 2003: 157–61; Lasker 1950: 52–5; Hane 2003: 208; Snouck Hurgronje 1923–24: II, 276–9.
[140] Reid 1983a: 32.
[141] Warren 1981: 208.
[142] Ileto 1971: 24–7
[143] Reid 1993: 69.
[144] Reid 1983a: 32; Anon. 1861: 335–6, 377; Snouck Hurgronje 1906: I, 20; Bigalke 1983: 347.

30 per cent in the Muslim zone of North Sulawesi, and two thirds or more in part of North Borneo in the 1880s.[145]

Orientalist contradictions

Western authors have generally supposed that Europeans imposed abolition on unwilling Muslims, and yet the late Edward Said remained curiously muted on this issue in his influential *Orientalism*. An American of Christian Palestinian origins, Said briefly lambasted Bernard Lewis, seen as an arch-Orientalist, for dwelling on Islam's 'racism, slavery and other more or less "Western" evils'. However, slavery did not make it to Said's index, and his citation of Chateaubriand's comment, that 'of liberty they know nothing', was not glossed in the light of social relations. There was a fleeting reference to slaves in Western sexual fantasies of the Orient, but no mention that Zaynab, Gérard de Nerval's 'Javanese' consort, was purchased in Cairo.[146]

For his part, Bernard Lewis wrote in the revised edition of his influential work on race and slavery in Islam: 'The abolition of slavery itself would hardly have been possible. From a Muslim point of view, to forbid what God permits, is almost as great an offense as to permit what God forbids—and slavery was authorised and regulated by the holy law. More specifically, it formed part of the central core of social usage'. This sweeping generalisation conflicts with an earlier warning against depicting a single Muslim point of view.[147]

Lewis did not innovate in taking this stance, for he echoed a host of earlier Western writers. Sir William Muir noted of the Prophet that, 'while lightening, he riveted the fetter'.[148] Étienne Berlioux opined that slavery was one with Islam.[149] Thomas Hughes thought that 'abolition would strike at the very foundations of the code of Muhammadanism'.[150] For Lucy Garnett, slavery was 'indispensable to the social system', based on the harem.[151] David Margoliouth even rashly asserted that 'the abolition of slavery was not a notion that ever entered the Prophet's mind'.[152] In the interwar years,

[145] Wertheim 1959: 241; Gullick 1958: 105; Dobbin 1983: 138; Ruibing 1937: 30.
[146] Said 1991: 182, 190, 294, 317–8; Nerval 1958: II, 194–5.
[147] Lewis 1990: 20, 78.
[148] DeJong 1934: 129.
[149] Berlioux 1870: 308.
[150] Hughes 1885: 600.
[151] Garnett 1891: II, 282–3.
[152] Margoliouth 1905: 461–2.

Robert Roberts declared, 'there is nothing whatever in Islam that tends to the abolition of this curse'.[153] Garrett DeJong considered that, 'the abolition of slavery would mean an upsetting of the entire system of Islam'.[154]

Even contemporary authors follow this line. John Hunwick and Eve Troutt Powell aver that, 'there was never any formal movement for the abolition of slavery, or even the suppression of the slave trade, in the Muslim world'.[155] Rodney Stark affirms that, 'the fundamental problem facing Muslim theologians vis-à-vis the morality of slavery is that Muhammad bought, sold, captured and owned slaves'.[156] Patricia Risso insists that, 'because the Qur'an sanctioned the institution of slavery, no human law could abolish it'.[157]

Historians of Africa and Southeast Asia concur. Paul Lovejoy maintains that 'strict adherence to law and tradition precluded any thought of abolition', while recognising the force of 'Islamic ideals' for reform.[158] Suzanne Miers and Richard Roberts argue that 'abolition ... was not an indigenous African concept. ... Full-scale abolition was a western European idea born of conflicts generated in the eighteenth-century and the expansion of capitalism'.[159] Anthony Reid considers that abolition had 'little to do with an increasingly sensitive moral conscience'.[160]

Dissenting voices arose early, even among Christian missionaries. Cardinal Charles Lavigerie, a doughty crusader against Islamic servitude, declared in 1888:

> The Quran does not enjoin slavery, but merely permits it. Indeed, the Quran goes further, because it places the liberation of captives at the top of the list of merciful deeds, through which believers may be worthy of heaven. Strictly speaking, nothing would prick the consciences of Muslims in the abolition of slavery. However, habits are there, and have acquired a sacred character through their very antiquity, so that one will not be able to get rid of them at once.

He went on to stress that Christianity had long faced the same problem, and sought to persuade enlightened Muslim monarchs to join

---

[153] Roberts 1925: 53.
[154] DeJong 1934: 143.
[155] Hunwick and Powell 2002: 181.
[156] Stark 2003: 338.
[157] Risso 1995: 94.
[158] Lovejoy 1981: 208; Lovejoy 1983: 264.
[159] Miers and Roberts 1988: 8–9.
[160] Reid 1983a: 33.

his campaign.[161] Samuel Zwemer, a fiery American Protestant, conceded in 1907 that 'some Moslem apologists of the present day contend that Mohammed looked upon the custom as temporary in its nature'.[162]

A few European officials and scholars made similarly perceptive comments. Britain's Sir Bartle Frere wrote in 1873 that 'the gradual extinction of slavery involves nothing repugnant to the law of the Koran, as interpreted by the most learned men in the best times, and under the most orthodox and best Mahommedan rulers'.[163] Christian Snouck Hurgronje, the great Dutch Islamist, remarked in 1886 that 'slavery would disappear, if ever Islam could draw near to its own ideals'.[164] Later he noted that 'according to Mohammedan principles, slavery is an institution destined to disappear ... [and is not] indispensable to the integrity of Islam'.[165] Georges Poulet, investigating slavery in French West Africa in 1905, wrote that, 'the religion of the Prophet could perhaps have contributed powerfully to the suppression of slavery, if the spirit of the Quran had been applied with wisdom by men whose fanaticism had not been accompanied by the pride of conquerors'.[166] Wilfrid Blunt mockingly recalled the shocked reaction of the secretary of the venerable British Anti-Slavery Society, when told that Ahmad 'Urabi was intent on rooting out slavery in Egypt: 'Mohammedans ... had no business to put down slavery on their own account, or what would become of the Society?'[167]

Western scholars of more recent times have demonstrated a similar awareness. Bertram Thomas stated baldly in the 1930s that, 'in the unabatement of slavery, Arabia has been false to her Prophet'.[168] Robert Brunschvig presented a brief outline of Islamic abolitionism in 1960, slightly amplified by Murray Gordon.[169] In the introduction to an edited collection on Africa, John Willis mused that, 'the voices of abolition come through faintly in these essays, but it is possible that we have not given them their due'.[170] Martin Klein

[161] Renault 1992: 566, 570.
[162] Zwemer 1965: 126–9.
[163] Frere 1873: 14.
[164] Snouck Hurgronje 1923–24: I, 273.
[165] Snouck Hurgronje 1916: 150–2.
[166] Poulet 1994: 40.
[167] Blunt 1907: 242–3.
[168] Thomas 1937: 69, 149, 267–8.
[169] Brunschvig 1960: 38; Gordon 1989: x–xi, 45–7, 208–9.
[170] Willis 1985: I, ix.

noted that some African and Asian reformers 'looked to their own traditions to sanction antislavery action'.[171] David Waines considered that 'slave ownership was not a badge of the truly pious', and that believers were urged to 'create the conditions of its ultimate dissolution'.[172]

The logic of Islamic abolition

Islamic abolitionists may have played little part in ensuring the passage of laws against slavery, but they played a vital role in turning the shadow of legislation into a lived reality. As long as significant numbers of Muslims believed that servitude was legitimate, suppression proved to be a labour of Sisyphus.[173] Slavery continued to function after secular laws had declared the institution to be defunct, with qadis or private arbitrators interpreting the holy law in private.[174]

A second basic assumption of this book is that the Muslim rejection of servitude was no simple response to Western pressure. It is impossible to know whether there would ever have emerged a powerful current of abolitionism without the Western challenge, but the Islamic debate was clearly rooted in arguments that stretched back to the origins of the faith. The foundations of slavery in the original texts were weak, exacerbating a permanent tension between religious belief and social reality. These internal contradictions facilitated the crafting of Islamic arguments for abolition.

A third characteristic of this book is the rejection of any single Islamic point of view, even in specific periods. From the time of the Prophet himself, believers held different views about social and political organisation. Slavery, even mitigated by ameliorationist tendencies, was the clearest negation of a socially egalitarian vision of the faith. Embarrassing to many of the faithful, servitude thus gave rise to a rich diversity of debates and interpretations.

The Quran, revealed by God to Muhammad, either failed to provide explicit guidance on slavery, or posed delicate problems of exegesis. The sayings and deeds of the Prophet and his companions, known as the Hadith or Traditions, clarified some points. However, even the half a dozen canonical collections presented

---

[171] Klein 1993: 25.
[172] Waines 1995: 31, 99.
[173] Beachey 1976a: 220–59; Salman 2001: 82.
[174] Snouck Hurgronje 1923–24: II, 281; Hunter 1964: 145, 153; Bonné 1948: 331.

uncertainties of transmission, coherence and interpretation. The early and approved biographies of the Prophet, notably that of Ibn Ishaq as transmitted by Ibn Hisham, introduced yet more diversity. A huge body of glosses, commentaries and fatwas completed these founding texts, applying analogy and consensus of the learned to resolve uncertainties, but often creating new doubts in the process.[175]

The approaches of the ulama were fully codified by the fifteenth-century. There were few differences between the Hanafi, Maliki, Shafi'i, and Hanbali schools of law in Sunni Islam, as shown in Chapter 2. However, sects outside the Sunni fold, together with early mystics and philosophers, treated servitude somewhat differently, as shown in Chapter 3. To the Druze sect, emerging from Isma'ili Islam, fell the honour of being the first Muslims to repudiate slavery.

Some aspects of social organisation did not originate in the sharia, but rather in customary and statute law. As William Robertson Smith (1845–94) put it in a book published in 1912, 'many of the prejudices which seem to us most distinctively Mohammedan have no basis in the Koran'.[176] Marshall Hodgson suggested the term 'Islamicate' for practices not derived from scripture, but culturally and historically embedded in 'Islamdom', another of his neologisms.[177] Particularly affecting enslavement and manumission, custom is covered in Chapter 4. Decrees of Muslim rulers added another layer of diversity, considered in Chapter 5. Sultan's law initially intensified slavery, but began to rein in the institution from the sixteenth-century.

The second part of the book moves on to responses to the external challenge from the late eighteenth-century. Chapter 6 looks at the ways in which imperialism, formal and informal, impinged on Islamdom. Although they were unbelievers, some Westerners engaged deeply with the holy law. The ulama in all traditions were thus pressed to re-examine slavery, a phenomenon appraised in Chapter 7. This occasionally gave rise to 'quasi-abolition', even when scholars only appeared to accept a tightening up in the enforcement of the holy law.

Other responses to the Western challenge were similarly ambivalent. Mystics and millenarians explosively increased rates of enslavement when they chose the way of the sword, as shown in Chapter 8.

---

[175] Hodgson 1974: I, 322–35.
[176] See Said 1991: 236.
[177] Hodgson 1974: I, 57–60.

However, subversive millenarians, claiming the right to abolish the law and reshape society, might oppose slavery. Peaceful mystics also did much to integrate former slaves into Islam. Literalists, the subject of Chapter 9, preached a reliance on Quran and Hadith, cutting out commentaries and mystical or millenarian accretions. They were equivocal and often divided about the legitimacy of servitude. Rationalists, the most consistent abolitionists in Islam, are examined in Chapter 10. While advocating a return to the founding texts, their chief concern was with the 'spirit' of the Quran. They fell into two broad camps on the issue of servitude. Radicals took the position that God had abolished slavery through his revelations to the Prophet, and that Muslims had wilfully refused to obey the divine command. Gradualists accepted that abolition was part of God's plan for humanity, but believed that the Prophet had judged conditions not to be ripe for immediate emancipation. They thought that modern times were suitable for grasping the nettle.

These various strands are woven together in Chapter 11, which attempts an overall chronology, followed by a comparison with other world religions. This exercise suggests many similarities, but also reveals a puzzling paradox. Islam was precocious in regulating slavery and exhorting the faithful to engage in manumission, and yet Muslim die-hards have generally lagged behind those in other faiths in endorsing complete emancipation. To understand the fractured Muslim response to abolition, it is essential to grasp the different ways in which the social obligations of the faithful have been construed over time.

Part I

THE CONTRADICTIONS OF SLAVERY

2

A FRAGILE SUNNI CONSENSUS

Slavery was neither taken for granted nor explicitly forbidden in the Quran. At first reading, Muhammad's revelations forbade anybody but himself to take slaves in war, while sanctioning no other method of acquisition. Combined with repeated exhortations to manumit existing slaves, this could have led to the institution dying out. However, passages regulating the treatment of slaves might be read as implying the existence of the institution. Indeed, one Hadith called for slaves to resign themselves to their fate.[1]

A compromise was hammered out by Sunni ulama by around 800.[2] They took human freedom to be the norm, and made no exceptions for foundlings, debtors or criminals. One mode of enslavement was the capture of obdurate infidels in holy war. The other was birth to a slave mother, unless she was a concubine whose master acknowledged paternity. Owners had to free any of their own slaves whom they wished to marry. Converting to Islam after enslavement was no passport to liberty, but manumitting slaves, especially Muslim ones, was a pious act, even a mandatory one to atone for certain sins. Finally, the law set out humane treatment in fine detail.[3] Rulings on slavery then came to be woven like a scarlet thread through the fabric of the holy law, making up about a third of the

[1] Awde 2000: 94; Abou El Fadl 2001: 246.
[2] Schneider 1999, 349–51.
[3] Brunschvig 1960.

text of the *Hidaya* code, an influential late-twelfth-century Hanafi jurisprudence commentary.[4]

Unhappiness persisted long after the 'gates of interpretation' allegedly slammed shut, at some time between the ninth and the eleventh century. The unavoidable contrast between servitude and egalitarianism grated on the pious.[5] As Franz Rosenthal puts it, 'the furthest jurists could go towards criticizing slavery was for them to look at the status quo with an uncomfortable feeling that its moral basis was shaky. In fact, this is what happened occasionally'.[6]

Unwilling to challenge bondage head on, the ulama disputed the 'technical' boundaries between free and slave.[7] While some scholars laid down that 'the basic principle for all the children of Adam is freedom', a few added 'as far as Muslims are concerned', a distinction that long bedevilled arguments.[8] Definitions caused much soul-searching when it came to 'bad Muslims', 'people of the book', and 'holy war'. Moreover, hallowed texts were deafeningly silent on acquiring slaves through purchase or tribute.[9]

Early uncertainties

Considerable hesitation appears to have prevailed at the dawn of Islam.[10] When the Prophet began to preach in Mecca, many of his earliest adherents were slaves, some of whom were singled out for persecution for lack of powerful protectors.[11] Revelations traditionally assigned to this period were generally more socially liberal than those attributed to the later era of the Prophet's rule in Medina.[12] Even a Hadith from the latter period told of Muhammad's daughter asking for a slave woman to relieve her of domestic duties, and receiving the answer that she would do better to pray.[13]

Euphemisms hint at early reservations. The Quran refers regularly to slaves either as 'necks', meaning people, or as 'those whom your right hand possesses', often used for concubines. A tradition recounted that the Prophet declared, 'Let no one say "my slave" or

[4] Hamilton and Grady 1870: xxxi.
[5] Mernissi 1987: 192.
[6] Rosenthal 1960: 29.
[7] Boisard 1985: 92–3.
[8] Rosenthal 1960: 31–2.
[9] Hunwick 1992: 10–11.
[10] Schneider 1999.
[11] Hodgson 1974: I, 71, 167, 170; Pipes 1981: 109.
[12] Na'im 1998.
[13] Awde 2000: 127.

"my slave girl," but rather "my boy" or "my girl.""[14] Muslim writers subsequently employed expressions such as 'children' and 'servants', although they also began to speak more pejoratively of 'captives', 'those under the yoke', 'property' and 'creatures'.[15]

Belief in the descent of all Arabs from Hagar the slave concubine might have predisposed Muslims to mercy.[16] The female line was subordinate, but not ignored by Arabs.[17] A Hadith told how the patriarch Ibrahim (Abraham), at the instigation of his free wife Sarah, repudiated Hagar.[18] Folk traditions embroidered on her tribulations in the desert with her young son Isma'il (Ishmael), ancestor of the Arabs.[19] The Quran, in 2:125–7, specified that Isma'il and Ibrahim were the founders of Mecca, and the builders of the sacred Ka'ba shrine.[20] To counter prejudice against caliphs born of slave mothers, scholars stressed that the Quraysh, the Prophet's own tribe, descended from Hagar the concubine, whereas the despised Jews were of the line of Sarah, the free woman.[21] Military slaves took Isma'il as one of their 'exemplars'.[22] Even non-Arab Muslims claimed descent from Hagar and Isma'il, as in Sumatra around 1500.[23]

The patriarch Yusuf (Joseph) was another patron of military slaves, and more widely of captives, underlining the significance of the story of Israel's bondage in Egypt.[24] Yusuf's enslavement by Pharaoh is related in 12:22–35 of the Quran, while 7:127, 23:47, and 26:22 refer to Musa (Moses) and Hebrew slaves in Egypt. Twentieth-century Muslims took these stories as a critique of slavery, perhaps following in the footsteps of earlier authors.[25]

In contrast, the example of the Prophet and his Companions tended to support slavery. Ibn Qayyim al-Jawziyya (1292–1350), a Hanbali *'alim* who may have sought to demonstrate the power and prosperity of the founder of the faith, listed 28 male and 11 female slaves belonging to Muhammad.[26] Another authority put the total

[14] Hunwick and Powell 2002: 2, 7.
[15] Brunschvig 1960: 24.
[16] Crone and Cook 1977: 121.
[17] Hodgson 1974: I, 259.
[18] Awde 2000: 143.
[19] Ruthven 2000: 13–18.
[20] Hodgson 1974: I, 179.
[21] Goldziher 1967: 116–19.
[22] Walker 1998: 335.
[23] Steenbrink 1993: 30.
[24] Walker 1998: 335; Rosenthal 1960: 67–8.
[25] Na'ini 2002: 121, 123; <http://www.central-mosque.com/fiqh/slav4.htm>
[26] Abd el-Schafi 2000: 153–5.

at 70, 'a very large holding in Arabia'.[27] Even the splitting up of families by sale was apparently accepted under the Prophet, for a Hadith told that, 'we used to sell the mothers of children in the time of the Prophet and of Abu Bakr, but 'Umar forbade it in his time'.[28] Appeals for the good treatment of slaves in Quran and Hadith were double-edged swords, for they seemed to presuppose the existence of slavery. Indeed, as manumission was the only prescribed way of atoning for certain sins, some ulama fretted as to what would happen if there were no longer any slaves. The drive to manumit should have led to a rapid withering away of existing stocks of slaves, but this left open the possibility of acquiring new ones.[29]

Taking infidels in holy war

The Quran is silent on the ordinary believer obtaining fresh slaves, and yet seizing hardened infidels in holy war came to be considered as the soundest form of enslavement. Quran 8:67—'It is not for any Prophet to have prisoners until he makes wide slaughter in the land'—concerns the Prophet alone. The same is true of 33:50, referring to, 'what thy right hand owns, spoils of war that God has given thee'. The most frequently cited text is thus 47:4: 'When you meet the unbelievers, smite their necks; then, when you have made wide slaughter among them, tie fast the bonds. Then set them free, either by grace or ransom, till the war lays down its loads'.

Jurists found reasons to nullify God's seemingly clear instructions to free prisoners after wars. The catch-all concept of 'public interest', drawn from repeated commands in the Quran to promote good and forbid evil, meant that men should not be released to fight again.[30] The enslavement of captives by infidels might be a further justification, given 16:126 in the Quran, 'And if you chastise, chastise even as you have been chastised', although this passage is followed by the admonition that it is better to be patient and self-restrained.

A common technique was to abrogate 47:4 with a later verse. This method of exegesis was justified by 2:106, and led to complex disputes about the chronological order of revelation in the Quran. It was alleged that 47:4 applied only to the battle of Badr in 624, and was nullified by later verses prescribing the treatment and manu-

[27] Pipes 1981: 140.
[28] Hughes 1885: 598.
[29] Brunschwig 1960: 25–7.
[30] Peters 1979: 26–8; Taleqani 1983: 191–2.

mission of slaves.[31] Alternatively, 8:67 was interpreted as a reproof to the Prophet for releasing prisoners to reinforce enemy ranks.[32] 'Sword verses' commanding the slaying of infidels, such as 8:39, were frequently used to annul 47:4, with enslavement then presented as a merciful substitute for death.[33]

Such exegetical exercises had the paradoxical outcome of seeming to mock the Quran. The instructions given to Muhammad al-Qasim, conqueror of the South Asian province of Sind in 710, read like a cruel parody of 47:4: 'When you encounter unbelievers, strike off their heads ... make a great slaughter among them ... bind their bonds... [and] grant freedom to no one of the enemy, and spare none of them'.[34]

Although ransom is specifically recommended in 47:4, the founder of the Hanafi school forbade the practice, and some later jurists even prohibited exchanges of captives.[35] In a Maliki fatwa from the fifteenth-century Maghrib, Ibn Siraj allowed exchanges, but disapproved of ransoming Christian slaves. While admitting that there was disagreement on such matters, he asserted that the enemy should not obtain valuable information and soldiers, placing slaves in the category of materials of war to be denied to the foe.[36] A Mauritanian scholar, Sidi 'Abdallah wuld al-Hajj Ibrahim al-'Alawi (1733–1818), prohibited the sale of slaves to those who might sell them on to Christians.[37]

Further problems arose from defining a properly constituted 'jihad of the sword'. Initially, the caliph sallied forth yearly against the infidel, with the task of 'voiding the earth of unbelief', and 'making Allah's word the highest'.[38] However, not every war against unbelievers was holy, for the ancient 'Constitution of Medina' indicated that a jihad had to be either 'in the path of Allah', or 'for religion'.[39] After the Mongols had destroyed the caliphate in 1258, some considered holy war to be in abeyance, although others believed caliphal duties to be delegated to any just ruler who enforced the sharia.[40]

[31] Ali 1883: 165; Ahmad 1967: 52.
[32] Peters 1979: 28; Ruud Peters, personal communication.
[33] Hughes 1885: 597–8; Azumah 2001: 65.
[34] Lal 1994: 21.
[35] Elwahed 1931: 131; Hughes 1885: 597–8.
[36] Wanscharisi 1908–9: I, 207–13.
[37] Wuld al-Bara 1997: 96.
[38] Peters 1979: 114.
[39] Firestone 1999: 123–4.
[40] Khadduri 1955: 65; Hodgson 1974: II, 472.

The next crucial step was to expand the category of the enslavable to the whole population of a conquered territory.[41] This furnished female captives, rare or non-existent on the field of battle, thus opening the way to hereditary slavery and concubinage.[42] The example of the Prophet and his Companions was vital. The Hanbali jurist Ibn Qayyim al-Jawziyya (1292–1350) stated that Muhammad had reduced prisoners of war to servitude, but never an adult male.[43] In particular, Muhammad had enslaved Jewish women and children in Arabia, sparing only tribes that submitted voluntarily.[44] However, the arbitrator who passed judgement against the Qurayza Jews did so in terms of Hebrew law.[45] Moreover, it was reported that two rightly-guided caliphs, 'Umar b. al-Khattab and 'Ali b. Abi Talib, rejected taking dependants as slaves.[46]

Abu Yusuf Ya'qub b. Ibrahim Ansari (731–98), adviser to the great Abbasid caliph Harun al-Rashid (r. 786–809), prudently declared that it was up to the commander of the faithful to determine the fate of non-combatants.[47] In practice, booty regularly came to include dependent women and children.[48] One author even attributed the debacle of the battle of Poitiers or Tours in 732, long believed to have prevented the conquest of Christendom, to the fear that the Franks would attack the Muslim camp, bursting at the seams with female captives.[49] Taqi al-Din Ahmad b. Taymiyya (1263–1328), the noted Hanbali jurist of Damascus, declared of a prisoner of war that it was 'lawful to take his offspring into captivity'.[50]

Slave raiding and kidnapping

From the ninth-century, jurists developed the fateful theory that the inhabitants of Dar al-Harb, the abode of war, 'were all potential slaves'. Also known as Dar al-Kufr, the land of unbelief, this area lay beyond Dar al-Islam, the abode of submission to God.[51] However, Shafi'i jurists conceived of an intermediary sphere, known as Dar

[41] Khadduri 1955: 127–32; Peters 1979: 21, 26.
[42] Gunasekara n.d.: 12–14.
[43] Charouiti Hasnaoui 2000: 4.
[44] Ruthven 2000: 54–7, 63; Guillaume 1955: 463–6.
[45] Muir 1877: 327–9.
[46] Hamidullah 1945: 172, 210, 235.
[47] Verlinden 1955: 183–4.
[48] Lal 1994: 55–6.
[49] Khan 1972: 39.
[50] Abd el-Schafi 2000: 150.
[51] Hunwick 1992: 11.

al-'Ahd or Dar al-Sulh, the abode of the covenant. Unbelievers who dwelled there, even Animists, were protected from arbitrary enslavement as long as they had concluded formal pacts with Muslims.[52] To convince waverers, the ulama developed the further argument that slavery was a form of divine retribution for unbelief. 'Abd al-'Aziz b. Ahmad al-Bukhari (d. 1330), declared that, 'freedom is the attribute par excellence of a living being in a secular jurisdiction, whereas slaves are in the category of the dead, for servitude is a vestige of obstinacy in refusing to believe in one God, and this in the eyes of the law is death itself'.[53] 'Ali b. Muhammad al-Jurjani (d. 1413) portrayed slavery as 'a debility theoretically produced by law, which originally was a penalty for unbelief'.[54] The most cited text was a fatwa from the pen of Ahmad b. Yahya al-Wansharisi (d. 1508). An Algerian scholar resident in Morocco, he described slavery as 'a humiliation and a servitude caused by previous or current unbelief, and having as its purpose to discourage unbelief'.[55]

From this, South Asian scholars deduced that jihad was irrelevant when seizing infidels, who were 'deprived of their rights of freedom without being possessed by anybody'.[56] It was unnecessary to invite infidels in the abode of war to embrace Islam before seizing their persons, because they were 'something which is the property of no particular person and may by law become the property of a Mooslim. ... They are classed with inanimate things ... thus liable to be reduced to state of property, like things which were originally common by nature'. For a raider, this entailed that 'such of the inhabitants, as have fallen into his hands, are at his absolute disposal, and may be lawfully reduced to slavery'.[57]

It has been asserted that Maghribi naval raiders engaged in jihad from the sixteenth to the nineteenth-century.[58] According to Khalifa Chater, Barbary corsairs 'considered themselves in a permanent state of war with Christian powers', had their expeditions blessed by ulama, and saw the Maghrib as part of Dar al-Jihad, the abode of holy war.[59] Barbary ships invoked Muslim saints and sailed with a

[52] Khadduri 1955: 261; Renault 1989: 31–2; Brett 2001: 384; Hunwick and Harrak 2000: 11–12, 38; Erdem 1996: 30.
[53] Forand 1971: 61.
[54] Rosenthal 1960: 25.
[55] Lewis 1990: 148; Wanscharisi 1908–9: II, 426–8.
[56] Ali 1883: 27–8.
[57] Baillie 1957: 363–5.
[58] Bennett 1960: 65; Kafadar 1995: 83.
[59] Chater 1984: 226, 261–2.

'scribe', and Muslims expelled from Iberia and Italy fought with particular fervour.[60] However, many Maghribi ulama stubbornly refused to accord the name of holy war to these piratical forays, for no caliph or Imam declared a jihad, and rapine was all too clearly the main motive.[61] The unusual notion of Dar al-Jihad seems to derive from a single letter by 'Umar Pasha, Dey of Algiers, desperate for Ottoman help after a British bombardment in 1816.[62] As for the 'scribe', he kept accounts and usually read books of divination and astrology, rather than consulting holy writ.[63] Sultans were rarely in a position to declare jihads, for the Ottoman and Moroccan sultans only exercised a loose suzerainty over 'corsair republics', which made and broke their own treaties from the 1570s.[64] At best, privateers preyed exclusively on unbelievers, and obtained licences to avoid being hanged as common pirates, though such documents were increasingly issued by corsair rulers themselves in the Ottoman zone.[65]

Men of dubious religious affiliation ruled Barbary states and crewed their ships. An Ottoman observed in the early eighteenth-century that 'these renegadoes are neither Christians, Musulmans, nor Jews; they have no faith, nor religion at all'.[66] Cosmopolitan bands even included the odd Japanese and Chinese adventurer.[67] Renegade Christians maintained close commercial links with their areas of origin, and might negotiate a further turning of their coats with the Holy Office of Inquisition or the Knights of Saint John in Malta. Whatever their nominal faith, many lived by the *usanza del mare*, Mediterranean lore pre-dating any world religion.[68]

While privateering retained aspects of a contest between faiths, it was also a business, rooted on both sides of the Mediterranean.[69] Commercial companies mounted expeditions out of Maghribi ports from as early as the tenth-century. Over time, financial backing for Muslim operations came mainly from Christians and Jews, the latter often from Livorno (Leghorn) and well connected in Marseilles, London, and Amsterdam. When the Dey of Algiers declared

[60] Bono 1964: 96; Clissold 1977: 33; Monlaü 1964: 73.
[61] Berque 1978: 166–7.
[62] Temimi 1971: 229.
[63] Bono 1964: 96–9; Clissold 1977: 35.
[64] Monlaü 1964: 61–4, 67, 70, 92–3, 97–8; Bono 1964: 101–3; Deardon 1976: 15–16.
[65] Monlaü 1964: 53, 57–8; Bono 1964: 92–4, Clissold 1977: 6; Colley 2002: 44–5.
[66] Clissold 1977: 101.
[67] Monlaü 1964: 75.
[68] Bono 1964: 91–2, 100, 256–66; Clissold 1977: 6, 93–8.
[69] Pennell 1989: 45–6.

war on France in 1681, he informed Marseilles merchants that they were still welcome to come and buy slaves.[70]

Kidnapping and raiding were far more common than holy war in Southeast Asia, although some authors have graced Moro naval raids from the southern Philippines with the name of jihads. At best, a religious specialist accompanied Moro fleets, to recite the Quran, lead prayers, and arbitrate in disputes over booty. The Iranun and Samal, the foremost raiders, were barely considered to be within the Islamic fold, and were quite prepared to take fellow Muslims as slaves. From bases in Mindanao and Sulu, they ravaged much of Southeast Asia from the seventeenth to the mid-nine-teenth-century.[71]

The element of raiding was clear elsewhere, for peninsular Malays made a distinction between people taken in war and inoffensive Animists, hunted down in the forests of the interior.[72] In Sumatra in 1823, Malays requiring Animist Batak slaves 'frequently seize their children straying near the banks of the river'.[73] Slave raiding grew out of the older practice of head-hunting, as rite of passage and proof of male bravery. In South Sumatra's Lampung districts, slave heads could substitute ceremonially for those of captured enemies.[74] In Southeast Sulawesi 'often some heads were taken and the rest of the inhabitants were taken away as slaves'.[75]

Similar problems arose in South India and the Caucasus. The Raja of Cannanore, the only Muslim ruler on the Malabar Coast of southwestern India, was not known ever to have declared a jihad. Nevertheless, a report of 1793 noted that Mapila Muslims were kidnapping Hindu children to sell to European traders, especially in the Dutch port of Cochin.[76] As for Chechen and Circassian clans in the Caucasus, they raided for slaves without religious sanction or leadership.[77]

Africa was no different. Al-Marwazi, writing in about 1130, recounted that traders in East Africa, seemingly Muslim by faith, 'repair to the meadows and hide in the woods carrying with them dates, of which they drop a little on the children's playing ground'.

[70] Monlaü 1964: 78, 84–5, 90–5.
[71] Warren 1981: 152–6, 182, 187–8.
[72] Winstedt 1981: 53.
[73] Anderson 1971: 321.
[74] Broersma 1916: 74.
[75] Velthoen 1997: 370.
[76] Day 1863: 171, 183–4, 367–8; Kusuman 1973: 41; Ramachandran Nair 1986: 49–50; Gabriel 1996: 115; Kelly 1968: 448.
[77] Majerczak 1912: 197; Erdem 1996: 46.

Having led the children a little further astray day by day, 'the traders leap on them, seize them, and carry them away to their land'.[78] This became a common story, told of Darfur in the nineteenth-century.[79] Ahmad b. Ahmad al-Takruri, a Maliki scholar of Timbuktu usually known as Ahmad Baba, reacted against this trend, but in vain. Responding to a query from the borderlands of southern Morocco in 1615, he insisted that Muslim rulers alone could legally enslave people, and only in holy wars to spread the faith.[80] However, African jihads were fated to 'yield place to the *ghazwa*—the expedition against the enemies of Islam was transformed into a foray for plunder'.[81] Fourteenth-century kings of Mali took slaves in holy wars, but this notion then receded into the background.[82] Hausa authors in West Africa argued that success in slave raiding was divinely ordained.[83] Leaders of East African razzias flew a white flag, inscribed with phrases from the Quran.[84]

Slave raiding in conjunction with infidels was perhaps the ultimate negation of the ideal of holy war. Around 1500, Muslims were accused of mounting such attacks with Animist Fulbe in West Africa.[85] A seventeenth-century Ottoman literary source described Christians and Muslims setting out on joint piratical expeditions in the Mediterranean.[86] Malays in nineteenth-century Borneo sallied forth on naval raids in partnership with Animist Sea Dayaks, and similar co-operation may have occurred in southeastern Sulawesi.[87]

Tribute, purchase and adoption

If unbelievers dwelling in the abode of war were at the free disposal of Muslim raiders, then they could also be procured through peaceful means, whatever the method of their enslavement. This conveniently overcame the silence of Quran, Hadith, and founders of the schools of law concerning the procurement of slaves through pur-

[78] Beg 1975: 107.
[79] Renault and Daget 1985: 52.
[80] Hunwick and Harrak 2000: 13, 23, 28, 43–4.
[81] Willis 1980: 189.
[82] Hunwick and Powell 2002: 53–64; Renault and Daget 1985: 25.
[83] Hiskett 1985: 123–4.
[84] Beachey 1976a: 197–8.
[85] Hunwick 1985: 86–7.
[86] Kafadar 1995: 83.
[87] Low 1968: 128–30; Velthoen 1997.

chase, gift or tribute.[88] Indeed, Muslims may have relied more on tribute to extract slaves than adherents of other religions.[89]

The precedent repeatedly cited for tribute was the treaty with Christian Nubia in 652, arranging for the transfer 360 slaves a year to the Muslim conquerors of Egypt.[90] However, the original treaty, drawn up after the inconclusive siege of Dongola, probably only regulated mutual trade. The text made public in the fifteenth-century, after the destruction of the original document, clearly incorporated elements posterior to 652. In all likelihood, Nubian tribute only began in the mid-eighth-century, and thus failed to benefit from association with the companions of the Prophet.[91]

Infidels not directly ruled by Muslims offered tribute in slaves when they had little else of value.[92] Africans often sent people to Muslim rulers, from as early as the ninth-century to Yemen.[93] Once Nubians had become Muslims, the burden of tribute owed to Egypt was transferred to Animists further up the Nile.[94] The Ottomans imposed levies of children on a number of vassal states, including Christian Georgia.[95] In Southeast Asia, the Moluccan sultans of Tidore and Ternate obtained drafts of Animists from Halmahera, western New Guinea, and northern Sulawesi. The ruler of Makassar, in South Sulawesi, relied on the Lesser Sunda islands, while Sumatran sultans received Animist Bataks from the highlands.[96] Marrying their daughters to Muslim Malays, Batak chiefs provided a dowry that included slaves, often sold forthwith.[97]

Infidels might enter servitude with Muslims as a matter of private contract. Deserters, such as those fleeing harsh conditions in Russia's Tsarist army, were one such group.[98] Some Christian Ethiopian women, vying with Circassians for popularity in Middle Eastern harems, were also said to offer themselves up to this fate, even if many were clearly sold by their parents.[99]

---

[88] Hunwick 1992: 10–11.
[89] Patterson 1982: 123.
[90] Hunwick 1992: 11; Fisher 2001: 295; Khadduri 1955: 259–61.
[91] Renault 1989: 11–23, 32–3, 92–5.
[92] Brett 2001: 249; Pipes 1981: 142–3.
[93] Bidwell 1983: 7; Azumah 2001: 122; Fisher 2001: 295–308; Lovejoy 1981: 236–7.
[94] Erdem 1996: 89–90.
[95] Papoulia 1963: 10, 14, 17, 57–9; Lang 1957: 22.
[96] Andaya, (Leonard) 1993: 90, 99, 177, 192–3, 198; Reid 1983a: 31; Dobbin 1983: 182.
[97] Anderson 1971: 315.
[98] Erdem 1996: 52.
[99] Fontrier 2003: 52–3.

Purchase, allegedly first permitted by the Ummayad Caliph Mu'awiya (r. 661–680), probably yielded the largest numbers of slaves.[100] In the eighth-century, Egyptian ulama declared it lawful for Muslims to buy people from Nubians, including 'if they desire ... their wives and children'.[101] The rider was sometimes added that such people should have been 'rightfully enslaved', although what this meant was far from clear.[102]

Attempts to restrict the buying of slaves from the infidel were few and half-hearted. From 1492 the Ottomans demanded proof that imported slaves were prisoners of war, but such documents were issued for a fee, in effect becoming an import duty.[103] For al-Wansharisi in Morocco, a believer should avoid acquiring slaves who had lived as free people in ethnic groups known to be Muslim. However, he allowed the benefit of the doubt to rest with the buyer, stressing that property rights were guaranteed in holy law.[104]

There was undoubtedly much purchasing of people forcibly enslaved by non-Muslims. From the fourteenth-century, Inner Asian dealers in Bukhara and Balkh bought unbelievers raided by Oyrat Mongols.[105] Many Georgian slaves from the Caucasus, including members of the clergy, were victims of civil wars between Christian lords, despite the strictures of the Patriarch of Antioch in the 1660s.[106] Ahmad al-Mansur (r. 1578–1603), sultan of Morocco wrote a letter to Egyptian ulama arguing that it was legitimate to buy 'originally unbelieving blacks from over there through purchase from those who neighbor them and raid them and campaign against them'.[107]

Modes of enslavement varied greatly. Al-Ya'qubi, a ninth-century geographer, reported that African kings sold their subjects without even the pretext of war or crimes.[108] Ibn Taymiyya permitted Muslims to purchase debt slaves from infidels who had no covenant with Muslims.[109] Christian Georgian lords handed over serfs for payment, while Armenians sold children in times of need.[110] During famines, Swahili, and Malay households purchased Animist

---

[100] Ali 1891: 379–80; Gordon 1989: 26.
[101] Renault 1989: 20.
[102] Fahmy 1990: 94.
[103] Erdem 1996: 19–20.
[104] Lewis 1990: 148; Wanscharisi 1908–9: II, 426–8.
[105] Levi 2002: 279; Cumming 1977: 86–7.
[106] Lang 1957: 69.
[107] Hunwick 1999: 53.
[108] Brett 2001: 250–1.
[109] Schneider 1999: 52–3.
[110] Lang 1957: 69; Erdem 1996: 51.

children.[111] Arabs in East Africa bought slaves condemned for witchcraft or non-payment of fines.[112] Mapila Muslims of southwestern India obtained Hindus reduced to servitude for sexual misconduct, often women in breach of caste rules.[113]

Nevertheless, the notion that a person should have been justly enslaved lingered on. Sidi al-'Arabi Burdalah issued a fatwa in Fez around 1708. He began by stating that trading in slaves was legitimate, for 'concerning the issue of ownership of slaves, it is based on the sale to the buyer. Opinions do not differ on this. Allah the Almighty said: whereas [sic] Allah hath permitted trade and forbidden usury'. However, he continued that 'evidence must establish beyond a shadow of a doubt that a person is originally a slave. The evidence should be in accord with the shari'a, free of bias, coercion and the like'.[114]

Uncertainty as to the acceptability of purchasing slaves was perhaps revealed by disapproving attitudes towards Muslim slave traders. The ulama failed to condemn them, and yet the occupation was often held to be reprehensible. A widely known saying of the Prophet declared that the seller of men was the worst of men.[115] Tradition also related that Muhammad's widow, 'A'isha, had denounced the sale of a slave, albeit possibly because the transaction involved the payment of interest.[116] The Prophet had exchanged Qurayza Jewish women and children for weapons and horses in Najd, and sold captives from the Ibn Harita group, but this was apparently seen as exceptional rather than exemplary.[117]

Dealers in slaves suffered from a generally poor reputation.[118] An influential South Asian ethical treatise from the 1390s commanded: 'Do not trade in slaves ... and you will not be an accursed regrater [profiteer]. In trading in slaves ... you will never find blessing'.[119] Ottoman guilds of slave merchants were little appreciated, and those selling Blacks in Egypt were of the 'cursed and impious guilds of low social status'.[120] Al-Nasiri, attacking slavery in late-nineteenth-

---

[111] Fisher 2001: 102; Anderson 1971: 297.

[112] Harries 1965: 206.

[113] Adam 1840: 157–8; Day 1863: 62; Kusuman 1973: 28; Ramachandran Nair 1986: 24–5.

[114] Batran 1985: 13–14.

[115] Kelly 1968: 595; Leitner 1893: 18; Cooper 1968: 115; Kake 1979: 164.

[116] Ali 1883: 152.

[117] Guillaume 1955: 463–6; Muir 1877: 331; Charouiti Hasnaoui 2000: 5.

[118] Brunschvig 1960: 32; Beg 1975: 108–9.

[119] Digby 1984: 111–12, 117–18.

[120] Erdem 1996: 34–9, 96; Garnett 1909: 212; Baer 1969: 174.

century Morocco, damned slave dealers as 'men of no morals and no religion'.[121] 'Slave dealer' was an insult, in areas as far apart as the southern Philippines and Somalia.[122] There was some evidence to the contrary. Those who sold Whites in Egypt were 'grouped with the highly respected guilds', possibly because Circassians were thought to enter slavery voluntarily.[123] A modern Moroccan historian writes that slave dealers were respectable folk.[124] One Western witness even alleged that 'sanctity and slave dealing may be considered somewhat akin in the Turkestan region, and, the more holy the person the more extensive are generally his transactions in flesh and blood'.[125] This may have reflected the high reputation of vendors supplying soldiers, as in Mamluk Egypt.[126] It was said that 'strong ties of affection and veneration' bound successful Turkic soldiers to the men who had sold them.[127]

Purchasing child slaves to adopt them was rare in Islamdom, compared to other civilisations.[128] Any kind of adoption was prohibited, in terms of 33:4 in the Quran: 'neither has He made your adopted sons your sons in fact'.[129] Adopting slave children was perceived as conflicting with holy law in India, although augmenting the size of the Islamic minority overrode Mapila scruples in the south.[130] Childless couples, widows and powerful men occasionally purchased children for adoption in the Ottoman lands and Egypt.[131]

The adoption of slave children was most characteristic of the Hui in China, but it probably served to evade Ming and Qing legislation. Chinese laws only tolerated sales of people if destitute children were thereby integrated into free households. This led to a widespread subterfuge, whereby Chinese owners called their slaves adopted children.[132] Hui increased their purchases of children of both sexes from the seventeenth-century, and settled some of them in satellite villages, perhaps as freed clients.[133] Many people came to

---

[121] Hunwick 1999: 61.
[122] Kiefer 1972: 85; Fontrier 2003: 190.
[123] Baer 1969: 174; Toledano 1998: 68, 70.
[124] Ennaji 1999: 110.
[125] Gardner 1898: 104.
[126] Ayalon 1951: 1–4.
[127] Wink 1999: II, 197–8.
[128] Patterson 1982: 232.
[129] Hodgson 1974: I, 181–2; Özbay 1999a: 6–9.
[130] Adam 1840: 63–4; Kumar 1993: 121; Day 1863: 369.
[131] Ayalon 1951: 22–4; Garnett 1891: II, 410; Chafik 1938: 52; Toledano 1998: 26.
[132] Tsai 1996: 27–8; Mazumdar 1998: 197–201; Lasker 1950: 52–3.
[133] Broomhall 1987: 57; Wei 1974: 8, 32; Anderson 1876: 228–9.

Islam in this way.[134] After an uprising in Gansu, an edict of 1784 prohibited Muslims from adopting children.[135]

The ulama forbade turning foundlings into slaves, but some believers took this to apply only to Muslim children.[136] Fulbe immigrants collected enslaved abandoned Animist infants in the Borgu area, west of the Niger. Parents exposed to the elements those children whose teeth had first appeared in their upper jaw, which was thought to be inauspicious.[137]

'People of the book'

There existed an early and clear prohibition on enslaving 'people of the book', or scriptuaries. These were initially Jewish and Christian monotheists living peacefully under Muslim rule, who paid special taxes. Zoroastrians were later included without too much protest, although Manichaeans were excluded. Some Muslims wanted Hindus and Buddhists to be classified as idolaters, enslavable at will, but this was eventually rejected.[138] Indeed, Ahmad Baba argued that the founder of the Maliki school of law had assimilated 'all the nations ... who do not have a book' to Magians, that is Zoroastrians.[139] In effect, scriptuaries became more or less coterminous with any infidel subjects, even Animists.

Such definitions mattered, because Muslims were prohibited from turning free scriptuaries into slaves through taxation. In reality, levies of slaves were raised from peaceful subjects, who were unlikely to be able to pay in existing or purchased slaves.[140] In late-fourteenth-century India, 'Sultan Firoz Shah Tughluq made special arrangements in the tax farm of the province of Gujarat for an annual supply of high-quality slaves'.[141]

The most striking example of such a deviation from sharia norms was the Ottoman *devshirme* tax in Christian youths, which probably began in the reign of Bayezit I (r. 1360–1403). Officials took male Christian children, usually adolescents but ranging in age from seven to 20. Recruitment was arbitrary, although the Janissary law of

[134] Hartmann 1921: 99–100; Anderson 1876: 228–9.
[135] Lipman 1997: 45, 113; Fields 1978: 68–9.
[136] Schneider 1999.
[137] Baldus 1977: 439–40.
[138] Hodgson 1974: I, 290–1; Lal 1994: 45; Wink 1999: I, 206.
[139] Barbour and Jacobs 1985: 136.
[140] Hunwick 1992: 10–11.
[141] Digby 1984: 117.

1402, or thereabouts, specified a lad from every 40 households, and not more than one from any given household. Officials toured every four to seven years. Towns were normally spared, though Athens was affected in the mid-sixteenth-century. Converted, circumcised, culturally assimilated and trained, youths were mostly incorporated into the Janissary infantry corps, with some destined for special cavalry units or palace duties.[142]

Basilike Papoulia concluded that the *devshirme* was an example of political prerogative exercised in violation of the rights of scriptuaries, but this provoked an apologetic response. Some challenged her citation of a long list of Balkan laments from 1395. They pointed out that most recruits were privileged and remunerated. They were rarely sold, and possessed and transmitted property, including their own slaves. Though ordered to cut all ties with their families, a few succeeded in dispensing patronage at home. Christian parents might thus implore, or even bribe, officials to take their sons. Indeed, Bosnian and Albanian Muslims successfully requested their inclusion in the system.[143]

The anguish was real, however, leading Christians in Albania and Epirus to rebel in 1565. Some parents bribed recruiters not to take their child, and only a few lads torn from their families rose far through the Ottoman ranks.[144] Youths were not regularly manumitted on completing their training.[145] Janissaries were subjected to ferocious discipline, and were forbidden to marry, measures tending to contribute to a homosexual culture in the corps.[146] Even boys taken legally could end up as slaves in private households, the usual fate of those snatched unofficially.[147] As for Albanian and Bosnian Muslims, they only agreed to send their sons to serve in the palace.[148]

Custom has sometimes been advanced to explain the system, but the evidence is thin. Turkish custom might have legitimised the

---

[142] Ménage 1965; Ménage 1956: 183; Papoulia 1963; Wittek 1955; Imber 2002: 134–40; Shaw and Shaw 1976–7: I, 46, 113–15; Sugar 1977: 55–9; Malcolm 1998: 95–6; Yarikayya 2004.

[143] Inalcik 1979: 46; Imber 1997: 78–9; Imber 2002: 135–7; Shaw and Shaw 1976–7: I, 114–15, 123; Sugar 1977: 57–8; Kunt 1982: 61; Erdem 1996: 4, 190; Malcolm 1998: 377.

[144] Malcolm 1998: 96; Papoulia 1963: 62–6, 109–16; Arnold 1913: 151–2; Sugar 1977: 57–9.

[145] Repp 1968; Erdem 1996: 11.

[146] Imber 2002: 138–41; Ménage 1965; Winter 1992: 9.

[147] Kunt 1982: 61–3.

[148] Shaw 1976–7: I, 114.

practice in places, but its status in the Balkans was weak.[149] Early
Ottoman slave law was provincial, based on the existing situation in
conquered lands.[150] This raises the question of Christian origins,
denied by Paul Wittek.[151] However, an eleventh-century Byzantine
text suggests that one child in five was taken into servitude from
Slavs and Albanians.[152]

Instead, Wittek argues ingeniously that Balkan Slavs were not
'people of the book' in Shafi'i terms, as they had converted to Christianity after the time of the Prophet. This is unlikely, for Greeks and
Armenians were sometimes recruited, and they had been monotheists since before the time of Muhammad. Furthermore, the pres-
ence in Istanbul of Shafi'i ulama, hailing from Syria or Egypt,
signally fails to explain why an officially Hanafi empire might have
turned to an arcane piece of Shafi'i law.[153]

The idea that peaceful Christians were slaves through conquest
was common, but it contradicted the sharia.[154] Hakan Erdem suggests more specifically that Christians without formal written pacts
remained collectively slaves. He notes that a 1430 treaty promised
the Greeks of one community in Epirus that, 'you shall have no
fear, either from enslavement or from the taking of your children'.
He further points out that communities yielding boys paid no taxes.
However, he admits that some communities had long been taxed
prior to having lads taken from them, notably in Anatolia.[155]

Other supposed Islamic justifications are scarcely more convincing. The levy was said to represent the fifth of the spoils of war owed
to the victor, but boys were taken from Christian communities that
had submitted peacefully, and booty was not due from generations
born into subjection.[156] Inalcik proposes that this tax was 'one of
the extraordinary services imposed by the state in an emergency',
in line with public interest. However, he fails to explain how an
'emergency' could have lasted for centuries.[157] Apologists further
protested that no youth was actually forced to be circumcised and
convert, but the pressure to do so was irresistible.[158]

---

[149] Kunt 1982: 56–7, 60; Wittek 1955: 275; Cahen 1970: 214–15.
[150] Fisher 1980a: 26–9.
[151] Wittek 1955: 275.
[152] Cahen 1970: 215–16.
[153] Wittek 1955; Papoulia 1963: 43–7.
[154] Ménage 1956: 181–3.
[155] Erdem 1996: 2–5.
[156] Wittek 1955: 271–4; Ménage 1965; Yarikkaya 2004.
[157] Inalcik 1979: 25, 46.
[158] Arnold 1913: 150–2.

Indeed, the element of forced conversion, prohibited in the sharia, loomed large. The *devshirme* was sometimes pictured as acceptable because Islam was the 'natural religion' of humanity, but the ulama did not concur.[159] A sixteenth-century author, Mustafa 'Ali, admitted that, 'the service assigned to them is at variance with the Divine Law. It was only adopted in the past out of need, as a means to increase the number of Muslims'.[160] Idris Bitlisi, Kurdish nobleman and historian, endorsed both this notion and the idea that infidels were slaves through conquest, appealing to sharia and reason. Some 70 years later, Sa'duddin transcribed much of his argument, but tellingly omitted passages affirming that the *devshirme* accorded with the sharia.[161]

More acceptable in holy law was the enslavement of dependants of scriptuaries who broke the terms of their subjection.[162] In the 1480s Muhammad b. 'Abd al-Karim al-Maghili, from Algeria, wrote an incendiary tract against Saharan Jews, accusing them of not paying canonical taxes. Despite strong local opposition, he called for the men to be killed and the women and children to be enslaved.[163] A Maliki mufti of Moroccan origins, in late nineteenth-century Cairo, held that Jews and Christians who broke their pact with Muslims could legitimately be either killed or enslaved.[164]

Nevertheless, Ebu's Su'ud [Abu al-Su'ud] (c. 1490–1574), a great Ottoman Hanafi jurist, rejected the penalty of enslavement for certain categories of rebellious scriptuaries. Defaulting on taxes, robbing believers, or fleeing to avoid oppression could not be punished in this way. Only if they took refuge among the infidel, or fought against Muslims, could they be reduced to servitude.[165] He also banned the enslavement of Armenian Christians in Persia, who had taken no part in war against the Ottomans.[166]

Conversion and freedom

Many believers were sorely troubled by the harshness of the sharia towards converts. Asking for a fatwa in fifteenth-century Morocco,

---

[159] Kafadar 1995: 83–4.
[160] See Erdem 1996: 6.
[161] Ménage 1956: 181–3.
[162] Hodgson 1974: I, 227.
[163] Hunwick 1985: 36–8.
[164] Delanoue 1982: 132, 166–7.
[165] Erdem 1996: 23.
[166] Imber 1997: 88.

one group inquired, 'How is it that the profession of the monotheistic creed, which saves from death and from punishment in the other world, does not save from the humiliation and suffering of slavery?' The answer, that servitude was a punishment for past unbelief, may not have convinced the doubters.[167]

Shaykh Burhanuddin 'Ali, Inner Asian author of the twelfth-century *Hidaya* Hanafi code mentioned above, even refused to release those who converted after defeat, but before being formally reduced to slavery. He explained that this was because their wickedness had existed up to the point of defying God's community. The shaykh admitted that his ruling contradicted passages in the Quran, the example of the Prophet after the battle of Badr, and the teachings of other schools of law. He argued his case on grounds of abrogation.[168] However, this still apparently contravened a 'sword verse', 9:5: 'Slay the idolaters wherever you find them, and take them and confine them, and lie in wait for them at every place of ambush. But if they repent, and perform the prayer, and pay the alms, then let them go their way; God is All-forgiving, All-compassionate'.

From a practical perspective, the men of the law feared that slaves would pretend to accept Islam to secure their release, causing social dislocation.[169] Indeed, doubts occasionally surfaced as to the sincerity of conversions. Ahmad b. al-Qadi al-Timbuktawi was shocked by the religious syncretism of freed Maghribi Blacks in 1808–9, and considered that they should be re-enslaved.[170] Numerous South Indian Hindus, from a servile and Dalit caste background, went over to Islam to gain emancipation. Complaints that they were not following their new faith provoked Sayyid Fadl b. 'Alawi b. Sahl, an early-nineteenth-century Hadhrami reformer in the region, to issue fatwas against their reprehensible practices.[171]

The ulama only accepted automatic liberation through conversion when slaves ran away from infidel owners to join the Islamic host.[172] The Prophet himself gave the example by freeing Abu Bakr, an Ethiopian who let himself down over the walls with a pulley at the siege of Ta'if.[173] Muhammad also freed the women of a tribe

[167] Lewis 1990: 148; Wanscharisi 1908–9: II, 426–8.
[168] Hughes 1885: 597–8.
[169] Hunwick 1985: 123.
[170] Montana 2004: 187–94.
[171] Panikkar 1989: 52, 62–3.
[172] Hamidullah 1945: 272; Awde 2000: 51.
[173] Lewis 1990: 25.

after their menfolk had joined the believers, although the ulama glossed this as an example of meritorious manumission.[174] Frontiers provided golden opportunities for infidel slaves and serfs to seek liberation, like the many Iberian Christians and Jews who deserted to become 'Allah's freedmen'.[175] A similar process seems to have been at work on the edges of Christian Ethiopia.[176] The North Caucasus mountains were a magnet for fugitive Russian serfs, although Muslim slaves fled in the other direction to join Cossack settlements.[177]

Matters were more complicated if owners of runaways were Muslims. Nevertheless, leaders of West African holy wars freed even these slaves when they fled to their standard.[178] A seventeenth-century Moroccan sultan did likewise when Christian captives escaped from their Barbary corsair owners, converted, and enlisted in his army. He was not amused when the privateers asked him for compensation.[179]

There was further dissension about slaves who embraced Islam while in the possession of a non-Muslim owner resident in an Islamic polity. Some opined that they should be freed immediately, whereas others argued that the owner should merely be forced to sell them to a Muslim. Either way, this might breach promises made to powerful infidel lords, who had submitted to Muslim rule on condition that they could keep their possessions, including slaves.[180]

Conversion came to be seen as its own reward, with enslavement portrayed as a golden opportunity to learn about the true faith.[181] Swahili poetry encouraged converted slaves to resign themselves to their fate and obey their owners.[182] Such ideas implicitly contravened 2:256 in the Quran which says, 'no compulsion is there in religion'. Nevertheless, an Uzbek general vindicated the mass enslavement of defeated Hindu rebels in the early seventeenth-century, saying that 'they all became Muhammadans. From their progeny there will be krors [tens of millions] by the judgement day'.[183]

---

[174] Ruthven 2000: 59; Hamidullah 1945: 209–10.
[175] Dozy 1913: 236–7.
[176] Miran 2004: 63.
[177] Barrett 1999: 35–6, 174–6.
[178] Klein 1998: 229; Ba and Daget 1962: 40.
[179] Berque 1978: 173.
[180] Erdem 1996: 27.
[181] Lewis 1990: 37–8; Brunschvig 1960: 35; Risso 1995: 94; Fisher 2001: 65; Kelly 1968: 594–5.
[182] Knappert 1979: 188.
[183] Kolff 1990: 13.

In other ways, slavery tended to work against proselytisation, for there emerged a deep reluctance to attempt to convert people living in servile 'reservoirs'. Ottoman sultans allegedly refrained from either directly ruling or converting Georgia, to keep the Christian kingdom in the Caucasus 'as a sort of nursery for slaves and for women for the sultan's seraglio'.[184] This problem was widespread in Africa, Inner Asia and Southeast Asia.[185] Stories about Nias, the island off West Sumatra that provided most of Aceh's Animist slaves, excused a lack of ardour in conversion by depicting islanders as descended from unclean animals and incestuous unions.[186] Slaving was judged a major impediment to the spread of Islam in Africa, which paradoxically only gathered pace after Western colonial conquest.[187]

Punishing 'bad Muslims'

Despite repeated prohibitions on reducing free Muslims to bondage, some ulama tolerated the enslavement of apostates, heretics, deserters, highway robbers, and those causing dissension, as long as they were taken in holy war.[188] However, many thought that it was illicit to condemn such people as infidels before the judgement day.[189] Jihads could certainly be declared against them, but the standard penalties were death, mutilation or exile. This reflected 5:33 in the Quran on apostates, who were to be 'slaughtered, or crucified, or their hands and feet shall alternately be struck off, or they shall be banished from the land'. The fate reserved for dependants of male apostates remained unclear, however, and some ulama agreed that they might be enslaved.[190]

Divisions persisted over apostasy. Muhammad b. 'Abd al-Karim al-Maghili, of Tlemcen (Tilisman) in Algeria, told the West African ruler of Songhay around 1500 that jurists remained undecided.[191] Ahmad Baba quoted well established precedent in 1615 against

---

[184] Lang 1957: 22.
[185] Gordon 1989: 28–9; Mahadi 1992: 115; Fisher 2001: 53–4, 65; Trimingham 1959: 29; Heers 2003: 59–61; Risso 1995: 109; Ceulemans 1959: 38–9; Levi 2002; Gregorian 1969: 37; Maxwell 1879: 46, 50; Loyré-de-Hauteclocque 1989: 128.
[186] Snouck Hurgronje 1906: I, 20–1.
[187] Forget 1900: 95.
[188] Fisher 2001: 28–9; Heers 2003: 44–5.
[189] Azumah 2001: 66–7.
[190] Khadduri 1955: 76–80; Hunwick 1985: 126–7.
[191] Hunwick 1985: 74.

enslaving them or their dependants.[192] Usuman dan Fodio, who founded the Sokoto caliphate in West Africa, listed deviants who could be attacked in holy war around 1800. He noted that only apostates might face enslavement, but that most Maliki scholars opposed this ruling.[193] In contrast, an 1855 fatwa of Shaykh Jamal, 'chief of the ulema of Mecca', declared that it was licit to kill Ottoman apostates and enslave their children.[194]

Defeated dissenters could also face servitude. A caliph imposed this sentence on Khariji captives in 740, and 'heretical' women from a rebellious Berber tribe were publicly auctioned in Cairo in 1077.[195] Sixteenth-century Inner Asian jurists pronounced it legal to enslave Iranian and Azeri Shi'a, who were outside the abode of Islam.[196] Afghan grandees of the 1830s even proclaimed it 'an act of merit to sell a Sheah into slavery'.[197] Shi'i believers thus came to dominate the servile masses of Bukhara and Khiva in the nineteenth-century.[198] Kurds of the Ottoman-Persian borderlands enslaved both Shi'i heretics and Yazidi syncretists.[199]

Such practices did not go uncontested. Ebu's Su'ud declared that war against the Shi'a was indeed obligatory, but that captives could not be enslaved. In particular, 'intercourse with slave girls' taken in such wars was sinful.[200] Confusingly, however, he seems to have issued another fatwa endorsing the enslavement of Shi'i foes in 1554. It was a 1736 peace treaty with Persia that ended the Ottoman enslavement of 'heretics' in war, at least on paper.[201]

Rulers were tempted to cast the net even more widely, despite a decision from the time of the rightly-guided caliphs that mere rebels should not be enslaved, recalled by sixteenth-century Ottoman and Maghribi scholars.[202] Complaints soared when recently converted Turks came to dominate the heartlands of Islam from the eleventh-century.[203] The Kazakh élite in Turkistan regularly sold the

---

[192] Hunwick and Harrak 2000; Barbour and Jacobs 1985; Willis 1980: 180; Hamel 2002: 37–8, 50.

[193] Bivar 1961: 240–2; Hunwick 1985: 74.

[194] Lewis 1990: 80–1.

[195] Pipes 1981: 142; Brunschvig 1960: 32; Heers 2003: 45.

[196] Petrushevsky 1985: 159.

[197] Harlan 1939: 66.

[198] Levi 2002: 279–87; Carrère d'Encausse 1966: 52, 145–7; Hodgson 1974: III, 39, 41.

[199] Erdem 1996: 46–7, 60; Garnett 1909: 224.

[200] Imber 1997: 86–9.

[201] Erdem 1996: 21.

[202] Charouiti Hasnaoui 2000: 7; Imber 1997: 84–5; Hunwick 1985: 74–5.

[203] Petrushevsky 1985: 158–9.

children of those 'in disfavour'.[204] An Ottoman general, sent to defeat Mamluk emirs in Egypt in 1786–7, sought to reduce their wives and children to servitude.[205] Civil wars led to mutual enslavement from as early as the sixteenth-century in the Hausa states of West Africa.[206] Around 1800, the ruler of Wadai, in modern Chad, punished Muslim women and children from Bagirmi in this way, for participating in the impiety of their sultan.[207] The sultan of Dar Sila, in the same area, enslaved rival sultans and their families in the 1890s.[208]

Even worse was the enslavement of free Muslims in raids, common in Southeast Asia.[209] At best, captors were more likely to ransom Muslims than infidels, and they released pilgrims and descendants of the Prophet.[210] The spread and deepening of Islam in Southeast Asia from the seventeenth-century led to a growing insistence that slaves should only be taken from unbelievers.[211] Early Modern sultans of Jambi in Sumatra, priding themselves on orthodoxy, thus sought to redirect their razzias.[212]

Pious descendants of the Prophet, immigrants from Hadhramaut, were agents of sharia-minded reform. They insisted that slaves be taken from groups such as Hindu Balinese and Animists from the Lesser Sunda islands, who, 'being infidels, are considered fair booty'.[213] One Arab publicly disowned his own son, Sayyid 'Abd al-Rahman al-Qadri, for ravaging the coasts of Borneo in the 1760s. After founding the new state of Pontianak in 1770–1, the sultan regularly visited his father's tomb to pray for forgiveness.[214]

Inner Asia suffered much from the scourge of Muslims enslaving fellow believers. Turkmen horsemen ingeniously asserted that Muslims could be enslaved because the Prophet Yusuf (Joseph) had suffered this fate, although, as an extra precaution, they forced captives

---

[204] Olcott 1987: 51.

[205] Winter 1992: 27–8, 146.

[206] Renault and Daget 1985: 37; Richardson 1853: II, 205; Fisher 2001: 121; Christelow 1994: 113.

[207] Tounsy 1851: 463–5.

[208] Bret 1987: 41.

[209] Warren 1981: 152–6, 182, 187–8; Rutter 1986: 28, 31–51, 92–5, 173; Loyré-de-Hauteclocque 1989: 100–4, 129–48; Kiefer 1972: 22–3, 84–5.

[210] Warren 1981: 199–201, 238–9; Rutter 1986: 40, 270–2.

[211] Reid 1993: 70; Reid 1983b: 169–70.

[212] Andaya (Barbara) 1993: 96.

[213] Raffles 1978: I, 76, 232–5.

[214] Moor 1968: Appendix, 101–2.

to declare themselves to be heretics.[215] Indian Muslims were often kidnapped when travelling in Turkistan.[216] Many Sunni Muslims were scooped up in expeditions against Animists and Shiʻi or Ismaʻili heretics in the high valleys where Afghanistan, Kashmir, and Turkistan met.[217] Khoqand raiders of the nineteenth-century, seizing Chinese slaves in East Turkistan, failed to differentiate between Hui Muslims and Han infidels.[218] Caucasus traditions envisioned both Muslims and unbelievers as legitimate victims.[219]

Complaints multiplied in Africa. A fourteenth-century king of Kanem, in the Lake Chad area, wrote to the Mamluk ruler of Egypt denouncing the arbitrary enslavement of free Muslims by Arab raiders.[220] There were growing abuses in West Africa, one of the reasons for Ahmad Baba's issuing of his famous fatwa in 1615.[221] The Hausa ruler of Zinder, heavily indebted to Maghribi merchants, seized peaceful subjects in the early nineteenth-century. He bought off the wrath of his overlord, the sultan of Borno, with a cut of the proceeds.[222] ʻAbd al-Rahman al-Jabarti (1754–1825), a distinguished scholar of Ethiopian origins, accused Muhammad ʻAli, Pasha of Egypt, of enslaving free Muslims in conquering the Sudan from 1820.[223] One shaykh in northern Mozambique was accused of kidnapping his own people 'indiscriminately' around 1880.[224]

Free Muslims illicitly taken into bondage might gain redress in qadi courts. Cases brought by those claiming to be have been wrongly enslaved were common in Cairo from at least 1749. Pious merchants paid the legal fees, and many petitioners were released.[225] Similarly, Zanzibar courts heard claims of wrongful enslavement of free Muslims in areas as far away as Manyema, in the Congo.[226]

Concubines and eunuchs

The ulama accepted that a male believer could have as many servile concubines as he desired, while neither encouraging the practice

[215] Letourneau 1897: 226; Ali 1891: 378.
[216] Levi 2002: 280–1.
[217] Harlan 1939: 44–5; Gardner 1898: 32–3, 103–5, 111, 119–25, 147–8; Levi 2002: 286–7; Noelle 1997: 80–3.
[218] Laura Newby, personal communication.
[219] Erdem 1996: 46.
[220] Renault and Daget 1985: 34.
[221] Hunwick and Harrak 2000; Barbour and Jacobs 1985; Lovejoy 1983: 71–2.
[222] Richardson 1853: II, 205, 221–3, 228–31, 238–44, 282.
[223] Delanoue 1982: 57.
[224] Duffy 1967: 85.
[225] Walz 1985: 147–9, 158.
[226] Harries 1965: 206–7.

nor allowing free concubines.[227] Verses from the Quran could be differently interpreted. Parts of 4:25–30 read: 'Any one of you who has not the affluence to be able to marry believing freewomen in wedlock, let him take believing handmaids that your right hands own'. As for 4:3, it commands, 'if you fear that you will not be equitable, then [take] only one [wife], or what your right hand owns'. Finally, 24:32 enjoins, 'Marry the spouseless among you, and your slaves and handmaidens that are righteous'. The Prophet had no concubines while married monogamously to Khadija, but was believed to have owned two in the later polygynous stage of his life.[228]

The ulama's resignedness could be seen as a pessimistic response to male lust, an 'attempt to deflect desire through a prophylactic approach to sexuality'.[229] Concubinage also eased the conversion of Animists, and may have attracted Jews and Christians.[230] The system overcame the 'four wives barrier' to embracing Islam, as among the Yao living to the east of Lake Malawi in Africa.[231] The ownership of concubines certainly became widespread in Islamdom, extending to men of quite modest means.[232]

Ulama were more likely to criticise the keeping of servile eunuchs.[233] The traditions were generally hostile to the practice, and a Hadith of the Prophet stated that, 'whoever castrates a slave, him also shall we castrate'.[234] Another canonical tradition taught that 'he is not of my people who makes another a eunuch or becomes so himself'.[235] Some scholars further interpreted 4:118 in the Quran, condemning those who 'cut off the cattle's ears ... and ... alter God's creation', as a general prohibition on emasculation, although others restricted it to animals.[236]

The problem was that no canonical text clearly forbade the purchase of male slaves emasculated by infidels, especially those that dwelled in the abode of war.[237] Indeed, the Prophet himself was said to have accepted a eunuch as a gift, although this Hadith was

---

[227] Hodgson 1974: II, 144; Fisher 2001: 181–2.
[228] Ruthven 2000: 57, 62–3; Awde 2000: 10; Zaidi 1935.
[229] Kandiyoti 1988: 37.
[230] Hughes 1885: 600.
[231] Willis 1980: 185–6; Baldé 1975: 205; Monteiro 1993: 198–9.
[232] Hodgson 1974: II, 65, 144; Ahmed 1992: 83; Adam 1940: 246–7; Baer 1969: 163; Mowafi 1981: 13; Strobel 1979: 49.
[233] Hodgson 1974: II, 144; Lal 1994: 116–17; Hambly 1974: 129; Winter 1992: 43–4.
[234] Hunwick 1992: 21; Kotb 1970: 48.
[235] Hughes 1885: 110; Juynboll 1912: 584.
[236] Juynboll 1912: 584; Levy 1957: 77; Meinardus 1969: 50–1; Pellat et al. 1978: 1,089.
[237] Brunschvig 1960: 26, 33.

excluded from canonical collections.[238] The responsibility for legitimating the practice was attributed to Caliph Mu'awiya (r. 661–680).[239] An early Arab geographer discussed castration by infidels dispassionately, as a scientific rather than a moral issue.[240]

Graver doubts surrounded unbelievers performing the grisly operation in the lands of Islam. In tenth-century Muslim Iberia, Jews castrated Slavs for export.[241] Hindu surgeons of the Baidya caste may have manufactured eunuchs in Muslim Bengal, a major source for South Asia.[242] Eastern Orthodox priests and monks operated on slave boys in Upper Egypt, especially in the Asyut region, usually practising complete removal. Stung by criticism, they retorted that their skills kept death rates low. One enquiry suggested that mortality in these centres was around 15 per cent, whereas it could reach 90 per cent elsewhere.[243]

The seeming Sunni consensus on slavery was full of fissures, from the time of the Prophet himself. An elaborate law of slavery was incrementally erected on foundations which were so flimsy as to pose a constant threat to the viability of the whole tottering edifice. There is little hope of ever ascertaining whether an abolitionist project existed at the dawn of Islam, but there is a pressing need to probe deeper into Sunni divisions over the issue, despite suggestions that the 'gates of interpretation' came to be firmly closed.

Determining who was legitimately a slave risked causing the *de facto* collapse of the institution. Definitions of Muslims bad enough to deserve such a fate varied greatly, as did those of 'people of the book' good enough to avoid it. Whether the latter, or indeed free unbelievers in general, benefited from the protection extended to free Muslims was particularly obscure. What defined a holy war, who decided the fate of captives, and whether non-combatants were legitimate victims, were issues shrouded in uncertainty. Obtaining slaves by purchase or tribute were dubious practices, all the more so when heathens enslaved people in ways diametrically opposed to Islamic norms.

---

[238] Pellat *et al.* 1978: 1,089; Millant 1908: 203.
[239] Ayalon 1999: 66.
[240] Muqaddasi 1950: 57–9.
[241] Constable 1994: 204–6; Wink 1999: I, 98.
[242] Hambly 1974: 130.
[243] Meinardus 1969; Baer 1969: 164; Juynboll 1912: 584; Hogendorn 2000: 62–3; Hunwick and Powell 2002: 99–105.

Supposed religious solutions to the problems encountered in acquiring infidel slaves were poorly grounded in the founding texts, notably the notion of the 'abode of war'. Slavery as punishment for unbelief covered every form of acquisition, and justified maintaining people in bondage after their conversion, but the notion emerged late, and lacked convincing canonical underpinnings. Other religious excuses were so lame that most ulama refused to acknowledge them, even if pious Muslims clung to them for centuries. Debates on these lines need to be unearthed from Sunni writings.

In regard to concubines and eunuchs, the canonical texts were either hard to interpret, or left awkward loopholes. Nevertheless, the tenor of Quran and Hadith appeared to be set against any employment of eunuchs, while limiting the incidence of concubinage. There is thus a need to examine more carefully whether casuistry elicited critical reactions.

Further work should help to fix trends over time more precisely, for there are unmistakable indications of a progressive hardening of hearts, as absolutism eroded early egalitarianism. Early Muslims appear to have been troubled that people should lose their birthright of freedom. Their Sunni successors comforted themselves with the mantra that not only rank unbelievers and seditious scriptuaries received their just deserts, but also evil Muslims.

3

DISSENTING TRADITIONS

Sects today account for around 15 per cent of Muslims, whereas most mystics and nonconformists have remained within the Sunni fold. Many dissenters had a libertarian agenda, with millenarian and antinomian groups particularly keen to stress social levelling. For them 'very shortly, the wicked great of this world would be humbled or destroyed, and the lowly ... would be exalted and share the good things of this world, free from oppressors'. In a famous prediction, the world 'would be filled with justice'.[1]

The Imam Mahdi, the focus of eschatological longings, was not clearly mentioned in the Quran, and traditions referring to him were weak. The title could simply designate a 'renewer of the faith', expected at the turn of each Islamic lunar century. However, many Muslims came to believe that the Mahdi would be the last caliph, as Muhammad had been the 'seal of the prophets'. For mystics, he would be the 'seal of the saints'. For Shi'i and Isma'ili groups, he would be the occulted Imam. The Mahdi was further thought to prepare the return of Nabi 'Isa, the Christian Jesus, to preside over the end of the world and the last judgement. Chiliastic expectations were strong in the ninth and tenth centuries, and flared up again around 1590–1, marking a thousand years since the Prophet's emigration to Medina.[2]

Maxime Rodinson has argued that despite libertarian tendencies, 'with rare exceptions, there was no question of contesting ... the hereditary status of slaves'.[3] This may be too strict a judgement. Even if social manifestations of bondage figured little as a direct preoccupation, slave rebellions indicate that there were practical interpretations of such doctrines. Moreover, sectarian ferment cul-

[1] Hodgson 1974: I, 252–5, 317, 320, 344, 369–70, 373–4.
[2] García-Arenal 2000; Halm 1991.
[3] Rodinson 1966: 86–7.

minated in the Druze abolition of slavery, a pioneering moment in Islamic history.

Ascetics and mystics

Despite a certain 'libertarian openness', early ascetics and mystics generally withdrew from the world to focus on their relationship with God.[4] Ascetics emerged from the late seventh-century, and gradually evolved towards Sufi mysticism. They propagated a disinterested love of God, motivated by neither desire for paradise nor fear of hell. Stressing the 'greater jihad' of the heart over the 'lesser jihad' of the sword, in terms of a Hadith of the Prophet, they spread Islam peacefully. They showed compassion for the wretched of the earth, and protested against injustice.[5]

The main impact of this kind of mystical thinking was probably to integrate slaves and former slaves more securely into the Islamic order, by encouraging adepts to accept their position in this world. Thus Suhaym (d. 660/1), a slave poet, wrote, 'If I am a slave, my soul is free, because it is noble. And if I am black in color, my character is white'.[6] This accorded with a Hadith of the Prophet, promising a double reward in heaven to 'a slave who discharges his duties fully to God and to his master'.[7]

Nevertheless, some early Sufis expressed social concerns. Many claimed a filiation to Abu Dharr al-Ghifari, a semi-mythical figure, later hailed as an early Muslim socialist. He was exiled for calling on believers to give away all their worldly goods, presumably including slaves, after the death of Muhammad in 632.[8] Another inspiring figure was Hasan al-Basri (642–728) of Iraq, said to have been a freed Persian slave of Christian origins, or the son of such a man.[9]

The story of Rabi'a al-'Adawiyya (717–801) neatly encapsulates Sufi ambivalence about servitude. Born to a poor family of Basra in the early eighth-century, Rabi'a was orphaned, kidnapped, and sold to a merchant. She prayed so earnestly for deliverance that her master freed her, awed by her piety and sanctity. Living in poverty and chastity, she built up a circle of devoted disciples. Her followers interpreted her initial loss of freedom as an opportunity to find

---

[4] Hodgson 1974: II, 455.
[5] Ruthven 2000: 222–30.
[6] See Rosenthal 1960: 91.
[7] Awde 2000: 94.
[8] Ruthven 2000: 176, 224; Rodinson 1966: 41–2.
[9] Ahmed 1992: 87; Ruthven 2000: 223–4; Hodgson 1974: I, 248–9, 394.

God, and her later refusal to accept the gift of a slave as a rejection of luxury.[10]

The life of the Tunisian ascetic Abu 'Abdallah b. Masruq, who died early in the ninth-century, was equally ambiguous. While his hagiographers underlined the saintliness of his poverty, they also hinted at unease about slavery. After his mystical conversion, he 'abandoned his whole inheritance to lead a life of prayer and total poverty'. He personally freed all the slaves that his father had accumulated.[11]

Abu Hamid Muhammad al-Ghazali (1058–1111) crafted a reconciliation between mystics and ulama, recognising the position of Sufi elites in the Islamic establishment. The Sufis were to obey the sharia, abandon monist or pantheist conceptions of God, and curb excessive ritual practices. For their part, jurists were to recognise the mystical contribution to piety. Sufi shaykhs and ulama began to overlap and intermarry, at least in towns. Loose Sufi brotherhoods emerged, although multiple affiliations were common, and the fundamental relationship remained that of master to disciple. Elite Sufis came to own many slaves, but others clung to poverty and succouring the underprivileged.[12]

A genre of Sufi philosophical writing in praise of liberty emerged at about this time, but authors mostly 'assumed that the search for absolute freedom would lead to absolute disaster'. The pioneer, al-Qushayri (986–1072), defined freedom as emancipation from the affairs of this world. He wrote that 'freedom means for a human being not to be under the yoke of created things'. Al-Jurjani (d. 1413) adopted current orthodoxy, describing slavery as 'a penalty for unbelief'.[13] Al-Ghazali himself, writing about the ethics of slavery, stressed good treatment over manumission.[14]

Jalal al-Din Rumi (1207–73), poet and founding figure of the Mawlawiyya order, was a Persian who settled in Konya, in Anatolia.[15] Metaphors of servitude abounded in his work, but he occasionally employed images illustrating the social realities of slavery, such as the charms of Bulgarian slave-girls symbolising the temptations of the world. In one parable, depicting the relative position of prophets, saints, and believers, he wrote that 'they bring boys as slaves

---

[10] Smith 1994; el-Sakkakini 1982; Knysh 2000: 26–9.
[11] Talbi 1981: 210–11, 215–16.
[12] Winter 1992: 130–1, 145–6, 149, 182; Willis 1989: 39–40; Hodgson 1974: II, 204–28; Ruthven 2000: 242, 251; Levi 2002: 278, 284.
[13] Rosenthal 1960: 25, 108–9, 119.
[14] Hunwick and Powell 2002: 7–9.
[15] Netton 1992: 167, 216.

from the lands of the unbelievers into the Moslem realm and sell them. Some are brought at five years of age, some at ten, and some at fifteen'.[16]

Early Ottoman Sufism had libertarian overtones. The son of a Turkish warrior and a Christian captive of the Edirne region, Bedreddin (1358–1419), was later hailed as an early socialist. Rejecting the resurrection of the body and the last judgement, he was executed for allegedly taking part in a rising in 1416. The rebels demanded universal brotherhood, equal property rights, simple living, and the recognition of Christians as worshippers of God. Whether this utopia included the abolition of slavery is unclear.[17] Musa, battling for the sultanate from 1410 and seeking Bedreddin's support, retained slave soldiers and administrators.[18]

Monist Sufis of the western Mediterranean implicitly questioned servitude. Ibn al-'Arabi [Ibn Arabi] (1165–1240), the Andalusian 'greatest master', acclaimed a slave woman of the Hijaz as a saint, 'unique in her time'. Tellingly, however, he omitted her name, simply calling her 'a slave girl of Qasim al-Dawlah'.[19] One of Ibn 'al-Arabi's Maghribi disciples, al-Harrali (d. 1240), wrote to the Catholic authorities in Tarragona, Spain, appealing for the freedom of his relatives enslaved there. His grounds were that there existed no real difference between religions. This evoked mystical notions that all historic faiths were external manifestations of a common 'kernel'.[20]

The Chishtiyya order of India voiced deep sympathy for the poor of all faiths, including a muted critique of slavery. A celebrated fourteenth-century Chishti, Nizam al-Din Awliya of Delhi, stressed service to the poor over prayers and spiritual exercises, forbade his followers from entering government service, and ministered to the spiritual needs of Hindus.[21] He told a story about his teacher, who freed a slave woman because she pined for her son back home. The ulama objected, because this meant that the woman would return to polytheism. Shaykh Nizam commented that, 'the externalist scholars [ulama] would deny this; but one can understand what

[16] Chittick 1983: 87, 157, 290.
[17] Shaw and Shaw 1976–7: I, 38–43, 144; Kafadar 1995: 143; Sugar 1977: 26–8; Hodgson 1974: II, 498–9.
[18] Shaw and Shaw 1976–7: I, 39.
[19] Austin 1971: 159
[20] Koningsveld 1995: 8–10
[21] Hodgson 1974: II, 206, 423; Knysh 2000: 281–2.

he did'.[22] He also told the story of Nur Turk, who allowed a slave
to buy his freedom with part of the money earned from carding
cotton.[23]

South Asian Sufi references to slavery often had a critical edge to
them. Shaykh Nasiruddin, whose order is not indicated, noted sar-
donically in the mid-fourteenth-century that the poor thought of
God, whereas the rich thought only of slave girls.[24] The *Tuhfa i
nasa'ih*, an ethical treatise composed in Persian by Yusuf Gada in
the 1390s and often attributed to the Chishtiyya, accepted slavery,
but condemned those who dealt in human flesh. This text was
much reprinted and translated.[25] Abul Fazl 'Allami (1551–1602),
Akbar's chief minister, portrayed his master's measures against slavery as the actions of a 'Sufi perfect man'.[26]

Theologians and philosophers

Sayyid Amir 'Ali provided no reference for his claim that Mu'tazili
theologians disapproved of slavery.[27] Mu'tazili thinkers certainly
imbibed a rationalist outlook from Greek and Indian mentors, but
this came with a highly elitist view of society. Although Mu'tazili
writers stressed the justice of God over his omnipotence, and
exalted a created Quran above the traditions, they were generally
mute on servitude. Moreover, the ninth-century Abbasid caliphs
who patronised them held many slaves.[28]

The prolific writer 'Amr b. Bahr al-Jahiz of Basra (776–869), was
an 'eager Mu'tazili'. Partly of African origin, al-Jahiz criticised aspects
of slavery, but scarcely condemned the institution as a whole.[29] His
famous defence of Turks and Blacks, the latter category embracing
Indians and Chinese, rested in part on the assertion that they were
not all slaves.[30] He noted that 'slaves do not suffer slavery except
when they have been captured', and yet he cited the common Arab
saying that 'the stick belongs to the slave'.[31] His story of an angry

[22] Habib 1988–9: 254–5.
[23] Habib 1988–9: 252–3; Kidwai 1985: 91.
[24] Moosvi 2003.
[25] Digby 1984: 111–12, 117–18.
[26] Hodgson 1974: III, 71, 73–9.
[27] Ali 1917: II, 32.
[28] Hodgson 1974: I, 433–8.
[29] Hodgson 1974: I, 466–7.
[30] Lewis 1990: 31–2.
[31] Rosenthal 1960: 92, 95.

wife, whose husband neglected her for a beautiful young concubine, was an ambivalent moral tale.[32] The epistle on singing-girls
contained satirical passages on slavery, particularly harsh on traders, and yet also condemned the wiles of the girls.[33]

Muslim philosophers and scientists, despite not being directly
acquainted with the *Politics* of Aristotle, generally agreed with their
'first teacher' that there existed 'slaves by nature'.[34] Abu'l Hasan
Muhammad al-'Amiri (d. 992) wrote of the natural superiority of
masters over slaves. Abu al-Nasr Muhammad al-Farabi (870–950),
exalted as the 'second teacher', stated that it was just to seize in war
people whose 'best and most advantageous status in the world is to
serve and be slaves'. The celebrated Persian physician, Ibn Sina
[Avicenna] (980–1037), insisted that 'there must be masters and
slaves'.[35] The famous Iberian opponent of al-Ghazali, Ibn Rushd
[Averroës] (1126–98), accepted the enslavement of captives, and
the distribution of women and children as war booty.[36]

That said, some philosophers cited liberal Greek texts on slavery,
possibly aware that Aristotle had quoted the Sophist Alcidamas,
who considered that 'nature has made no one a slave'. They may
also have been acquainted with Stoic critiques of servitude. Some
Islamic philosophers certainly cited Aristotle's advice to Alexander
the Great that 'governing free men is nobler than governing slaves',
and Plato's opinion that 'he is no ruler who rules slaves'. A clearer
reference to social bondage emerged from the story that Alexander
had once refused to enslave war captives, because he had no wish to
become a 'ruler of slaves'.[37]

Interpreting slavery as punishment for sin, or as a divine dispensation unfathomable for mortals, may have accompanied the decline
of rationalist thinking from the thirteenth-century. Determinism triumphed, emerging from the theological arguments of Abu al-Hasan
'Ali b. Isma'il al-'Ashari (873–935).[38] To the extent that they survived, Mu'tazili and philosophical ideas came to be associated with
sectarian Islam, notably of the Shi'i and Zaydi variety.[39]

---

[32] Fahmy 1990: 107–8.
[33] Jahiz 1980: 1–5, 20, 26, 34–8.
[34] Rosenthal 1960: 31, 91; Davis 1984: 14.
[35] Lewis 1990: 54–5.
[36] Kelsay 1993: 62–3.
[37] Rosenthal 1960: 31, 102–3.
[38] Ruthven 2000: 194–6.
[39] Crone and Cook 1977: 134.

Establishing a Shiʻi consensus

The Shiʻa considered that supreme power was due to the descendants of Fatima, the Prophet's daughter, and her husband, 'Ali b. Abi Talib (r. 656–61). Imams in this line were infallible, and thus had the power to modify the holy law, with an emphasis on restoring justice. However, once the twelfth Imam had become occulted in 873–74, Shiʻi scholars in this 'Twelver' strand could only interpret the law.[40]

Liberal traditions on servitude were attributed to Shiʻi Imams. 'Ali b. Abi Talib banned the enslavement of the womenfolk of defeated foes, except for female slaves captured in the enemy camp.[41] He was also reported to have said, 'I would be ashamed ever to take as a slave a man who said that Allah was his master', probably referring to enslaving fellow Muslims, but possibly authorising liberation after conversion.[42] It was related that 'he was hard-working, and would never support himself from the labour of others'.[43] He purchased slaves to free them, demonstrating his piety.[44] However, he reputedly owned 17 concubines.[45]

The evidence for later Imams is ambiguous. Husayn, son of 'Ali, was given a slave girl by the 'usurper' Muʻawiya. Horrified to realise that she could recite the Quran, he freed her immediately.[46] Zayn al-'Abidin, grandson of 'Ali, liberated many slaves. However, there is no compelling reason to believe the claim that, 'If he had lived for a longer time, he would have freed all the slaves'.[47]

Jaʻfar al-Sadiq (d. 765), sixth in line, was known as the lawgiver for his crucial role in the elaboration of Shiʻi law. He 'preached against slavery', and attested to the Prophet's saying that the man who dealt in slaves was an outcast of humanity.[48] Jaʻfar ordered the freeing of Muslim slaves after seven years, although later Shiʻi scholars interpreted this as 'a highly recommended deed of virtue', rather than a binding obligation.[49] He repeatedly declared that 'all

[40] Halm 1991: 29–155.
[41] Hamidullah 1945: 172.
[42] Chafik 1938: 37.
[43] Nurbakhsh 1980: 2.
[44] Rizvi 1987: ch. 3.
[45] Blank 2001: 77.
[46] Mernissi 1987: 192–3.
[47] <http://www.balagh.net/english/ahl_bayt/zayn_al_abidin/03.htm>
[48] Ali 1917: II, 31–2.
[49] Brunschvig 1960: 31; Rizvi 1987: ch. 3.

people are free except someone who acknowledges his own enslavement', but this could have allowed for self-enslavement.[50]

In practice Shi'i approaches to slavery came to differ only in matters of detail from those of their Sunni rivals. For the Shi'a, birth as a slave depended on the servile status of both parents, and only Muslim slaves could be manumitted.[51] In theory, there could be no jihad of the sword after the occultation of the twelfth Imam, so that war captives could not be enslaved.[52] However, the Buyid dynasty, ruling Iraq and western Iran from 932 to 1055, obtained a ruling that they could declare holy war because they were 'guarding the frontier'.[53] They employed military slaves.[54]

A millenarian and mystical current flowed through Shi'i channels from the fourteenth-century, notably in Iran and India, with a stress on protesting against social injustice.[55] The most famous Shi'i Mahdi was of Azeri Turkmen background, and he led the Safaviyya mystical order. He initially presented himself as the reincarnation of 'Ali and a divine emanation, but was astute enough to accept the judgement of those who hailed him as the instrument of imposing Twelver doctrines on Persia.[56] As Shah Isma'il (r. 1501–24), he claimed the right to declare holy war, due to his alleged descent from the Imams.[57] Shah Isma'il spurned military and administrative slaves, but he owned domestic ones. His successors soon restored elite slavery, turning their backs on any millenarian flirtation with freedom.[58]

Isma'ili divisions

Isma'ili sects, disagreeing with Twelvers about the succession to Ja'far al-Sadiq, were generally libertarian, antinomian, and millenarian, but most were also small and ephemeral. Many believed that the Mahdi would abrogate the law, introducing the religion of paradise.[59] Thus, Abu Ya'qub al-Sijistani (d. c. 990) foresaw that the Mahdi would restore the religion of Adam. He cited 7:157 in the

---

[50] Taleqani 1983: 193.
[51] Brunschvig 1960: 31; Petrushevsky 1985: 158.
[52] Peters 1979: 171; Khadduri 1955: 67; Kohlberg 1976: 69–70, 78–80.
[53] Kohlberg 1976: 80–1.
[54] Hodgson 1974: II, 35–6.
[55] *Ibid*.: II, 493–7.
[56] Roemer 1986: 209–11, 336–7.
[57] Kohlberg 1976: 81.
[58] Babaie *et al.* 2004.
[59] Hodgson 1974: I, 490–2; Halm 1991: 169.

Quran, speaking of the 'Prophet of the common folk ... relieving them of their loads, and the fetters that were upon them'.[60]

Sayyid Amir 'Ali declared that Hamdan Qarmat, the semi-legendary founder of Qarmati (Carmathian) groups in Iraq from the 860s, 'held slavery to be unlawful', but cited no source.[61] More prudently, Leila Ahmed opines that the Qarmati sect rejected concubinage and polygyny.[62] Some adepts certainly owned slaves, and tentative negotiations with Iraqi slave rebels did not lead to any formal alliance.[63]

Abu Sa'id al-Jannabi, the Mahdi of the Bahrayn Qarmati community, was no abolitionist. He built up a state from the 890s, extending into al-Hasa. The form of government was quasi-republican, there were no taxes, and the poor benefited from generous social services. However, this precocious 'welfare state' depended on a servile underclass, mainly consisting of purchased Blacks, and estimated to number some 30,000 in the eleventh-century. Al-Jannabi himself was assassinated by a slave.[64]

The Bahrayn Qarmati enslaved Muslim enemies false to the faith.[65] In about 925, they attacked the pilgrim caravan returning to Syria from the Hijaz, capturing some 2,200 men and 500 women. Among them was a scholar, al-Azhari, who became the slave of a Bedouin family. Some five years later, they seized Mecca itself, removing the sanctuary's sacred black stone as an idol, and enslaving numerous inhabitants of both sexes.[66] However, Bedouins overran the remnants of the Bahrayn Qarmati state in 1077, and the sect disappeared without a trace.[67]

Fatimid Isma'ili missionaries broke away to take their version of the Mahdist message to the Maghrib, where their revolutionary propaganda 'promised an equal share for all in the Sun of God, symbolized by the Mahdi'.[68] However, 'Abdallah (r. 910–34) took over many of the concubines, eunuchs, and Black and White slaves of his vanquished opponents in Qayrawan, Tunisia. At best, he expressed some objections to administrative and military slavery.[69]

---

[60] Halm 1985: 140.
[61] Ali 1917: II, 32.
[62] Ahmed 1992: 66.
[63] Rodinson 1966: 43–4; Popovic 1976: 122, 167.
[64] Goeje 1886: 69–70, 150–1, 155–6, 178; Brett 2001: 68–72.
[65] Thomas 1937: 150; Brett 2001: 62.
[66] Goeje 1886: 85, 106–7.
[67] Ruthven 2000: 206.
[68] Talbi 1981: 220, 224.
[69] Brett 2001: 144; Halm 1996: 121–2, 137.

Most later Fatimid caliphs, ruling the largest Ismaʻili state that ever existed up to its collapse in 1171, displayed even fewer qualms about servitude. The son and successor of the Mahdi called himself the Qaʻim (r. 934–46), the 'judge at the end of the world'. He surrounded himself with slave soldiers and officials, mainly 'Slavs'. One of them, the eunuch Jawdhar, became the most powerful man in the realm. To obtain fresh supplies, the Fatimids scoured the Adriatic for captives, and imported Blacks from the south.[70]

Nuʻman b. Muhammad al-Tamimi (d. 974) composed *The pillars of Islam*, the Fatimid code, which was close to Twelver Shiʻi law.[71] He not only permitted slavery, but also legislated for it in some detail.[72] Slaves also figured in the condensed version of this code, used for teaching purposes in Cairo.[73] To be sure, Nuʻman ordered that no free person should be reduced to slavery, but he probably meant free Muslims.[74] The Ismaʻili scholar Hamid al-Din al-Kirmani (d. 1021), heading the Fatimid mission organisation in Cairo, dismissed Turks, Blacks, and Berbers as intellectually inferior, possibly justifying their enslavement.[75]

Of the Ismaʻili groups to survive the collapse of the Fatimid caliphate, the Mustaʻli remained truest to their roots. Loyal to the occulted child Caliph al-Tayyib, victim of usurpation in 1130, they vested authority in a line of semi-hereditary and divinely inspired Daʻi. They came to be centred in Yemen and Gujarat, and split into two sects.[76] They retained Nuʻman al-Tamimi's code, and thus explicitly held fast to slavery.[77]

The Nizari Ismaʻili, breaking with the Fatimids over an earlier succession dispute in 1094, took refuge in Syrian and Iranian eyries. There they became the 'Assassins', champions of 'ordinary people' and 'determined to be free'.[78] Whether freedom extended to slaves is unclear. Nadir al-Din al-Tusi (1201–74), a Persian writer on ethics sympathetic to Ismaʻili doctrines, described slaves as the gifts of a beneficent God to mankind. Some slaves were admittedly free 'by

---

[70] Brett 2001: 144–5, 148; Halm 1996: 220, 279–80, 339.
[71] Halm 1996: 174.
[72] Fyzee 1969: 30–1, 88–9; Abu-Izeddin 1984: 122.
[73] Dodge 1961: 16.
[74] Schneider 1999: 50.
[75] Lewis 1990: 55.
[76] Halm 1991: 193–200.
[77] Fyzee 1969.
[78] Halm 1991: 185–93; Hodgson 1974: II, 59–61; Hodgson 1955: 148.

nature', and yet he recommended that they be well treated rather than liberated.[79]

Servitude was probably questioned in a millenarian and libertarian phase in Iran.[80] When Hasan II (r. 1162–66) declared himself to be the Qa'im and annulled the sharia, he liberated captives, although it is unclear whether he freed all slaves. He further proclaimed that paradise on earth was at hand, where 'there will be neither work nor illness'. After his murder, his son Muhammad II (r. 1166–1210) claimed to be the Imam, the infallible descendant of Nizar. The following ruler kept the title, but abandoned the millenarian promises.[81] Shortly afterwards, the castles of the Assassins fell, to the Mongols in Persia in 1256, and to Egyptian *mamluk* forces in Syria in 1271–3.[82]

The great Fatimid exception on servitude was Caliph al-Hakim (r. 996–1021), who ruled from Cairo and sought to be the perfect Isma'ili leader. He became so eccentric that he was thought to be insane, but there was a certain method in his madness. Pursuing social justice and a puritanical lifestyle, he freed all his slaves, male and female, in 1013, albeit without commanding his followers to do likewise. In 1021, he rode out from Cairo into the desert on his humble donkey and vanished without a trace.[83] Those who believed him to be a divine manifestation called themselves the Muwahhidun (Unitarians), but the name Druzes, from one of their early leaders, has stuck to them. Defeated in rebellion, they settled in the mountains of Greater Syria to await al-Hakim's return, developing their own scriptures.[84]

The Druzes copied most of their *al-Shari'a al-Ruhaniyya*, the spiritual law, from al-Tamimi's Fatimid code, and yet they expressly banned slavery, concubinage, and polygyny.[85] Baha' al-Din explained this in an epistle dating from the earliest years of the faith. The covenant, by which believers bound themselves to the community, was incompatible with slavery, because adherents needed to be completely free and able to determine their conduct.[86] Moreover, 'In Druze religious teaching all human souls are given an equal op-

[79] Tusi 1964: 181–4.
[80] Jambet 1990.
[81] Hodgson 1955: 148–219.
[82] Halm 1991: 185–200.
[83] Abu-Izeddin 1984: 74–86; Hodgson 1974: II, 26–7.
[84] Halm 1991: 181–5.
[85] Abu-Izeddin 1984: 122, 230.
[86] *Ibid.*: 122.

portunity in their transmigration from one body to another; thus, the Unitarians ... are free as human beings the moment they choose the Unitarian doctrine'. However, Druze egalitarianism never went so far as to dissolve 'the differential ranks and classes within society'.[87]

The wider impact of precocious Druze abolition remains uncertain. Endogamous and refusing to accept converts, the Druzes 'may be said to constitute a separate religion'. Hiding away in their mountains, they were prone to conceal their dogmas from outsiders as a defensive tactic. Indeed, the majority of the community were called the 'ignorant ones', because they knew so little about their faith.[88]

Other sects

Zayd b. ʿAli, great grandson of ʿAli b. Abi Talib, broke away from the Shiʿi mainstream in 740. He was killed in that same year, but his ideas lived on, notably his insistence that the Imam should be chosen from among the most qualified descendants of ʿAli b. Abi Talib. The Imam was no more than a fallible political leader of the faithful, a position reinforced by the later adoption of Muʿtazili rationalism. Ejected from various areas, Zaydi believers at last found a permanent refuge in the highlands of Yemen from the 890s.[89]

Zayd himself had been taunted because of his mother's servile origins, and his followers were credited with a certain distaste for slavery, but Zaydi ulama did not formally reject the institution.[90] Adepts occasionally owned slaves, including concubines and eunuchs, even if they were mentioned more frequently in the context of Sunni or Ismaʿili believers in Yemen.[91] A seventeenth-century Zaydi Imam employed Ottoman captives as 'agricultural workers'.[92] Even an austere seventeenth-century leader, who 'was so determined never to touch state funds that he earned his living by making caps that go under turbans', still lived with a female slave and a single wife.[93]

Nusayri believers, also called Alawites but differing from others of that name, originated in 859 and later took refuge in the Syrian mountains. They had Shiʿi roots, but accepted the transmigration

[87] Firro 1992: 23.
[88] Ruthven 2000: 207–8.
[89] Halm 1991: 206–11; Bidwell 1983: 9–10.
[90] Rouaud 1979: 132; Elwahed 1931: 35–6; Bernard Haykel, personal communication.
[91] Bidwell 1983: 11–13, 25–7, 127; Heyworth-Dunne 1952: 14, 40.
[92] Jane Hathaway, personal communication.
[93] Bidwell 1983: 25.

of souls. Their trinitarian doctrine of divine emanations associated the Prophet, 'Ali b. Abi Talib, and Salman al-Farisi. The latter was a famous Persian slave, or freed slave, who had been a companion of Muhammad.[94] The ninth-century *Book of shadows*, a sacred Nusayri text, declared that those with true knowledge were free of slavery. This was probably meant metaphorically, and yet the words used for slavery were *al-mamlukiyya* and *al-riqq*, rather than the usual word in this context, *al-'ubudiyya*.[95]

Khariji believers, emerging in 658, rejected Shi'i approaches entirely. Priding themselves on their social inclusiveness and egalitarianism, they rejected the hereditary principle, arguing that the best man should be elected caliph. Extreme groups acted violently, and were soon suppressed. However, the moderate Ibadi sect survived, taking refuge in the Maghrib and Oman.[96]

Ambivalent about slavery, Khariji scholars were fond of quoting the Prophet's saying that obedience was required from the faithful, even if an Ethiopian slave was placed in charge of them.[97] They also proclaimed that a Black slave might be elected caliph.[98] This appealed to 'oppressed and marginal groups'.[99] However, there was no Khariji rejection of servitude as such. The 'sixth pillar of the faith' was holy war, including against Muslims who shunned them. The radical Azraki sect executed the vanquished, but others declared their womenfolk forfeit.[100] Even Ibadi leaders, rebelling in the tenth-century Maghrib, promised the dependants of their foes to their followers.[101] Ibadi ulama also allowed taxes in slaves to be imposed on non-Muslims as a transitional measure pending their conversion, and permitted the Imam to purchase slaves with funds from the state treasury.[102]

Slavery was administered in ways that were both more and less liberal than in the majority Sunni community. Khariji groups in eighth- to tenth-century Iran may have given slaves greater property rights than was usual, and refused to sell slave women, or possibly even to own them at all.[103] This may be the source of the dubious

---

[94] Halm 1991: 156–61; Ruthven 2000: 203, 210, 212; Pipes 1981: 111.
[95] Halm 1985: 137–9; Rosenthal 1960: 25.
[96] Hodgson 1974: I, 214–6, 256–8; Risso 1986: 22–4, 31; Zeys 1886.
[97] Talhami 1977: 455.
[98] Brett 2001: 63; Netton 1992: 145–6.
[99] Ruthven 2000: 177.
[100] Shinar 1961: 97; Popovic 1976: 178; Brett 2001: 62, 167.
[101] Zeys 1886: 17–18; Brett 2001: 167; Talbi 1981: 215; Wilkinson 1987: 180–1, 189.
[102] Wilkinson 1987: 178, 180; Schwartz 1983: 70, 245.
[103] Madelung 1988: 58–9, 61, 76.

assertion that there was no Khariji concubinage.[104] A tenth-century summary of Ibadi law held that a person who had contracted to pay for freedom in instalments was no longer a slave, but that a concubine who had given birth to a child might yet be sold.[105]

Ibadi ulama not only objected to the emergence of a hereditary dynasty of rulers of Oman from the seventeenth-century, but also denounced their standing army of slaves and mercenaries. This reflected Khariji norms that no potentate should be able to prevent the faithful from deposing him, were he to stray from the path of righteousness. However, the sultans eventually prevailed, splitting religious and political roles and building up a substantial maritime and slaving empire in the Indian Ocean.[106]

Indeed, Ibadi entrepreneurs came to figure particularly prominently among Muslim traders in Black slaves. They virtually monopolised a number of trans-Saharan trade routes, notably those from the Niger bend and Lake Chad.[107] Those who took refuge in the Mzabi oases of modern Algeria, centred on Ghardaya, relied on slave labour to cultivate date palms.[108] The Omani Ibadi were pioneers of the East African slave trade, and also employed slaves to produce dates.[109]

Emancipatory zeal was absent among Moroccan millenarian movements from the twelfth-century, despite a tenth-century prophecy that the Mahdi's mother would be a slave.[110] The Almohads, Berbers of the Atlas mountains, developed Mahdist doctrines from 1121. They displayed a certain austerity and restricted the use of Black slave soldiers, but they enslaved numerous Christian Iberians.[111] The dynasty stuck closely to Maliki law in social matters, and returned to Sunni orthodoxy in 1227.[112] The Sa'di dynasty renewed Mahdist claims in 1511, but without breaking with the Maliki establishment.[113] Maghribi slave markets were once more flush with captives, as the dynasty defeated the Portuguese in 1578, patronised

[104] Ahmed 1992: 66, 71.
[105] Zeys 1886: 67–8.
[106] Risso 1986: 27, 46.
[107] Brett 2001: 165–6, 249–50, 264; Renault and Daget 1985: 21–2, 33.
[108] Shinar 1961: 98–9.
[109] Risso 1995: 14, 93; Wilkinson 1987: 222.
[110] Margoliouth 1915: 13.
[111] Verlinden 1955: 201–3; Clissold 1977: 8; Hunwick 1992: 19.
[112] Bel 1938: 245–59; Huici Miranda 2000: II, 576.
[113] Brett 2000: 103.

corsair raids from Sale and Tetuan, and conquered the middle Niger in 1590–1.[114]

Libertarian Mahdism was more in evidence in India. Sayyid Muhammad al-Jawnpuri (1443–1505) came from a Chishti Sufi background. He declared himself the Mahdi in 1495, encouraged flight from corrupt society, and died in exile in what is today Afghanistan. After unsuccessful attempts at gaining political power through holy war, his followers formed righteous Islamic communities, forecasting the arrival of Nabi 'Isa a thousand years after that of the Mahdi. Recruiting among the poor, Mahdawi preachers renounced worldly goods, meditated, lived communally, and sought complete social equality, although there is no mention of condemning slavery.[115]

Slave revolts

Exhibiting a heady mixture of millenarianism and sectarianism, slave rebellions rarely, if ever, appear to have been truly abolitionist. That said, the sources for these violent episodes are fragmentary and biased, depending on the accounts of the victors. The very occurrence of slave revolts challenged the notion of a meekly accepted servitude in Islam.

Two slave risings broke out in southern Iraq in the seventh-century, a small one around 689–90, and a more serious one in 694–5.[116] The second rebellion was probably led by a Black slave, Rabah Shirzanji. It coincided with Khariji insurgents taking refuge in the region's swamps, and there may have been some connection between slaves and sectarians, even if chroniclers of the time failed to make the connection.[117]

'Ali b. Muhammad, leader of southern Iraq's third and much larger Zanj rebellion of 869 to 883, grasped opportunistically at a number of religious ideologies to shore up his position. He proclaimed himself to be the Mahdi, inscribing the title on all his surviving coins. However, some of these also carried Khariji slogans. For a while, he espoused the Zaydi position that the most able person in the Prophet's tribe should rule, claiming filiation to Muhammad through 'Abbas. In a genealogical shift, he asserted his descent

[114] Clissold 1977: 29; Monlaü 1964: 54, 65–6, 86, 97; Heers 2003: 41–2, 59; Ruiz de Cuevas 1973: 17–23.
[115] MacLean 2000; Hodgson 1974: III, 70–1; Margoliouth 1915: 17–19.
[116] Popovic 1976: 62–3.
[117] Rotter 1967: 105–6; Beg 1975: 115.

from Husayn, suggesting identification with Shi'i and Isma'ili notions of the infallible Imam.

Despite temporarily threatening the foundations of the caliphate, 'Ali b. Muhammad was no Muslim Spartacus. He was a free man, possibly of Persian origins, and some of his followers were also free, whether pastoral Bedouins or settled farmers. He reserved high positions for them, even though Black slaves, employed to remove the saline crust from the land, formed the bulk of his forces. Despite the appellation Zanji, many of them probably came from the Horn and the Sahel, rather than from East Africa. A few White slaves joined the movement, including eunuchs and soldiers.[118]

Turning slaves into slave-owners was 'Ali b. Muhammad's interpretation of justice, a paradox which has been widely noted. Michael Brett suggests that unjustly deprived Muslims would thereby taste the fruits of conquest and empire.[119] Some have alleged that 'Ali b. Muhammad wished to abolish plantation slavery, but he appears only to have criticised poor conditions. He certainly owned slaves, and sold defeated foes.[120] To the horror of pious critics, he even enslaved Arab women descended from the Prophet, after taking Basra in 871.[121]

Egypt's slave rebellions are much less well known. 'Abdallah b. Ahmad b. al-Arqut led a movement in the ninth-century, claiming the title of Mahdi and filiation to the Prophet. He promised that he would turn former slaves into slave-owners, but enjoyed less success than the 'lord of the Zanj', perhaps because there were fewer concentrations of agrarian slaves in the Nile valley.[122] Some 500 Black slaves, employed to care for horses near Cairo, rebelled in 1146. They briefly set up their own state, but their religious beliefs are not mentioned.[123]

The study of dissenting groups in early Islam is somewhat frustrating, as the sources rarely reveal directly what these people thought about servitude. Nevertheless, this is an important task to undertake, for these groups displayed the most libertarian sentiments in Islam. How far they went in opposing slavery remains to be securely established.

[118] Popovic 1976; Halm 1967; Rotter 1967; Talhami 1977.
[119] Brett 2001: 57–8.
[120] Halm 1967: 40–1.
[121] Popovic 1976: 160; Talhami 1977: 456, 460.
[122] Brett 2001: 57, 128, 471.
[123] Heers 2003: 237.

Other-worldly ascetics and mystics may have underpinned servitude, by offering a spiritual refuge from drudgery and violence, but they also pricked elite consciences. This remained the case even after some Sufis had drifted closer to the establishment. Writings on early Islamic mysticism are voluminous, but authors say surprisingly little about the social content of this strand of thought, and even less about the Sufi impact on the real world.

Philosophers, scientists, and rationalist theologians seem unlikely to have condemned slavery at this stage, for they were heavily influenced by Aristotle's elitist and utilitarian views. As has often been pointed out, classical Athens was a striking example of the coexistence of servitude and rational investigation. However, there is a faint possibility that Greek and Roman authors opposed to Aristotle on this issue were more influential among Muslim thinkers than has generally been realised.

Claims about sectarian hostility to servitude need to be taken with a large pinch of salt, and yet more probing might reveal some surprises. It would be particularly helpful to know what happened to captives and born slaves when the Persian Assassins experienced their millenarian convulsion. How the Druzes took their decision to abolish slavery, and whether it affected other Muslims at all, remains to be fully elucidated. It is unclear whether Khariji egalitarianism ever resulted in any abolitionist tendencies, especially in the period before this strand of thought became restricted to the Ibadi sect.

Millenarian elements in dissent might repay special attention, as Mahdism clearly contributed to slave rebellions. To be sure, no systematic abolitionist doctrine emerged from a vision of an earth filled with justice. However, rebels may have sowed ideological seeds of self-liberation. For example, the extent to which folk traditions about the great Iraqi rebellion of the late ninth-century inspired later generations of slaves remains quite unclear.

Libertarian tendencies appear to have run into the sands in the middle centuries of Islam. At present, it seems as though the Druzes withdrew into isolation, Isma'ili influence reached a nadir, and the sixteenth-century resurgence in Shi'i political fortunes only gave rise to a tidal wave of enslavement. As for Ibadi survivors within the Khariji fold, they became great traders in Black slaves. Nevertheless, a subterranean current of ideas may have survived to motivate abolitionists of a later age.

4

CUSTOMARY LAW

The ulama recognised a subordinate place for custom and precedent from early in the history of Islam. These terms covered everything from unwritten local lore to the elaborate codes of conquered peoples. The ulama upheld the primacy of the sharia in case of conflicting interpretations, but local communities were not necessarily of the same opinion, especially in regions where conversion to Islam had been peaceful, recent, and gradual.

Custom meshed with the holy law in complex ways. Kazakh qadis in Inner Asia dispensed an amalgam of Turkic custom, Mongol law, Russian codes, and the sharia, only fully codified in the 1820s.[1] A proverb from Aceh, Sumatra, held that holy law and custom (*adat*) were 'like the pupil and the white of the eye', both emanating from God.[2] Snouck Hurgronje commented acidly that *adat* was really the 'mistress', and sharia 'her obedient slave'.[3] This was a problem all over Islamdom, for Bedouin 'customary law could be as distant in Arabia itself from the Shari'ah law of the books as in the remotest corner of the hemisphere'.[4]

Local conventions allowed for forms of servitude which made pious ulama shudder. Enslavement through crime, debt, and the sale of children was particularly common, and women laboured under a number of specific disadvantages. The spread of sharia-mindedness led to gradual reform, but customary resistance could be tenacious.

In other instances, custom was more forgiving than the holy law, acting to restrict slavery in significant ways. Local habits allowed for liberation on conversion, after a fixed period, or because of ethnic factors. Second and subsequent generations of slaves were often

---

[1] Olcott 1987: 19.
[2] Ali 1969: 29.
[3] Snouck Hurgronje 1906: I, 153, 168.
[4] Hodgson 1974: II, 10.

treated differently. In Iraq aspects of Babylon's ancient Hammurabi code continued to be enforced, limiting the activities that slaves could perform.[5]

Liberation after a fixed term or on conversion

Obligatory emancipation after a fixed time was praiseworthy in both Shi'i and Sunni Islam, and may have derived from the Jewish precedent of freedom in the seventh year, considered in chapter 11 below.[6] In the nineteenth-century Balkans and Anatolia, the seven-year rule was usually reserved for Blacks, cheap and adversely affected by cold weather, whereas more resistant, and expensive, White slaves completed nine years.[7] Manumitting a couple when they married was another norm in Anatolia.[8]

Opinions differed as to the enforcement of these customs. One author claimed that 'masters who do not conform to this requirement are severely punished'.[9] A former member of the Ottoman imperial harem described the process as automatic, and enforced by qadis.[10] However, refusal was possible, if rare.[11] Heirs might seek repossession through a sharia court, while owners could demand compensation, refuse liberation if the purchase price had not been redeemed, or sell a slave just before the fixed time was up. Officials also unilaterally extended the term of service, for example in Crete in 1860.[12]

In the wider Turkic world, a similar custom prevailed. Crimean Tatars freed most of their slaves after six years.[13] Chinese military slaves in East Turkistan were released after 12 years.[14] Khan Nadir Muhammad of Bukhara (r. 1642–5) wrote more vaguely of Russian slaves who 'have served out their work'.[15] Most Uzbek slaves seem to have been freed after about 10 years, but release could be made conditional on the agreement of the owner.[16]

---

[5] Jwaideh and Cox 1989; Albertine Jwaideh, personal communication.
[6] Ali 1883: 171; Heers 2003: 10; Hellie 1993: 294.
[7] Erdem 1996: 111, 152–64; Hanimefendi 1994: 66–7, 71, 76.
[8] Young 1905–06, II, 168.
[9] [Quilliam] 1895: 55
[10] Hanimefendi 1994: 66.
[11] Garnett 1891: II, 412.
[12] Erdem 1996: 155, 158–9, 162–4.
[13] Fisher 1972: 585; Hellie 1982: 517.
[14] Kuropatkin 1882: 199.
[15] Allworth 1994: 32.
[16] Burton 1998: 347–8.

Elsewhere, liberation after a fixed term was rare, and often influenced by Turkic norms. In Egypt the only slaves freed after seven or nine years in the nineteenth century were those employed by the state, run on Ottoman lines.[17] In Algeria, subject to centuries of Ottoman suzerainty, an observer in the 1850s noted that 'scrupulous Mussulmans think themselves bound to offer liberty to their slaves after nine years' good service, because it is thought that after that time they have paid their value in labour'.[18] However, Syrian Arabs resented high-handed Ottoman attempts to impose the practice on them at this time.[19] Samory Ture worked for a nineteenth-century West African chief for seven years to gain his mother's freedom, perhaps a reflection of the custom across the Sahara.[20]

A more prevalent expectation among Arabs was that devout believers would free slaves after an indeterminate number of years, especially if they had converted to Islam. Muhammad al-Anbabi, Egyptian Shaykh al-Azhar in the late nineteenth-century, spoke of 'advice to pious persons among the captors to give them at the end of a few years their freedom'.[21] A similar precept was recorded in Tunisia.[22] Bedouins often freed slaves, though they continued to control them through clientage.[23]

'Limited service contracts' were at the discretion of owners, and thus acceptable in sharia terms. Such documents were popular in Turkistan and the Ottoman empire.[24] In the great Anatolian manufacturing centre of Bursa in the fifteenth-century, masters of workshops guaranteed freedom after the completion of a specified task, or after a period of time, enhancing productivity among servile artisans, and lowering costs of supervision.[25] Similar cases were recorded for sixteenth-century Ankara, Edirne, and Sofia, although heirs sometimes managed to obtain a reversal of liberation through the courts.[26]

Some Western observers opined that emancipation merely stimulated fresh imports of slaves. Conversely, restricting imports made

---

[17] Walz 1985: 147.
[18] Morell 1984: 342.
[19] Erdem 1996: 157–8.
[20] Fisher 2001: 188.
[21] Baer 1969: 188.
[22] Brown 1974: 185.
[23] Burckhardt 1992: I, 181–3.
[24] Levi 2002: 287; Inalcik 1997: 284.
[25] Inalcik 1979: 27–9.
[26] Fisher 1980b: 49–56.

owners unwilling to release existing slaves.[27] Anatolian enthusiasm for liberation after a fixed term shrank in tandem with imports.[28] Limited service contracts lapsed in late-nineteenth-century Hadhramaut, following treaties with Britain to prohibit the trade.[29] Many Russians languished in captivity in nineteenth-century Turkistan, even after conversion to Islam.[30]

When much of the local population was not Muslim, custom was prone to be generous to slaves who embraced Islam. In the Christian Balkans, Ottoman officials encouraged converts to apply for manumission, contributing to the growth of a Bosnian and Albanian free Muslim population.[31] Ottoman palace slaves also expected liberation if they converted on the birth of an imperial child, though they were disappointed in 1762.[32] The Soninke, inhabiting areas of the upper Senegal and Niger basins where Animists were numerous, freed any slave who became a Muslim, even if seized in holy war.[33]

Military slaves were especially likely to earn their liberty.[34] A popular literary genre portrayed freedom as a reward for heroism in battle. The *Sirat 'Antara b. Shaddad*, frequently re-issued and probably dating in part from the eighth-century, tells the story of a pre-Islamic hero. The son of an Ethiopian slave mother, 'Antara earned his freedom by his bravery.[35] The chivalric ideal of his emancipation as a recompense for daring resonated throughout Islamic history, summed up in his father's famous cry, 'Charge and be free. You shall be a slave no longer'.[36]

However, custom could be to the disadvantage of slaves wishing to gain freedom through conversion. Indeed, Barbary corsairs discouraged, or even banned their slaves from converting, because it entailed a customary exemption from rowing the galleys. Among the Christians and Jews who were allowed to adopt Islam, skilled workers and concubines were those most likely also to be liberated.[37]

[27] Douin 1936–41: III/2, 655.
[28] Young 1905–06, II, 166–8.
[29] Berg 1886: 11, 69–70.
[30] Hopkirk 2001: 85, 148.
[31] Malcolm 1994: 66–9; Fisher 1980b: 54.
[32] Erdem 1996: 31.
[33] Sy 2000: 47.
[34] Pipes 1981: 22.
[35] Hamès and Ould Cheikh 1991: 67–73; Hodgson 1974: II, 156.
[36] Norris 1980: 46.
[37] Clissold 1977: 4–5, 91–2; Bono 1964: 250–3, 256–7; Wolf 1979: 164–5; Davis 2003: 21–3.

In South India some local Muslims clung to caste beliefs that certain people were inherently servile by birth.[38]

The ambiguities of ethnicity and race

Any recourse to ethnic and racial notions, whether favourable to slaves or not, conflicted with Islamic universalism.[39] Black and Persian slaves, or freed slaves, were numbered among the prestigious companions of the Prophet, who himself repeatedly rejected discrimination on such grounds.[40] Ethnic and racial stereotypes, however common in popular culture, were thus akin to dynastic, sectarian, and nationalist loyalties, tearing apart the seamless robe of God's community.[41]

From one perspective, ethnicity might limit the incidence of enslavement. Caliph 'Umar b. al-Khattab (r. 634–44) was said to have prohibited enslaving male Arabs, even if many ulama rejected this tradition as uncanonical.[42] Sales of Arabs certainly persisted, including girls obtained by West African potentates in the fourteenth-century.[43] Indeed Ibn Butlan's eleventh-century buyer's manual described the qualities of Arab slave women from the holy city of Mecca.[44] Even the custom that Arab slaves should never be castrated was not always respected.[45]

This casts doubt upon claims that ethnic groups of lesser standing were immune from slavery. Nevertheless, the Somali of the Horn of Africa were routinely credited with this privilege, not only by Somali authors.[46] Of the Javanese in the 1810s it was written that, 'if they should happen to be seized and sold by pirates, a satisfactory proof of their origin would be sufficient to procure their enfranchisement'.[47]

The Timbuktu Berber scholar, Ahmad Baba, drew up a famous list of which ethnic groups could not be enslaved in West Africa in 1615. This may have been a response to his own capture in 1593,

---

[38] Kusuman 1973: 24, 35.
[39] Lewis 1990; Elwahed 1931: 159–69.
[40] Rahal 2000: 18–20; Ruthven 2000: 212; Norris 1978: 111–16.
[41] Piscatori 1986.
[42] Khadduri 1955: 131–2.
[43] Beg 1975: 108; Battuta 1983: 334; Rutter 1986: 140.
[44] Müller 1980: 66–71.
[45] Ayalon 1999: 75.
[46] Cerulli 1957–64: II, 19–20; Cattelani 1897: 71; Beachey 1976b: 107; Nicholls 1971: 231.
[47] Raffles 1978: I, 75.

followed by imprisonment and house arrest in Morocco till 1607.[48] Ahmad's criteria were religious rather than ethnic, for at one point he allowed the enslavement of two peoples whose Islam was 'shallow'. However, the list became enshrined in local lore, and even the enslavement of Animist Fulbe came to be condemned.[49]

More problematic is the contention that the customs of some Muslim peoples prevented them from owning slaves. The French believed this to be true of 'republican' Berber communities of North Africa.[50] However, Algerian Kabyles enslaved shipwrecked Christians when they could, and Moroccan Berber villages owned slaves collectively.[51] Another group allegedly without slaves were the mountaineers of northern Albania, organised in tight-knit clans.[52] It is possible that their concubines were widows of relatives, according to local custom, and that they paid bride price to obtain wives from Catholic neighbours.[53] However, in more socially stratified southern Albania, the nineteenth-century elite imported Black slaves from Egypt, and Circassian concubines from Istanbul.[54]

The Muslim Hui of China supposedly held no slaves, for they lacked an Islamic state and lived in relatively densely populated areas, but the waters have been muddied by Communist theoreticians equating slavery with backwardness.[55] Muslim merchants in fourteenth-century China bought girls from infidel parents.[56] The Hui purchased numerous children, and it seems unlikely that they freed them all through adoption, as noted in Chapter 2.[57] Eighteenth- and nineteenth-century jihads probably gave rise to enslavement, as will be discussed in Chapter 8. As late as 1930 the founder of the northwestern rebel state of Islamistan seized youths as soldiers, and handed over enemy women to his men.[58] Hui 'brigand chiefs' in Yunnan were kidnapping and enslaving people at around the same time.[59]

[48] Zouber 1977: 26–32.
[49] Hunwick and Harrak 2000; Barbour and Jacobs 1985; Kake 1979: 164–5; Hunwick and Powell 2002: 61.
[50] Emerit 1949: 35.
[51] Clissold 1977: 67, 145, 153; Michaux-Bellaire 1910: 425.
[52] Reclus 1883: 186.
[53] Durham 1909: 36, 208.
[54] Vlora 1911: 45–6; Vlora 1968: I, 70.
[55] Jiangping Wang and Jake Whittaker, personal communications.
[56] Battuta 1983: 286, 292.
[57] Broomhall 1987: 57.
[58] Cable and French 1942: 222, 231, 239.
[59] Dymond 1929: 10, 56–62.

Much more in evidence was the manipulation of ethnicity and race to justify enslavement. Ibn Sina, the famous Persian physician and philosopher encountered in Chapter 3 defending natural servitude, further propounded that extremes of temperature produced temperaments suitable to slavery among the fairer and darker peoples, notably Slavs, Turks and Africans.[60] Seventeenth-century Algerians likened the pink skin of European captives to that of the proscribed pig.[61] As for Black Africans, they 'were predestined to servility'.[62] Black Papuans and Melanesians were probably also regarded as natural slaves in Southeast Asia.[63]

For the dark-skinned there was the additional problem of stories that the biblical Ham and his descendants had been cursed with both servitude and blackness for laughing at the nakedness of his father Noah. The curse originally fell on Ham's son Canaan with no hint of pigmentation, but Jewish, Christian and Muslim writers embroidered the story. Ham's progeny was sometimes divided between the offspring of Canaan in darkest Africa, Kush in the Horn of Africa, and Fut in South Asia. The great Tunisian historian Ibn Khaldun (1332–1406) was among Muslim intellectuals who refused to accept such tales, while endorsing Ibn Sina's climatic determinism.[64]

Slavery by birth

Local custom might mitigate the lot of those born to slave parents, especially Muslims. Manumission on birth occurred, notably in the Balkans.[65] Among the Minangkabau of West Sumatra, grandchildren were freed.[66] Custom more commonly imposed a lesser improvement in status. Pre-Islamic Arab norms, influential in the Middle East, held that a slave born in the owner's house should not be sold, and should be treated better than raided or purchased outsiders.[67] Reformers in sixteenth-century Songhay unsuccessfully tried to overlay West African conventions of this type with a more Islamic system.[68] Special treatment of second and later generation

---

[60] Lewis 1990: 5, 18, 54–5.
[61] Colley 2002: 115.
[62] Willis 1985: I, ix.
[63] Ufford 1856: 70; ANRI 1836–9.
[64] Braude 2002; Davis 1984: 36, 43, 86–7; Lewis 1990: 53, 55, 123–5; Rotter 1967: 141–4; Colley 2002: 115.
[65] Hellie 1993: 296; Sugar 1977: 13.
[66] Lasker 1950: 32
[67] Brunschvig 1960: 25.
[68] Olivier de Sardan 1975: 112–13, 119–22.

slaves, notably protection from sale, persisted in West Africa.[69] A similar situation was recorded in northwestern India in the 1840s.[70] In contrast, such slaves could be sold without problem in the Sudan, and in the Gayo highlands of Sumatra.[71]

Amelioration in status over generations was a double-edged sword, for subordination easily became permanent in systems close to serfdom.[72] Tuaregs of the Ahaggar distinguished between recently obtained slaves, who tended herds, and born slaves, who worked the soil in perpetuity.[73] West Sumatran freed slaves and their descendants formed 'impure clans', owing labour duties to local rulers.[74] They lived in satellite villages, could not marry 'proper people', and were euphemistically called 'nephews below the knees'.[75] The Alas and Gayo of North Sumatra distinguished between slaves who were adopted into clans after emancipation, equal to free people, and those who were merely liberated.[76]

Children of a servile mother by a free man, not her owner, were of servile status in Sunni Islam, but free in Shi'i Islam.[77] If the man married the woman, Shafi'i and Hanafi ulama imposed liberation as a precondition, so that any children were automatically free. Maliki ulama, who unrealistically attempted to limit such marriages to men beyond the age of fathering, could not agree as to the status of children.[78]

Customary deviations from this pattern were legion.[79] A free Circassian man might marry a slave woman without freeing her, and her offspring were then servile.[80] On the fringes of West Sumatra, a free man marrying a slave woman himself adopted her status, as did their children.[81] Under customary law, children of a free man and a slave woman were free in Aceh, whereas they were alternately

---

[69] Trimingham 1959: 133–5; Hill 1976; Azarya 1978: 35; Christelow 1994: 5–6; Stilwell 1999: 174–5; Caro Baroja 1955: 48.
[70] Burton 1973: 253.
[71] Spaulding 1982: 12; Snouck Hurgronje 1903: 63.
[72] Baldé 1975: 200–1.
[73] Bourgeot 1975: 92–3.
[74] Moszkowski 1909: 229.
[75] Verkerk Pistorius 1868: 437–43; Graves 1984: 13–14; Young 1994: 48.
[76] Iwabuchi 1994: 94, 158; Snouck Hurgronje 1903: 60, 63–4, 269.
[77] Brunschvig 1960: 31.
[78] Fahmy 1990: 96–7, 100
[79] Adam 1840: 68–72.
[80] Young 1905–06: II, 169.
[81] Moszkowski 1909: 236.

slave and free in South Sulawesi.[82] Uncanonical 'half-slaves', emerged from such unions in East Africa.[83]

The children of recognised concubines might be treated contrary to sharia provisions, notably in Southeast Asia and Africa.[84] In Aceh, descendants of a concubine retained the 'taint' of slavery for several generations. Men thus practised birth control or infanticide, both of which violated holy law.[85] To the horror of pious ulama, men sometimes took free concubines, notably in the Balkans, Africa and Southeast Asia. Adding insult to injury, the children of such unions were often considered inferior to those of free wives.[86]

Self-enslavement and the sale of relatives

Muslims might enslave themselves or their children because of abject poverty, but also because this was a customary way to achieve upward social mobility through army, bureaucracy, or harem. Recent and imperfect converts often specialised in selling their offspring. They often ceased to do so as they became more thoroughly Islamised.

Turkic steppe tribes, gradually entering the Islamic fold, were famed for providing boys as military slaves from the ninth to the fourteenth-century. In some cases, they invoked destitution to explain their actions.[87] However, they also portrayed themselves as supplying soldiers for the noble cause of Islamic military supremacy.[88]

Circassians of the northwestern Caucasus, gradually embracing Islam from 1717, continued to sell servile soldiers and concubines after conversion, which was more or less complete around 1850. Some were constrained by poverty, but others wished to better the lot of their children.[89] Their greatest hope was that a daughter might become 'the mother of sultans'.[90] Under local custom, a man who had lost both parents could even sell his unmarried sisters, or

---

[82] Loeb 1972: 230–1; Sutherland 1983: 276.
[83] Lodhi 1973: 12–13; Mirza and Strobel 1989: 19.
[84] Lasker 1950: 32–3; Djajadiningrat 1929: 90; Lodhi 1973: 12–13.
[85] Snouck Hurgronje 1903: 63; Snouck Hurgronje 1906: I, 22, 359.
[86] Durham 1909: 36; Fisher 2001: 181–2; Hunwick 1985: 71; Linehan 1973: 129; Snouck Hurgronje 1906: I, 360; Jacobs 1894: I, 78; Winstedt 1981: 54; Kumar 1997: 62.
[87] Wink 1999: II, 147–8, 197–8; Jackson 1999: 63–4.
[88] Ayalon 1951: 1–4.
[89] Toledano 1998: 36–40; Jaimoukha 2001: 149–52, 169.
[90] Morell 1984: 340.

his adulterous wife, as long as the family of the latter agreed.[91] Purchasers in the cities asked no questions, attributing blame to dealers, and finding it hard to distinguish between Circassians of free and servile origins.[92] Traders assuaged their consciences by affirming that they were rescuing children from a life of grinding poverty.[93] When Circassians fled the advancing Russians and flooded into the Ottoman empire from the late 1850s, complaints grew apace. Balkan Muslims, notably in Kosovo, were horrified that Circassians sold free children.[94] Some free Circassian parents thus obtained false certificates, stating that their children were slaves.[95] Anatolian Turks, who described their new compatriots unflatteringly as 'wild, savage, vile and uncivilised', portrayed this as an outlandish custom of improperly Islamised people.[96] Poverty, intensified by uprooting, was also blamed.[97]

Kurds were another group known for selling their children. Indeed, Kurdish children were occasionally passed off as Circassians.[98] Muslims in the largely Kurdish Mosul area were reduced to selling their children in 1841, 'on account of their extreme poverty'.[99] Kurds more generally traded their daughters for domestic and factory work in Iran in the nineteenth-century.[100]

Some Muslims in South Asia, Southeast Asia and Africa voluntarily became slaves, or sold their children, usually for reasons of debt, hunger, and chronic insecurity.[101] Self-enslavement and the sale of children by parents was allowed by the eighteenth-century Luwaran code of the southern Philippines.[102] The South Asian *Mohit-u-Surakhsi* declared that Muslims could sell themselves or their children, if there was no other way of staying alive, apart from 'eating a dead body'. This was contested, however, and did not appear in the

[91] Jaimoukha 2001: 169.
[92] Garnett 1909: 211–12.
[93] Vlora 1968: I, 72.
[94] Malcolm 1998: 214–15; Popovic 1978: 168; Jaimoukha 2001: 169.
[95] Erdem 1996: 48–50.
[96] Toledano 1998: 105–9.
[97] Hanimefendi 1994: 59; Sagaster 1997: 43–4.
[98] Hanimefendi 1994: 68.
[99] Erdem 1996: 197.
[100] Migeod 1990: 333; Polak 1865: I, 249.
[101] Chattopadhyay 1977: 175; Kidwai 1985: 188–9; Adam 1840: 64–7; Miers 2003: 306; Loyré-de-Hauteclocque 1989: 151; Sutherland 1983: 275; Broersma 1916: 74–6; Moszkowski 1909: 236; Harries 1965: 206–7; Fisher 2001: 102–3.
[102] Warren 1981: 215–17.

Fatawa Alamgiri, an authoritative collection of legal opinions from the time of Awrangzib (r. 1658–1707).[103] The ulama frowned upon breeding children for sale, although no text was cited to prohibit the practice. Circassians courted further infamy by encouraging their slaves to produce children for the market.[104] One Barbary entrepreneur outside Algiers sold mulatto children, resulting from forced mating between purchased Black women and European captives.[105] Slave breeders in Nias island were Animists, but they were supposedly encouraged by Muslim traders from Aceh.[106]

Debt bondage and serfdom

The earliest Muslims probably tolerated the imposition of slavery for unredeemed debt. Indeed, the Surraq Hadith told of the Prophet selling a debtor, although this weak tradition was not included in canonical collections.[107] The enslavement of Muslims for debt persisted *de facto* in the Middle East after the ulama had prohibited it, for example in eighteenth-century Egypt.[108] It was common in Bukhara, Inner Asia, in the nineteenth-century.[109]

Debt bondage was particularly widespread in Southeast Asia, where many Muslim societies failed to make a clear distinction between this status and slavery proper.[110] The laws of Melaka (Malacca) allowed enslavement for debt in the fifteenth-century, albeit with limitations for victims of natural disasters, and this famous code served as a model in the archipelago for centuries.[111] The eighteenth-century Luwaran code of the southern Philippines enshrined the principle.[112] Only in Java was the transition from debtor to chattel 'out of the question', reflecting Javanese legal principles.[113] That said, Java's debt peons were worked hard, for example in Cirebon's weaving workshops around 1800.[114]

---

[103] Adam 1840: 23, 48, 67–8, 246; Baillie 1957: 365–6.
[104] Erdem 1996: 52–3; Jaimoukha 2001: 169.
[105] Clissold 1977: 46–7.
[106] Loeb 1972: 143.
[107] Schneider 1999: 15, 56, 277; Elwahed 1931: 120–2.
[108] Winter 1992: 69.
[109] Khan 1998: 57–8.
[110] Reid 1983b: 160–1.
[111] Thomaz 1994: 261, 285–6, 292; Matheson and Hooker 1983: 184–6.
[112] Warren 1981: 215–17.
[113] Hoadley 1983: 99.
[114] Burger 1975: I, 58.

Elsewhere in Southeast Asia, unpaid debts were 'the most common origin for the heritable slaves found in many societies'.[115] High levels of indebtedness were made worse by usurious interest rates, themselves an overt breach of sharia principles. Among the Maranao of Mindanao, a loan could allegedly double in size in as little as 10 days.[116] Malays recognised that the sharia only allowed the seizure of debtors' property, not their person, but they appealed to the authority of Malay custom, and presented children as collateral for loans.[117] A response to growing sharia-minded criticism was to insist that debtors were technically free, being merely under an obligation to repay the sum owed.[118] In reality, selling unredeemed debtors, and treating their descendants as chattels, was commonplace.[119] An Indonesian official, working for the Dutch, therefore argued that replacing customary law with the sharia would eradicate persistent servitude in South Sumatra.[120]

Sir Bartle Frere's surprising statement that Islam authorised the enslavement of 'insolvent debtors' may have reflected his long experience of British India.[121] The *Mohit-u-Surakhsi* held that a free man, hard pressed by his creditors, could sell himself. A tradition of the Prophet was invoked, presumably the discredited Surraq Hadith. Although numerous South Asian ulama contested this ruling, Muslims regularly owned such slaves.[122] Many debtors were doubtless Hindus, but Ibn Battuta reported a fourteenth-century trade in indebted women in the entirely Muslim Maldive Islands.[123]

Islam did not eliminate enslavement for debt in Africa, although default might give rise to pawning rather than slavery proper in West Africa. Redemption thus remained a possibility.[124] Nevertheless, the sultan of Wadai around 1870 'does not delay in announcing clearly to the negligent debtor, whether a high official or a slave, "If you have not satisfied your creditor by such and such a date, you will go with him [across the Sahara] as a slave, as a substi-

---

[115] Reid 1983b: 160–1.
[116] Loyré-de-Hauteclocque 1989: 145–6, 151.
[117] Bird 1883: 370–5.
[118] Reid 1993.
[119] Maxwell 1890: 247–8; Endicott 1983: 217; Mahmud 1954; Gullick 1958: 101–5; Clifford 1913: 121–5; Linehan 1973: 128–9; Andaya (Barbara) 1993: 85; Thosibo 2002, 97; Worcester 1913: 5.
[120] Djajadiningrat 1929.
[121] Frere 1873: 14.
[122] Adam 1840: 23, 48, 67; Baillie 1957: 365.
[123] Battuta 1983: 244.
[124] Trimingham 1959: 30, 134–5, 147.

tute for the money you owe him.'"[125] When Arab slavers in East Africa sought to buy Swahili debtors, their kin sometimes paid off the debt.[126]

An example of sharia-minded reform of debt bondage in West Africa came from Futa Jalon, where a regime born of holy war imposed Islamic norms from the 1720s. Muslim debtors were then freed from enslavement. Defaulting debtors were still beaten, however, and this punishment was not condoned in Maliki law.[127]

Tying people to the land, with an obligation to work for the owner, was unacceptable to the ulama, because it infringed the rights of free Muslims and scriptuaries.[128] However, wherever custom prevented the sale of rural slaves born in captivity, their de facto status was close to that of serfs, as indicated above. The late seventeenth-century laws of inheritance in Makassar, South Sulawesi, even distinguished between chattel slaves, movable property, and those attached to the land.[129] Areas recently conquered from Christians showed signs of adopting similar arrangements, especially in Balkan and Caucasus frontier areas. They were influenced by the repressive 'second serfdom', developing in eastern Europe from the fifteenth-century.[130]

Crime and taxes

Discussing judicial condemnation to bondage, Patterson concludes that 'the introduction of Islam to a country usually terminated this means of enslavement', but this is an exaggeration.[131] In reality, enslavement for crimes persisted where customary law was strong, for example in Inner Asia, where the highway robbers of Afghanistan were regularly sold into slavery.[132] The Shi'i Hazara of Afghanistan, of Mongol origin, reduced to servitude those merely convicted of 'lasciviousness' and other misdemeanours.[133]

Sentencing free Muslims to slavery was common in Southeast Asia. In Banten in the 1780s, theft and simply 'contravening a pro-

[125] Fisher 2001: 32.
[126] Harries 1965: 206–7; Mirza and Strobel 1989: 24, 39.
[127] Rodney 1968: 281–2; Fisher 2001: 117.
[128] Pipes 1981: 98; Rosenthal 1960: 78.
[129] Gervaise 1971: 114.
[130] Shaw and Shaw 1976–7: I, 50–1, 104; Malcolm 1994: 93–4; Gammer 1994: 246.
[131] Patterson 1982: 128.
[132] Gardner 1898: 121–2.
[133] Harlan 1939: 122.

hibition' were punished in this way.[134] Felonies leading to loss of freedom in South Sulawesi in 1863 included adultery, eloping with slaves, and incest.[135] Children born out of wedlock became state slaves on the fringes of West Sumatra, together with those who did not pay fines.[136] Servitude was the usual penalty for many crimes in the eighteenth-century Luwaran code of the southern Philippines.[137] This punishment might even fall upon the relatives of criminals, which was 'grossly at odds with the Islamic system of justice'.[138] Among the Maranao of Mindanao, rape was one offence for which a man's whole family could be enslaved.[139]

Similar examples came from Africa. In thirteenth-century West Africa, thieves could be either killed or enslaved. In Senegal, two centuries later, women and children were sent into bondage 'for the slightest fault'.[140] Making an unmarried woman pregnant was punished by a fine of three slaves, failing which the guilty party was himself enslaved.[141] In Zinder, crime was 'a lucrative source of supply for the prince. ... A boy steals some trifling articles—a few needles; he is forthwith sold in the souk; not only he, but if the Sarkee wants money, his father and mother, brothers and sisters'.[142] Theft, banditry and disobeying royal orders were major causes of enslavement in the Oromo kingdom of Jimma in Ethiopia.[143]

There was sharia-minded opposition. In Futa Jalon, a European observer in 1803 praised the 'abolition of those African laws which make slavery the punishment of almost every offence'.[144] However, even in this case a judge enslaved a Muslim who killed his own son in the 1820s. This was because he could discover no penalty in the Quran for this crime.[145]

Taxes levied in slaves might be paid by dipping into existing stocks of slaves, but free Muslims were also reduced to servitude in this manner. There were bitter complaints that Arabs continued to demand a tax in children from Maghribi Berbers after their conver-

---

[134] Kumar 1997: 269–70.
[135] Sutherland 1983: 275.
[136] Moszkowski 1909: 235.
[137] Warren 1981: 215–17.
[138] Federspiel 1998: 351.
[139] Loyré-de-Hauteclocque 1989: 145.
[140] Heers 2003: 45–6.
[141] Fisher 2001: 119, 121.
[142] Richardson 1853: II, 231.
[143] Lewis 1965: 112–13.
[144] Rodney 1968: 281–2.
[145] Canot 1940: 81–2.

sion, till the pious Caliph 'Umar b. 'Abd al-'Aziz (r. 717–20) stamped out this abuse.[146] Inner Asian taxes in slaves exacerbated local wars, feuds and raids.[147] Non-payment of taxes in Bukhara resulted in the enslavement of Muslim children.[148] The Egyptian conquerors of the Sudan from 1820 were accused of taxing in slaves, or enslaving Muslims for failing to pay uncanonical taxes.[149]

An astute doctrine to warrant taking free Muslims as tax was to declare that they had converted too late. Fulbe élites denied free status to West Africans who stuck to Animism at the time that jihads were declared, but adhered to Islam later. As 'their servile status preceded their adoption of Islam', there was no harm in collecting tribute in slaves from them.[150] A reforming sultan of Dar Sila, Chad, freed one such community around 1900.[151] A similar situation developed in the Sudan–Ethiopia borderlands from the 1720s.[152] The sharia-minded grandees of Banten, in West Java, took concubines only from 'those villages which during the period of Islamisation had refused to embrace the new religion, and had thereupon been declared to be slaves'.[153]

Female and mutilated slaves

Bondwomen might benefit from custom, for example in the limitation of concubinage. Muslims of Sri Lanka and parts of India established an upper limit of forty concubines per man, although it is unclear how this figure was arrived at, or when this rather generous restriction dated from.[154] In Shi'i Persia, some 'respectable' men entered a contract for 99 years with a concubine, 'which is equivalent to a permanent marriage'.[155] Tribesmen of the remote Arabian mountains of Dhofar exclaimed contemptuously in the late 1920s, 'let the nobility—the saiyids and the merchants of the coast—use their slave girls as concubines at their pleasure'.[156]

---

[146] Wilkinson 1987: 180–1; Papoulia 1963: 58; Hodgson 1974: I, 269.
[147] Wink 1999: II, 198; Levi 2002: 287; Noelle 1997: 83; Harlan 1939: 82, 127; Gregorian 1969: 34–5.
[148] Khan 1998: 57.
[149] Ali 1972: 19; Peters 1979: 68–9; Spaulding 1982: 4, 10–12.
[150] Azarya 1978: 25, 35.
[151] Bret 1987: 43–4.
[152] Trimingham 1965: 219–20.
[153] Kumar 1997: 62.
[154] Bevan Jones 1941: 209.
[155] Wills 1891: 326.
[156] Thomas 1938: 67.

Free wives were the most consistent opponents of concubinage, although it is unclear what arguments they deployed.[157] Moral tales criticising the custom showed wives as victims from quite early on.[158] In late-seventeenth-century South Sulawesi, some free women went as far as to murder their husbands' concubines.[159] The wife of 'Umar Pasha, Mamluk governor of Baghdad (r. 1764–75), 'did not even allow him to have a concubine, and 'Umar died childless'.[160] Prostitution was explicitly prohibited in 24:33 of the Quran.[161] However, the legal fiction of short-term sales disguised the practice in Ottoman lands, and probably elsewhere.[162] Accusations were made against Ibadi believers in Libya in the twelfth-century, and Egyptians and Sudanese in the nineteenth-century.[163] Servile prostitution flourished in the Malay peninsula, albeit 'not sanctioned by law or custom'.[164] The same problem arose in Sumatra.[165] South Asian Muslim prostitutes even bought other girls to work for them.[166]

There was weak scriptural backing for female circumcision, let alone infibulation, and no particular mention of slaves.[167] This was a pre-Islamic Arabian custom, 'and the more careful legists could not regard it as fully binding'.[168] However, slave girls from the interior of Borneo were circumcised as part of their conversion to Islam in the nineteenth-century.[169] The same was true of slave girls from Nubia, and later from the Nilotic Sudan.[170] Under British pressure, the Sudanese ulama produced a 'tentative religious ruling against infibulation', but not circumcision.[171]

Custom contributed to an uneven distribution of eunuchs across Islamdom. Many Arabs in the central lands, including Bedouins, frowned on the practice.[172] However, Omani sultans employed them,

---

[157] Goldziher 1967: 116–17; Lane 1895: 147; Walz 1985: 151; Burckhardt 1993: 186–7; Fahmy 1990: 107–8; Hanimefendi 1994: 65–6; Findley 1995: 169.
[158] Fahmy 1990: 107–8.
[159] Gervaise 1971: 115–16.
[160] Nieuwenhuis 1981: 24.
[161] Brunschvig 1960: 25; Arberry 1969: II, 50.
[162] Erdem 1996: 34–5.
[163] Hunwick 1992: 16.
[164] Sullivan 1982: 56.
[165] Andaya (Barbara) 1993: 96.
[166] Burton 1973: 201; Adam 1840: 68–9.
[167] Awde 2000: 126, 192, 199.
[168] Hodgson 1974: I, 324.
[169] Low 1968: 119.
[170] Heers 2003: 193; Hunwick and Powell 2002: 94, 155–6.
[171] Hargey 1981: 70, 298.
[172] Pellat *et al.* 1978: 1091; Lane 1895: 147; Jwaideh and Cox 1989: 55–6.

and Morocco remained a consumer into the twentieth-century.[173] Arabs in Mukalla, Hadhramaut, even asked a Western visitor in 1843 how many eunuchs Queen Victoria maintained at her court.[174] Turkic and Iranian custom may have made these peoples receptive to Byzantine, Persian and Chinese precedents.[175] Of ancient date in West Africa and the Horn, eunuchs appeared late in East Africa.[176] Numerous in early Islamic Java and Sumatra, they inexplicably vanished from the record thereafter.[177] Chinese Muslims probably had none, although Zheng He [Cheng Ho] (1371–1435), a Muslim boy captured and castrated by Ming forces in Yunnan in 1381–2, rose to lead China's maritime expeditions in the Indian Ocean from 1405 to 1433.[178]

The castrating of slaves by Muslims clearly violated the sharia, and yet this occurred in eleventh-century Iberia, and later in Sub-Saharan Africa.[179] A few Muslims competed for this function with Egyptian Christians in the nineteenth-century.[180] In the Atlas Mountains of Morocco in 1881 no less a personage than a Sharif 'rendered young boys into eunuchs with considerable skill, so that there were few fatal cases, and developed a lucrative trade'.[181] According to one victim, Chamba Arabs of the Algerian Sahara recited 'in the name of God, the Beneficent, the Merciful', as they chopped off a slave boy's testicles with a knife.[182]

Penal emasculation, common in many civilisations, remained highly unusual in Islam. A Hadith of the Prophet clearly forbade this practice, stating that 'he is not of my people who makes another a eunuch'.[183] However, Iranian Safavid rulers imposed castration as a punishment, gelding a man for homosexuality.[184] Their Qajar successors were also prone to imposing this disability on potential claimants to the throne.[185]

---

[173] Beachey 1976a: 38, 52; Schroeter 1992: 200.

[174] Bidwell 1983: 41–2.

[175] Zambaco 1911; Kidwai 1985: 77; Renault 1989: 55–8; Battuta 1983: 149; Beachey 1976a: 39, 45; Millant 1908: 173–6, 228–33; Saltana 1993: 113.

[176] Heers 2003: 193, 203; Meillasoux 1991: 185–91, 196, 365; Olivier de Sardan 1975: 128; Fisher 2001: 280–94; Renault and Daget 1985: 37–8; Lewis 1965: 70–1; Trimingham 1965: 66; Beachey 1976a: 172, 287; Sheriff 1987: 50–1.

[177] Hambly 1974: 125–6; Lombard 1967: 81, 97, 138, 148, 230.

[178] Tsai 1996: 55–60, 153–64.

[179] Constable 1994: 206; Hunwick 1985: 71; Baldé 1975: 203; Zambaco 1911: 46, 59.

[180] Meinardus 1969: 49–54.

[181] Beachey 1976a: 172.

[182] Hunwick and Powell 2002: 105–6.

[183] Hughes 1885: 110.

[184] Baghdiantz McCabe 1999: 39.

[185] Polak 1865: I, 256.

Sharia-minded distaste for emasculation was heightened by the homosexual abuse of slaves, for castration served to preserve a 'boyish and beardless appearance'.[186] Although a flagrant breach of holy law, sexual relations with slave boys were often tolerated.[187] Indeed, some Barbary corsairs kept veritable harems of 'male concubines', and the prostitution of eunuchs was denounced in Lucknow in 1855.[188]

Customary law threatened to choke God's word and the Prophet's teachings in prolific and hardy Islamicate weeds. Sharia-mindedness could therefore restrict, or even eradicate, aspects of 'folk slavery' that threatened the rights of freeborn believers and scripturaries. Reform could also protect particularly vulnerable groups, notably females and young boys. More research on the dynamics of this process might reveal the impact of waves of religious revivalism, especially in corners of Islamdom where custom was tenacious.

Practical considerations may have reinforced the persistence of non-sharia forms of enslavement. Making slaves of criminals and debtors was a convenient alternative to putting them in prison, even a humane alternative under certain conditions of incarceration. Similarly, self-enslavement and the sale of children in times of want mitigated the nefarious effects of natural disasters and social crises. There were other ways of dealing with such problems, however, and reducing people to chattels may have inhibited reform.

Less is known about advantages for slaves resulting from customs more liberal than the holy law. Unconditional liberation after a fixed term was the most valuable right that they stood to lose through sharia-minded reform. Folk pressures to free slaves on their conversion to Islam were great, but were fiercely resisted as undermining the entire edifice of servitude. More work is thus required to establish where such rights existed, how they evolved over time, and to what extent they were accepted in qadi courts.

Ethnicity and race have stirred much interest among scholars investigating slave systems, but they appear to have been marginal in Islam. In part, this was because Muslims took people from so

[186] Sourdel *et al.* 1965: 1082; Hodgson 1974: II, 145–6.
[187] Patterson 1982: 421; Pipes 1981: 99; Toledano 1998: 73; Zambaco 1911: 77; Willis 1980: 185; Laffin 1982: 58, 104–6; Segal 2001: 41–2; Romero 1997: 82–3; Snouck Hurgronje 1906: I, 21, 361.
[188] Clissold 1977: 42–3; Millant 1908: 205.

many origins, including the noble Arabs themselves. However, credit should also be given to the ulama's unyielding refusal to take such factors into consideration, whatever the prejudices of secular élites and the general populace.

5

SULTAN'S LAW

Secular legislation encroached on the sharia, especially in powerful and bureaucratic states. Although politics and religion were not clearly demarcated at the dawn of Islam, pre-existing Roman and Persian notions of monarchs as founts of justice re-asserted themselves from Umayyad times. The Saljuq Turks formally split secular and religious roles in the eleventh-century, and the Mongols symbolically destroyed the vestigial caliphate in 1258, imposing their own legal code.[1] Rulers converting outside the frontiers of the old caliphate introduced further diversity, notably in Southeast Asia.[2]

Monarchs legitimised their role by stressing the catch-all concept of public interest (*maslaha*), based on repeated injunctions in the Quran to command good and forbid evil. The ulama reacted by treating edicts as administrative decrees, tolerated if they accorded with sharia principles. Over time a separate system of secular justice emerged, but family law, in which slavery was included for most purposes, remained most firmly in the domain of sharia courts.[3]

Élite slavery became a major source of friction between rulers and the ulama.[4] To frustrate the ambitions of nobles and tribal leaders, and indeed religious notables, Muslim potentates built up disciplined corps of military and administrative slaves. Political opportunities also emerged for concubines and eunuchs. The ulama acquiesced with bad grace, and played a part in reversing the process, even if royal fears of political usurpation by élite slaves may have been more significant. Attempts to restrict élite servitude began in the thirteenth-century, perhaps reflecting Mongol distaste for the system, and gath-

---

[1] Hodgson 1974: I, 347–50, II, 291–2, 405–6, 412; Hourani 1970: 10–21; Shaw 1976–77: I, 62, 134.
[2] Thomaz 1994; Matheson and Hooker 1983.
[3] Anderson 1976; Hooker 1988.
[4] Pipes 1981: 60.

ered momentum from the sixteenth-century. Slave armies were moribund in larger Islamic polities by 1800, and concubines and eunuchs were largely confined to the harem, although administrative slavery limped on.[5]

Restricting illicit forms of enslavement sprang from a similar mix of sharia-mindedness and pragmatism. This preoccupation developed from the thirteenth-century, once it became evident that numerous infidels in newly conquered lands were resisting conversion to Islam. Rebellion was feared, notably among East European Christians, South Asian Hindus and Jains, East Javanese Hindus, and Animists in scattered locations. At the same time, a stricter application of rules protecting 'people of the book' brought Muslim regimes into line with holy law.

A few monarchs even envisaged complete emancipation. This suggests that scholars may have underestimated the role of the religious input into the process of reform, for such cases are difficult to explain purely in terms of social or political imperatives. That said, there were hardly any attempts actually to get rid of slavery, and they proved to be ephemeral.

Military slavery

Although the Prophet and his companions attracted individual slaves and freed slaves to fight for them, they did not make use of servile regiments. It was later rulers, from Umayyad times, who adopted Byzantine, Persian, and Chinese models of imperial military slavery.[6] Indeed, Abbasid caliphs developed the strategy to such a degree that this became a striking example of an Islamicate institution amounting to much more than the fossilised relics of older cultures.

Specialised military slavery grew fast from the early ninth-century, with an emphasis on recruiting Turks and Africans. Arab tribes had become unruly and unreliable, foreign mercenaries were untrustworthy, and the pious were increasingly withdrawing from the public arena, or turning to sects. Slaves thus appeared to be the best option, as long as the thorough indoctrination of impressionable infidel youths overcame the danger of servile mutinies. Military slaves never rose against Islam itself.[7]

[5] Inalcik 1979: 25–6; Philips 2000.
[6] Philips 2000; Pipes 1981; Crone 1980; Peirce 1993; Babaie *et al.* 2004.
[7] Pipes 1981; Crone 1980: 74–81; Bacharach 1981.

That said, monarchs frequently lost control of the Frankenstein's monster they had created, initially allowing servile officers to become the power behind the throne.[8] Self-perpetuating *mamluk* regimes then emerged, in which rulers were typically bought infidel slaves, selected to succeed by predecessors or peers. This was clearest in Egypt from 1250 to 1382 under Turkic slaves, and then up to 1517 under Circassian slaves.[9] The Ottomans allowed a subordinate Circassian regime to persist in Egypt after 1517, and a similar and largely Georgian one to bloom in Iraq from 1749 to 1831.[10] Turkic slaves also rose to power in thirteenth-century North India.[11] Africans dominated other *mamluk* regimes, notably in parts of Yemen, Ethiopia, and India.[12]

Military slaves might be ceremonially liberated on graduation, but this expectation probably declined over time. Moreover, officers were always more likely to be freed than troopers.[13] Pipes estimates that roughly half the military slaves of the early centuries were emancipated.[14] Egyptian sultans turned the manumission of trained infidel boys into a central ritual from 1250, but this fell into disuse after the Ottoman conquest of 1517.[15] There was little systematic liberation of military slaves in thirteenth-century India, the sixteenth-century Ottoman empire, or eighteenth-century Iraq.[16] However, successful military slaves might accumulate sufficient booty or power to gain their freedom.[17]

Although common, this military system 'could never be specifically Islamic'.[18] The ulama almost invariably objected to it, as did other Islamic intellectuals, despite the conversion of military slaves and attempts to show that they were good Muslims.[19] Caliph al-Amin created three corps of military eunuchs on Chinese lines in the early ninth-century, and it may have been sharia-minded objections that prevented his successors from following suit.[20]

---

[8] Gordon 2001.
[9] Ayalon 1951.
[10] Winter 1992; Nieuwenhuis 1981.
[11] Jackson 1999.
[12] Trimingham 1965: 61, 95; Renault and Daget 1985: 53.
[13] Crone 1980: 78–9; Patterson 1982: 288.
[14] Pipes 1981: 22.
[15] Ayalon 1951; Winter 1992: 2–3, 47, 66.
[16] Jackson 1999: 64; Repp 1968; Nieuwenhuis 1981.
[17] Pipes 1981: 10, 20–3; Baldé 1975: 203.
[18] Crone and Cook 1977: 125.
[19] Gordon 2001: 129–35; Pipes 1981: 157–8.
[20] Pipes 1981: 142, 145.

More broadly, the ulama taught that bondservants should not fight in offensive operations.[21] Professional soldiers, whether slaves or mercenaries, prevented free Muslim men from carrying out their obligation to fight in holy war.[22] To follow the example of the Prophet, thirteenth-century Hanafi jurists required those who battled for Islam to be free. Believers also had to refrain from needlessly putting property at risk, including slaves. Shafi'i ulama only allowed slaves to fight in defence of the Muslim community, or in exceptional circumstances.[23]

In eighteenth-century Morocco, the ulama apparently objected to the deracination and brutalisation of military slaves.[24] However, there is no evidence of scholars showing concern elsewhere, despite often harsh and difficult conditions of service. As slave soldiers were generally paid, and had a chance of manumission and upward social mobility, their lot may not have been seen as too harsh.[25]

Administrative and harem slavery

The ulama were hostile to the employment of servile officials. Such people were neither authorised by the founding texts of Islam, nor employed by the Prophet and his companions.[26] Less numerous and more privileged than slave soldiers, bureaucrats were often selected from the most able boys obtained for military duties.[27] The servile status of numerous senior administrators depressed the status of all officials over time, probably buttressing the despotic nature of political systems.[28]

Many senior officials were castrated into the bargain. Originally employed to watch over the harem, eunuchs became involved in palace administration, and then in running the state.[29] One particularly exalted group guarded the holiest places of Islam, the Prophet's tomb in Medina and the great mosque in Mecca, from the eighth-century.[30] Jalal al-Din al-Suyuti (d. 1505), a great Egyptian scholar, inveighed against this practice as an unauthorised innovation.[31]

---

[21] Khadduri 1955: 85–6; Hamidullah 1945: 152.
[22] Schleifer 1983: 187.
[23] Pipes 1981: 54, 94–5.
[24] Heers 2003: 208.
[25] Gordon 2001; Pipes 1981.
[26] Philips 2000: 215, 232.
[27] Papoulia 1963; Miura and Philips 2000.
[28] Toledano 1993: 39–42.
[29] Toledano 1984.
[30] Marmon 1995.
[31] Tounsy 1845: 269–70.

Mass royal and noble concubinage dated from Abbasid times.[32] Caliph Harun al-Rashid (r. 786–809) already owned 'hundreds' of concubines, and Caliph al-Mutawakkil (r. 847–61) was said to have possessed 4,000.[33] A rival Umayyad caliph in Iberia, 'Abd al-Rahman III (r. 912–961), allegedly held over 6,000 in the tenth-century.[34] Muhammad Rimfa (r. 1465–99), ruler of Borno in West Africa, supposedly purchased a thousand women for this purpose on a single occasion.[35] There were even attempts to give the practice religious sanction in South Asia, where Ziya-ud-Din Barani (1285/6–1356) wrote that the collection of large harems helped sultans to 'exhibit divinity' as vice-regents of God.[36]

Early Ottoman court practice seriously undermined the sharia norms of family life. From the late fourteenth-century, sultans restricted the succession to sons of concubines, each of whom was only allowed to have one male child. After that, a concubine dedicated her life to scheming in favour of her boy, whose most likely fate was death at the hands of a rival. If her son was successful, she might become the veritable ruler of the empire. From the mid-fifteenth-century, sultans even ceased to contract legal marriages. Süleyman the Lawgiver, or the Magnificent, (r. 1520–66) thus caused astonishment by falling in love with his Ruthenian concubine, Hurrem or Roxelana, and marrying her.[37]

The Ottoman system was extreme, but by having sexual relations with a handful of women drawn from a vast harem, a master denied a family life to numerous unwanted concubines. In effect, he condemned them to a 'system of involuntary imprisonment', together with their many female slaves.[38] Chafing against enforced chastity, women might commit adultery, or engage in homosexual relations, violating the sharia.[39]

For the sharia-minded, vast numbers of servile consorts flouted repeated recommendations in the Quran to treat slaves and wives well.[40] The ulama favoured the seclusion of women, but they could not approve of the excessive development of the harem system,

---

[32] Peirce 1993: 30; Khan 1972: 35–9.
[33] Ahmed 1992: 83, 86.
[34] Heers 2003: 193.
[35] *Ibid.* 193.
[36] Rizvi 1978–83: II, 357.
[37] Peirce 1993: 29–31, 39, 44, 58–9, 62.
[38] Elbashir 1983: 127; Gervaise 1971: 83–5; Montesquieu 1960: 241.
[39] Tounsy 1851: 404–5; Ingrams 1970: 29.
[40] Khan 1972: 35–9; Kidwai 1985: 85.

which was 'seriously alien to the Shar'i sense of human dignity'.[41] Implicitly, enormous harems breached the command in 7:29 of the Quran, 'be you not prodigal; He loves not the prodigal'.

Mughal reforms

Among the 'gunpowder empires' of Islam, the Mughals moved most decisively against slave élites from the sixteenth-century.[42] The imperial nobility and army of the new dynasty consisted essentially of free men. At most, individual nobles might field their own military slaves. Palace slavery became essentially domestic in nature, even if some eunuchs continued to straddle the private and public spheres.[43]

The great emperor Akbar (r. 1556–1605) stood out in tackling aspects of servitude out of kilter with the sharia, from the time that he assumed real power in 1560.[44] He forbade the enslavement of women and children in war in 1562, on grounds both temporal and religious.[45] He also prohibited the enslavement of non-Muslim subjects in arrears on their taxes.[46] This followed a turbulent period, when 'peaceable inhabitants' had frequently been enslaved.[47] Akbar was probably, in part, seeking to limit unrest among his Hindu subjects, a majority in his realm.[48]

He went further, however, exhibiting a personal distaste for the entire institution. He freed thousands of slaves in his own household in 1582, stating that 'it is beyond the realm of justice and good conduct for me to consider as my slaves those whom I have captured by force'.[49] He also banned the sale of slaves in public markets.[50] Though much hagiography accumulated around Akbar, even critics acknowledged his attempts to stem the tide of slavery.[51]

Nevertheless, Akbar's reforms were tarred with the brush of heterodox religious opinions, and were not always consistent. He may have kept his concubines after 1582, and he authorised slave trad-

---

[41] Hodgson 1974: II, 143–4.
[42] Sourdel et al. 1965: 1084–5; Hardy 1972: 14.
[43] Richards 1993: 60–2; Pipes 1981: 50, 92; Sourdel et al. 1965: 1084–5.
[44] Hodgson 1974: III, 71.
[45] Abul Fazl 1972: II, 246–7; Nizami 1989: 106.
[46] Lal 1994: 72–3.
[47] Balfour 1885: III, 673.
[48] Ruthven 2000: 272–4.
[49] Moosvi 1998: 88.
[50] Hodgson 1974: III, 71.
[51] Moosvi 2003.

ing in areas affected by severe famine.[52] He issued an edict in 1568 for the imprisonment of families of executed rebels, which came perilously close to permitting their enslavement.[53] Some of his generals continued to enslave women and children in conquered territories.[54] On one occasion, a slave tried to shoot him, although the arrow merely grazed his skin.[55]

There was a return to older patterns after Akbar's death, although not all was lost. Under Jahangir (r. 1605–27), 'Abdallah Khan Firuz Jang, an Uzbek commander, seized throngs of Indian 'rebels' in 1619–20, many of whom were exchanged in Iran for horses.[56] However, sales in public markets continued to be forbidden, and Nur Jahan, Jahangir's wife, liberated all her female slaves after her marriage in 1611.[57] Jahangir himself prohibited castration in 1608, citing the need to augment the Muslim population. Awrangzib, keen on Islamic orthodoxy, deployed religious arguments to justify the repetition of this prohibition in 1668. However, he did not prevent the importation of servile eunuchs, and he enslaved 'recalcitrant peasants and rebels'.[58]

Even during the eighteenth-century dismemberment of the empire, tax collectors were less likely to seize family members as slaves from Hindu defaulters than in pre-Mughal times.[59] However, the Shi'i Nawabs of Awadh (Oudh) employed eunuchs, bought young girls from poor parents, and enslaved tax defaulters. They seem to have been oblivious to any potential conflict with the holy law.[60]

The turning of the Ottoman tide

Ottoman sultans sought fatwas on aspects of enslavement from the late fifteenth-century. They 'wished to establish a legitimate basis for the ownership of slaves and goods taken in war, for frontier raids contradicted formalistic Hanafi rules'. When planning an attack on Cyprus in 1570, which was to yield many female slaves, the sultan hesitated to break a treaty with Venice. Ebu's Su'ud declared

---

[52] Khan 1972: 39; Moosvi 2003.
[53] Nizami 1989: 107, 383–4.
[54] Lal 1994: 73; Kolff 1990: 12.
[55] Law 1916: 167.
[56] Kolff 1990: 12–13; Levi 2002: 283–4.
[57] Moosvi 2003.
[58] Lal 1994: 116–17; Kidwai 1985: 87; Hambly 1974; Moosvi 2003.
[59] Lal 1994: 72–3; Levi 2002: 282, 286, Knighton 1921: 229.
[60] Ahmad 1971: 91; Knighton 1921: 134–8; Blank 2001: 323–4.

the campaign acceptable as holy war, because the treaty was detrimental to Muslims. However, he cautioned that not all attacks on Christians automatically qualified as jihads.[61]

As was shown in Chapter 2, the Ottoman ulama prohibited the seizure of Muslim rebels, apostates, and heretics, as well as infidel non-combatants in enemy lands. However, the 1791 Sistova (Swischtow) peace treaty caused a furore, because it enjoined that all Austrian slaves in Ottoman hands should be freed and returned. This breached the convention that Muslim converts should never be given up, even if they had embraced Islam as children or under duress.[62]

The infamous *devshirme* tax in Christian slave boys ebbed from the 1570s, ceased to be regular from the 1630s, and was last mentioned in 1738, although the causes of its disappearance remain controversial.[63] The system may have withered away as slave prices fell, but the sharpest price rise came when the *devshirme* was already decaying, in the early seventeenth-century.[64] Islamic misgivings motivated sultans who sought to align their laws with the sharia, as levies of adolescents taken from peaceful scriptuaries were an embarrassing anachronism.[65] However, one might have expected reform to occur earlier, in the reign of Süleyman the Lawgiver (r. 1520–66).[66] Reform may simply have aimed to keep the non-Muslim population quiescent.

Policies on military and administrative slavery remained hesitant and unsystematic. No formal text ever ended the Janissaries' technically servile status, even though the decline of the *devshirme* was accompanied by an influx of free volunteers into the corps. Soldiers could now marry, obtained tax advantages, and were not subjected to former levels of discipline.[67] Around 1700, there was an attempt to resurrect military slavery with Circassian and Georgian boys, obtained from the Caucasus.[68] The number of freeborn administrators increased, and yet it was estimated in 1832 that four-fifths of ministers had been purchased as slaves.[69]

---

[61] Imber 1997: 84–5.
[62] Heyd 1961: 88; Erdem 1996: 31.
[63] Ménage 1965; Sugar 1977: 56.
[64] Papoulia 1963: 52, 61; Fisher 1980a: 35.
[65] Imber 1997: 78–9; 134, 141; Imber 2002: 134; Kunt 1982: 64.
[66] Hodgson 1974: III, 109–11.
[67] Imber 2002: 141–2; Shaw and Shaw 1976–7: I, 187.
[68] Nieuwenhuis 1981: 13.
[69] Toledano 1993: 42, 54–5.

Religious motives have been neglected in explaining the loss of power by concubines and eunuchs in the course of the eighteenth-century, usually attributed to Western threats to the empire's survival. However, some Ottoman ulama publicly castigated 'the political activity of royal women,' for example a mufti named Sunullah in 1599. A Sufi shaykh from southeastern Anatolia, who mounted another attack in 1653, was declared to be deranged. Leslie Peirce may be unfair in attributing such criticism solely to misogyny, citing a Hadith of the Prophet that a 'people who entrusts its affairs to a woman will never know prosperity'.[70]

Ottoman doubts concerning eunuchs emerged clearly in 1715, when the sultan sent a decree prohibiting castration to Egypt, to be publicly displayed. It came with a fatwa from Istanbul's Shaykh al-Islam, declaring castration to be a prohibited innovation, inhumane, and contrary to the sultan's orders. The document graphically described as 'slaughterhouses' the 'terrible places' where castration was practised in Egypt, including in Cairo itself. However, the decree precluded neither imports from the abode of war, nor the employment of existing eunuchs. Indeed, Istanbul sent urgent requests for palace eunuchs in 1722 and 1737, specifying in the latter case that they be drawn from the households of recently deceased emirs.[71]

Iran, Morocco, and other gunpowder states

The Safavid Shi'i state in Iran, encountered as a radical millenarian regime in chapter 3, suffered from growing social inequality.[72] A tidal wave of bonded people flowed into the empire, captured from the Caucasus or purchased from India and Africa. Many were eunuchs, concubines, officials, and soldiers.[73] Persian armies seized not only infidels but also Muslim heretics. Intervening in an Omani civil war from the 1720s to the 1740s, the Persians were accused of slaughtering Ibadi children and enslaving women.[74]

Shah Abbas I (r. 1587–1629) turned his back on the dynasty's origins, crushing a rival Mahdist rebellion in 1590–1, and developing élite slavery. A servile army, equipped with firearms, was the key to his military success, and he appointed slave governors in all the provinces. Under Shah Safi (r. 1629–42), concubines replaced

[70] Peirce 1993: 267, 282.
[71] Winter 1992: 43–4.
[72] Hodgson 1974: III, 6.
[73] Baghdiantz McCabe 1999: 38–46.
[74] Risso 1986: 31.

princesses as the mothers of rulers, and hereditary families of élite administrative slaves emerged. There were estimated to be a thousand military slaves and three thousand eunuchs serving the Shah in Isfahan, with an Azeri eunuch, Saru Taqi, wielding real power as grand vizier from 1634 to 1645.[75] This tremendous growth of élite slavery provoked a religious backlash. Shah Abbas II (r. 1642–66) ordered Saru Taqi's murder in 1645, and undertook a return to Shi'i orthodoxy. The ulama objected strenuously to the political dominance of Georgian and Armenian converts, perhaps because they doubted their sincerity. Military and administrative slavery thus declined, albeit without disappearing.[76]

The Qajar dynasty, of Turkmen origins and in power from the 1790s, further reduced the influence of élite slaves.[77] Sons of concubines could no longer succeed to the throne, even though this conflicted with the practice of the Shi'i Imams themselves.[78] Moreover, eunuchs were confined to the harem.[79] However, the Qajar did not oppose slavery as such, keeping a largely Georgian servile bodyguard till the 1810s, and assiduously mounting slave raids in the Caucasus.[80] Lacking any claim to descent from the Imams, Qajar rulers persuaded the clerical hierarchy to allow them to wage 'defensive' jihads, widely interpreted, thereby justifying the enslavement of war captives.[81]

Morocco employed firearms to revive its military fortunes and take numerous slaves. Ahmad al-Mansur (r. 1578–1603) first expelled the Portuguese from many of their footholds, taking copious levies of captives in the process. He then deployed musketeers, serving under an Iberian eunuch, to conquer the middle Niger in 1590–1. This stimulated a wave of servile imports. Moroccan seamen also took part in the rising tide of Barbary incursions, with one Dutch renegade based in Sale raiding Iceland in 1627.[82]

Al-Mansur wrote an undated letter to some Egyptian ulama to justify developing a Black *mamluk* army. He stressed the pressing

[75] Babaie *et al.* 2004; Baghdiantz McCabe 1999: 39.
[76] Baghdiantz McCabe 1999: 173, 175, 178–9.
[77] Hambly 1991a: 159–60; Sourdel *et al.* 1965: 1083.
[78] Brunschvig 1960: 36; Haeri 1993: 139–40.
[79] Polak 1865: I, 261.
[80] Hambly 1991a: 159–60; Hambly 1991b: 583.
[81] Lambton 1970; Kohlberg 1976: 81–6; Peters 1979: 171; Halm 1991: 104–5.
[82] Monlaü 1964: 65–6, 86, 97; Clissold 1977: 29; Heers 2003: 41–2, 59; Hodgson 1974: II, 555; Renault and Daget 1985: 31–2.

danger from Christian unbelievers on all sides, and affirmed that all his soldiers either had been legally purchased, or had been taken as runaways.[83] However, his own ulama expressed doubts as to the legality of enslavement in naval raids.[84]

The employment of slave soldiers reached a peak under his successor, Mawlay Isma'il (r. 1672–1727), but this provoked a religious response. Isma'il rounded up free Blacks to serve as military slaves, arguing that they were runaways and 'natural slaves', who were needed to defend the realm against Christians. He sought support from the al-Azhar *madrasa* in Cairo, and bullied most Moroccan ulama into accepting his claims. However, 'Abd al-Salam b. Jasus, an *'alim* of Fez, denounced this flagrant violation of the holy law, arguing that even a voluntary acknowledgement of servile status by a free Muslim was inadmissible. Imprisoned in 1708, he took up the cause again on his release, and was executed by strangulation in 1709.[85] Explaining his refusal to back down, he wrote: 'I would have betrayed God, his Messenger and his law. And I would have feared eternity in hell because of it'.[86]

Slave soldiers interfered in succession disputes for three decades after Isma'il's death, leading Mawlay Muhammad III (r. 1757–90) sharply to curtail the size of the corps, while retaining some military and administrative slavery.[87] According to Jacques Heers, some ulama protested against the rigorous isolation and training of slave soldiers, held to be contrary to the sharia, though he cites no source. He also notes that the system had alienated influential urban merchants.[88]

South of the Sahara, Askia Muhammad I (r. 1493–1528), of Songhay in West Africa, expressed uncertainty as to the legality of some forms of enslavement. Attempting to bolster his usurpation of the throne by excelling in piety, he criticised his predecessor for enslaving Muslims, and released those of doubtful status. He then obtained confirmation of his actions from three religious authorities, the ulama of Timbuktu, Muhammad b. 'Abd al-Karim al-Maghili in Algeria, and Jalal al-Din al-Suyuti in Egypt.[89] However, Askia Muhammad took thousands of slaves in a 1498 jihad against the Animist Mossi,

[83] Hunwick 1999: 52–5.
[84] Berque 1978: 166–73.
[85] Hunwick 1999: 56–9; Hamel 2002: 46–8; Batran 1985: 7–9; Sikainga 1999: 63–4.
[86] Munson 1993: 51.
[87] Hunwick 1999: 59; Hunwick 1992: 20; Michaux-Bellaire 1910: 424–5.
[88] Heers 2003: 208.
[89] Willis 1980: 189–90; Olivier de Sardan 1975: 110–12; Hunwick 1985: 25–7, 71, 75–7.

and no long-term reform occurred.[90] On the other side of the continent, Somali rulers claimed the right to free slaves by decree, but it is not clear whether they ever exercised this privilege.[91]

An exceptionally bold royal assault on slavery occurred in Southeast Asia, although it proved to be a flash in the pan. In the first zealous flush of Islamisation, which began around 1610 in the Bugis state of Bone in South Sulawesi, La' Ma'daremmeng (r. 1631–44) interpreted the holy law as commanding the liberation of all bondservants, or perhaps of all foreign slaves. The neighbouring sultan of Makassar asked him whether this was 'by command of the Prophet, or on the basis of traditional custom, or according to his own will and pleasure'. Receiving no reply, he invaded Bone and revoked the emancipation edict.[92] However, sharia rules on enslavement were carefully enforced in Makassar. The sale of children and self-sale were not tolerated, and most slaves were Animists taken in war.[93] The dangers posed by discontented helots were illustrated by a serious rising of 'Javanese' slaves, presumably Hindus, in the Malay sultanate of Patani in 1613.[94]

Monarchs bore a heavy responsibility for building up an intricate system of élite slavery, but it is an exaggeration to assume that the ulama merely responded by withdrawing from an impious world. It seems more accurate to say that many ulama opposed these developments, and that a few occasionally brought their doubts into the public arena. There is scattered evidence of ulama remonstrating with rulers, protesting against excesses in the accumulation of soldiers, officials, eunuchs, singing-girls and concubines. What is required is a systematic piecing together of such objections into a coherent and documented narrative of religious opposition.

The role of 'gunpowder emperors' in repressing élite slavery is much better known, but the religious elements in this about-turn have been neglected, or even denied. It may well be that monarchs sought to end these kinds of servitude mainly for temporal reasons, notably to guard against usurpation and to modernise their armed forces and bureaucracies. Even so, rulers sought religious justifications for their actions, and these need to be better understood.

---

[90] Hunwick 1985: 27; Azumah 2001: 147.
[91] Cerulli 1957–64: II, 24.
[92] Pelras 2001: 230; Reid 1983b: 169.
[93] Gervaise 1971: 81–5.
[94] Lombard 1990: II, 148–9.

As for less common attempts to reform ordinary slavery, the religious dimension has again been disregarded. To be sure, it can be argued that the driving force was a fear of alienating numerous non-Muslims. Showing no signs of turning to Islam, they threatened the stability of some states, even their very survival. Nevertheless, religious justifications and motivations need to be better grasped. Moreover, research should not be confined to the three great gunpowder empires, for humbler monarchs displayed liberal attitudes towards servitude.

Part II

THE ROADS TO ABOLITION

6

IMPERIALISM AND SECULARISM

The demise of slavery has traditionally been ascribed to imperialism and secularism, as 'one of the most typical examples of the transformation that the Muslim world has undergone, through European pressure or example'.[1] Western ideologists denounced slavery as a root cause of Islamic moral decadence and social decay, justifying diplomatic bullying or colonial conquest.[2] For Adu Boahen, 'The readiness with which the Sultan of Turkey and the Bey of Tunis granted the British Government's urgent requests, and the refusal of the Shah of Persia and the Sultan of Morocco, show quite clearly that the determining factor in these negotiations was not a ruler's religious convictions, but rather his political and bargaining power *vis-à-vis* the British Government'.[3]

As for Western example, nineteenth-century Muslim élites were undoubtedly exposed to secular ideas such as humanitarianism, natural law, and utilitarianism. There was a parallel acceleration of the process of statute law encroaching ever more on the sphere of the sharia. However, the language of abolitionist legislation suggests that Muslim bureaucrats borrowed eclectically from secular and Islamic motifs. At the same time, some educated Muslims were swayed

---

[1] Brunschvig 1960: 36.
[2] Daniel 1966; Reclus 1883: 237; Muir 1891: 594; Cooper 1968: 130; Salman 2001: 95; Zwemer 1965: 126–9.
[3] Boahen 1964: 148.

by Social Darwinist notions, spreading from the 1860s, which held that 'biologically inferior' peoples were better off as slaves.[4] Sayyida Salme, a renegade Zanzibar princess living in Germany, was a good example of this tendency.[5]

Despite presenting the evils of servitude as a routine justification for conquest, colonial administrators hesitated. Underfunded, understaffed, and unfamiliar with local conditions, bureaucrats hoped that suppressing raiding and trading would suffice.[6] Some manipulated Islamic beliefs and institutions to delay the enforcement of legislation imposed by the metropolis, to the extent that, 'colonial regimes became the defenders of slavery, and the greatest single impediment to full emancipation'.[7] However, other officials studied Islam to foster its abolitionist potential, attempting to give legislation an Islamic gloss that would render it acceptable.

Independent Muslim rulers moved legislation further away from Islamic norms, as radical secularism took root after 1918. Prohibiting slavery became an unthinking reflex in the era of decolonisation and socialism, when brave new constitutions specified individual freedoms in borrowed garb. Laws were sometimes copied verbatim from Western codes, and became integrated into an expanding framework of international law developed by the West.[8] Even so, the input of Islamic notions never ceased entirely, and began to revive from the 1970s.

The Maghrib between colonialism and secularism

As the Napoleonic Wars dragged to a close in Europe, Western newspapers called vociferously for naval action to liberate the Christian slaves of Maghribi corsairs.[9] At the Congress of Vienna in 1814–15, the assembled powers decided to end Mediterranean slave raiding by both Muslim and Christian privateers. On the one hand, the Knights of Saint John were not allowed to regain Malta, and Muslim merchant ships were to ply their trade peacefully. On the other hand, Anglo-Dutch and Anglo-French naval forces attacked Barbary ports in 1816 and 1819 respectively, while the United States imposed a treaty on Algiers in 1815. The French seizure of Algiers

[4] Lewis 1990: 82–4.
[5] Salme 1993: 152, 327–33, 441–2, 500.
[6] Miers and Roberts 1988: 17, 19–21.
[7] Lovejoy 1983: 247.
[8] Awad 1966.
[9] Chater 1984: 220; Marques 1999: 120.

in 1830 ended a process of cajoling, intimidating, or battering the Barbary states into freeing Christian slaves.[10] Although the French presented liberation of Christians as a justification for taking Algiers, they failed to extend their liberality to Muslim and Animist slaves as they pushed further into Algeria. When a French official, on his own initiative, freed tribal slaves in the Oran region in 1840, Mustafa b. Isma'il complained that, 'this measure harms our religion and destroys our power. We have heard it said that the King of the French declared that nobody can destroy our religion, our law, and our power'. The Ministry of War ordered the return of the slaves, because France had guaranteed security of property to the vanquished.[11]

Shamed by Tunisian abolition two years previously, the French Republicans prohibited slavery on seizing power in 1848, ordering the law to be read in all Algerian mosques.[12] As compensation was rejected, however, the governor-general advised officials to 'close their eyes'.[13] Napoleon III left the law on the statute book, but liberation only occurred in areas under civilian rule, and on a case by case basis.[14] The Third Republic returned to the question, after receiving reports of up to 2,000 slaves a year transiting through the Mzab.[15] The high court in Algiers issued a decree in 1880, underlining that the relation between owner and slave was not recognised in law.[16] In the same year, Governor-General Albert Grévy reminded judges of their obligation to enforce the law on servitude. However, many Algerian Muslims still owned slaves in 1905–6, even in the Department of Algiers, when Governor-General Charles Jonnart sought to stamp out the institution.[17]

Ahmad Bey of Tunisia (r. 1837–55) was the first modern Muslim ruler to embrace abolition. On acceding to the throne, he refused to parade manumitted slaves in his predecessor's funeral procession, because 'manumission is an act dedicated to God, and not to gain glory through the number of slaves freed'.[18] In 1841–2, he banned foreign trade in slaves and birth as a slave, closed slave markets,

[10] Chater 1984: 213–57; Valensi 1969: 62–9; Deardon 1976: 243–4; Clissold 1977: 158–64; Monlaü 1964: 117–23; Bono 1964: 69–76.
[11] Emerit 1949: 36–7.
[12] Cordell 1999: 38–40; Emerit 1949: 41.
[13] Emerit 1949: 40–2; Jennings 2000: 256; Christelow 1985a: 119–20.
[14] Cordell 1999: 44–8; Christelow 1985a: 120–1.
[15] Renault and Daget 1985: 162.
[16] Sikainga 1999: 65.
[17] Dermenghem 1954: 258–9.
[18] Temimi 1985: 215.

liberated his own dependants, and ceased to send slaves as tribute to Istanbul. Lacking funds for compensation, he initially hesitated to abolish the institution itself. However, in 1846 he ordered manumission documents to be issued on request.[19] An estimated 6,000 to 30,000 people gained their freedom, imports of Black slaves slowed to a trickle, and White slaves ceased to enter the realm.[20]

Reasons of state supposedly explained this radical act. Ahmad Bey sought complete political autonomy from the Ottomans, who had imposed direct rule on neighbouring Libya in 1835. Even more threatening was French expansion into Algeria from 1830, for Ahmad feared that France would exploit the problem of runaway slaves to intervene in his domains. The British were the best allies he could hope for, and he shrewdly realised that abolishing slavery would win them over.[21]

This cannot explain everything, for the British consul worried that Ahmad was rushing the attack on slavery, having 'come to a fixed resolution of putting a total end to it in his Dominions'.[22] Ahmad's mother was a Sardinian slave, probably seized in a brutal raid, which may have given him an emotional commitment to the cause.[23] He was also fascinated by Western power, wanting to be known as a 'civilised monarch'. Indeed, he greatly enjoyed a state visit to Paris in late 1846, during which liberals lionised him for abolishing slavery before France.[24]

Nevertheless, Ahmad wanted his decrees to accord with Islam. He declared that slavery was 'contrary to religion', and referred to a 'desire for liberty of the ultimate lawgiver'. Citing Ahmad Baba, he stressed the dubious provenance of most slaves. Ahmad Bey further extolled the virtues of manumission, and condemned the terrible sufferings endured in crossing the Sahara. He contended that the sharia imposed freedom for ill-treatment, although sale to another owner was a canonical alternative. As the ulama remained hesitant, he took it upon himself to act in the public interest.[25]

Reforms broadened after Ahmad's death. Muhammad Bey (1855–9) rather reluctantly followed the Ottoman pattern in 1857, with

---

[19] Brown 1974: 322–5; Chater 1984: 550–3; Temimi 1985: 215–16; Awad 1966: 134; Boahen 1964: 140.

[20] Emerit 1949: 39; Temimi 1985: 217–18; Brett 1982: 18.

[21] Boahen 1964: 137–41; Brown 1974: 323–4; Montana 2001: 9–11.

[22] Erdem 1996: 48.

[23] Brown 1974: 30–1.

[24] Brown 1974: 322, 324–5, 328–89; Chater 1984: 553.

[25] Montana 2001; Hunwick and Powell 2002: 183–4; Khuri 1983: 152–4; Brown 1974: 324; Chater 1994: 45; Awad 1966: 134.

'public interest' guaranteeing human freedom. Under Muhammad al-Sadiq (1859–82), equality before the law was guaranteed in 1861, in the Islamic world's first modern constitution.[26] Husayn Pasha, minister of education, roundly declared in 1863 that countries without slavery were more prosperous, cultured, just, and egalitarian. He also quoted a man of letters exclaiming: 'Your shari'ah aims at liberty; the enslavement of a human being is a disaster'.[27]

Resistance prevented complete success. Overt opposition to abolition was initially confined to Bedouins and southern farmers, notably in the island of Jerba.[28] When tax increases led to great rural rebellion in 1864, insurgents demanded the cancellation of reforms not in line with Islam. These included the constitution and the abolition of slavery.[29] The rising was crushed, but with difficulty. The constitution was withdrawn in 1866, and some illicit slavery continued.[30]

An increasingly powerful figure was Khayr al-Din (1810–89), a Circassian slave purchased for Ahmad Bey in Istanbul around 1839. He sought to avoid the Scylla of popular protest and the Charybdis of Italian or French conquest. In a book published in Tunis in 1867, and later reissued in Istanbul, he stressed freedom of the person, albeit without mentioning slavery.[31] As chief minister from 1873 to 1877, he was instrumental in getting the bey to sign a treaty with Britain in 1875. Tunisia promised to implement the 1846 decree, actively suppressing slavery and punishing offenders.[32]

Failure to eradicate slavery entirely helped to justify the imposition of a loose French protectorate in 1881. Six years after that date, the bey freed the women of his harem.[33] In 1890, penal sanctions were decreed for buying, selling, or keeping slaves.[34] The French called this the 'second abolition', although few people were affected, most of them in southern oases.[35]

Morocco was far more dilatory. Sultan 'Abd al-Rahman of Morocco famously proclaimed in 1842 that slavery was a matter on which 'all sects and nations have agreed from the time of the sons of Adam'.

---

[26] Hourani 1970: 64–5; Green 1978: 104.
[27] Khuri 1983: 154.
[28] Chater 1984: 553; Montana 2001: 16.
[29] Valensi 1977: 360–1; Slama 1967: 34–7.
[30] Green 1978: 104; Fisher 2001: 339; Erdem 1996: 89.
[31] Khayr ed-Din 1987: 148; Green 1978: 120; Leone 1973: 10; Hourani 1970: 84–7, 90.
[32] Brunschvig 1960: 37.
[33] Gordon 1989: 163.
[34] Dermenghem 1954: 258.
[35] Larguèche 2003: 336.

He continued that not only the making of slaves but also 'trading therewith' were sanctioned by the Quran, which 'admits not either of addition or diminution'.[36] The sultan declined to meet envoys from the Anti-Slavery Society in 1844.[37] His chief minister, Muhammad b. Idris, wrote to the British in the following year, 'as we do not interfere in religious principles which you profess, likewise you should not interfere in our religion'. Pursuing his universalist claim, the sultan even secured a ruling on slavery from Jewish rabbis.[38]

Later Moroccan leaders moved slowly. Sultan Muhammad b. 'Abd al-Rahman's decree of 1863 cited ill-treatment to justify the retention of slaves who fled to the authorities, with compensation paid to owners. However, a Moroccan minister declared in 1884 that abolishing slavery conflicted 'with the bases of Muslim law'. Slaves were well treated, and the institution protected the poorest. Possibly influencing the official mind were tax revenues, and the South's dependence on slave labour.[39] Military slavery disappeared from the central state, but Ba Ahmad b. Musa, regent from 1894, inherited both his servile status and his elevated position from his father and grandfather.[40] At best, the authorities episodically closed public slave markets.[41]

Ahmad Sikainga asserts that the declaration of a loose Franco-Spanish protectorate in 1912 completed the abolition process.[42] In reality, cases of slavery were left to qadis.[43] The French did at least issue a circular in 1922, reminding officials that public dealing in slaves was prohibited, and that anybody asking for freedom would receive it.[44] The Spaniards also admitted that they had in fact failed to ban the status of slavery in their two Moroccan zones.[45]

Even the Rif Republic only timidly raised the abolitionist flag, despite the declaration of Liazid b. Haj, minister of home affairs, that he had 'emancipated the slaves'.[46] Muhammad b. 'Abd al-Karim al-Khattabi, charismatic rebel leader from 1921 to 1926, claimed to be restoring the sharia, which had been distorted by Sufi excesses.

[36] Boahen 1964: 141–4.
[37] Ennaji 1999: 115.
[38] Schroeter 1992: 202–3, 212.
[39] Ennaji 1999: 116, 120, 122.
[40] Michaux-Bellaire 1910: 424–5; Schroeter 1992: 201.
[41] Schroeter 1992: 203–5; Ennaji 1999: 122.
[42] Sikainga 1999: 65.
[43] Lapanne-Joinville 1952: 153–6.
[44] Brunschvig 1960: 39; Ennaji 1999: 114–15.
[45] Greenidge 1958: 37.
[46] Sheean 1926: 142.

However, he was also influenced by exposure to Spanish culture, and inspired by the example of Kemal Atatürk, secular president of Turkey.[47] Moreover, al-Khattabi needed recognition from the world, so that an appeal to the League of Nations included a promise to abide by international treaties.[48] Nevertheless, Western visitors met Black slaves and eunuchs, and noted that slave markets remained open. A local leader even described Spanish prisoners of war, toiling on public works, as 'slaves' of the emir, a claim echoed by Spanish propaganda.[49]

Maghribi independence witnessed the confirmation of emancipation on secular lines. Habib b. 'Ali Bourguiba, president of Tunisia, declared that slavery and polygyny 'made sense at an earlier stage in human history, but were offensive to the civilised conscience today'.[50] The king of Libya, head of the Sanusi Sufi order considered here in Chapter 8, guaranteed personal liberty in the constitution of 1951.[51] Muammar al-Qaddafi, who seized power in Libya in 1969, went further. His 'Third Universal Theory', elaborated from 1976, canvassed support for his ambitions in Africa. Portraying true Islam as the bastion of equality between races, sexes, and classes, he misleadingly denounced 'the latest age of slavery' as that of White capitalists enslaving Blacks.[52]

From reform to revolution in the Ottoman empire

The looming threat of military annihilation led Mahmud II (r. 1808–39) to accelerate the pace of Ottoman reform, even if his delegates at the Congress of Vienna refused to sign a declaration against the slave trade in 1815.[53] He swept away the relics of military servitude in 1826, creating a new model army on Western lines, and sharply pruned administrative slavery in 1831–3.[54] From Syria, a force was despatched to snuff out Iraq's autonomous *mamluk* regime in 1831.[55]

To parry any overspill from the Western crusade against Barbary slavery, Mahmud ceased to enslave war captives, and ordered the

[47] Pennell 1986.
[48] Madariaga 1987: II, 259–61, 269–72.
[49] Sheean 1926: 47, 55, 126, 142, 247–8, 284, 294; Furneaux 1967: 101, 110.
[50] Anderson 1976: 63.
[51] Brunschvig 1960: 39.
[52] Qaddafi 1987: 77, 121.
[53] Erdem 1996: 71.
[54] Erdem 1996: 11; Cleveland 1994: 76–7; Sourdel *et al.* 1965: 1091.
[55] Niewenhuis 1981.

freeing of Christian slaves in 1830.[56] He justified this unusual preference for unbelievers over Muslims by questioning the purpose of keeping stubborn infidels under the yoke.[57] Those emancipated were mostly Greek women and children, captured in the bitter war of independence of 1821–9.[58] For good measure, Mahmud also swept away relics of 'serfdom' in the Balkans, turning Christian peasants fully into sharecroppers.[59]

Sultan Abdülmecit I (r. 1839–61) launched the Tanzimat reform programme, ending relics of administrative servitude.[60] He also banned keeping eunuchs, although enforcement was patchy.[61] The Crimean War of 1853 to 1856 was the first major conflict in which regular Ottoman troops did not reduce prisoners to slavery, although Bashibozuk irregulars 'saw no reason not to enslave enemy subjects as they had done before'. Embarrassed officials were obliged to return 'kidnapped' Christians to the Russians. The Bashibozuk repeated this performance in the 1877–8 war against Russia, seizing numerous Bulgarians.[62]

Relief of suffering, evinced in religious terms, was Abdülmecit's main justification for acting against slave trading. The Gulf decree of 1847 noted that slaves were treated in ways 'harsh and bereft of mercy'. Proscribing the trans-Saharan trade in 1849, he cited appalling mortality, while cautiously affirming that 'our holy law permits slavery'.[63] He declared in 1851, 'It is a shameful and barbarous practice for rational beings to buy and sell their fellow creatures ... Are not these poor creatures our equals before God? Why then should they be assimilated to animals?'[64] In 1854, he opined that 'selling people as animals, or articles of furniture, is contrary to the will of the sovereign creator'.[65] Some high-ranking officials expressed similar feelings, though others did not.[66] Further decrees outlawed the Caucasus trade in 1854–5, and exports from Libya to Crete and Epirus in 1855. The entire African trade was prohibited

[56] Vlora 1968: I, 68; Erdem 1996: 30.
[57] Young 1905–6: II, 171–2.
[58] Erdem 1996: 20, 26, 59.
[59] Malcolm 1994: 93–4, 129.
[60] Toledano 1998: 24–6.
[61] Zambaco 1911: 40; Renault 1971: II, 60–2.
[62] Erdem 1996: 44–5, 196.
[63] Lewis 1990: 160–1.
[64] Toledano 1998: 117–19.
[65] Gordon 1989: 47.
[66] Toledano 1998: 117–18.

in 1857, albeit with exemptions for the Red Sea trade, after revolts had broken out in the Hijaz and Massawa.[67] Commercial and criminal law, codified from 1839, dealt further blows to the slave trade. The 1858 penal code imposed punishments for kidnapping and enslaving people, which were added to in 1867.[68] Article 210 of the 1869 'Book of Trade' specified that 'a free man cannot be sold or exchanged for something else'.[69]

A further twist in the saga of Circassian slavery threatened public order. Fleeing Russian conquest, free Circassians flooded into the empire in the late 1850s and early 1860s, bringing with them throngs of slaves, held under their harsh customary code.[70] Appraised of milder local customs of servitude, notably liberation after a fixed term, as discussed in Chapter 4 above, these slaves began to clamour for their liberty. In 1867, Istanbul reacted by decreeing that they should be freed on payment of a mutually agreed sum. Owners resisted, and the authorities deployed field artillery to oblige some Circassian beys near Edirne to free their slaves in 1874. However, the latter still had pay for their emancipation in instalments.[71]

Reformers balked at complete abolition, for not even Abdülmecit was prepared to condemn a status enshrined in holy law. This dashed the expectations of the British Anti-Slavery Society, which had hoped that the caliph, as a kind of Muslim 'pope', might declare abolition throughout Islamdom. In 1840 Lord Palmerston minuted sarcastically that one might as well ask the sultan to become a Christian. The Ottoman foreign minister's widely touted promise to abolish slavery, contained in a diplomatic note of 1857, resulted from a faulty translation from the Turkish.[72]

Furthermore, Abdülmecit's death in 1861 signalled a slackening in the campaign against the slave trade. British consular reports from 1869 revealed that imports from Africa were growing again, facilitated by the opening of the Suez Canal in that year and the use of steamers.[73] Ottoman officials allowed the resumption of imports from the Caucasus, alleging that suppression, decreed under duress,

[67] Erdem 1996: 66–76, 107, 129, 177–8; Young 1905–6: II, 172–4; Lewis 1990: 78–81; Ewald and Clarence-Smith 1997: 290–1; Beachey 1976a: 157–8.
[68] Toledano 1998: 33.
[69] Erdem 1996: 189.
[70] Toledano 1993: 44; Toledano 1998: 81–2; Erdem 1996: 53; Young 1905–6: II, 166–7.
[71] Erdem 1996: 114–21, 156–7, 161; Toledano 1998: 99–101.
[72] Erdem 1996: XX, 70–1, 110–11.
[73] Douin 1936–41: III–2, 653–91; Erdem 1996: 63–4, 155–6; Beachey 1976a: 167; Toledano 1982: 44–5.

was invalid. Instructions issued in 1864 tolerated Circassian parents selling their children, as long as they were neither tricked nor coerced, merely threatening miscreants with the 'wrath of God'.[74] When Abdülhamit II came to the throne in 1876, he disappointed his liberal supporters. Midhat Pasha (1822–84), chief minister and leading reformer, inserted a commitment to the gradual abolition of slavery in the speech from the throne, but the sultan omitted it. Although Abdülhamit reluctantly promulgated a constitution asserting the equality of citizens before the law, specific legislation on slavery did not follow.[75] He dismissed Midhat Pasha in 1877, and suspended the constitution the following year.[76] The dreams of one woman were shattered. Believing herself to be free, she left Istanbul and married a farmer. Her master hauled her in front of a qadi, who ordered that she be restored to her rightful owner. She ran away, but was brought back by the police.[77]

Abdülhamit rapidly became the bugbear of abolitionists. The sultan stubbornly refused to prohibit the renewed traffic from the Caucasus, and his 'freedom-loving acts' of 1877 and 1889 merely re-iterated existing bans on the African slave trade, as did an 1880 convention with Britain. These prohibitions were poorly enforced, even after the sultan had officially committed himself to 'strive for the suppression of slavery, and especially the Negro slave trade' at the Berlin Conference of 1885. Only diplomatic arm-twisting persuaded Abdülhamit to ratify the Brussels General Act of 1890 a year later, despite a clause permitting 'domestic slavery'.[78] The status of exemptions granted for the Red Sea trade remained unclear, and an Italian traced the movement of slaves from Eritrea to Syria, and on to Istanbul in 1908.[79]

Internal reform stalled. In 1882, the sultan rejected a draft law from the Council of State, whereby the empire would have ceased to recognise the legal status of slavery.[80] At best Circassian and Georgian youths were freed before enrolment into the army from that year.[81] On the advice of the Shaykh al-Islam, the sultan ordered the cessation of all work on codifying Hanafi family law in 1888,

[74] Toledano 1998: 31–2, 89–92.
[75] Erdem 1996: 125–9, 205; Zambaco 1911: 65; Sagaster 1997: 18.
[76] Erdem 1996: 130.
[77] Zambaco 1911: 64–5.
[78] Erdem 1996: 130–46.
[79] Lenci 1990: 41.
[80] Erdem 1996: 137–9.
[81] Toledano 1993: 44.

leaving slavery unreformed and subject to sharia courts.[82] In 1901 Abdülhamit refused to punish Yemenis discovered re-enslaving persons freed three years earlier.[83]

The resurgence of harem servitude was a further sign of the times.[84] In 1903, there were 194 eunuchs and up to 500 women in the imperial harem.[85] The number of eunuchs illegally entering the empire rose after 1876, many of them destined for the imperial household.[86] Coded missives ordered the governor of Konya to procure Circassian girls for the palace in 1891–2. They were to be blonde, blue-eyed, to speak no Turkish, and they did not need to be drawn from the slave class.[87]

Some highly placed Ottomans supported the sultan's reactionary stance. The Ottoman foreign minister defended slavery as bringing infidels to the true faith, in correspondence with his Persian opposite number in 1882.[88] At the time of Cardinal Lavigerie's attack on Muslim slavery in 1888, Kara Teodori (1833–1906), a French-educated Greek Christian from Edirne, was Ottoman ambassador in Brussels. He diligently defended the empire's 'mild' slavery. A flurry of apologetic articles claimed that slaves were well treated, upwardly mobile, and often manumitted, while admitting that the institution was doomed in the long term.[89]

Conversely, liberal members of the élite refused to give up the struggle. Midhat Pasha, demoted to governor of Syria, unsuccessfully tried to suspend the annual pilgrim caravan in 1879, to prevent slave imports from the Hijaz.[90] He was accused of donating two female slaves to a religious dignitary, but this seems to have been a trumped-up charge.[91] Among those who made real attempts to stamp out the infamous traffic were Arifi Bey, governor of Jidda in the 1880s, and Ahmad Rasim Pasha, governor of Tripoli, Libya, from 1881 to 1896.[92]

Once Young Turk rebels had forced the restoration of the constitution in 1908, several newspapers took advantage of freedom of

[82] Kandiyoti 1991: 27; Sagaster 1997: 18.
[83] Erdem 1996: 177–8.
[84] Hanimefendi 1994; Croutier 1989.
[85] Toledano 1984: 300–1.
[86] Toledano 1984: 382–5, 390; Toledano 1998: 48–52.
[87] Toledano 1998: 36–40.
[88] Vanessa Martin, personal communication.
[89] Sagaster 1997: 31–7.
[90] Toledano 1998: 119.
[91] Erdem 1996: 131–2.
[92] Toledano 1998: 119; Martin 1985.

expression to appeal for purification from the stain of slavery, thereby enhancing the empire's standing in Islamdom.[93] The satirical press lampooned Abdülhamit's eunuchs as an 'image of obsolescence', and Young Turk authors called Abdülhamit an apologist for slavery: for example, Osman Nuri, in a book published in 1911–12.[94] 'Ziya Gökalp (1876–1924), 'mentor of the nation', criticised slavery in 1909. He was motivated by ethical Sufism, romantic notions of freedom-loving ancient Turks, and a belief that 'the basis of democracy is equality; the basis of a republic is liberty'.[95] Circassian intellectuals, ashamed of their people's reputation, agitated for abolition.[96]

Despite all this commotion, little was achieved. Imports of slaves from the Caucasus were prohibited for the second time in 1909, and Abdülhamit's personal slaves were freed on his deposition in that year. Nevertheless, members of the dynasty were allowed to keep their slaves, as were high officials.[97] Generals instructed their troops, fighting with Germany from 1914, to abide by international conventions on prisoners of war.[98] The family code of 1917, a tortuous compromise, probably allowed a wife to prevent her husband from taking concubines, but it was suspended a year later.[99]

Although Hakan Erdem contends that slavery had become 'moribund' by the First World War, there was one last burst of mass enslavement[100] After a number of Armenians had risen in rebellion, the Ottoman authorities deported millions to Syria from 1915, resulting in a humanitarian disaster of epic proportions. Among the survivors were women and children, enslaved by Kurds, Turks, and Arabs. Other Christians considered to have sided with the enemy, such as Greeks and Assyrians, shared the same fate.[101] The slave markets of Syria were glutted with Armenian girls, some of whom ended up in Central Arabia.[102]

The dictator Kemal Atatürk ended legal slavery in the Turkish Republic, but in an ambivalent and shamefaced manner. The 1926 civil code, copied almost verbatim from that of Switzerland, denied

[93] Zambaco 1911: 60–3.
[94] See Brummett 2000: 95, 293, 376; Erdem 1996: 128, 206.
[95] Parla 1985: 38–41, 62, 114, 121.
[96] Erdem 1996: 128, 147–8.
[97] Erdem 1996: 148–51.
[98] Yucel Yanikdag, personal communication.
[99] Fahri 1936: 37–8, 55.
[100] Erdem 1996: xvii.
[101] Morgenthau 1918: 316–21, 324–5; Shemmassian 2003; Miller 1993: 94–136.
[102] Jaussen 1927: 129–30; Rihani 1928: 152.

legal status to servitude.[103] However, Turkey waited till 1933 to ratify the 1926 League of Nations convention on the suppression of slavery.[104] Illicit sales of girls were reported in the early 1930s.[105] This may have referred to the *evlatlık* system, under which young girls, including Muslims, were fostered in a state of unpaid quasi-slavery until they were married off. Indeed, the words for 'slave' and 'foster child' became almost interchangeable. Specific legislation against both slavery and *evlatlık* only came in 1964.[106] In the 1990s, no day existed to commemorate abolition, and there were no references to the embarrassing institution in school textbooks.[107]

Hesitation on the Nile

Abolition in the Nile valley consisted of a series of false starts. Having seized Lower Egypt in 1798, Napoleon Bonaparte issued a bold proclamation in Arabic, declaring all men to be free and equal. This followed the 1794 abolition of slavery in the French empire, and might have signalled the end of servitude on the Nile. However, the French bought males as soldiers and females as concubines.[108] Moreover, Napoleon personally opposed abolition, and restored colonial slavery in 1802, a year after the capitulation of his troops in Egypt.[109]

Muhammad 'Ali (r. 1805–48) massacred Circassian slave officers in 1811, but attempted to conquer the Middle East with a Black servile army, recruited in the Sudan from 1820. He abandoned this strategy in the late 1830s because of high Sudanese mortality and a surprisingly good performance by Egyptian peasant conscripts.[110] However, he retained numerous slaves in the Sudan, to garrison the region, work in agriculture and pastoralism, and service the booming ivory trade.[111]

Raiding in the Sudan usually stayed just within the letter of the most traditional interpretation of the sharia. The succinct instructions to the Egyptian conqueror of Kordofan were that 'the end of

[103] Fahri 1936.
[104] Awad 1966: 267.
[105] Jomier 1954: 232.
[106] Özbay 1999a: 10, 12–14, 17–24; Özbay 1999b: 558.
[107] Erdem 1996: xix.
[108] Hourani 1970: 49–50; Renault and Daget 1985: 178–9.
[109] Jennings 2000: 3.
[110] Baer 1969: 161, 164; Beachey 1976a: 123; Philips 2000: 232–3.
[111] Gray 1961.

all troubles and this expense is to procure negroes'.[112] While avoiding attacking known Muslims, generals rounded up Animists like cattle, with no suggestion that they might convert or live as peaceful tributaries.[113] Cowed survivors then furnished a regular tribute in slaves.[114] The autonomous sultanate of Darfur ran raiding as an organised business. Licences were issued annually, surprise was of the essence, and there was no attempt to summon victims to the faith.[115]

British pressure from 1837 led to token concessions.[116] On a visit to the Sudan in 1838, the aged Muhammad 'Ali was allegedly 'moved to pity' by the plight of slaves.[117] He gained favourable publicity in Europe by freeing some 500 recently seized captives, and forbidding his troops from foraging for slaves. However, once he had returned to Egypt, raids began again. European complaints met with the official answer that military expeditions were responses to appeals from friendly tribes, and that since 'the people of these countries are savages, humanity cannot approve leaving them in that state'.[118]

The prejudices of the Egyptian élite, for whom slavery was in conformity with Islam, were advanced as an excuse for inaction.[119] Muhammad 'Ali also declared that he could do nothing without the sanction of the Ottoman sultan and the Shaykh al-Islam in Istanbul.[120] At best, he prohibited castration in 1841, and closed Cairo's infamous slave market the following year, neither measure having much real impact.[121]

Muhammad 'Ali's successors from 1848 achieved little. To be sure, Ibrahim Pasha freed his own slaves, prohibited purchases for the state, and 'conceived a policy for the general abolition of slavery and the slave trade', but he died suddenly.[122] 'Abbas I (r. 1848–54), relapsed into inactivity, and 'was murdered in his bath by two young slaves, whose morals he had corrupted'.[123] Sa'id Pasha (r. 1854–63) undermined his own laws. He banned imports from the

---

[112] Elbashir 1983: 28–9.
[113] Hunwick and Powell 2002: 53–4.
[114] Baer 1969: 164–5.
[115] Tounsy 1851: 465–90.
[116] Mowafi 1981: 45–6, 54–5.
[117] Delanoue 1982: 479.
[118] Gray 1961: 6–7.
[119] Baer 1969: 176; Tucker 1985: 173; Mowafi 1981: 46, 55.
[120] Hunwick and Powell 2002: 188, 193.
[121] Hogendorn 2000: 67; Elbashir 1983: 31.
[122] Meinardus 1969: 58.
[123] Hardinge 1928: 32.

Sudan and the payment of soldiers in slaves, and in 1856 granted freedom to those wishing to leave their owner. However, in 1860 he placed an order for a bodyguard of 500 'Negroes' with the al-'Aqqad brothers, infamous slave traders of Cairo.[124]

Publicly denouncing slavery in fashionable Western jargon, Isma'il Pasha (r. 1863–79) seemed to herald a new age. He hired foreigners to suppress the slave trade in the Sudan, and assured an American visitor in 1869 that he considered abolition 'the swiftest mode of reviving the material prospects of his Central African domains'.[125] Sir Bartle Frere put it to him in 1873 that, 'according to strict Koranic law most of the children sold as slaves in Cairo are not lawful slaves but simply stolen chattels', because slave razzias were unlawful.[126] John Scott, of the Egyptian Court of Appeal, backed the ulama who declared in 1877 that the Quran did not sanction slavery.[127] Manumission Bureaux issued freedom papers to some 18,000 slaves from 1877 to 1889.[128] Isma'il also adopted French civil law, as the ulama refused to codify the sharia.[129]

Despite this progress, Isma'il prevaricated. He complained of opposition from local Muslims, adding, somewhat inconsequentially, that slavery went back to the times of the Pharaohs.[130] Said to be the largest owner of slaves in the country, he had some 2,000 servile domestics in his household, including eunuchs. His favourite Circassian concubine herself owned some 50 Circassians and 30 Ethiopians.[131] There were an estimated 500 eunuchs in Cairo, and imports of slave soldiers from the Sudan swelled once again.[132] Lady Duff Gordon commented acidly, 'With 3,000 in his hareem, several slave regiments, and lots of gangs on all his sugar plantations, his impudence is wonderful'.[133]

Cairo found it particularly hard to control distant adventurers in the Sudan and beyond. Al-Zubayr al-Mansur, a Sudanese Arab, dominated the Bahr al-Ghazal from 1856. He not only gathered countless slaves in brutal razzias, but also flouted the sharia by forcing them to convert at the point of the sword. When Isma'il Pasha

[124] Ali 1972: 19–20; Baer 1969: 175; Gray 1961: 52–3.
[125] Elbashir 1983: 40.
[126] Frere 1873: 14.
[127] Beachey 1976b: 33.
[128] Walz 1985: 147; Tucker 1985: 177–8, 187–8.
[129] Badawi 1978: 102.
[130] Frere 1873: 8–9.
[131] Beachey 1976a: 130–1, 135, 171; Fredriksen 1977: 177.
[132] Beachey 1976a: 172; Baer 1969: 164.
[133] Tucker 1985: 174.

finally called these rascals to heel in 1877, Rabih b. Fadlallah (d. 1900) swept westwards to Lake Chad, enslaving thousands in his wake.[134] While al-Zubayr generally stuck to capturing Animists, Rabih was remembered for seizing mainly Muslims in Dar al-Kuti and Borno.[135]

Once Isma'il had been deposed in 1879, Muhammad Tawfiq Pasha (r. 1879–92) ascended the throne with a liberal reputation. He owned no slaves, opposed the slave trade, had a single wife, and was 'very unfavourable to the system of the harem'. However, he balked at abolishing slavery proper.[136] It was Ahmad 'Urabi, Minister of War and virtual dictator by 1882, who promised to eliminate the embarrassing institution.[137] Wilfrid Blunt, trying to ensure the success of 'Urabi's regime, urged that the al-Azhar ulama be encouraged to issue abolitionist fatwas. More ambitiously, he hoped that a caliph of the tribe of the Prophet would call a general council of ulama in Mecca, to issue an internationally binding prohibition of servitude.[138]

In the event, slavery helped to vindicate Britain's 'veiled protectorate' from 1882. Sir Evelyn Baring, later Lord Cromer, castigated Islam as a 'complete failure', in part because it accepted slavery.[139] He argued that the institution was recognised by 'Mahomedan religious law'. Since 'any measure likely to lead to a recrudescence of Mahomedan fanaticism is much to be deprecated', servitude was to be gradually eliminated by repressing imports and granting manumission on demand.[140] Neither the 'religious party' nor the political élite were to be provoked by precipitate action.[141] He forbade castration in Upper Egypt, although this merely displaced the activity to Darfur and Kordofan.[142]

Disagreement within the Egyptian élite persisted. 'Abdallah al-Nadim, exiled in 1882 for his role in the 'Urabi regime, returned ten years later and set up a newspaper, *al-Ustadh*. He published a sharp critique of servitude, in the form of a fictional debate between two slaves. However, several high-ranking Egyptians, including the

---

[134] Spaulding 2000: 126; Mowafi 1981: 52–3; Renault and Daget 1985: 194.
[135] Cordell 1985: 53–8, 206.
[136] Elbashir 1983: 120–1; Fredriksen 1977: 177; Erdem 1996: 89.
[137] Blunt 1907: 210–11; Powell 2003: 143–4; Tucker 1985: 178; Baer 1969: 188.
[138] Blunt 2002: 149–50.
[139] Hourani 1970: 251.
[140] Erdem 1996: 91–3.
[141] Tucker 1985: 176–8.
[142] Zambaco 1911: 46, 59.

president of the legislative council, were arrested for buying slaves in 1894. Their show trial resulted in a single conviction, and revealed much support for buying slaves, albeit not for selling them.[143]

This was the last gasp of pro-slavery opinions, for élite mentalities were changing. The legislative council meekly accepted abolitionist legislation in 1895, even though the delegates usually vociferously opposed any British proposal. Slavery was now seen as expensive, as rural labour surpluses emerged and the dissolution of guilds in 1887–90 reduced urban labour costs.[144] Baer makes no mention of Islamic reformism, but it probably played a part in this change of heart. A guarantee of individual liberty was then inscribed in the 1923 constitution.[145]

Progress was slower in the Anglo-Egyptian Sudan. Officials enthusiastically steeped themselves in the holy law, but the effect was to buttress servitude. 'Ironically, slavery became more "Islamic" under the British regime than previously'.[146] Left to reconstituted sharia courts from 1902, bondage was bolstered by the surprising British decision to treat all female slaves as concubines.[147] The ending of raiding and trading, and the revocation of slave officials, were thought to be sufficient. As late as the 1940s Lord Kitchener's memorandum of 1899 discouraging interference unless complaints were received 'still governs the official attitude on slavery'.[148]

Paradoxically, the 'principal thorn in the flesh of the Sudan government' was the Egyptian Slavery Repression Department, initially entrusted to an energetic Scot, A. M. McMurdo.[149] The Sudan administration therefore took over the Department in 1911, only to then abolish it in 1922, despite persistent reports of flagrant abuses.[150]

Middle Eastern stragglers

In the lands between India and the Red Sea, some Muslim statesmen, desiring to participate in the new dispensation after the First World War, portrayed anti-slavery agreements as the 'premature

[143] Powell 2003: 147–9, 150–5.
[144] Baer 1969: 181–9.
[145] Brunschvig 1960: 39.
[146] Lovejoy 1983: 264–5.
[147] Hargey 1981: 419–53; Sikainga 1996: 54–7; Warburg 1981: 258–66; Beachey 1976a: 144–7.
[148] Trimingham 1965: 23.
[149] Collins 1992: 151–5.
[150] Daly 1986: 235–6, 444.

anticipation of a future political and social development', to be ratified at a later date by the community.[151] Where slavery persisted, despite treaties prohibiting the slave trade, the British Foreign Office declared itself powerless to act, because even formal protectorate arrangements left internal affairs in the hands of rulers.[152]

Afghanistan was a model of the first approach. Abd al-Rahman Khan (r. 1880–1901) prohibited slave trading, enslavement, and emasculation in 1895. In that same year, he conquered Kafiristan, the main reservoir of Animist slaves, forced the inhabitants to convert, and renamed the area Nuristan.[153] His successor, Habibullah Khan (r. 1901–19), banned concubinage.[154] Amanullah Khan (r. 1919–29), inspired by Kemal Atatürk and gaining Turkish assistance, abolished slavery in 1921. Freedom of the person was inscribed in the 1923 Afghan constitution, itself a striking innovation. However, Amanullah was forced to abdicate in 1929, having been called a deranged infidel for emancipating women.[155] Muhammad Nadir Shah Ghazi (r. 1929–33) promulgated a new constitution in 1931, establishing security of the person, equality before the law, and freedom from forced labour.[156] In 1935, the Afghan government adhered to the 1926 League of Nations convention on slavery.[157]

Persia's Muhammad Shah (r. 1834–48) long resisted British pressure. Justin Sheil, British minister in Tehran, set out to prove that 'the sacred law distinguished between slaves bought in commercial transactions and captives made in war'. However the shah responded that, 'buying women and men is based on the Shari'a of the last Prophet. I cannot say to my people that I am prohibiting something which is lawful'. He also considered that by abolishing the slave trade, 'I would prevent five thousand people a year from becoming Muslims. This would be a great sin, and I would get a bad name'. Told of progress accomplished by other Muslim monarchs, he lambasted the Ottomans as schismatics, and the Omani sultan as 'a Kharijite, and as such little better than a kafir'. However, he issued a vaguely worded prohibition on importing slaves by sea shortly before his death.[158]

---

[151] Snouck Hurgronje 1916: 151–2.
[152] Brunschvig 1960: 39; Gordon 1989: 229–34.
[153] Gregorian 1969: 37, 139; Ahmad 1934: 6.
[154] Gregorian 1969: 198; Iqbal 2002: 308.
[155] Poullada 1973: 71–7, 89–90, 96, 129–30.
[156] Ahmad 1934: 73–4, 97, 103.
[157] Awad 1966: 166.
[158] Kelly 1968: 495, 594–604; Mirzai 2000.

A complete prohibition on imports followed the Brussels General Act in 1890, but Iranian officials did little to enforce the measure, believing the trade to be religiously licit. Slaves dismissed without a letter of manumission suffered from social death, as nobody would employ them. At best, Sunni captives might be freed on adopting the Shi'i creed.[159] That said, Taj al-Saltana, a Persian princess born in 1884 and educated on French lines, criticised the treatment of those 'bought and sold like so much cattle'. She wrote of the Black slaves of the palace as 'creatures whom God has made no differently from others except for the colour of their skins—a distinction that in all honesty does not exist at the divine threshold'.[160] An anti-slavery society was founded in Tehran in March 1903, to succour an estimated 38,000 people, but the president of the provisional committee was Western, and it is not clear what the society achieved.[161]

After the promulgation of an Iranian constitution in 1906, fundamental laws of 1907 established equality before the law and individual freedom, albeit without expressly mentioning slavery.[162] It was left to Reza Shah to enact specific abolitionist legislation in 1928–9, as part of a programme of radical secular modernisation on Turkish lines initiated in 1921.[163] However, weak Persian authority in Baluchistan, partitioned with British India, allowed the persistence of clandestine slave exports to Arabia.[164]

The Fertile Crescent came under League of Nations mandates after 1918. Despite the British legally ending slavery in Jordan in 1929, a report to the League openly discussed the slaves of Bedouin shaykhs in 1934.[165] Slavery often survived under the guise of clientage, as among the Bedouin tribes of northern Palestine.[166]

Treaties from the nineteenth-century prohibited the slave trade in the Gulf, but rulers long refused to end slavery. African and Baluchi slaves continued to trickle in, and Western oil companies hired those no longer needed for pearling. Anxious not to introduce religiously improper innovations, the Shaykh of Bahrayn issued a proclamation in 1937, 'reminding the public that owning

---

[159] Migeod 1990: 330–3, 339–40; Polak 1865: I, 248–9, 252–3; Kelly 1968: 594–6; Douin 1936–41: III/2, 664.
[160] Saltana 1993: 113.
[161] *Anti-Slavery Reporter*, 1903, 23/2, 70.
[162] Aubin 1908: 210–12; Brunschvig 1960: 38–9.
[163] Awad 1966: 77; Brunschvig 1960: 39.
[164] Miers 2003: 166, 306–9.
[165] Bonné 1948: 330–1; Brunschvig 1960: 223.
[166] Ashkenazi 1938: 80–1.

slaves was forbidden'. The Trucial Council, in what are today the United Arab Emirates, copied this subterfuge in 1963, stating that 'slavery, like the slave trade, had long been forbidden in their territories'. The Shaykh of Kuwayt declared slavery unrecognised in law in 1952, and promised to free anybody on application.[167] The Emir of Qatar took the plunge the same year, explaining that slavery was 'forbidden in all civilized countries' and 'contrary to the principles of human dignity and social justice', but mentioning no Islamic principles.[168]

The sultan of Oman clung to slavery the longest, with a Black slave governing a province in the 1930s.[169] It was not till 1970 that a palace coup placed the Western-educated Sultan Qabus on the throne, resulting in the official ending of servitude.[170] However, the decision was taken by an Interim Advisory Committee under *de facto* British control. The 1971 programme of the People's Front for the Liberation of Oman and the Arabian Gulf still called for 'the eradication of slavery and the abolition of slave relationships'.[171]

The Qu'ayti sultan in Hadhramaut built up an African slave army in the nineteenth-century, to reduce dependence on unreliable tribal levies.[172] Slaves remained significant for security and administration in the 1930s.[173] From the lands of the Hadhrami diaspora came Chinese, Southeast Asian, Indian and African slaves, while free Arabs were occasionally kidnapped locally. The sultan recognised that most slaves had not been canonically taken as war captives, and both he and his Kathiri rival made the possession of slaves a criminal offence prior to 1967. However, other local potentates under British protection failed to follow suit.[174] It was left to Yemen's Marxist ruling party, the National Liberation Front, to eradicate slavery in 1967.[175]

In Britain's Aden Protectorate, rulers warned in the 1930s that the ulama would reject proposals to prohibit slave sales at fairs, and to give slaves the right to manumission on demand. Sultans would have to pretend to be acting under colonial duress. At best, they

---

[167] Miers 2003: 164–5, 263–7, 340–5.
[168] Awad 1966: 149; Miers 2003: 340–1.
[169] Harrison 1939: 208.
[170] Miers 2003: 347.
[171] Townsend 1977: 79, 114–15.
[172] Gavin 1975: 161.
[173] Stark 1946: 49, 140.
[174] Miers 2003: 268–71, 351; Ingrams 1942: 154; Stark 1946: 28, 38, 128–9, 194, 249.
[175] Miers 2003: 352.

decreed the ending of slave imports by sea, but only the sultan of Lahij had proclaimed it an offence to own slaves by 1939. However, this very sultan later stood accused of including a slave girl in his retinue at a London hotel. When the British ignominiously withdrew from Aden in 1967, the National Liberation Front imposed emancipation.[176]

The Zaydi Imam of North Yemen, independent from 1918, failed to adhere to the international anti-slavery convention of 1926, did not prohibit imports of slaves till exchanging diplomatic notes with Britain in 1934, and refused to answer a United Nations questionnaire in 1948.[177] Servitude remained legal, manumission declined, and clandestine imports continued.[178] When abolition was announced during the 1962 revolution that overthrew the Imam, 'nobody dared openly to criticise'.[179] The regime did not reply to a further United Nations questionnaire, but non-governmental sources considered that the illegal trade in slaves had dwindled.[180]

Backsliding Middle Eastern governments, especially those that refused to ratify anti-slavery documents of the United Nations, found themselves chivvied by Dr Muhammad Awad. An Egyptian geographer and former rector of Alexandria University, he had become interested in slavery as a student in London. For many years, he headed international efforts to enforce abolition.[181]

Abolition from Inner to Southeast Asia

The Russians initially prevaricated. They forbade Tatar nobles from exporting Christian serfs to the Caucasus in 1838, but violently repressed an 1853 rising by Christian serfs against their Armenian Muslim lord, close to the North Caucasus.[182] Beyond their frontiers, the Russians sought from the 1810s to gain freedom for Christian slaves held in the Caucasus, and acted likewise in Turkistan from the 1840s.[183]

Systematic Russian attempts to obtain the liberation of all slaves began later. On finally crushing Circassian resistance in 1864, 'the

---

[176] *Ibid.*: 268–9, 304, 351–2.
[177] Brunschvig 1960: 39; Rouaud 1979: 132.
[178] Dresch 2000: 65, 233; Heyworth-Dunne 1952: 14; Miers 2003: 261; Greenidge 1958: 39–43, 56; O'Callaghan 1961, 45, 82–4, 113.
[179] Defarge and Troeller 1969: 56.
[180] Awad 1966: 180.
[181] Miers 2003: 361.
[182] Kolchin 1987: 41–6, 145, 310.
[183] Gammer 1994: 40; Allworth 1994: 33; Hopkirk 2001: 203, 222–6, 297, 351.

triumphant tsar issued an edict prohibiting slavery'.[184] In 1873 the defeated khan of Khiva signed a treaty in which he confirmed an abolitionist proclamation, issued earlier in the year to stave off a Russian assault. The emir of Bukhara, intimidated by these events, undertook to end the slave trade in a treaty signed in the same year. Separately, he promised to end slavery itself within ten years. On acceding to the throne in 1885, Emir 'Abd al-Ahad made good his father's promise by proclaiming the abolition of slavery, and yet he kept servile officials and concubines.[185] Certificates of manumission were still being issued in 1885–6.[186] Although overt field slavery ended and public slave markets closed, covert sales, especially of women, continued.[187] Many Persian slaves and ex-slaves fell victim to an anti-Shi'i pogrom in 1910.[188] As late as 1914 a Russian veterinary surgeon witnessed a man selling his daughter to pay a debt.[189]

Qing emperors of China, gradually taking over East Turkistan (Xinjiang), forbade trading in slaves in 1778–9. This followed the assassination of a Muslim merchant of Yarkand by his slaves. The repetition of similar edicts in later years indicates problems in enforcing the ban.[190] Under British pressure, the Chinese issued a decree banning slavery itself in 1897, 'larded with expressions of moral indignation', and ordering owners to free their slaves without compensation.[191] This preceded the 1906–10 process of abolition in China proper, discussed in chapter 11 below.

Britain initially attempted to achieve reform in India by persuading the old Mughal ruling élite and curbing trade. The East India Company decided in 1772 that slavery should be governed by either Islamic or Hindu law.[192] Two years later, Warren Hastings wrote optimistically that leading Muslims in Bengal 'condemn the authorised usage of selling slaves as repugnant to the particular precepts ... of the Koran'. The Company then banned the maritime slave trade of the Bengal Presidency in 1789, a measure only applied to the whole British empire in 1807–8.[193]

[184] Jaimoukha 2001: 156.
[185] Becker 1968: 76–8, 200; Khan 1998: 151, 254; Olufsen 1911: 351.
[186] Adeeb Khalid, personnal communication, summarising Turgun A. Fayziev (1990) *Bukhara feadal jamiyatida qullardan faydalanishga dair hujjatlar (XIX asr)*, Tashkent: Fan.
[187] Levi 2002: 285; Cumming 1977: 156–7.
[188] Carrère d'Encausse 1966: 145–7.
[189] Khan 1998: 57.
[190] Laura Newby, personal communication.
[191] Skrine and Nightingale 1973: 89–90.
[192] Adam 1840: 25–6.
[193] Chattopadhyay 1977: 83–6, 158.

John Richardson, district judge in central India, demanded the ending of slavery proper in Company territory in 1808. His letter was sent for comment to the muftis attached to the Company's high court in Calcutta. The muftis' 1809 ruling, discussed further in Chapter 7, strictly circumscribed the sources of enslavement to capture in war and descent.[194] Although disappointed that maltreatment was rejected as grounds for obligatory manumission, Richardson considered these opinions greatly superior to those of the Hindu pandits. He thus requested that Muslim law be applied exclusively to slaves, but in vain.[195] Gyan Prakash contends that the British urged the muftis to assert that freedom was the natural human condition, but Muslim jurists had taken this position for centuries.[196]

Officials and politicians hoped that such reformism would suffice to extinguish Muslim ownership of slaves.[197] An 1830 appeal case in Calcutta confirmed the validity of the 1809 fatwa.[198] In 1841, the muftis of the Company's Madras court confirmed the ruling of their Calcutta colleagues.[199] Lord Auckland optimistically reported in 1839 that 'all slavery is excluded from amongst Muhammadans by the strict letter of their own law'.[200]

The British stance became more confrontational, under pressure from Christian missionaries and their allies. They singled out slavery as a particularly objectionable feature of Muslim social relations, together with polygyny, female seclusion, and ease of divorce.[201] In 1843–4, the Company therefore decided to cease recognising slavery in law in directly ruled India, without paying compensation. Similar legislation for indirectly ruled princely states, some of them under Muslim monarchs, was gradually introduced from 1855.[202] This contributed to the alienation of Muslim élites, culminating in the 1857–58 'Indian Mutiny' discussed in Chapter 8.

This great rebellion led to Crown rule, and owning slaves or trading in them became illegal in terms of a penal code drawn up in 1860, and effective from 1862. However, debt bondage was not affected.[203] A new edition of the *Hidaya* in 1870, first mentioned in

---

[194] Chattopadhyay 1977: 170–80; Chatterjee 1999: 183.
[195] Chattopadhyay 1977: 181–4; Banaji 1933: 248, 252–3; Adam 1840: 66–7; 196–207.
[196] Prakash 1990: 145–7.
[197] Adam 1840: 23, 42–8.
[198] Banaji 1933: 43–4.
[199] Chatterjee 1999: 213.
[200] Leitner 1893: 18.
[201] Hardy 1972: 99.
[202] Chattopadhyay 1977: 250–3; Hjejle 1967: 98.
[203] Chattopadhyay 1977: 253; Chatterjee 1999: 219–24; Dingwaney 1985: 313.

Chapter 2, omitted as irrelevant the voluminous sections of Islamic law concerning slavery.[204] However, aristocratic Muslim families continued to possess slaves, 'who seem willingly to assent to their condition of bondage'.[205] Legislation against debt bondage, initiated in 1920, continued till 1976, long after Indian independence.[206] Secularist Muslims in Pakistan after 1947, such as Muhammad Munir, continued the colonial struggle against slavery.[207]

British efforts in Sri Lanka and Southeast Asia were also protracted. A 'free womb' law was passed in Sri Lanka in 1816, affecting the Muslim minority as both owners and slaves.[208] Thomas Stanford Raffles promulgated regulations against slavery in Singapore in 1822, contributing to the murder of a senior official the following year.[209] Slavery was not mentioned in treaties signed with Malay sultans from 1874, but British officials were verbally instructed that 'no slavery could be permitted to exist in any state under British protection'.[210] Charles Brooke, the 'White Raja' of Sarawak in North Borneo, feared the reactions of 'Moslem aristocrats'. He thus issued a cautious circular on slavery in 1868, introducing nonbinding regulations, which 'after a certain time may become custom'. More traditions were invented in 1882, but slavery only legally ended in 1928.[211]

Loopholes permitted debt bondage and military slavery to continue in British territories in Southeast Asia, and the possession of slaves only became illegal in 1935.[212] A late-nineteenth-century British expert called Malay debt bondage an 'unauthorised and illegal innovation' in terms of Islamic law.[213] In seeking to resolve this widespread social problem, officials stressed that the Quran urged the remission of debts.[214]

The process of abolition in Indonesia is a minefield for the unwary. In directly ruled areas the Dutch banned the maritime trade in 1818, the internal trade in 1855, and slavery proper in 1860, while excluding debt peons and slaves of uncompensated

---

[204] Hamilton and Grady 1870: xxxi.
[205] Hughes 1885: 599.
[206] Dingwaney 1985: 324.
[207] Ahmed 1987: 168.
[208] Adam 1840: 277–8.
[209] Trocki 1979: 50–1, 208.
[210] Andaya and Andaya 1982: 160.
[211] Pringle 1970: 176–7.
[212] Yegar 1975; Loh 1969: 184–6; Endicott 1983: 236; Lasker 1950: 49–50, 55–6.
[213] Winstedt 1981: 54–5.
[214] Loh 1969: 189–90.

'native' owners.[215] In some cases, notably the West and North Sumatran holy wars discussed in Chapter 8, the Dutch were only able to
emancipate slaves after long and bloody struggles. As late as 1909,
the Dutch turned South Sulawesi's slaves into debtors, obliged to
repay owners in cash or labour services within two years.[216]

In areas of indirect rule, slavery persisted even longer. A code of
Shafi'i law, published in Batavia 'by order of the government' in
1882–4, thus contained a detailed section on servitude.[217] A scandal
erupted in the late 1870s, when it was discovered that Dutch plant-
ers and officials were hiring slaves from sultans in eastern Indonesia. The latter were thus paid to abolish the institution, although
the sultan of Tidore refused to extend the measure to his possessions in New Guinea.[218] Slavery remained legal in some principali-
ties till the eve of the First World War.[219]

That said, Indonesia's Muslim princes sometimes took the initiative. The sultan of Sumenep, on Madura, freed his slaves around
1814, writing that, 'for long have I felt shame, and my blood has run
cold, when I have reflected on what I once saw at Batavia and Sema-
rang, where human beings were exposed for public sale, placed on
a table, and examined like sheep and oxen'.[220] The sultan of Tidore,
animated by 'philanthropic ideas', ceased to demand an annual
tribute in Papuan slaves from New Guinea and Halmahera in the
1850s.[221] However, the system had been re-established by the 1870s.[222]

Rejection of abolition was violent in the southern Philippines,
initially under Spanish rule and passing to the Americans after
1898. Asked to give up his slaves in 1861, the sultan of Magindanao
replied 'that he would rather give up his wife and children than his
slaves, for lacking the latter he simply would cease to be a sultan'.
The sultan of Sulu wrote to the American authorities in 1902, insisting that slaves were held 'according to Moro law, custom, and the
Mohammedan religion', in that order. Moreover, 'slaves are part of
our property. To have this property taken away from us would mean
a great loss to us'.[223]

[215] Lasker 1950: 31, 36, 122, 340; Sutherland 1983: 274–8; Reid 1993: 77; Hasselt
     1882: 190–1; Verkerk Pistorius 1868; Burger 1975: II, 20; Taylor 1983: 125, 129.
[216] Bigalke 1983: 347.
[217] Berg 1882–4: II, 452–99.
[218] ANRI 1876–9.
[219] *Encyclopaedie van Nederlansch-Indië* 1917–21: III, 807.
[220] Raffles 1978: 78.
[221] ANRI 1859.
[222] Reid 1993: 78.
[223] Salman 2001: 66, 81.

One Republican congressman argued that 'domestic' slavery among the Moros was so mild that there was nothing to abolish, although the numerous slaves who risked their lives to flee to the protection of colonial garrisons refuted this meretricious argument. Indeed, the United States public was scandalised to learn that Moros held numerous Christian Filipinos as slaves.[224] A plan to place the Sulu sultanate under indirect rule had to be shelved, and there followed long years of warfare.[225] General George W. Davis commented that slavery 'will never be eradicated in these islands until public sentiment in the community is opposed to it, and this sentiment will be of slow growth'.[226]

Nevertheless, Muslim élites of the southern Philippines were not united over the issue. Datu Mandi, seeking to carve out an autonomous fiefdom with American backing, prohibited slavery in the Zamboanga region of western Mindanao in 1901. He made no reference to Islam, merely referring to colonial law. He also stated that 'slavery never has and never will bring any progress with it'.[227]

Conflicting experiences in Africa

The Zanzibar sultanate was the scene of a prolonged tussle. To justify signing the 1822 Moresby Treaty with Britain, Sayyid Sa'id b. Sultan Al Bu Sa'id (r. 1806–56), declared that he was prohibiting the sale of slaves 'to Christians of all nations'. While this undoubtedly conformed with the sharia, his predecessors had shown no qualms in selling to the French from the 1780s. The 'Moresby Line' of 1822 restricted exports of slaves to a mainly Muslim zone of the Indian Ocean. When the line was altered in 1839, the newly excluded areas of Kutch and Kathiawar (Saurashtra) were predominantly Hindu.[228]

Ending the trade with Islamic lands was another matter. Sayyid Sa'id wrote plaintively to Bombay in 1826 that he would be forced into exile, as 'all Muslims would be his enemies'. The British consul noted in 1844 that there existed no 'party favourable to the abolition of slavery'.[229] The sultan even ordered his subjects to pray that Westerners should come to their senses.[230] His private secretary

---

[224] *Ibid.*: 47–8, 53, 74–85.
[225] Gowing 1983.
[226] Salman 2001: 82.
[227] Salman 2001: 77, 284–5; Gowing 1983: 55–6.
[228] Nicholls 1971: 222–4, 231; Nicolini 2002: 138, 140; Bhacker 1992: 103.
[229] Nicholls 1971: 226, 244.
[230] Nicolini 2002: 154.

exclaimed that, 'Arabs have carried on the trade since the days of Noah. Arabs must have slaves'.[231] The 1845 treaty, prohibiting all exports of slaves beyond coastal waters, prompted the Sharif of Mecca to send an envoy to remonstrate with the sultan in 1850.[232]

Sultan Barghash (r. 1870–88), faced with the novel demand to end slavery itself, pleaded for time, because of 'the weight of Muslim opinion [and] the advice of the leading Arabs'.[233] In 1872 his 'council of shaikhs was unanimous in refusing to "commit suicide".'[234] Barghash opined that 'the Koran sanctions slavery', even if it earnestly enjoined manumission, and his subjects protested that abolition amounted to 'force and plunder'.[235] At best, the sultan threatened prison sentences for those caught kidnapping Muslim children on the coast.[236]

After Zanzibar had adhered to the Brussels General Act in 1890, Sultan 'Ali b. Sa'id (r. 1890–3) was derided as the *mamluk* of the British for issuing a restrictive proclamation, which was torn down.[237] Up the coast the governor of Lamu raised the spectre of insurrection.[238] Conservative British officials delayed full abolition by raising the twin perils of economic chaos and the undermining of indirect rule.[239] Sir Arthur Hardinge argued that the measure would be regarded as 'manifest despoliation' by the Arabs.[240]

Sultan Hamid b. Muhammad (r. 1896–1902) finally proclaimed the abolition of slavery in Zanzibar and Pemba in 1897. When chosen by the British to succeed to the throne, he owned no slaves, which the American consul attributed to poverty.[241] Personal conviction seems a more likely explanation, as even the poorest free family owned a slave in Zanzibar at the time.[242] Sultan Hamid presented abolition as Islamic, but also as a generous personal act, and one necessary to obtain free labour for clove and coconut plantations.[243] In a preamble to his decree, he said: 'And whereas the

[231] Bhacker 1992: 129–30.
[232] Beachey 1976a: 52–3.
[233] Kelly 1968: 632.
[234] Sheriff 1987: 236.
[235] Frere 1873: 51, 54.
[236] Harries 1965: 206–7.
[237] Gordon 1989: 213; Bennett 1978: 165–6.
[238] Romero 1997: 112.
[239] Cooper 1980: 34–68.
[240] Beachey 1976a: 295.
[241] Bennett 1978: 179.
[242] Bhacker 1992: 132.
[243] Hardinge 1928: 197; Hollingsworth 1953: 217.

Apostle Mohamed ... has set before us as most praiseworthy the liberation of slaves, and We are Ourselves desirous of following his precepts ...'[244] Enforcement was another matter, especially on the mainland, to which application of the measure was extended in 1907. Concubines were explicitly excluded, because they might turn to prostitution, their children would become illegitimate, and fathers would lose rights in their children, thus causing a revolt.[245] An amendment facilitated the departure of concubines from masters on the mainland in 1909.[246] The authorities long left cases of slavery to Islamic justice, so that a British judge was scandalised to hear a man declare in court 'she is my slave' in 1922.[247]

Italy moved slowly, repressing the trade in Eritrea and Somalia, but continuing to recognise 'domestic slavery'. A serious Somali rebellion followed mild attempts by the Società del Benadir to manumit slaves with compensation in 1903–4. The Italians waited till 1908 before taking further measures, and seem generally to have been content with allowing 'free womb' laws to reduce bondage in their colonies.[248] However, an Italian Fascist decree of 1936 freed an estimated 420,000 slaves, in both Christian and Muslim areas of Ethiopia, in an attempt to gain international backing for the invasion of 1935.[249]

The German authorities tried suspected East African slave traders in summary courts from 1885, and hanged those convicted. They believed that the institution would die a natural death, once sources of new slaves had been choked off. Hermann von Wissman, sent to crush the Arab Revolt of 1888–9, regarded the slave trader as 'the enemy of the human race'. Abushiri b. Salim, who defended traditional Islamic servitude in this revolt, gained support from caravan slaves and maroons, but the issue divided Muslims and contributed to the revolt's collapse.[250]

Portuguese difficulties in repressing the illegal slave trade from northern Mozambique to Arabia partly reflected a lack of commitment to the cause.[251] Ernesto de Vilhena, representing the char-

---

[244] See Beachey 1976b: 125.
[245] Cave 1909–10: 29–33; Romero 1997: 130.
[246] Mirza and Strobel 1989: 130.
[247] Trimingham 1964: 137–8, 148; Strobel 1979: 51.
[248] Salvadei 1927; Cassanelli 1988.
[249] Brunschvig 1960: 39; Greenidge 1958: 46.
[250] Beachey 1976a: 199–200; Iliffe 1979: 92–7.
[251] Duffy 1967: 67, 83–5, 91–5, 161.

tered Companhia do Nyassa in the north, criticised 'philanthropic' British measures against slavery in Zanzibar. He alleged that the institution was useful, helping to civilise barbarous Africans, and providing much needed labour. Moreover, slavery was 'domestic', and concubinage was the basis of the Muslim family.[252]

When King Leopold II of the Belgians, sovereign of the Congo Free State, appointed Hamid b. Muhammad al-Murjebi governor of Stanley Falls (Kisangani) province from 1887 to 1892, Western journalists wrote that the fox had been put in charge of the hen coop. However, al-Murjebi, better known as Tippo Tip, sought to implement his instructions to end the slave trade. Of mixed Omani and African origins, he had earlier ruled Manyema under loose Zanzibari suzerainty.[253] Primarily an ivory trader, he owned few concubines, and considered that slave porters and agricultural workers were prone to desert or die.[254] Discreet as to his motives for repressing the slave trade in his autobiography, he made no appeal to Islam, but seemed fascinated by the power of the West.[255]

The issue of abolition encouraged Muslim resistance to European conquest in West Africa. Senegalese notables attacked French measures in 1848 as 'an attempt to diminish their wealth'.[256] The Mauritanian leader Shaykh Ma' al-'Aynayn (1831–1910) justified holy war against France and Spain, in part because infidels were liberating slaves.[257] Agostinho Coelho, Portuguese governor in Bissau from 1879, invoked progressive sentiments to aid slaves fighting Fulbe masters, although his successors switched sides.[258]

French and Spanish officials trod softly, exploiting Islamic motifs. French conventions with chiefs from 1890 turned slaves into 'servants like those of whom it is spoken in chapters 24 and 43 of the Book of God'. Self-liberation for a fixed sum became mandatory, with certificates of freedom signed by a qadi.[259] In Chad, a 1912 convention with Dar Sila stated that the French would hand over runaways to the sultan, 'who will act according to the prescriptions of the Book'.[260] As late as the 1960s, the authorities in the Spanish

[252] Vilhena 1906: 198–200.
[253] Kinenge 1979; Ceulemans 1959: 102, 106–7; Renault 1987: 165, 168, 241–5.
[254] Northrup 1988: 466–8.
[255] Murjebi 1974.
[256] Willis 1989: 71.
[257] Wuld al-Bara 1997.
[258] Hawkins 1980: 169–74.
[259] Deherme 1994: 136–7; Klein 1968: 167.
[260] Bret 1987: 50.

Sahara pointed to 'the merit gained, according to the Koran, from freeing a slave'.[261] Even after French West African slaves had been formally freed in 1905, the authorities stalled.[262] Futa Jalon's slaves, facing a particularly well entrenched aristocracy, found it hard to shake off their dependence before the social reforms of the 1950s.[263] An official in interwar Timbuktu advised a runaway to pay his Tuareg master for his freedom, to avoid complications.[264] In the Adrar region of Mauritania, the French tolerated slavery by birth in 1918, and allowed sales of slaves under a qadi's supervision, as long as both parties were from the same district.[265]

Lord Lugard warned against ending northern Nigerian slavery prematurely in 1906, asserting that 'slavery is an institution sanctioned by the law of Islam, and property in slaves was as real as any other form of property among the Mohammedan population'.[266] He left the sharia courts to regulate slavery.[267] Although decreeing freedom for all those born after the first of April 1901, the British did nothing about concubines, allowing transactions in women to continue.[268] Even administrative slavery was not finally repudiated in the Kano emirate until 1926.[269] Sir Ahmadu Bello, Sardauna of Sokoto, premier of Northern Nigeria, proclaimed in 1955: 'As regards slaves, it is only because the Moslem power is not strong here that we have not got the slaves to sell'. In a barely audible Hausa aside, he added 'and they are there.'[270] In neighbouring Cameroon, a Norwegian film crew showed the world the slaves of a Muslim lord of Adamawa in 1966.[271]

Colonial abolition might appear to be a field so thoroughly trampled by scholars that there is nothing left to discover. However, the manipulation of Islamic beliefs and institutions to delay emancipation requires both more research and more publicity. It neatly turns on its head the patronising view of unwilling Muslims forced to accept abolition by upright Westerners.

---

[261] Mercer 1976: 130.
[262] Klein 1968: 169–70, 198–9.
[263] Azarya 1978: 74–8, 184–5, 196; Marty 1921: 447–52; Baldé 1975: 214.
[264] Maugham 1961: 166.
[265] McDougall 1988: 368.
[266] Lovejoy 1983: 265.
[267] Christelow 1994: 113–16.
[268] Lovejoy and Hogendorn 1993; Lovejoy 1983: 265; Hill 1976: 407–10.
[269] Stilwell 1999: 175–84.
[270] Mark Smith, personal communication, citing Northern House of Assembly Debates, 10 March 1955.
[271] Derrick 1975: 72–5.

As for the contrasting colonial stratagem, to hasten abolition through Muslim channels, it underscores the significance of Islamic agency. Too little work has been done on the ways in which Western notions of freedom had to be expressed in Islamic terms to become effective. More needs to be known about the considerable colonial efforts made to define and explain the suppression of slavery in ways acceptable to Muslims. In the Indonesian case, a Dutch obsession with customary law, perpetuated since independence, has almost obliterated the Islamic dimensions of this process.[272]

It remains unclear when Muslim secular élites really turned against bondage. One Western abolitionist asserted in the 1870s that, 'an intelligent Mohammedan ... will probably frankly tell you slavery is an evil institution which must be abolished'.[273] Some Western-educated Muslims declared slavery, polygyny, and male divorce to be 'incompatible with the modern society they wished to create'.[274] By 1925, there existed a kind of club of 'the more advanced Muhammadan princes' opposed to slavery.[275] However, Sir Arthur Hardinge was of the view that 'liberal and Europeanized Mohammedans' simply sought to curry favour by pretending that slavery was not a 'fundamental principle of the social system of Islam'.[276] A Christian missionary took the same line in 1907.[277] Modern authors still consider that 'an exculpatory counterthrust arose from a few western-educated Muslims'.[278]

Assumptions that Westerners bullied Muslim rulers have led scholars to neglect those rulers' relationship with religious scholars. Burgeoning legal autonomy clearly shaped the ending of slavery, but nineteenth-century monarchs made repeated attempts to gain the support of the ulama, drafting legal instruments along sharia lines. The standard argument, that the ulama would accept no restrictions on servitude, cannot be accepted at face value. There is an even greater paucity of information on Islamic reactions to abolition by secular politicians in the twentieth-century, notably Kemal Atatürk. To understand when laws ending the institution were deemed to be religiously legitimate, it is necessary to turn to the differing strands of the Islamic renaissance.

---

[272] Ruibing 1937; Thosibo 2002.
[273] Cooper 1968: 114.
[274] Gordon 1989: 45–6.
[275] Rutter 1933: 323–4.
[276] Hardinge 1928: 355.
[277] Zwemer 1965: 126–9.
[278] Miller 1992: 249.

7

THE ULAMA AND QUASI-ABOLITION

Responding to the shock of Western demands, backed by unprece-
dented military might, Islamic scholars undertook a painful reap-
praisal of servitude from the late eighteenth-century. The ulama
tackled the problem by re-examining their own traditions, however.
Their lack of interest in Western ideas, and their failure to refer to
them, were striking.

Numerous ulama accepted no more than rectifications in the law
of slavery, to bring it in line with underlying principles. Regulations
pertaining to servitude accounted for a large proportion of the
sharia, and scholars were uneasy about jettisoning too much of what
their illustrious predecessors had elaborated. Property rights were
guaranteed in holy law, and the Prophet and his companions had
owned slaves. Those released from bondage might become vagrants,
or otherwise undermine social order. Slavery was necessary to gain
merit from manumission, and was effective in bringing infidels
to Islam.

A few scholars went further, sometimes as far as adopting a quasi-
abolitionist stance. They reaffirmed the limitation of legitimate slave
origins to capture in properly constituted holy war, commanded
the faithful to check servile filiation stringently, and called insis-
tently for manumission. These requirements were at times framed
in such a rigorous manner that, in effect, slavery could no longer
reproduce itself.

However, this nearly always remained abolition by the back-door,
for the abstract legitimacy of slavery was rarely questioned. Reformist ulama might downgrade servitude from the 'neutral' to the 'discouraged' level in the fivefold Islamic ethical system. Merit was then
earned by abstaining from such actions, but they were not actually
sinful. The crucial final step, demoting the embarrassing institution to the 'forbidden' category, was most likely to be contemplated
by dissenters, possibly renewing old libertarian traditions.

Dissenting reformers

The quixotic British campaign to prove that Shi'i Islam did not countenance slavery, noted in Chapter 6, divided the ulama. In 1847, six Persian interpreters of the law cited the Hadith that 'the seller of men is the worst of men', and deduced from this that the slave trade was an 'abomination'. However, a more eminent *mujtahid* pronounced that infidels taken in war could be enslaved. The chief *mujtahid* of the holy city of Najaf, in Iraq, agreed that slavery was 'discouraged', and that the Hadith condemning 'the seller of men' was valid. However, in a deft piece of casuistry, he asserted that the buyer of slaves was exempt from the censure proclaimed upon the seller.[1]

Shi'i circles in India and Lebanon contributed to the debate. A pamphlet, published in Calcutta in 1871, argued that holy war had been suspended since the occultation of the Twelfth Imam, and that the making of new slaves in war was thus illegitimate.[2] The influential Shaykh Husayn al-Jisr (1845–1909), from Tripoli, in Lebanon, published a book in Beirut in 1887, dedicated to the Ottoman Sultan Abdülhamit II. Open to modern ideas, al-Jisr taught that non-combatants should be spared enslavement, while clinging to the notion that infidels taken in a properly constituted jihad could be enslaved.[3]

The question of freedom agitated Iranian ulama in the context of the constitutionalist revolution of 1905–6, albeit almost exclusively from a political perspective.[4] A famous 1909 text by a leading constitutionalist from Najaf, Muhammad Husayn Na'ini, attacked traditionalists repeatedly for defending political 'slavery'. However, he also ridiculed opponents who said that the constitution would erase a set of differences between people, including those between 'the free and the coerced'. 'All these issues', he exclaimed, 'are further from the quest for constitutionalism than the sky is from the earth'.[5]

In contrast, the *mujtahid* 'Ali Nur 'Ali Shah issued an uncompromising fatwa in 1912. He stated that 'the purchase and sale of human beings is contrary to the dictates of religion and the practice of civilisation; and therefore in our eyes any persons, men or women alike, who are claimed as slaves, are in legal fact completely

[1] Kelly 1968: 495, 594–7; See also Mirzai 2000.
[2] Hunter 1964: 85–7.
[3] Snouck Hurgronje 1906: II, 345–8; Hourani 1970: 222–3.
[4] Martin 1989: 113–38, 165–200.
[5] Na'ini 2002: 124.

free, and the equals of all other Muslims of their community'. There had been no properly constituted jihad after the last Imam had been occulted, and it was impossible to prove unbroken descent from legal slaves on the maternal and paternal side over a millennium.[6] He must have been the same person as Wafa 'Ali Shah (1847–1918), both *mujtahid* and head of the Nimatullahi Sufi order, who supported the constitution and was a 'model for the lovers of freedom'.[7]

'Ali Shah's fatwa appears to have had little impact, perhaps because he was a Sufi, or perhaps because it was in advance of its time. He was poisoned in 1918, for reasons that are not clear. In 1970, his own grandson queried the validity of the fatwa in terms of Shi'i law, while stressing the good intentions that lay behind it. Two kinds of slavery were still licit. Anybody 'taken prisoner fighting against Islam with a view to its extirpation, and [who] persisted in his sacrilegious and infidel convictions' would still be a slave. So would anyone for whom there was 'legal proof that all his ancestors without exception had been slaves descended from a person taken prisoner'. Rather feebly, he fell back on the virtues of manumission.[8]

Shaykh Fadhlalla Haeri, raised in the holy Iraqi city of Karbala and educated in the West, remained ambivalent as late as 1993. In a publication intended for a Western audience, he restricted the sources of slavery to capture and birth. However, he noted that servitude gave a person a chance to learn about Islam. He stressed the mildness of Muslim slavery, noting that several Shi'i Imams were born of slave mothers. He ended lamely and inconclusively by observing that, 'except for isolated instances, the slave trade had died out by the twentieth-century'.[9]

Zaydi ulama, ensconced in the highlands of northern Yemen, found slavery distasteful rather than actually illegitimate. An Italian explorer asserted in 1877–8 that highland tribes round Sana'a kept no slaves, concubines or eunuchs of any kind, in contrast to ruling 'Turks' and lowland Shafi'i tribes.[10] A British report of 1936 was more cautious, estimating that Zaydi owners held about a tenth of the slaves in Yemen.[11] An academic writing at about the same time stated that, 'slaves as such, proper Africans, are almost unknown on

[6] Tabandeh 1970: 26–7.
[7] Pourjavady and Wilson 1978: 160–3; Nurbakhsh 1980: 113–14.
[8] Tabandeh 1970: vii–viii, 27.
[9] Haeri 1993: 139–40.
[10] Manzoni 1884: 190, 196, 199–201.
[11] Miers 2003: 261.

the plateau. In the city of Sana'a they are exceedingly rare, and owned by but a few extremely wealthy families'.[12] Moreover, Zaydi adepts generally left the slave trade to their Shafi'i compatriots.[13] However, as late as 1947, the great Zaydi jurist Ahmad b. Qasim al-'Ansi referred to the law of manumission, while noting that slavery had become 'very uncommon'.[14]

Musta'li Isma'ili or Bohra believers were centred in Gujarat by the nineteenth-century. Merchants of this community dominated the slave trade from Mozambique to Madagascar in 1873, at a time when Sir Bartle Frere wrote that no Indian trader in East Africa regarded slavery as a 'moral crime'.[15] Even after slavery had been 'abrogated by statute' in British India in 1843–4, the institution was valid in the community's religious law, This remained the position in the 1960s.[16] At best, a cautious gradualist position was espoused by some Bohra in the 1990s.[17]

The winds of change blew more precociously through the Nizari Isma'ili or Khoja community, by this time also centred in Gujarat and implicated in the East African slave trade. As religious decisions were in the purview of the living Imam, the advent of the Western-educated and liberal Aga Khan III (r. 1885–1957) was decisive. He spent much of his time in Europe, befriended South Asian Islamic modernists opposed to servitude, and publicly praised the British in 1909 for abolishing slavery in India.[18] The British knighted the great Khoja entrepreneur Tarya Topan in 1890, for contributions to the repression of the East African slave trade, indicating that the turning point came shortly after 1885.[19] Known as an opponent of servitude, Aga Khan III campaigned for the League of Nations after the First World War.[20]

Druze opposition to slavery became better known in modern times. C. H. Churchill, a British explorer of the 1840s, published news of their rejection of concubinage and polygyny, in an influential account, first published in 1853.[21] Druzes began to leave their mountain fastness in increasing numbers from the 1860s, not only

[12] Coon 1968: 199.
[13] Rouaud 1979: 132.
[14] Bernard Haykel, personal communication.
[15] Frere 1873: 107, 150.
[16] Fyzee 1969: ix–x; Blank 2001: 76.
[17] <http://www.dawoodi-bohras.com/perspective/methodology.htm>
[18] Aga Khan III 1998: I, 117–18, 310.
[19] Mangat 1969: 20–1.
[20] Rutter 1933: 323–4; Aga Khan III 1998.
[21] Churchill 1994: II, 294.

going down to expanding coastal cities such as Beirut but also participating in the 'Syro-Lebanese' diaspora around the world.[22] The central figure in the Ibadi renaissance in Algeria was Muhammad b. Yusuf Atfayyish (1820–1914), who seems not to have opposed slavery.[23] This may have reflected persistent slave trading. In 1858 a group of Mzabi merchants wrote indignantly to the French authorities, protesting against the liberation of slaves in one of their caravans, and asking what else they could possibly buy in the lands of the Blacks.[24] Mzabi involvement in the trans-Saharan slave trade remained considerable in 1880.[25] As late as the 1920s, Mzabi men kept concubines, albeit only with the consent of their single wife, and 'exchanged' slaves. Servitude was not harsh, but slaves longed for their homelands.[26]

Mutawwa revivalists in Oman and Zanzibar were favourable to slavery.[27] This nineteenth-century movement sought to return to the fundamentals of the Ibadi creed, notably by downplaying divisions between tribes and electing an Imam. When a governor of Suhar signed an agreement with Britain to stop imports of African slaves, his family had him murdered in 1849.[28] The Banu Riyam tribe, alienated by 1890s measures against trading in slaves and firearms, supported the Imam's cause against the sultan.[29] In 1909, the Ibadi chief qadi of Zanzibar, Shaykh 'Ali b. Msellum al-Khalassi, 'dared to stand alone in open defiance against the ban on the status of slavery', imposed in 1897. This probably contributed to British threats to abolish his position.[30]

Attitudes in Zanzibar and Oman gradually became more critical of servitude. The Ibadi chief qadi of Zanzibar in 1914, Shaykh 'Ali b. Muhammad al-Mundhiri, stated that slaves freed by the government could not become clients of their former owners, but that it was legitimate for infidels to buy slaves and emancipate them, even if owners objected, for 'the aim was honourable under Islam'. Such liberated individuals were entitled to all the rights of free persons. In a more pragmatic vein, he noted that any qadi who opposed the authorities risked dismissal.[31]

[22] Hourani and Shehadi 1992.
[23] Powels 1987: 204–6; Wilkinson 1987: 243–5.
[24] Dermenghem 1954: 258.
[25] Christelow 1985a: 119; Renault and Daget 1985: 162.
[26] Goichon 1927: 73, 119–20.
[27] Sheriff 1987: 218–20.
[28] Pouwels 1987: 204–5; Wilkinson 1987: 232–3, 236–8, 354.
[29] Allen 1987: 59.
[30] Pouwels 1987: 120, 191.
[31] Strobel 1979: 52.

'Abdallah b. Hamid al-Salimi (1869/70–1914), a blind scholar influential in Oman's Ibadi revival, was asked by Zanzibari petitioners whether it was lawful to hire slaves freed by the Europeans without the consent of owners. They also wanted to know whether such slaves were allowed to marry without their owner's permission. Al-Salimi answered that 'this is a scourge that has stricken Zanzibaris as a punishment for the injustice they inflicted upon the slaves', without specifying whether he meant bad treatment or illegitimate enslavement. He ruled that if the intentions of Christians were honourable in freeing slaves, then the measure was acceptable, whereas if 'extortion and injustice' were their motives, then it was not legitimate.[32]

It was not until 1963 that an Ibadi Imam, once more fighting a sultan of Masqat, actually 'repudiated slavery'.[33] The reasons for this decision were not made clear. However, it may have been intended to gain support from Prince Faysal b. 'Abd al-'Aziz, who had abolished the institution a year earlier in Saudi Arabia (see Chapter 8 below).

South Asian Sunni pioneers and their opponents

British India was an early testing ground for the Sunni world. When the East India Company's muftis issued a fatwa on slavery in 1809, discussed in Chapter 6, they stated that it was only legal to enslave 'infidels fighting against the faith'. This did not clearly distinguish between captives taken in battle and non-combatants. Such slaves, and their descendants, could be transferred by sale, gift, or inheritance. Sale of self or children was prohibited, as was slavery originating in debt, kidnapping, fraud or life-long labour contracts, whether those involved were Indian or African.[34] Bengali ulama even stated in 1825 that slavery had effectively been 'almost extinct in this country for generations'.[35]

Other jurists backed the stance of the Calcutta muftis. The *Hidaya* code, translated from Persian into English in 1791 (see above), implicitly legitimised the servile status of descendants of those enslaved before the advent of Islam. Following an appeal to the Calcutta court in 1830, judges chose the 1809 fatwa over the *Hidaya*. More-

---

[32] Amal Ghazal, personal communication, citing 'Abd Allah al-Salimi, ed. (1999), *Jawabat al-Imam al-Salimi li'l-Imam Nur al-Din 'Abd Allah b. Hamid al-Salimi*, [n.p.], 2nd ed., V, 396.

[33] Miers 2003: 360.

[34] Adam 1840: 64–7; Chattopadhyay 1977: 170–7.

[35] Bevan Jones 1941: 204.

over, they added that owners must prove servile origins.[36] In 1841, the muftis of the Company's Madras court declared that only captives in war and their descendants were 'true' slaves in Islamic law.[37] In Sind in the 1840s, slaves 'must have been duly paid for, inherited or taken in warfare, provided that in this case they refuse to become Moslems'.[38]

Muslims in much of the subcontinent refused to accept narrow definitions. Waji al-Din Saharanpuri headed a group of ulama who issued a fatwa, probably in the 1830s, justifying the enslavement of men and women who 'sought refuge' with the victors after the battle. Sayyid Imdad 'Ali Akbarabadi, Deputy Collector of Kanpur (Cawnpore), led conservative ulama in producing a stream of publications defending traditional forms of slavery.[39] Sayyid Muhammad 'Askari, of the same town, roundly denounced progressive notions of abolition in the 1870s.[40]

Consensus long remained conservative. In 1926 Sayyid Muhammad Kifayatullah, president of the Jamiat ul-Ulama, stressed the need to observe sharia rules on slavery, interpreted in a fairly restrictive manner.[41] In a book published in Lahore in 1946 Mawlana Sa'id Ahmad Akbarabadi, of the influential and conservative Deobandi school, denied that the Prophet had ever ordered the abolition of slavery, or even inspired it. At most, Islam improved the status of slaves and recognised their humanity, making their lot superior to that of subject peoples in Western colonial empires.[42] He repeated this argument in a publication of 1957.[43]

Religious publications, even those emanating from moderate groups, took slavery for granted. 'Abd al-Hayy, of the Farangi Mahall school of Lucknow, published a compendium of fatwas around the 1880s. In it, he ruled on the question, 'whether the owner of a male slave may arrange the marriage of his slave'.[44] Similarly, fatwas of Shah 'Abdu'l-'Aziz Waliyullah (d. 1761), translated into Urdu and published in Kanpur in 1905, included sections on female slaves and servile marriages.[45]

[36] Banaji 1933: 43–4; Leitner 1893: 18.
[37] Chatterjee 1999: 213.
[38] Burton 1973: 242.
[39] Powell forthcoming; Avril Powell, personal communication.
[40] Ahmad 1967: 63.
[41] *Oriente Moderno*, 1926, 6/7: 358; Sékaly 1926: 201.
[42] Ahmad 1967: 254–5.
[43] See Mujeeb 1967: 450.
[44] See Hardy 1972: 173–4.
[45] Claudia Preckel, personal communication.

Collections of fatwas dealing with practical aspects of slavery long continued to be published in India. Arun Shourie, an ardent Hindu politician, quoted a set of opinions from the pen of Sayyid 'Abd al-Rahim Qadri, from Gujarat, which appeared between 1975 and 1982. One passage reads: 'A slave-woman does not need marriage for the reason [that] the Shari'ah has made the possession of a slave-woman the substitute of marriage ceremony, and the legal permit for coition with her'. The mufti merely noted that 'it is difficult to come by slave-girls in the present times, for the conditions required for lawful slave-girls are difficult to obtain now'. The problem was not secular legislation, but doubtful provenance. A slave woman had to be captured in a jihad in the abode of war, brought to the abode of Islam, and apportioned as booty.[46]

Apotheosis in the Maghrib

Tunisia's ulama exhibited great caution during Ahmad Bey's drive for abolition in the 1840s, discussed in Chapter 6, although they later drew praise from Ottoman secular abolitionists.[47] Those on the bey's newly formed religious council agreed that the monarch's will should be respected, and that his decrees were in conformity with the sharia. The Hanafi chief mufti, Shaykh Bayram, further noted that Muslims might have been improperly enslaved.[48] His Maliki colleague, Ibrahim al-Riyahi (d. 1850), did not go so far, although he had a reputation as a progressive and modernising scholar.[49]

An open letter, in Arabic, circulating in Tunisia at this time, demonstrated that Quran and Hadith did not preclude abolition. However, this document was probably written in Malta by a Christian reformer from Lebanon, Faris al-Shidyaq (1804–87), who only later converted to Islam. Distributed by the British Anti-Slavery Society, the letter's impact remains to be ascertained, even if al-Shidyaq enjoyed good personal relations with Tunisia's Muslim reformers.[50]

A few Algerian qadis co-operated with the suppression of slavery in the two decades following the French decree of 1848. Christelow speculates that this sprang from interpretations of abolition conforming to the spirit of the Quran, but the dates seem too early for such an explanation.[51] In any event, most Algerian ulama were slow

[46] Shourie 1995: 5–11, 531, 533–4.
[47] Sagaster 1997: 33.
[48] Montana 2001: 3–7, 15; Chater 1984: 553.
[49] Green 1978: 105–6.
[50] Chater 1984: 552; Hourani 1970: 97.
[51] Christelow 1985a: 121.

to accept the legitimacy of French measures.[52] The French complained that Algerian qadis were returning slaves fleeing from Morocco in 1880, and that they were attesting that female slaves were wives in 1893.[53]

It was a Moroccan scholar from Sale, Ahmad b. Khalid al-Nasiri (1834–97), who brought quasi-abolitionism to a climax in the late nineteenth-century. A religious specialist and minor official, he was influential in the emergence of conservative modernism.[54] His arguments were rooted in Maliki conventions and Sufi piety. He wrote his attack on slavery in 1881, as part of a history of the Maghrib, and his opinions were more widely disseminated through a posthumous publication in Paris in 1906. Al-Nasiri rehearsed established arguments, rejecting the curse of Ham and denouncing uncertain conditions of enslavement. His real bombshell was the affirmation that no wars after the time of the Prophet and his companions could be called holy wars, and that this effectively challenged the status of all existing slaves.[55]

Al-Nasiri's uncompromising stance on slavery was contested, for many Moroccans still believed the institution to be legitimate on the eve of the declaration of the Franco-Spanish protectorate in 1912. Indeed, one pessimistic European observer thought that freeing ill-treated slaves was the best that could be hoped for.[56] French hesitations after 1912 sprang partly from apprehension as to the ulama's reactions.[57]

These fears may not have been entirely justified. Some Moroccan jurists declared slave trading to be illegal in 1894, as people could no longer be captured in holy war after the French conquest of West Africa.[58] Many Moroccan ulama maintained the abstract validity of the institution, but believed that it should disappear because conditions were no longer suitable. Most slaves in Morocco in 1952 had been kidnapped as children, in flagrant violation of the sharia, an argument that convinced some Muslims to free their remaining slaves. Qadis also undermined slavery by treating concubines as a special category of wife without a dowry.[59]

[52] Dermenghem 1954: 258–9.
[53] Cordell 1999: 48–50.
[54] David Gutelius, personal communication.
[55] Ennaji 1999: 121; Hunwick 1999: 60–3; Hunwick and Powell 2002: 44–8; Toledano 1998: 125; Willis 1980, 193–4, 196; Willis 1985: I, 7; Lévi-Provençal 1960: 290–1.
[56] Michaux-Bellaire 1910: 423–7.
[57] Ennaji 1999: 114–15; Lapanne-Joinville 1952: 153–4.
[58] Ennaji 1999: 114.
[59] Lapanne-Joinville 1952: 154, 156.

Wider Arab reformism

The Egyptian ulama, some of whom were substantial slave owners, remained circumspect.[60] Edward Lane reported in the 1830s that 'the slave is either a person taken captive in war or carried off by force from a foreign hostile country, and being at the time of capture an infidel; or the offspring of a female slave by another slave, or by any man who is not her owner, or by her owner if he does not acknowledge himself to be the father'. This wording allowed for the enslavement of non-combatants, while saying nothing about tribute and purchase.[61] Conservatives defended slavery more crudely in 1869. Sanctioned by the sharia, the institution was both ancient and mild, women were needed for harems, and barbaric Blacks benefited.[62]

The issue came to a head with the establishment of Manumission Bureaux in 1877, discussed in Chapter 6. Some ulama backed the government, citing 47:4 and 24:33 to prove that the Quran did not sanction slavery in modern times, although the latter passage merely recommended the manumission of worthy slaves.[63] However, some Cairo qadis refused to allow the marriage of slave women freed by the secular bureaux, insisting that they had to obtain their owners' consent in terms of the sharia, and allegedly driving them into prostitution.[64]

As a showdown with Britain loomed in 1881, opinions seemed divided. The Shaykh al-Islam refused to concede 'the civil rights of a person born free' to those liberated by the state. Having consulted the most learned scholars, he declared that he 'would be overriding the law in decreeing the abolition of slavery'. At best, he admitted that tribute in slaves from the Sudan was illegal, because people lived in peaceful treaty relations with Egypt.[65] Muhammad al-Anbabi, Shaykh al-Azhar in 1882, considered existing slavery to be a perversion of the institution as permitted in holy law, which only sanctioned the enslavement of idolaters in war for the purpose of converting them. He added that reducing captives to slavery was not directly enjoined in holy law, but was a matter of custom.[66]

---

[60] Crecelius 1972: 169–70, 178, 186–7; Winter 1992: 69, 116–17.
[61] Lane 1895: 115.
[62] Douin 1936–41: III–2, 672–3.
[63] Beachey 1976b: 33.
[64] Baer 1969: 183–5; Tucker 1985: 177–8, 187–8.
[65] Erdem 1996: 89–90.
[66] Baer 1969: 188; Tucker 1985: 178.

After the British conquest in 1882, the Egyptian ulama declared that as the Prophet had not prohibited slavery, neither could they.[67] Shaykh Muhammad Ahmad al-Bulaqi, of al-Azhar, refuted modernist theses on women in 1899, by implication defending concubinage.[68] However, pious ulama refrained from taking as concubines girls who might have been wrongly enslaved.[69] Although traditionalists continued to hold that what the Quran specifically permitted could not be outlawed, abolition caused little overt contestation. This reflected 'the power of the great international opprobrium felt for the institution'.[70]

Eunuchs were one subject on which the ulama were prepared to accept reform. Snouck Hurgronje, following his visit to Mecca in the 1880s, wrote of castrati as 'the great abuse condemned even by Islam'.[71] A congress of Islamic scholars was held in Egypt in 1908, pronouncing that the sharia prohibited not only the making but also the owning of eunuchs. However, despite the citation of a long list of weighty authorities, this ruling was contested.[72]

An undated text from around this time blamed the use of eunuchs on the Turks:

> We found the institution of eunuchs among the Greeks, Romans and other peoples who preceded us. ... The eunuch is contrary to Islam, its principles, and its ethics. Did our blessed Prophet need eunuchs? Does the Arab of the desert and the tent make use of these incomplete men? One can only blame the inconsiderate use that the Turks make of White and Black eunuchs, as this tends to perpetuate the abominable practice of castration. But who does not know that the Turks have long since wandered from the straight path of Islam to follow a tortuous trail which will eventually make them, if they are not careful, blind schismatics, unworthy of the religious and political preponderance that they have desired to exercise over the sons of Islam?[73]

As far as ordinary slaves were concerned, an observer of the Middle East in the late 1940s thought that, 'the institution of slavery leads a

[67] Erdem 1996: 92.
[68] Ahmad 1963: 101, 104–5.
[69] Chafik 1938: 49.
[70] Eccel 1984: 417.
[71] Snouck Hurgronje 1931: 20.
[72] Zambaco 1911: 36–8.
[73] Millant 1908: 203.

by no means illegitimate existence even today'.[74] The Arabian peninsula was an area of particular uncertainty. Slaves in the Gulf perceived the 'iniquity' of their condition in the 1920s, and 'progressive leaders frequently admit that slavery is inconsistent with the solidarity of Mohammedanism', albeit without daring to say so in public.[75] A decade later, 'the finer spirits of the community ... agree that slavery is an evil system, and assert that it is out of harmony with the spirit of their religion. The slave holders on the contrary ... assert roundly that slavery comes direct from the deep counsels of God, and represents His revealed will'.[76] In Hadhramaut in 1938, Bedouins drove their agricultural slaves harshly, 'so that the Arabs of the towns are loud in blame'.[77]

Al-Azhar prevaricated for decades. A fatwa of 1939 declared that a father could not sell his son, but only because no free child should be sold.[78] An undated publication by a leading teacher stuck to the notion that slavery was licit for infidels captured in war and their descendants.[79] Nevertheless, the third edition of a textbook of Maliki law, published in Cairo in 1980, held that Islam had set out to 'cure' slavery. Avoiding any 'counterreaction that would shake the pillars of society and tear apart its structures', the ulama recognised the rights of owners and the dangers of vagrancy. Islam thus proceeded by 'reducing the avenues to enslavement and closing them off', while gradually preparing slaves for freedom.[80] An al-Azhar fatwa, available on the internet in Indonesian in 2001, simply relegated slavery to the domain of history.[81]

Ottoman conservatism

The Ottoman ulama 'upheld the legality of slavery because it was sanctioned by Islam'.[82] At best, they endorsed the sultan's elimination of the relics of military servitude in 1826, and proposed reforms to administrative slavery.[83] However, they refused Young Ottoman

---

[74] Bonné 1948: 351.
[75] Harrison 1924: 257–8.
[76] Harrison 1939: 207–8.
[77] Stark 1945: 216.
[78] Jomier 1954: 232.
[79] Abd el-Schafi 2000: 149.
[80] Hunwick and Powell 2002: 17–19.
[81] <http://members.tripod.com/skypin/fatwa/fatwa17.html>
[82] Toledano 1998: 96.
[83] Heyd 1961.

demands for fatwas declaring slavery to be illegitimate.[84] They accepted capture in war, birth, and purchase as causes of slave status in 1869, and stressed that slavery was authorised by Quran and Hadith.[85] Qadis refused to liberate slaves without their owners' consent, except in cases of proven ill-treatment.[86] Some ulama even queried the manumission of some Circassian immigrants, because the Russians had obliged their owners to free them.[87]

A conservative Palestinian *'alim*, Yusuf b. Isma'il al-Nabhani (1849–1932), would go no further than restricting enslavement to war against infidels, and encouraging manumission. Educated at al-Azhar, he spent some time at court in Istanbul, and became a senior judicial figure in Ottoman Syria. In a little book published in 1908 he argued that the West was manipulating abolition as a weapon against Islamic influence. Believers might not comprehend why God allowed slavery, but there was a link with the divine dispensation that there should be rich and poor. Moreover, slaves stood to lose most from abolition.[88]

The Syrian paper *al-Haqa'iq* not only published the views of al-Nabhani, but also reprinted an article by one Muhammad Ragheb in 1911, in which he criticised the abolitionist views of a certain Ahmad al-Mahmasani. Upbraiding his opponent for reading too much into a Hadith, Ragheb made the telling point that God would have revealed the need to end slavery directly, had that been his intention. Servitude was an inherent part of the law, necessary to allow believers to atone for certain sins, and providing men too poor to marry with a legitimate sexual outlet. Europeans were merely trying to divide Muslims and stop the spread of Islam through conversion, each year depriving some 100,000 people of a chance of salvation.[89]

Following the Young Turk revolution, Istanbul's Shaykh al-Islam confirmed in 1909 that the 'basic principle of the House of Islam is liberty'. However, this only authorised freeing 'those persons who were not claimed by anybody as being slaves'.[90] The Shaykh al-Islam continued to issue decisions concerning servile marriages as late as 1916.[91] Armenians, together with other Christian 'rebels' enslaved

---

[84] Sagaster 1997: 33, 45; Erdem 1996: 150.
[85] Douin 1936–41: III–2, 662, 679.
[86] Toledano 1998: 93–9; Erdem 1996: 94, 151; Zambaco 1911: 64.
[87] Toledano 1998: 39–40.
[88] Ghazal 2003; Ghazal 2001.
[89] Ghazal 2003.
[90] Erdem 1996: 150.
[91] Sagaster 1997: 18–19.

during the First World War, were 'people of the book' who had broken their contract.[92] In the 1920s a Palestinian shaykh expressed the view that pious Muslims could therefore buy Christian girls on the slave markets of the Fertile Crescent.[93]

Some ulama persisted in recognising the validity of slavery after the fall of the Ottoman empire in 1918. In republican and secular Turkey, sharia norms for dealing with slaves continued to appear in specialised Islamic literature, as though nothing had changed.[94] In the new state of Yugoslavia a storm erupted in 1935, when a qadi allowed a Circassian slave youth to marry a free woman. From the subsequent inquiry it emerged that Circassian slaves were turning to secular Yugoslav courts to avoid buying their freedom.[95]

Evolution in Southeast Asia

Influenced by Egypt, some Southeast Asian ulama displayed reformist tendencies. A mufti of Batavia [Jakarta] issued a fatwa in the 1880s, answering a query about the legality of purchasing Chinese girls as concubines from Chinese dealers in Singapore. He began by stressing the consensus that the root of legal slavery was capture in holy war. Buying a slave from an unbeliever was only possible if the initial owner was a Muslim, who had acquired the slave legitimately. A free father, even a non-Muslim, could not sell a child, although the services of such a child could be obtained in return for a loan. Marriage of under-age girls was only valid if the child's father or legal guardian allowed it, and a slave trader could not stand in as such.[96]

The author of this fatwa was almost certainly Sayyid 'Uthman b. 'Abdallah b. 'Aqil b. Yahya (1822–1931). Of mixed Hadhrami and Egyptian parentage, this scholar was appointed chief mufti of Indonesia by the Dutch.[97] He was known for narrowly restricting the conditions under which a holy war could be waged.[98] Although argued in terms of contesting colonial power, such views of jihad simultaneously limited the scope for enslavement.

Reform was one thing, but the legitimacy of slavery was another. A collection of fatwas, published in Mecca in 1892, answered ques-

[92] Kamal-ud-Din 1925: 273–4.
[93] Jaussen 1927: 129–30.
[94] Sagaster 1997: 19.
[95] Popovic 1978: 168; Malcolm 1998: 215.
[96] Snouck Hurgronje 1923–4: II, 276–9.
[97] Stauth 1992: 74–5.
[98] Azra 1995.

tions from the region, especially Sumatra. Ahmad Dahlan (1817–86), Meccan head of the Shafi'i school of law from 1871, wrote most of the 130 opinions. Seven of them referred wholly or partly to slavery, treating the institution as a routine aspect of sale, inheritance, marriage, and manumission.[99] In 1915–16, a scholar of Lampung, South Sumatra, who had studied in Mecca, issued a similar fatwa on servile marriages.[100] Sharif Tuan, an 'Arab priest', backed the struggle against the Americans in Mindanao. He declared in 1904 that 'the Moros would not submit to any interference with their slave trading and holding'.[101]

Slavery continued to be seen as licit long after formal colonial abolition. Owners issued manumission certificates to slaves in South Sulawesi in the 1930s, even though such documents were not recognised in colonial courts.[102] Ex-slaves needed such certificates to gain access to land.[103] Purchases of Chinese slave girls did not cease, some of them being re-exported to Hadhramaut as concubines and domestics in the interwar years.[104] The Maranao of Mindanao took slaves during the Japanese invasion of the Philippines from late 1941, and attempted to retain them after independence in 1946.[105] Servitude also continued to affect marriages and ritual status across Southeast Asia.[106] East Javanese in the 1950s declared that slaves could not perform the pilgrimage to Mecca.[107]

It was not until opposition to military rule grew in Indonesia after 1965 that the men of the law showed interest in abolition. Abdurrahman Wahid [Gus Dur], from a distinguished family of Javanese ulama, received education in Cairo and Baghdad. He headed Indonesia's Nahdatul Ulama, possibly the largest single organisation in the Islamic world, and became president of Indonesia from 1999 to 2001. He considered that social aspects of the sharia should change according to period and culture, and stressed the virtues of freedom.[108] He accepted the 1948 Universal Declaration of Human Rights, of which article 4 bans slavery, as applicable to believers.[109]

[99] Kaptein 1997.
[100] Djajadiningrat 1929: 87–8.
[101] Salman 2001: 114.
[102] Chabot 1996: 160.
[103] Putra 1988: 15; Bigalke 1983.
[104] Lasker 1950: 53–5; Snouck Hurgronje 1906: I, 23; Ingrams 1970: 26–7.
[105] Mednick 1965: 31–2, 36, 61–5, 163, 165.
[106] Lasker 1950: 31, 77–8.
[107] Geertz 1960: 205.
[108] Riddell 2001: 249–53.
[109] Muhammad 1999: 190.

Mixed responses in Africa

West African reform was initially couched in terms of implement-
ing particular aspects of the sharia. In the late 1890s Muhammad
al-Sanusi b. Ibrahim al-Jarimi, an obscure *'alim*, probably from
Timbuktu, rejected skin colour or an alleged incapacity for self-
government as justifications for enslaving free Black Muslims.[110] A
qadi of Futa Jalon protested when a man gave a slave child to a chief,
because the sharia forbade the separation of mother and child.
When his arguments were rebuffed, he went to study in the Maghrib for several years, and re-opened the case on his return.[111] A
French report of 1905 suggested that 47:4 in the Quran was sometimes taken as a command to free captives.[112]

Shaykh Musa b. Ahmad al-Futi, known as Musa Kamara (d. 1945),
took a more systematic line, inspired by the Moroccan writings of
al-Nasiri.[113] Originating from Futa Toro, between Senegal and Mauritania, Musa Kamara stated the absolute freedom of all human
beings in unconditional terms.[114] He published his main work in
1925, and it was probably there that he cited a tradition that the
Prophet had liberated all his slaves before he died. He commented
that Muhammad 'inspired a desire among the people to manumit
slaves to the point where someone would say that he was forcing
them, that he was compelling them to do so'. Rejecting the curse of
Ham, Musa Kamara mused whether abolition by Christian infidels
might not have fulfilled a deep desire of the Prophet.[115]

Reformist views persisted in West Africa, When Mauritania promulgated its third formal abolition of slavery, in 1980–1, some
ulama gave the decrees their cautious endorsement. Given that the
country was completely Muslim, no new slaves could be made by capture. Furthermore, bad treatment justified the liberation of those
born into slavery.[116] In the 1980s ex-slaves of Futa Jalon themselves
engaged in an intense study of the sharia, to claim equality in land
distribution, marriage, and political and religious employment.[117]

Nevertheless, most West African ulama fiercely opposed abolition, even censuring colonial measures as a plot to undermine the

---

[110] Hunwick 1999: 61–3.
[111] Derman 1973: 29; Klein 1998: 230–1.
[112] Poulet 1994: 40–1.
[113] Willis 1980: 197–8.
[114] Samb 1980: 94.
[115] See Hilliard 1985: 162.
[116] Messaoud 2000: 337.
[117] Botte 1994: 109–10.

faith. They argued that slaves were necessary to enable scholars to concentrate on learning and devotion.[118] In the 1950s it was reported that, 'jurists do not recognize the suppression of slave status by colonial governments'. Concubinage therefore remained legitimate with women of servile descent, and slaves could not marry free people.[119] The pilgrimage was limited to free people, unless slaves accompanied owners.[120]

Tuareg ruling clans clung to slavery.[121] Indeed, a servile rebellion against them erupted as late as 1946 in the Timbuktu area.[122] A former qadi issued a letter of manumission, in Arabic, to a male slave in 1961.[123] In the same year slaves expressed the fear that their masters would repossess them once the French left, unless they had paid for their freedom.[124]

Fulbe élites had a similar reputation.[125] Slaves in Futa Jalon were told that those who failed to stay with their owners faced death and eternal torment in hell, and that wicked European impostors merely sought dependants for themselves.[126] Northern Nigeria's sharia courts slowed the pace of emancipation and refused to oblige owners to release slaves.[127] Masters still took concubines from their 'clients', and inherited from slaves without heirs.[128] The 'redemption' of slaves for a payment left them free in law, but in local eyes they became the slaves of their redeemers.[129] African judges, convinced that slavery was sanctioned by Islamic law, overstepped the mark, leading to a scandal in Kano in 1921.[130]

Mauritania became the best known case of resistance to abolition.[131] Although often presented as a racial conflict, buttressed by a persistent acceptance of the 'curse of Ham', free Blacks and people of mixed race were among the owners of slaves.[132] Mauritania

---

[118] Sanneh 1989: 215–16, 237; Sanneh 1997: 62–6.
[119] Trimingham 1959: 168, 213.
[120] Klein 1993: 190.
[121] Botte 1999.
[122] Klein 1998: 234.
[123] Bernus 1975: 35–6.
[124] Maugham 1961: 164–5, 170–2, 207, 215.
[125] Azarya 1978: 74–8, 184–5, 196.
[126] Barry 1997: I, 308.
[127] Christelow 1994: 113–16.
[128] Trimingham 1959: 133.
[129] Christelow 1985b: 62–3.
[130] Fika 1978: 198–202.
[131] Ruf 1999: 291–2.
[132] McDougall 1988; Caro Baroja 1955: 48, 97, 188.

adopted the sharia as the country's 'main law' in 1981, leading some owners openly to press claims against their slaves in front of qadis.[133] Reports told of slaves bought and sold, compelled to work for no pay, imprisoned, beaten, obliged to make owners their heirs, forced to marry, taken as concubines, and required to pay for their freedom.[134]

Many Mauritanian ulama refused to accept the legitimacy of abolition. One group from Futa Toro indignantly protested against the 1981 abolition proclamation, arguing that only owners could legitimately free their slaves, and that a supposedly Islamic regime was 'breaking the most elementary religious rules'.[135] A Mauritanian scholar opined in 1997 that abolition 'is contrary to the teachings of the fundamental text of Islamic law, the Koran ... [and] amounts to the expropriation from Muslims of their goods, goods that were acquired legally. The state, if it is Islamic, does not have the right to seize my house, my wife or my slave'.[136]

East Africa seems not to have hosted reformist ulama. A qadi in Mombasa ruled in 1911 that no government could free a slave without the owner's consent, an opinion endorsed by Kenya's Shaykh al-Islam and a qadi of Lamu.[137] The chief qadi in Khartoum in 1925 objected to 'any unwarranted dilution of Islamic law' resulting from forced manumission.[138] Sudanese mosques were themselves endowed with slaves in charitable trusts.[139]

Some East African owners, fearing a loss of merit accruing from manumission, refused British compensation. Others took the money, but argued that the Europeans had bought their slaves, who could therefore not become clients of former owners.[140] Even slaves themselves 'believed that waiting for their master to manumit them would improve their social status more than the piece of paper provided by an alien authority'.[141] Muslims generally spurned manumission certificates signed by officials, or even by the sultan of Zanzibar, so that the latter persuaded owners to sign instead.[142]

[133] Ould Ahmed Salem, forthcoming.
[134] Messaoud 2000.
[135] Kamara 2000: 266.
[136] Segal 2001: 206.
[137] Strobel 1979: 52–3.
[138] Targey 1981: 279–80.
[139] Karrar 1985: 142, 156–7.
[140] Salim 1973: 112, 114; Cooper 1980: 52, 74–6; Romero 1997: 123, 129–30; Hardinge 1928: 362–3.
[141] Cooper 1980: 76.
[142] Beachey 1976b: 38–9; Hardinge 1928: 363–4.

Religious courts continued to deal with slavery, affecting the right to take concubines, the authorisation of marriage in return for a fee, inheriting from slaves who lacked an heir, and allocating land.[143] According to Spencer Trimingham: 'The social status of former slaves still remains in the "Arab" areas of the coasts and islands ... Religious law supports this distinction. Descendants of slaves, though free according to secular law, are still slaves according to the shari'a and subject to disabilities in a shari'a court, from which freedom can only be obtained by the process of manumission in such a court'. Masters continued to take concubines from servile families, and slaves had to obtain permission from their owners to marry, or their children would be illegitimate.[144]

Similar problems arose elsewhere. When the French ended slavery in the Comoro Islands in 1904, 'slaves were not freed, in Comorian eyes, by European emancipation decrees, but only by the individual action of their masters'. At the time, an abundance of servile dependants was credited with making the Comoros East Africa's main centre of Islamic learning.[145] Many of those liberated by the Italians in Somalia from 1903 drifted into vagrancy and crime, as they were seen as slaves of a government that was failing to provide for them.[146] The largely Islamised Makua of northern Mozambique, still deemed slavery to be 'legitimate' in the 1960s.[147]

Muslims in Christendom

In lands where owners were overwhelmingly Christian by faith, Muslims apparently did not oppose slavery on religious grounds, even when Western abolitionism became influential. Rather, Muslim leaders 'fully recognised and sanctioned slavery'.[148] When Muslims gained their freedom in such areas, some therefore became owners of slaves, if local laws permitted it.

There were Muslim slaves in western Europe from at least the ninth-century, and some remained in Italy in the early nineteenth-century.[149] Muslims in independent realms developed a tradition of

---

[143] Cooper 1980: 189–90, 229; Romero 1997: 130–1, 147, 158–9; Mirza and Strobel 1989: 23–4; Strobel 1979: 51–4.
[144] Trimingham 1964: 137–8, 148.
[145] Shepherd 1980: 86–7, 95–6.
[146] Cassanelli 1988: 319.
[147] Machado 1970: 273.
[148] Lovejoy 2004: 8–11.
[149] Koningsveld 1995: 5; Prud'homme 2002: 75–6.

redeeming them from servitude, for it was considered meritorious to engage in this activity. However, no critique of the institution of slavery appears to have emerged. Slaves were only emancipated if they converted, so that the question of freed Muslims owning slaves did not arise.[150]

The same appears to have been true of Muslim slaves in North America, concentrated in Louisiana, Georgia, and the Carolinas.[151] Umar b. Sayyid [Sa'id?], of Futa Toro and resident in North Carolina, wrote a letter in Arabic in 1819, addressed to his owner's brother, Major John Owen, requesting his freedom. However, his citations from the Quran referred to good treatment rather than to abolition.[152] The Muslim leader of Sapelo Island, Georgia, was Bilali, or Muhammad b. Ali, a Fulbe from Timbo in Futa Jalon. Around 1840, he wrote down from memory excerpts from a standard Maghribi exposition of Maliki law, the *Risala*, presumably the tenth-century text by Ibn Abi Zayd al-Qayrawani. Whether Bilali transcribed passages relating to servitude is not clear, but his choice of text implied acceptance of the institution.[153]

Richard Madden corresponded with free Jamaican Muslims in 1834. Among them was Sharif Abu Bakr Sidiqi, born in Timbuktu and raised in Jenne, and Muhammad Kaba Saghanugu, a Mandingo from beyond Futa Jalon. Both came from élite slave-owning families. Their summaries of Islamic beliefs noted God's command to care for the poor, but Madden upbraided them for remaining mute on slavery.[154] Saghanugu's Arabic discussion of duties incumbent on a pious Muslim failed to mention servitude.[155] Islam may have been an effective ideology of resistance on the island, but Sultana Afroz provides no evidence for the further statement that, 'the existence of the slave system was an antithesis to the concept of Islamic freedom'.[156]

A Quaker delegation to Trinidad discussed slavery in 1840 with the leader of the Muslim community, Emir Samba Makumba. He told them that slavery was legitimate in Islam, as long as sharia precepts were scrupulously observed, notably the prohibition on enslaving fellow Muslims. Prior to emancipation in 1834, some free

---

[150] Koningsveld 1995.
[151] Austin 1997; Lovejoy 2004: 18.
[152] Hunwick 2003.
[153] Judy 1993: 248, 327; Gardell 1999: 422–3; Austin 1997: 6.
[154] Madden 1835: II, 157–60, 183–9, 197–8, 203–7, 214.
[155] Addoun and Lovejoy 2004.
[156] Afroz 1999: 175.

Muslims on the island owned slaves, although they reputedly treated them well. They also pooled their resources to liberate Muslim slaves and help them to return to Africa.[157] Muslims were particularly numerous and combative in parts of Brazil. They played the leading role in a great slave rebellion in Baía in 1835, led by Malam Abubakar from Kano and possibly influenced by jihads at home.[158] A detailed police investigation revealed that some Muslim freedmen owned slaves, and that the plotters had planned to enslave mulattos, at least according to one witness.[159] Hausa freedmen, probably Muslims, figured prominently in Rio de Janeiro, where they manumitted slaves, including some from their own ethnic group.[160] A number of Brazilian Muslim ex-slaves returned to West Africa, especially to the Bight of Benin, where 'Brazilians' continued to be involved in the slave trade for decades.[161]

Most free Muslims in South Africa owned slaves. Indeed, there were some in the retinue of Shaykh Yusuf of Makassar, political exile and originator of Cape Islam in 1694. Tuan Guru, released from prison in 1793 and a second founding father, owned slaves, and avoided condemning the institution.[162] Achmat van Bengalen, leader of the Auwal mosque from 1822 to 1843, set out appropriate rules for owners, enjoining good treatment and prohibiting the sale of Muslim slaves to unbelievers. Muding, heading another mosque, declared in 1825 that, 'their bodies are in slavery, but we teach them to believe that their souls are free'.[163] Nevertheless, slaves converted to Islam on quite a scale, because Muslim owners treated them well, refused to sell them, and sometimes freed them on conversion.[164] Some Cape Muslims purchased 'aged and wretched creatures, irrespective of their religion, to make them free', following a well established tradition of Islamic charity.[165]

Dissenters may have progressed slightly more rapidly than their Sunni rivals along the abolitionist road, raising thorny questions as to the influence of these minorities. However, it is far from clear

[157] Trotman and Lovejoy 2004: 225–7.
[158] Lovejoy 2004: 19.
[159] Verger 1968: 341, 521–3, 528–32; Reis 1986: 147–51.
[160] Florentino 2002.
[161] Verger 1968: 603–4, 613, 618; Marty 1926: 16–19, 51–2.
[162] Mason 2003: 184–9.
[163] Davids 1980: 95–7.
[164] Mason 2003: 184–5, 198–207.
[165] Watson 1990: 174–5.

whether the 1912 abolitionist fatwa in Iran was generally accepted in Shi'i circles, let alone outside them. The wider impact, if any, of Druze and Nizari views remains to be ascertained, and it is uncertain whether any Aga Khan issued a condemnation of slavery in doctrinal terms. Ibadi reconciliation to the ending of slavery remains shrouded in obscurity.

The Sunni drift towards quasi-abolition has received less attention than it may deserve, for the ulama might have created consensus around this position over time. The shaky foundations for slavery in the sharia made it possible to question the decisions of earlier generations of scholars. The ulama, 'those who bind and loose', could have achieved a literal release of slaves. Reformers criticised the ulama as steeped in tradition and hypocritical in their refusal to condemn slavery *per se*, but some rationalist views of slavery owed more to traditional doctrines than is often realised. Furthermore, the ulama probably reached more believers than any other group. They also offered practical avenues for upward social mobility to people of unfree origins, within an Islamic structure of manumission and clientage.

That said, conservative positions were clearly more common, persisting well into the twentieth-century, and in some cases into the twenty-first century. A great deal more research is required to determine who among the ulama contemplated going right down the abolitionist road, who would only go a certain distance, and who refused to set out on the journey at all. It is necessary to gauge how much support each group commanded among the faithful in different parts of the Islamic world, and how this changed over time. The boldness of some scholars was striking, but the reserve shown elsewhere was even more conspicuous.

8

MYSTICS AND MILLENARIANS

The growth of Neo-Sufism, broadly defined, had explosive consequences from the late seventeenth-century. Abandoning other-
worldly reticence, Neo-Sufis sought to make the sharia triumph.
They stressed social and political reconstruction rather than personal salvation, and reserved esoteric study for the élite. They built
up ever more exclusive and tightly knit brotherhoods, transcending family and tribe. Pitting their energies against backsliding Muslims and resurgent infidels, these revivalists frequently turned to
holy war.[1] They not only fought Western imperialists around the
world, but also Ethiopian Orthodox Christians, Sikhs, Hindus in
India and Southeast Asia, Theravada Buddhists, and Chinese and
Vietnamese Confucianists.[2]

Mahdist movements also erupted, as chiliastic expectations reached
a crescendo between 1785 and 1883. This was the thirteenth Islamic century, when many preachers prophesied that the world would
pass away. The Shi'i looked specifically to the 1840s, marking a
thousand lunar years since the twelfth Shi'i Imam's occultation.
Apparently irresistible advances by infidels made it seem all the
more likely that the end times were nigh.

The consequences for slavery were contradictory. Neo-Sufis and
Mahdists initially strove to preserve free Muslims from enslavement,
and sometimes took a reformist stance on servitude. However, revivalists also tended to protect property rights in people. More seriously, successful movements punished countless 'bad Muslims' by
reducing them to servitude, together with hosts of hostile unbelievers.

Some mystics and millenarians swam against the tide of violence.
For those living in powerful Muslim states, force was not an option,

[1] O'Fahey and Radtke 1993; Martin 1976; Sirriyeh 1999;
[2] Beachey 1990: 37–8; Gaborieau 2000; Ricklefs 1993: 135; Andaya and Andaya 1982:
119–20; Wyatt 1982: 172–3; Lipman 1997; Dharma 1987: I, 141–63.

and they sought rather to influence rulers. Even in less tightly governed areas, some mystics and millenarians rejected the jihad of the sword as a matter of principle, often acting as arbitrators. Particular Sufi orders chose different strategies under different conditions, notably the Naqshabandiyya and the Tijaniyya.

Once revivalist polities had been crushed by around 1900, the 'greater jihad' against the base self could flourish. Millenarians, faced with the failure of eschatological predictions, formed new sects and sought social insertion. There was a return to traditional Sufi policies of proselytisation and social inclusion, with ex-slaves figuring prominently in such programmes. These movements thus played an important part in helping Muslim societies to avoid the social tensions that bedevilled the West after emancipation.

Early Sufi reformism in West Africa

West Africa's holy wars, probably the most extensive in Islamdom, were mystically inspired from the outset. They witnessed a slow progression from the influence of individual shaykhs to that of the Qadiriyya, in turn partly supplanted by the Tijaniyya. Leaders were typically rural preachers, and abuses involving slavery commonly justified holy war.

The process began in the far west. Nasir al-Din al-Daymami, a Berber Mauritanian holy man, led a jihad from around 1645, blaming Blacks from south of the Senegal river for enslaving free White Muslims.[3] In Senegal itself, the extortions and abuses committed by slave soldiers, hard-drinking infidels or nominal Muslims, were another source of early reformist zeal.[4] In late-eighteenth-century Futa Toro, Almamy 'Abd al-Qadir bi-Hammadi prohibited slave raiding and prevented foreign raiders from crossing his territory.[5]

Futa Jalon emerged from 1725 in the plateau south of the Senegal river, through a defensive jihad partly aimed at preventing the enslavement of Muslims. War captives were released, as long as they could recite the short Muslim creed in Arabic.[6] Less Sufi oriented than many in West Africa, this state made a particular effort to apply the holy law to matters concerning servitude.[7]

The vast Sokoto caliphate, spilling over the limits of modern northern Nigeria, grew out of a jihad launched in 1804 by Shehu

[3] Norris 1969: 515.
[4] Klein 1968: 63, 69–70.
[5] Hilliard 1985: 160; Martin 1976: 16.
[6] Baldé 1975: 188–9.
[7] Rodney 1968: 281–2; Fisher 2001: 117.

Usuman dan Fodio [Shaykh 'Uthman b. Fudi] (1754–1817). A rural Fulbe preacher, influenced by at least three Sufi orders, he had a vision in 1794, in which the founder of the Qadiriyya placed a green turban on his head as the 'Imam of the saints', and girded him with the 'sword of truth'. However, he did not exploit the loosely structured Qadiri order for military or bureaucratic purposes, treating Sufism as a matter of personal devotion. Moreover, he was learned in Maliki law, and influenced by millenarian and literalist currents of thought.[8]

Oral traditions that Shehu Usuman freed all Muslim slaves are erroneous, even if his desire to reform slavery was evident.[9] Justifying holy war against Hausa rulers, he cited the enslavement of free Muslims among a plethora of offences. He freed slaves who fled to join the cause, as well as Muslim slaves taken as booty, and he encouraged the manumission of all slaves who converted. He eschewed military and administrative servitude, as it did not figure in the Prophet's state. He renounced attacks on Animists in treaty relations with Muslims, and rejected the enslavement of 'bad Muslims'. When military success led superficially Islamised and Animist Fulbe pastoralists to join his cause for the sake of booty, Shehu Usuman was so upset that he retired from public life.[10] His own few slaves were treated with 'strict regard for the law', and some refused to accept manumission.[11]

Other early leaders of the Sokoto caliphate demonstrated unhappiness with aspects of servitude. Abdullahi dan Fodio, Usuman's brother, criticised the reduction of free Muslims to servitude in a famous poem, and temporarily withdrew from leadership of the movement on this account.[12] Muhammad Bello, Usuman's son, declared in 1812 that no slave should be sold to unbelievers, whether directly or indirectly.[13]

Inspired by Shehu Usuman, Muhammad al-Jaylani (c. 1777–c. 1840), probably a Qadiri, launched a jihad in the Tuareg region of Adar in the 1810s. Al-Jaylani sought to settle and urbanise his people, imposing 'the social ideal of the equality of all classes and

---

[8] Levtzion 1987: 32–5; Martin 1976: 13–15, 18, 35; Sirriyeh 1999: 13–16.
[9] Yamba 1995: 212.
[10] Martin 1976: 15–35; Fisher 2001: 71, 173–4; Willis 1985: I, 21–3; Lovejoy 1981: 210–13; Mack 1992: 89–90; Clarke 1982: 113–14; Philips 2000: 222–4; Stilwell 1999: 169; Bivar 1961.
[11] Hiskett 1994: 31–2.
[12] Mahadi 1992: 114; Azumah 2001: 105–6.
[13] Lovejoy 1981: 213–14.

ethnic groups in the jihad in God's way'.[14] Peter Clarke glosses this
as a wish to eliminate the distinction between noble, labourer, and
slave, but equality may have been more religious than social.[15] In a
letter to Muhammad Bello, written after defeat in 1816, al-Jaylani
noted ominously that, 'the property of the doers of iniquity ... [is]
not inviolate nor sacrosanct-not even mothers of children'.[16]

Probably the most radical state was Masina, on the Upper Niger.[17]
Shehu Ahmadu Lobo was a Qadiri Sufi, although the order figured
little in his administrative system. He launched his struggle around
1818, gaining much initial support from slaves, and liberating those
who fought for the faith, those who formed his personal share of
booty, and pious captives allocated to the state treasury. He refused
to give the name of holy war to offensive operations, and stressed
that Animists living peacefully under Muslim rule, or allied to Muslims, should not be disturbed. On one occasion, he even berated
the 'men of books and pens', saying to them, 'Forget the treatment
that the law demands for prisoners of war who do not believe in one
God, and apply that which is inspired by mercy'.[18]

Some council members in Masina suggested the complete abolition of slavery and caste, because the Quran enjoined the brotherhood of man. However, Ahmadu Lobo demurred. He endorsed the
legality of enslaving Animists taken in holy war, appointing a few to
high office. Moreover, he owned some slaves, including at least one
concubine, despite his austere lifestyle.[19]

Al-Hajj 'Umar b. Sa'id Tal (1794–1864), from Futa Toro, was
Masina's nemesis. He built up a vast state from 1852, basing the
legitimacy and organisation of his state squarely on his position as
West Africa's Tijani leader. He fulminated against the enslavement
of peaceful Animist subjects, and the sale of slaves to infidels. He
freed slaves, Muslim or not, who fled to join him, and refused to
return them to Muslim owners who later came over to his side.
More controversially, he 'silkened the fetters of bondage' by pro-
moting numerous slaves as governors, generals and Tijani shaykhs.[20]
Ma Ba, a Tijani supporter who fought his own holy war in Senegal

---

[14] Norris 1975: 147–9.
[15] Clarke 1982: 123–5.
[16] Norris 1975: 157.
[17] Fisher 2001: 71–3, 249.
[18] Ba and Daget 1962: 40, 52, 62, 66–7, 72, 147, 165, 280–1.
[19] *Ibid.*: 52, 67–8, 133, 147.
[20] Willis 1989: 72, 138–9, 159–60, 205–6; Willis 1980: 192; Willis 1979: 30–1.

from 1861 to 1867, confined enslavement to Animists and freed slaves who fought with their masters.[21]

Sufi retrogression in Africa

Regimes born of holy war became less liberal over time.[22] Scruples dwindled, as leaders sought to obtain vital firearms and horses by selling slaves, or by employing them to produce commodities.[23] Underpinning this evolution were facile definitions of 'bad Muslims'. Ahmad b. al-Qadi al-Timbuktawi, writing around 1810, reduced unbelief meriting enslavement to a simple failure to practise Maliki rituals.[24] In Masina 'Islam started as a liberating force and ended up rationalizing slaving military activity'.[25]

Futa Jalon provided a precocious example of hardening hearts. Conquered groups became servile tribes, instead of living peacefully under Muslim rule and paying the canonical tax. Almamy Ibrahima Sory turned from holy war to razzias from the 1750s, garnering ever more Animist slaves to sell to Western traders.[26] The élite's sparing use of slave soldiers arose from fear of uprisings, and did not preclude the employment of servile officials.[27]

So oppressive did slavery become in Futa Jalon that it provoked resistance. A major servile rebellion broke out in 1785, and was only crushed with considerable loss of life.[28] Mahmadu Juhe withdrew to the mountains in 1841 to found the Hubbu movement, 'those who pray to God'. He freed slaves who joined him, albeit without abolishing servitude as such, and his movement held out for decades.[29] Alfa Molo, son of a Mande slave, led another slave uprising in the western part of Futa Jalon from 1870. He created a state along the south of the Gambia river, and was succeeded by his son Musa Molo. However, both rulers themselves owned slaves.[30]

A reactionary drift became evident in Sokoto, once Muhammad Bello emerged as sole ruler after 1817. He cited the slave origins of Hausa rulers to justify their overthrow, and accepted the enslave-

[21] Klein 1968: 73–4, 77; Searing 2002: 47.
[22] Willis 1989: 70–1; Azumah 2001: 103.
[23] Klein 1998: 43, 51–3; Person 1968–75: 924–9.
[24] Mansour and Harrak 2000: 27–34.
[25] Klein 1998: 48.
[26] Baldé 1975: 189–95, 205; Barry 1998: 98–101; Canot 1940: 81–2, 130.
[27] Azarya 1978: 29–30.
[28] Baldé 1975: 207.
[29] Klein 1998: 46; Baldé 1975: 207.
[30] Klein 1998: 146; Botte 1999: 68.

ment of 'bad Muslims'.[31] Manumission, especially for field slaves, declined, and he excused the capture of Animists on the hoary old pretext of giving them the chance to convert. Tribute in slaves became institutionalised, with about 5,000 a year coming to the subordinate emir of Adamawa alone in 1851.[32] Bello also re-appointed slaves to high administrative and military positions on pragmatic grounds, although they were more prominent in some constituent emirates than in others.[33]

The rising power of the Tijaniyya signalled harsher attitudes. Al-Hajj 'Umar was more conservative on the issue than either Usuman dan Fodio or Ahmadu Lobo. When 'Umar set out on pilgrimage to Mecca in 1825, he took slaves to sell at intervals. Stopping in Sokoto on his return, he took part in razzias, receiving slaves as presents. After launching his holy war, he seized numerous slaves on flimsy pretexts, including 'bad Muslims' from Masina, and interpreted his wealth in captives as a sign of God's favour.[34] He viewed slaves as legitimate booty, and repressed slave flight.[35] About half his army consisted of slaves.[36]

A Mande trader from the eastern fringes of Futa Jalon, Samory Ture (c. 1830–1900), built up the last great conquest state of West Africa, gradually moving eastwards into northern Côte d'Ivoire. Neither a Sufi shaykh nor an *'alim*, he experienced only a short period of religious enthusiasm, and mainly played off Tijani against Qadiri shaykhs. Although born of a slave mother, he enslaved copious numbers of Animists, while generally refraining from taking Muslims.[37]

The British gave the pejorative name of 'Mad Mullah' to Sayyid Muhammad b. 'Abdallah Hasan (1864–1920) of Somalia. A Salihi Sufi, he was also influenced by literalist and millenarian ideas, prohibiting *qat* (*Catha edulis*), tea, coffee, drumming, dancing, and intercession through dead saints. He used the Salihiyya to unite feuding Somali clans around his austere programme, declaring jihads against the Ethiopians, British, and Italians from 1899 till he succumbed to influenza in 1920. However, the international head of the Salihiyya washed his hands of his fiery lieutenant in 1908.[38]

[31] Clarke 1995: 43; Lovejoy 1981: 213–14.
[32] Lovejoy 1981: 214–15, 220–1, 236–7; Mack 1992: 93, 96–7; Azarya 1978: 34.
[33] Philips 2000: 222–7; Azumah 2001: 106; Stilwell 1999: 169–73; Stilwell 2004: 89–90, 94–7; Azarya 1978: 30.
[34] Martin 1976: 69, 74–83, 86.
[35] Klein 1998: 51–3; Willis 1989: 130, 145.
[36] Berlioux 1870: 46.
[37] Person 1968–75: 251–5, 881–3, 924–32.
[38] Beachey 1990; Martin 1976: 179–201; Bemath 1992; Samatar 1992: 55–7.

The Salihi cause gained considerable support from fumbling colonial attempts to end slavery. The powerful Bimayaal [Bimal] clan was angered by the Società del Benadir's refusal to return runaways, or pay for them, from 1903.[39] A letter to an Italian commission of inquiry in that year stated that some slave-owners, especially poorer ones, 'pray for the coming of Sheikh Muhammad bin Abdullah, and invoke his name day and night'.[40] A 1905 peace treaty with Italy included an oath before God that Sayyid Muhammad would stop the slave trade, but there was no sign of compliance.[41] Writing to the British in 1917, he stated that 'it is you who have joined with all the peoples of the world, with harlots, with wastrels, and with slaves'.[42]

Sayyid Muhammad even seemed prepared to break the strong customary taboo on enslaving fellow Somalis. His enemies accused him bitterly of seizing their womenfolk, and of believing it licit to capture free Muslims.[43] In 1912 he distributed the women and children of one group among his men.[44] In a poem, castigating those who supported the infidel, he wrote about 'treading on their necks', probably a euphemism for enslavement.[45]

From an old Omani family, Muhammad b. Khalfan al-Barwani, better known as Rumaliza, carved out a principality along the northeastern shore of Lake Tanganyika from 1879. He raided and traded in slaves far and wide, and combated German and Congo Free State forces. He became a Qadiri shaykh at an unknown date, and circulated an intriguing letter in 1908, 'the dream of Shaykh Ahmad'. This missive was interpreted either as a call for religious purification, or as a Pan-Islamic blueprint for opposition to European rule.[46]

Varieties of African Mahdism

In 1881 the Sudan fell to a Mahdi, Muhammad b. Ahmad (1848–85). Of the former Egyptian rulers, he said that they 'used to drag your men away in fetters and keep them imprisoned in chains, and used

---

[39] Cassanelli 1988: 319, 324; Martin 1976: 188; Caroselli 1931: 164–5; Sheik-'Abdi 1993: 108.
[40] Cassanelli 1988: 318.
[41] Caroselli 1931: 86; Martin 1976: 186; Sheik-'Abdi 1993: 155.
[42] Sheik-'Abdi 1993: 97.
[43] Bemath 1992: 42; Samatar 1992: 55, 66; Martin 1976: 197–8.
[44] Caroselli 1931: 150.
[45] Martin 1976: 193.
[46] Martin 1976: 158–60, 168–71, 175; Constantin 1987: 90–2; Northrup 1988: 469.

to capture your wives and children'.[47] Slaves were promised 'freedom in this world and paradise in the next', if they would fight under his flag. Freeing the militiamen of slave merchants, he enrolled them into his army. He exhorted his followers to treat slaves properly and not to enslave fellow Muslims. Ceasing to employ servile officials, he banned private slave razzias and slave exports.[48] Western observers agreed that the intensity of slave trading fell under the Mahdi's rule, albeit possibly because he lost control over southern areas.[49]

The Mahdi never questioned slavery's status as a religiously ordained institution, and some of his measures intensified its incidence. Those smarting at Egypt's hiring of Western officials to suppress slave raiding and trading supported him. Even if he did not deliberately court these men, he rescinded impious certificates granted by Egypt's secular Manumission Bureaux from 1877, returning slaves to their former owners. Acknowledging only Quran, Hadith and his own divine inspiration, the Mahdi enslaved Muslims who refused to accept his exalted mission, including their wives and children. He distributed numerous female captives to his followers after the fall of Khartoum in 1885.[50] Indeed his sudden death a few months later was attributed to poisoning by a concubine.[51]

Any residual hesitations were swept away by the Mahdi's successor, 'Abdallah al-Ta'a'ishi, known as the Khalifa. Under his rule, 'the buying and selling of slaves ... was regarded as a charitable solution of the problem of prisoners of war and surplus women, who were thus at least provided with a home and means of sustenance'.[52] The Khalifa revived administrative slavery, and boasted of a harem containing some 500 women. Imports of eunuchs picked up, though castration was restricted to areas outside the state, and female slaves were circumcised and infibulated. There was little manumission, and even poor Muslim families were said to possess a slave girl. Slave exports moved back towards former levels, despite problems in subduing southern Animists and trading with Egypt. At best, the Khalifa continued to free male slaves enrolled into his army, many of whom bravely fought and died for the regime.[53]

[47] Peters 1979: 68–9.
[48] Hargey 1981: 56–7; Sikainga 1996: 29–30.
[49] Renault and Daget 1985: 193.
[50] Hargey 1981: 55–8; Sikainga 1996: 29–30; Warburg 1981: 245–7, 250–9; Layish 2000: 223–6; Beachey 1976a: 136, 139–40; Fredriksen 1977: 181–2.
[51] Ruthven 2000: 293.
[52] Theobald 1951: 184.
[53] Hargey 1981: 58–62, 69–72; Sikainga 1996: 29–34; Beachey 1976a: 140–2; Collins 1992: 150–1.

The Mahdiyya survived British persecution after defeat in 1898. Millenarian die-hards portrayed the Europeans as the Dajjal, the Antichrist, and eagerly awaited the arrival of Nabi 'Isa. The Nyala rebellion of 1921, in the west, was precipitated by officials freeing slaves and raising taxes, and small uprisings persisted to the early 1930s. However, Sayyid 'Abd al-Rahman al-Mahdi, son of the Mahdi, prudently disowned violence, and gradually improved his relations with the colonial authorities.[54]

Sudanese Mahdists attempted to retard the process of abolition. After two idealistic young British officials denounced laxity in repressing slavery and the slave trade in 1923, the colonial government reminded its subordinates that those born after 1898 were free. Moreover, runaways should not be returned to owners, slaves should not have to buy their liberty, and no official could refuse to issue freedom papers. This triggered the intervention of the 'Three Sayyids' in 1925, including Sayyid 'Abd al-Rahman al-Mahdi, who warned the authorities that hasty liberation would undermine both agrarian output and social order.[55]

Somali millenarians also supported slavery. In 1924, Shaykh Aji Hasan, leader of a Somali clan, predicted the imminent end of the world. He then complained to the Italians:

All our slaves have escaped and fled to you, and you have commanded that they be freed. We are unhappy about this. This is not in accordance with our law, because, according to our law, we can imprison slaves and force them to work. We are true Muslims, following the Prophet Muhammad and all the saints. The government has its laws and we have ours. We accept no law other than our own. Our law is that of God and the Prophet.[56]

West African notions were similar, in part because some Nigerian millenarians were influenced by the Sudanese Mahdiyya.[57] In Futa Jalon, Tcherno Aliou announced the imminent arrival of the Mahdi around 1911. He declared: 'Since we have not been heard on the question of slavery, which has made us rich, we must chase off the French'.[58]

Nevertheless, the borderlands of Nigeria and Niger harboured a group of Mahdists who actively opposed slavery, as part of filling the

[54] Daly 1986: 119–29, 278–86, 335–9, 391–5.
[55] Hargey 1981: 268–85; Daly 1986: 443–4; Jok 2001: 102–3.
[56] Vecchi di Val Cismon 1935: 27–8.
[57] Clarke 1982: 201–2.
[58] Sanneh 1997: 86.

world with justice. The chief of Satiru, close to Sokoto, proclaimed himself the Mahdi in 1904, designating his son as Nabi 'Isa. The Mahdi was arrested by the Sokoto authorities, and died in prison before he could be tried, but his son raised the standard of revolt in 1906. The rebels defeated a detachment of British mounted infantry, capturing a maxim gun, although a larger force soon avenged this humiliation. The British destroyed the movement's rustic capital, and had five 'ringleaders' executed by the Sokoto authorities. However, the movement spread quite widely across British, French, and German territory, arousing colonial fears.

The leaders of the Satiru Mahdists, notably the blind scholar Saybu dan Makafo, taught that slavery was 'a prime example of the injustice of caliphate society'. They abolished the institution, encouraged slaves to leave their masters, and liberated the inhabitants of slave villages. Refusing to pay taxes or perform corvée labour, the faithful awaited a great Muslim army, which would come from the East to deliver God's oppressed.[59] Some Nigerian millenarians continued to seek inspiration in Satiru and its abolitionist programme after 1906.[60]

Maghribi holy warriors

Algerian Mahdism flared up following French advances from 1830. Bu Ma'za declared himself 'lord of the hour' in 1845 between Algiers and Oran. According to his detractors, he abolished the law, prayed and fasted little, and 'seized women in razzias, had sex with them, and did not hide it'.[61] A year after the unpopular French abolition decree of 1848, colonial officials refused to return a fugitive slave woman. This was the spark that led Bu Ziyan to raise the Mahdist standard in the eastern Biskra area.[62]

'Abd al-Qadir b. Muhyi al-Din (1807–83) formed an Islamic state in western Algeria from 1832 to 1847, on the basis of his hereditary status as Qadiri shaykh. He had also been influenced by the Naqshabandiyya in the Middle East.[63] In gilded exile in Damascus after his defeat, he acquired a reputation as a progressive scholar and nationalist hero, obscuring his involvement in slavery. In 1839 he demanded the return of a Black slave woman, together with her

[59] Lovejoy and Hogendorn 1990: 217–43; Lovejoy and Hogendorn 1993.
[60] Shobana Shankar, personal communication.
[61] Nadir 1972: 858–60.
[62] Clancy-Smith 1994: 87–92.
[63] Martin 1976: 36, 48–9, 66.

freed mother. The pair had fled to Algiers, accused of facilitating the infidelity of 'Abd al-Qadir's wife. The governor-general agreed to return them, despite impassioned pleas, causing the head of the Direction des Affaires Arabes to resign in disgust.[64] More controversially 'Abd al-Qadir sought to enslave Muslims who opposed him. He wrote three letters to Islamic scholars in the late 1830s, one of them to 'Ali b. 'Abd al-Salam al-Tasuli, Maliki Shaykh al-Islam of Morocco.[65] Al-Tasuli responded that 'Muslims may attack traitors and their associates, spies and connivers, or those who shelter them. With full justification, and without remorse, they may be extirpated and their women and children taken, like their property'.[66] The second letter was destined for Muhammad b. Ahmad 'Illaysh ['Ilish] (1802–82), a Maliki mufti of Moroccan origins in Cairo, and a fervent adept of the Shadhili order. He also authorised killing collaborators and enslaving their families.[67] However, 'Abd al-Hadi b. 'Abdallah al-Husayni, chief qadi of Fez and recipient of the third missive, disagreed. He opined that 'even if they were apostates, it would be forbidden to seize their wives and children'.[68]

'Abd al-Qadir certainly took captives from France's indigenous Muslim allies, but it is uncertain whether he enslaved them. A contemporary source recorded that 'their girls and possessions are seized ... [and] they are conscripted by force'.[69] On a single expedition in 1835, he seized 95 male prisoners and 260 women and children. A year later, he proposed an exchange of captives to the French general in Oran, who refused, stating that prisoners held by France were not slaves.[70]

The Sanusiyya was initially more liberal. Muhammad b. 'Ali al-Sanusi (1787–1859), also from western Algeria, preached universal brotherhood, modelled on the Prophet's ideal community. His order took root in Cyrenaica from the 1840s, and eventually overflowed the boundaries of modern Libya.[71] Al-Sanusi declared no holy wars, prohibited weapons in and around his missionary lodges, mediated between tribes, and preached against the enslavement of

[64] Emerit 1949: 36; Emerit 1951: 182–3; Julien 1964: 332–3.
[65] Tsouli 1907–09.
[66] Martin 1976: 66, 211.
[67] Peters 1979: 58; Delanoue 1982: 164–5.
[68] Chater 1994: 44.
[69] Danziger 1977: 202, 204.
[70] Emerit 1951: 155–6; 210.
[71] Vikør 1995; Martin 1976: 100–18.

Muslims. Some Europeans spoke of his 'abhorrence' of the slave trade and attempts to stop it.[72] The Sanusiyya purchased Africans from caravans, freed them, educated them, and sent them back as missionaries to their communities of origin.[73]

That said, there is no evidence that al-Sanusi ever preached against slavery or the slave trade, and caravans from Wadai to Benghazi brought mainly slaves in al-Sanusi's time.[74] Some Europeans alleged that al-Sanusi benefited from the infamous commerce. They also accused him of supporting 'Abd al-Qadir's jihad in Algeria, with its ambiguous impact on slavery. Moreover, the policy of freeing slaves to act as missionaries may have been initiated by his son, Muhammad al-Mahdi.[75]

Under the protection of al-Sanusi's successors, the slave trade undoubtedly blossomed along the Wadai–Benghazi route, which lasted longer than any other trans-Saharan artery.[76] The British consul in Benghazi said in 1892 that 'slave dealing is considered by the Mussulman population a perfectly legitimate trade'.[77] The sultan of Wadai to the south, a Sanusi adept, regularly sent slaves as gifts to the head of the order.[78] Although the Sanusiyya did not directly engage in the trade, slaves became embedded in the state. There were about a hundred Black slaves acting as domestics and herdsmen in the central lodge by the 1870s.[79] In 1877, each lodge contained 'Black slaves, camels and horses'.[80]

When Ahmad al-Sharif succeeded to the leadership in 1902, the Sanusiyya drifted further away from the ideals of the founder. Known for his love of luxury, Ahmad asked for supplies of eunuchs and numerous 'young, skilful and pretty female captives'. He also employed many slaves as agricultural workers and soldiers in a growing network of lodges in Borku, northern Chad, which became his 'granary'.[81] The Sanusiyya became more violent after the 1911 Italian invasion of Libya, justified in part by the need to repress the slave trade.[82] Ahmad al-Sharif published a call to jihad

---

[72] Vikør 1995: 184–212, 266; Martin 1976: 109, 123.
[73] Forget 1900: 59.
[74] Richardson 1853: I, 19.
[75] Vikør 1995: 188, 211–12.
[76] Wright 1989: ch. 5; Triaud 1995: I, 415, 446.
[77] Erdem 1996: 86.
[78] Triaud 1995: I, 164, 466, 552–3, 582; Renault 1971: II, 15.
[79] Rinn 1884: 505, 507–7.
[80] Triaud 1995: I, 224.
[81] *Ibid*.: I, 509–12; II, 647–8, 653–9.
[82] Salvadei 1927: 168.

in a Cairo journal in 1913–14, drawing heavily on al-Tasuli's 1830s Moroccan treatise, and thus probably condoning the enslavement of collaborators.[83] After the dust had settled, slavery remained part of life in Sanusi oases.[84] The Sufi contribution to Tunisian abolition was ambivalent. The Shadhili order encouraged Ahmad Bey to care for the poor and needy, possibly influencing his 1840s abolitionist decrees, discussed in Chapter 6.[85] Conversely, rebels in the great 1864 revolt sought to reverse the abolition of slavery, and were led by 'Ali b. Ghadahum, with strong Tijani links. Two Sufi shaykhs, of uncertain affiliation, were prominent rebel commanders in Sfax.[86]

Jihads from the Balkans to Yunnan

Sufis provided support to Ottoman Balkan wars, in which numerous Christians were reduced to servitude. Founded in Azerbaijan around the fourteenth-century, the Khalwatiyya encouraged anti-Christian operations from the sixteenth-century. As the tide of war turned, a new offshoot, the Jerrahiyya, preached jihad and strict adherence to the sharia. The heterodox Bektashiyya, displaying Christian and Shi'i tendencies, was associated with the Janissary infantry, initially formed of slave youths, till the violent dissolution of the corps in 1826.[87]

In the northeastern Caucasus, Naqshabandi Sufis were the catalyst for jihad against Russia from 1830 to 1859. Imam 'Ali Shamil united ethnically fragmented peoples of Daghestan and Chechenya around the Khalidi branch of the order, imposing the sharia and stamping out rampant blood feuds. In a famous incident in 1839, Shamil prevented a Chechen from selling a free Muslim woman as a slave.[88] He also liberated the serfs of hostile khans in Daghestan, emancipated Russian prisoners who converted, and treated freed slaves as full members of society.[89] Furthermore, he rejected the use of force to bring Circassian Muslims into his new state.[90]

There was a darker side to Shamil's jihad. To launch his movement, he exploited resentment against the Russian refusal to return run-

[83] Peters 1979: 87–8.
[84] Levy 1957: 86.
[85] Brown 1972: 82–3.
[86] Valensi 1977: 363–4; Temimi 1971: 20–3.
[87] Clayer 1994; Shaw and Shaw 1976–7: I, 123; II 21; Malcolm 1998: 190.
[88] Zelkina 2000: 190.
[89] Gammer 1994: 246, 252–3; Baddeley 1999: 455; Majerczak 1912: 197.
[90] Gammer 1994: 170; Zelkina 2000: 200.

aways, and their attempts to prevent the enslavement of Christian Armenians and Georgians, sold to the Ottomans.[91] Shamil's favourite wife was an Armenian captive, Anna Uvarova, taken in a raid on a Russian fort in 1840 and converted under the name of Shuanet.[92] Shamil ransomed captured Russians who refused to convert, but if no money was forthcoming, he sold them as slaves.[93] He did not liberate all serfs who came under his control, killed Muslims who failed to join his cause, and enslaved their wives and children.[94]

As the war dragged on, a Qadiri leader arose among the Chechens, Kunta Haji. He preached non-violent self-purification, religious devotion and withdrawal from the world. Because he was gaining support among a weary population, Shamil forced him to go on a second pilgrimage to Mecca in 1859.[95] However, Qadiri Sufis joined their Naqshabandi rivals in 1877–8, fighting a holy war against the Russians in Daghestan.[96]

Although Naqshabandi shaykhs remained subservient to Uzbek rulers of centralised states, mystics were active elsewhere in Turkistan. They animated Turkmen resistance to the Russians till 1885, with slave raiding as a major bone of contention.[97] Naqshabandi Sufis were prominent in the struggle against piecemeal Chinese conquest from 1697. In the greatest jihad, from 1862 to 1878, East Turkistan forces 'obtained the women and children of the Chinese'.[98] The leader of this jihad, Yakub Beg from Tashkent, in 1864 sent 'nine Chinese damsels' to a Muslim chief fighting the Russians. Yakub Beg offered Chinese male captives the choice between execution and converting to serve as soldiers for 12 years, doing 'all the menial tasks'. Moreover, he enrolled 'a considerable number of slaves who had been taken in wars with the various independent and minor potentates, whose territories bordered on the west and south of Kashgaria'.[99]

Hui Muslims suffered from a rising tide of Han Chinese settlement, notably in Yunnan, Gansu, and Shaanxi. Many turned to the reformist teachings of the Jahriyya, a Naqshabandi offshoot. Vio-

---

[91] Gammer 1994: 40; Sirriyeh 1999: 39.
[92] Zelkina 2000: 199; Gammer 1994: 120, 397; Baddeley 1999: 456.
[93] Barrett 1999: 157–61, 176.
[94] Gammer 1994: 245–6, 252–3, 256; Zelkina 2000: 193, 224; Leone 1973: 93, 102.
[95] Zelkina 2000: 229–30; Gammer 1994: 295.
[96] Zelkina 2000: 237; Sirriyeh 1999: 42.
[97] Yemelianova 2002: 61, 66; Bacon 1980: 104–5.
[98] Hamada 1990: 486.
[99] Kuropatkin 1882: 145, 164–5, 199.

lence erupted in the northwest in 1781–4, 1861–73, 1895, and 1914, sometimes taking the form of holy war led by Sufis. Hui leaders forcibly enlisted captives and conquered peoples, including Muslims fighting for the enemy, and seized their dependants, although there were no explicit references to permanent servitude.[100] A similar pattern emerged during the southwestern Hui rebellion of 1855 to 1873, when Du Wenxiu founded a Yunnanese sultanate centred on Dali [Tali].[101]

Risings in South and Southeast Asia

A famous Sufi shaykh and reformist *'alim* of Delhi, Shah 'Abdu'l-'Aziz Waliyullah, issued a fatwa in 1803. In it he declared India to be part of the abode of war, where it was legitimate to 'hold slaves unconditionally'.[102] He inspired Sayyid Ahmad Barelwi (1786–1831), who was initiated into the Naqshbandi, Qadiri and Chishti orders, and then founded his own austere Muhammadi order to enforce the sharia. Influenced by the Mahdist expectations of his followers, he declared a jihad against the Sikhs of the Punjab in 1826. Booty was promised, although slaves were not specifically mentioned. After his death in 1831, low-level guerrilla operations, including kidnapping for ransom, continued for decades in the northwest.[103]

There were two other South Asian examples of mystical and millenarian conflicts, possibly involving slaving. Titu Mir led a jihad in Bengal in 1831, having earlier accepted Sufi investiture from Sayyid Ahmad Barelwi in Mecca. Titu Mir planned on seizing Hindu girls for his followers, but was soon defeated and killed.[104] An altogether more momentous event was the 'Indian Mutiny' of 1857–8, which, for some participants, was a holy war to restore Mughal power. Shah Ahmad Sa'id, an influential Naqshabandi shaykh, affixed his seal to a fatwa declaring the conflict to be a jihad, as he had earlier done to a fatwa justifying slavery.[105]

A heady mixture of Neo-Sufi revivalism, Mahdism and holy war spread through Southeast Asia from the eighteenth-century. 'Abd

---

[100] Lipman 1997: 68–9, 100, 111, 113, 186; Fields 1978: 68–9, 71, 93–4, 102; Dillon 1999: 71–2, 146–7; Bonin 1910: 217; Kuropatkin 1882: 112, 121.

[101] Wei 1974; Anderson 1876: 233–4; Garnier 1996: 156, 224–6.

[102] Metcalf 1982: 47–52.

[103] Gaborieau 2000; Hardy 1972: 51–5, 58, 82–4, 173–4; Hunter 1964: 5, 14; Rizvi 1978–83: II, 381.

[104] Dutta 1987: 25; 90, 108–11, 165–6.

[105] Powell forthcoming.

al-Samad al-Palimbani (c. 1704–89), of Arab origins and propagator of the Sammaniyya order in Palembang and beyond, wrote a famous and influential tract commending holy war towards the end of his life, which circulated widely for over a century. Significant reformist conflicts broke out in southern Thailand, Sumatra, Java, southeastern Borneo, South Sulawesi, and Lombok, influenced by the Sammani, Shattari, Khalwati and Naqshabandi orders.[106]

West Sumatra's Padri Wars raged from 1803 to the late 1840s. This civil war sprang from numerous abuses, including 'bandits' enslaving free Muslims. Young Minangkabau radicals of the Shattari order, influenced by literalist ideas, proclaimed a jihad.[107] Local tradition and Dutch documents attest that the 'white time' of the Padris marked a high point in enslaving indigenous 'bad Muslims', or at least their womenfolk.[108] Padri forces also seized Animist Batak to the north, and forced them to pay tribute in slaves.[109] Imam Bonjol, a famous Padri leader, reputedly owned 70 slaves, and rejected his own shaykh's call for gentle persuasion.[110] The servile population of eastern villages cultivated fields and mined for gold in the 1860s.[111] Most slaves freed by the Dutch in 1876 had entered servitude through war.[112]

The eradication of the slave trade was one of three Dutch demands that contributed to the outbreak of war with the Sumatran sultanate of Aceh in 1873.[113] Asked for succour, the United States consul in Singapore insisted on 'measures against piracy and slavery'. Aceh's negotiators replied that the Americans should 'let us know if we have at any time dealt with our countrymen in selling them to other nations as slaves'. Further, a Dutch allegation that Aceh 'has carried on trade by selling and buying slaves is untrue, the said Government never having done and is [sic] unwilling now to carry on such trade'. This was disingenuous, for slaves were imported not exported, and by private traders not by the state.[114]

The Dutch instituted a naval blockade to prevent slave imports from Nias, and decided to ban slavery itself in 1874, at least in Aceh

---

[106] Azra 1992; Riddell 2001: 184–6; Pelras 2001; Ricklefs 1993: 119–47.
[107] Dobbin 1983: 128–87; Kraus 1984: 51–62.
[108] Verkerk Pistorius 1868: 435–6; Loeb 1972: 108; Dobbin 1983: 137–8; Steenbrink 1993: 75.
[109] Dobbin 1983: 180–2.
[110] *Ibid.* 1972: 7, 10, 20–1.
[111] *Ibid.* 1983: 138.
[112] Hasselt 1882: 191.
[113] Veth 1873: 119–20; Collet 1925: 101; Juynboll and Piekaar 1960: 743–4.
[114] Reid 1969: 83, 90–1, 96, 100.

proper. This contributed to the bitterness of the 'Thirty Years War' which ensued, at a time when the main Sufi order in Aceh was the Sammaniyya.[115] Resistance quickly turned into an Islamic struggle, inspired by al-Palimbani's tract on jihad, *nasihat al-Muslimin.*[116] A long poetic call for holy war lamented that 'who is a noble, who a slave, who a lord—this is no more to be known, as the unbeliever levels out all social differences'.[117]

Similar forces were at play in Pahang, in the Malay peninsula, where Sultan Ahmad refused to accept a British Resident till 1887. The subsequent registration of slaves helped to spark off a rebellion from 1891 to 1895, portrayed by later nationalists as a rising 'to safeguard Malay tradition'.[118] The rebels declared their struggle a holy war in 1894, backed by a 'saint' from Trengganu to the north. They apparently took slaves from hostile villages.[119]

Sufi 'jihads of the tongue'

Little is known of pacific Sufis at the time of the great holy wars. One example was the Mukhtariyya, a Qadiri branch in West Africa. founded by Sidi al-Mukhtar al-Kunti (1729–1811) of Mauritania. Influential in Timbuktu, this sub-order preached the superiority of the 'jihad of the tongue' over that of the sword. They mediated between Arab and Tuareg desert tribes, and called for clemency as holy wars engulfed the region. That said, Ahmad al-Bakka'i al-Kunti blessed the rebellion which led to the death of al-Hajj 'Umar in 1864, because the latter's attack on Masina had been unlawful.[120] Moreover, a European observer noted in 1860 that Qadiri shaykhs of Mauritania 'are all very concerned with worldly goods and have many slaves'.[121]

Once defeated by Europeans, the West African Tijaniyya backtracked rapidly. Al-Hajj Malik Sy, leader of a branch of the order in Senegal from 1891, called for obedience to Europeans in 1912, in part because they had stopped the Wolof from 'enslaving one another'.[122]

---

[115] Kreemer 1922–3: II, 201–2; Snouck Hurgronje 1957–65: I, 383; Collet 1925: 520; Kraus 1984: 101.
[116] Azra 1992: 551; Riddell 2001: 185; Risso 1995: 91.
[117] Damsté 1928: 595.
[118] Andaya and Andaya 1982: 160–1, 167–70.
[119] Linehan 1973: 140–2, 153, 161–2.
[120] Martin 1976: 31–2, 75–6, 92–3; Knysh 2000: 260–1; Levtzion 1987: 34; Azumah 2001: 78–9; Vikør 2000: 445.
[121] McDougall 1992: 74.
[122] Searing 2002: 131–2, 271–2.

His disciple, al-Hajj Seydou Nourou Tal (c. 1880–1980), toured French Africa in the interwar years, spreading a new Tijani message that the Europeans had done great things by freeing slaves. Ironically, he was a grandson of al-Hajj 'Umar Tal.[123] Shaykh Ahmad Hamahu'llah b. Muhammad (d. 1943) developed the Hamawiyya in the Upper Niger region, deriving his initiation from a Tijani centre in Tlemcen, Algeria, in 1909. The son of a slave woman, this reclusive mystic and ascetic concentrated on the recently converted, the illiterate, the poor, and the disenfranchised. He 'urged former slaves to reject the claims of their masters' and welcomed 'slaves fleeing from their patrons'. The French exiled him in turn to southern Mauritania, Côte d'Ivoire and France, where he died.[124]

The influence of the Uwaysi branch of the Qadiriyya helps to explain why holy war figured little south of central Somalia. Shaykh Uways b. Muhammad al-Barawi (1847–1909), of Brava (Baraawe) in Somalia, became a Qadiri initiate in Baghdad. After his return in 1881, he sent missionaries as far as Rwanda, the Congo, Mozambique, and Madagascar. Zanzibar became his second centre from 1884, and large numbers joined the order on the mainland after the failure of the Maji Maji uprising against the Germans in 1905–7. He named his new southern Somali capital the 'town of peace' in 1898–9, before suffering martyrdom at the hands of Salihi followers of Sayyid Muhammad in 1909.[125] However, although the founder of the Qadiri order was widely revered as the 'saint of the oppressed' in East Africa, Shaykh Uways was accompanied on his many trips by 'slave and free'.[126]

Sudanese Sufism, outflanked by Mahdism, remained peaceful and conservative on slavery. Sayyid Muhammad b. 'Uthman al-Mirghani (1793–1853) founded the Khatmiyya, also active in the Hijaz and Eritrea. He appointed as deputy a slave owned by a woman, but hagiographers boasted of his numerous concubines.[127] Yusuf bin Ahmad al-Hindi, leading the Hindiyya offshoot from the Sammaniya, owned 'hundreds and hundreds' of slaves.[128] After the British had destroyed the Mahdi's regime in 1898–9, runaways captured in Kordofan in 1906 were found to belong to Sayyid al-Makki Isma'il

[123] Garcia 1997: 253.
[124] Klein 1998: 229–30, 313; Vikør 2000: 453.
[125] Samatar 1992: 51–4, 60; Vikør 2000: 447.
[126] Pouwels 1987: 196–8, 200–1; Constantin 1987: 89; Martin 1976: 163.
[127] Karrar 1985: 143; Grandin 1987: 48.
[128] O'Fahey and Radtke 1993: 80.

al-Wali, leader of the traditionalist wing of the Isma'iliyya.[129] Heads
of the Khatmiyya and Hindiyya were the other two Sayyids pleading
for a slower tempo of slave emancipation in 1925.[130]

Some Sufis in the Ottoman empire may have evinced critical attitudes towards slavery. The Naqshbandi and Mawlawi [Mevlevi]
orders endorsed measures against military and administrative slavery
from the 1790s, whereas 'popular orders' and 'unattached itiner-
ant dervishes' opposed them.[131] Naqshbandi Sufis in Bosnia succoured the poor, and Shaykh 'Abdul Vehhab b. 'Abdul Vehhab,
better known as Ilham Baba, was executed in 1821 for criticising
social injustice.[132]

The Nimatullahiyya, a Shi'i order developing from the fourteenth-
century, was most obviously liberal on slavery. Rooted in Iran and
India, the order overcame eighteenth-century Persian persecution
of Sufis, gradually gaining adepts in high places.[133] Haji Mirza Aqasi
served as both first minister and Sufi shaykh for Muhammad Shah
in the 1840s. Personally opposed to the slave trade, Aqasi successfully encouraged his imperial master to end imports of slaves by sea
in 1848.[134]

Dual allegiances have obscured later mystical contributions to
abolitionism. Of the ulama treated in Chapter 7, the Iranian *mujtahid* 'Ali Nur 'Ali Shah was a Nimatullahi shaykh, Al-Nasiri reformed
Moroccan Sufism and wrote a hagiography of the Nasiriyya order,
and Musa Kamara of Senegal was probably a Qadiri.[135] Mystical
thought might seem less relevant to secularists and rationalists, but
among those deeply influenced by Sufism were the secularist Turk
Ziya Gökalp, considered in Chapter 6, together with the Tatar
teacher Musa Jarullah Bigi and the Sudanese reformer Mahmud
Muhammad Taha, both covered in chapter 10.[136]

Renewers of Sufism in modern times, spreading to the West from
the 1960s, called for greater social responsibility.[137] Although slavery was not overtly attacked by those retelling the famous story of

---

[129] Warburg 1981: 260; Vikør 2000: 460.
[130] Hargey 1981: 268–85; Daly 1986: 443–4; Jok 2001: 102–3.
[131] Heyd 1961: 68–9, 73–4.
[132] Cehajic 1990: 667.
[133] Martin 1989: 19–21; Petrushevsky 1985: 298; Hodgson 1974: II, 496, III, 38.
[134] Mirzai 2000; Kelly 1968: 594.
[135] Tabandeh 1970: 26–7; David Gutelius and Constance Hilliard, personal
communications.
[136] Parla 1985: 38–41, 114; Rorlich 1986: 61; Taha 1987.
[137] Sirriyeh 1999: 140, 151–2.

Rabi'a for Western audiences, an implicit opposition was clear.[138] More explicit was M. R. Bawa Muhaiyaddeen, a Sri Lankan Tamil Sufi, settled in Philadelphia from 1971 to his death in 1986. He advocated religious pluralism and 'proclaimed an Islam of mercy and compassion'. Allowing only for the narrowest defensive concept of holy war, he censured the enslavement of enemies.[139]

Peaceful millenarianism

'Ali Muhammad (1819–50) declared himself to be the Bab or 'gate' of the Mahdi in 1843–4, marking the millennium of the occultation of the twelfth Imam. He claimed to be the Mahdi himself in 1847, abrogating the holy law. The authorities executed him in 1850, and harshly suppressed the movement.[140] The Bab does not appear to have directly opposed slavery. Originating from a southern Iranian mercantile family, he possessed at least one Black slave, who probably witnessed his master's first revelations.[141]

It was Baha'u'llah (1817–92) who developed the Bab's notions of social justice, having received revelations of his own. In 1863, he proclaimed himself to be the prophet foretold by the Bab, and those who accepted his leadership were called Baha'i.[142] In Palestinian exile, Baha'u'llah wrote to Queen Victoria in 1869, praising her for abolishing the trade in male and female slaves, which accorded with his revelations. In a publication of 1873 he forbade trading in slaves, for 'all are but bondslaves before the Lord'.[143] His successor, 'Abdu'l Baha, glossed this as a prohibition of slavery itself, perhaps on a visit to the United States in 1912.[144] By this stage, however, the Baha'i faith had become a separate religion.

In contrast, Mirza Ghulam Ahmad (1839–1908) strove to remain within the Islamic fold. He proclaimed his mission in British India in 1889, claiming to be both Mahdi and Messiah. He declared himself free to assume the title of Messiah because Nabi 'Isa [Jesus] had not been bodily assumed into heaven to return for the last judgement, but had died a natural death in Srinagar, Kashmir. Ghulam Ahmad also claimed to be a prophet, a renewer of religion, one to

---

[138] Smith 1994; el-Sakkakini 1982.
[139] Muhaiyaddeen 2002: i, 22, 66, 81.
[140] Halm 1991: 109–10.
[141] Lee 1999.
[142] Hodgson 1974: III, 305.
[143] Lee 1999: 2–3.
[144] Baha'u'llah and 'Abdu'l Baha 1956: 53, 269.

whom God or angels speak, and an avatar of the Hindu god Krishna. Orthodox Muslims most resented the claim to prophethood, which negated the belief that Muhammad had been the 'seal of the prophets'.[145] Ghulam Ahmad's views on slavery were probably moderately reformist. He denounced 'empty-headed maulvis' for issuing fatwas that declared it 'lawful to seduce or seize the women of unbelievers or heretics', but he also criticised 'advanced Muhammadans' for rejecting Medinan verses of the Quran.[146] He interpreted jihad as peaceful striving, relegating holy war to purely defensive struggles, and repeatedly protesting his loyalty to the British.[147]

When the Ahmadiyya split in 1914, the Qadiyani branch continued the messianic tradition, taking a relatively conservative line on slavery. Ghulam Ahmad's son, Mirza Bashir-ud-Din Mahmud Ahmad, was the divinely inspired leader for over 50 years. Treated as an apostate by most Muslims, he energetically spread the sect's teachings around the world.[148] He maintained that infidel aggressors could rightly be enslaved in defensive holy wars.[149] Mawlana Sher 'Ali stated in 1934–5 that concubinage was licit, as long as concubines were 'women taken prisoners in war', presumably meaning female inhabitants of conquered countries.[150]

Qadiyani attitudes towards servitude changed after 1945, for Muhammad Zafrulla Khan (1893–1985), highly placed in the sect, opposed slavery unconditionally. He was Pakistan's first foreign minister, and later led his country's delegation to the United Nations.[151] Qadiyani believers in the United States and Nigeria also rejected slavery from the 1950s, in the latter case taking the stance that Islam could only gradually get rid of slavery.[152]

The other Ahmadi branch, known as Lahori from their headquarters, restricted Ghulam Ahmad's role to that of a restorer of the faith, and turned against servitude more rapidly and more radically. In an English-language commentary on the Quran, first published in 1916 and re-issued four years later, Muhammad 'Ali interpreted 47:4 in the Quran as an unconditional order to release

---

[145] Friedmann 1989; Walter 1998.
[146] Walter 1998: 68–70.
[147] Friedmann 1989: 172–80; Walter 1998: 38, 71–3; Hardy 1972: 172–3.
[148] Friedmann 1989; Walter 1998.
[149] Mahmud Ahmad 1924: 331–3.
[150] Bevan Jones 1941: 208.
[151] Khan 1976: 66–72.
[152] Balogun 1975: 165; Saifi 1956: 13–15.

unransomed captives. He stressed manumission, and traditions
that the Prophet had freed all his slaves before his death. Slavery
should have withered away rapidly, had Muslims obeyed God and
his Prophet.[153] Returning to the fray in 1936, Muhammad 'Ali
included an incisive and lengthy attack on concubinage.[154] In that
same year, Abdul Karim, President of the Muhammadan Educational Council of Bengal, linked an intransigent stand against slavery to the Prophet's 'declaration of the equality of man'.[155]

Khawaja Kamal-ud-Din took the Lahori message to England in
1912, where he gained support from an influential convert, Lord
Headley.[156] Kamal-ud-Din published a confused and contradictory
appendix on slavery, in a book appearing in 1925. The 'ignoble
institution' was a 'curse', and 'it is apparent that from the teachings
of the Prophet no Muslim is permitted to bring any person into
slavery, and that Islam and the Qur-an [sic] give no countenance to
anything like the institution of slavery'. The Prophet and his close
companions freed all their slaves, encouraged manumission, and
rejected concubinage. However, they faced practical problems, as
slavery was deeply ingrained in Arab society. Enslaving captives was
better than killing or mutilating them, so the Quran permitted it,
albeit only in defensive wars. Kamal-ud-Din pessimistically envisioned that, 'as long as war continues in the world the system must
continue', and yet predicted that slavery would die a 'natural death'.

Further dubious notions appeared in this tract. He denied accusations that the Ottomans had enslaved Armenians in the First
World War, and yet considered Armenian slave girls in Turkish
households to have been legitimately captured in a defensive war
against the infidel. The best solution to the lingering slave trade
would be to convert all barbarous Blacks to Islam. Upward social
mobility and alleged good treatment proved the superiority of Muslim slavery. Polemical attacks on Christians degenerated into accusations of responsibility for the international traffic in prostitutes.[157]

Lahori Ahmadi missionaries spread to Africa and Southeast Asia.
Entering Java in 1924, they translated texts opposing slavery, although
it is not certain how much was published. Mirza Wali Ahmad Baig
began rendering Muhammad 'Ali's annotated English version of
the Quran into Malay, but only three instalments had appeared by

[153] 'Ali 1920: 78, 975, 1192.
[154] 'Ali 1936: 587, 661–70.
[155] Karim 1936: 62–4.
[156] Greenidge 1958: 59–61.
[157] Kamal-ud-Din 1925: 245–74.

1928. Further progress was blocked by influential Islamic intellectuals, who held Lahori to be heretics. Translation into Dutch continued, but it is unclear how much was published.[158] West African millenarian sects probably appealed to former slaves. Seydina Mouhamoudou Limamou Laye (1845–1909) of Senegal declared himself the Mahdi and the Prophet reincarnated in 1884. Instead of the 'jihad of the sword', he preached fear of God, respect for rulers and parents, purity, conjugal fidelity, and the use of the Wolof language.[159] In the 1940s, Muhammad Jumat Imam declared himself Mahdi and Messiah in Ijebu, a Yoruba region much influenced by both branches of the Ahmadiyya. Seeking to bring Muslims and Christians together in a new 'religion of the spirit', the movement was initially dominated by the poor and marginal.[160]

Integrating former slaves

Sufi orders were particularly well equipped to deal with the social and religious problems of former slaves. These became acute when abolition was enforced around the world from the late nineteenth-century. In sharia terms, ex-slaves became clients of their former owners. The relationship was in theory perpetual between families, although in practice it rarely extended beyond three generations.[161] The taint of servitude might be considered ineradicable, especially where racial prejudice intervened.[162] The belief that marriage partners should be socially equal was exploited to prevent marriages with former slaves, as in Mauritania.[163]

Freed persons reacted by creating their own organisations. Africans in nineteenth-century Istanbul formed mutual-aid lodges, under female leadership. They followed the religious cult of priestesses of the 'infant Lord', involving spirit possession, divination, and fetishes. Although a thin Islamic veneer was retained, pious Muslims were shocked. Sultans exiled priestesses, but lodges and their cults persisted, especially as official measures to care for former slaves were half-hearted and ineffective.[164] Similar cults in other

---

[158] Noer 1973: 150–1; Bousquet 1938: 20–1.
[159] Azumah 2001: 185–6.
[160] Clarke 1995.
[161] Hunwick 1992: 30; Forand 1971; Mitter 2001.
[162] Jwaideh and Cox 1989: 47–8; Jaussen 1948: 60–1; Loyré-de-Hauteclocque 1989: 104, 113.
[163] Ould Ahmed Salem, forthcoming.
[164] Garnett 1891: II, 415–7; Hanimefendi 1994: 71–5.

cities, for example in Tunisia, Morocco, and Albania, met with episodic repression.[165]

Sufi orders took up the task of steering former slaves more firmly into the Islamic fold. To attract former slaves of African descent, adepts invoked the memory of Bilal b. Rabah, the Ethiopian freedman who acted as the *muezzin* of the Prophet. Ecstatic rituals and indigenous customs drew criticism from some ulama.[166] Mauritanian brotherhoods had most success in attracting those who had been freed the longest.[167]

Ahmad Bamba Mbacké (d. 1927), a Wolof teacher, placed more emphasis on material factors. A Qadiri from the late 1880s, he founded Senegal's Murid [Mouride] order around 1905.[168] Opposing the 'jihad of the sword', he attracted slaves and ex-slaves to cultivate groundnuts in rural communities, where complete equality reigned between disciples.[169] Despite caustic French comments that Murid disciples became slaves of their autocratic shaykhs, one informant recalled the attraction of leaders 'who did not categorize people as masters and slaves'.[170] That said, Ahmad Bamba never explicitly denounced servitude, and on one occasion ordered the return of a slave to his masters, as property rights could not be violated.[171]

In the Horn of Africa, Somalia's main orders, especially the Ahmadiyya, Salihiyya, and Qadiriyya, formed similar large agricultural settlements. Ex-slaves, whose position as clients of former owners was disadvantageous, flocked to join these establishments.[172] A certain ecological division of territory was possible, as agricultural settlements were often in areas infested by tsetse flies, and hence unattractive for Somali pastoralists.[173]

Of Kenyan Sufis it was written that their 'popular teachings challenged the political élite's hegemony in religious matters, and legitimised the social and economic aspirations of those excluded from power'.[174] The best known was Sayyid Salih bin 'Alawi Jamal

[165] Erdem 1996: 173–4; Montana 2004; Mansour and Harrak 2000: 36–43; Larguèche 2003: 337–8; Vlora 1911: 45–6.
[166] Dermenghem 1954: 261–94; Michaux-Bellaire 1910: 426; Hunwick 1992: 28; Schroeter 1992: 206; Christelow 1985a: 121; Rahal 2000.
[167] Kamara 2000: 284.
[168] Vikør 2000: 449.
[169] Searing 2002: 47, 102, 130–6, 180–3, 246–8; Cruise O'Brien 1971: 38–57.
[170] Moitt 1989: 44–5.
[171] Searing 2002: 247–8.
[172] Cassanelli 1988: 322–3; Trimingham 1965: 238–44.
[173] Salvadei 1927: 166–7.
[174] Morton 1990: 183–5.

al-Layl, or Habib Saleh, who came to Lamu from the Comoros around 1880. Unusually he allowed those not descended from the Prophet to join the exclusive 'Alawiyya brotherhood, at least as ordinary members. Known as the 'saint of Lamu', or the 'sharif of the coconut cutters', he persuaded former slaves and masters to frequent the same mosque, and allowed singing and dancing. The renown of his Riyadha religious school and mosque radiated over East Africa and Arabia, and his disciple, 'Abdallah Ba Kathir, took the message to South Africa.[175] That said, Habib Saleh is said to have owned slaves, and to have employed some to build his mosque and school.[176]

'An egalitarian brand of Sufi mysticism' developed around Bagamoyo, 'attracting ex-slaves with dancing and elaborate celebrations of the Prophet's birthday'.[177] A former slave from the Congo, Yahya b. 'Abdallah (d. 1931), known as Ramiya, obtained an initiation from the Middle East, and spread the Qadiriyya from 1905. He made a fortune in trade, followed in the footsteps of his former owner as governor of Bagamoyo, and dabbled in nationalist politics. He was a model of assimilation through Sufism, symbolically transcending the past by becoming a Qadiri shaykh on a par with Rumaliza, the Omani former slave trader.[178]

In the Lake Malawi area, a woman of servile origins was prominent. Mtumwa binti 'Ali b. Yusufu (d. 1958) was born of a slave mother and a free Swahili father. Allegedly she married a District Commissioner, studied in Zanzibar, and became a Qadiri shaykh. She returned to Lake Malawi to spread the Qadiriyya, although her position was usurped by an Arab in the 1930s.[179]

Zanzibar and Pemba provide a rare example of social incorporation that may have failed. From 1908 a Qadiri shaykh, Zahor Mohammed, spread his peaceful message of economic and social justice among the numerous former slaves, accounting for 85 per cent of the population according to the 1895 census.[180] This did not prevent the massacre of some five thousand Arabs in the revolution that followed independence in 1964, in a welter of rhetorical denunciations of the iniquities of Arab slaving. However, the lead-

[175] Zein 1974: 117–43.
[176] Romero 1997: 99–102, 168–9.
[177] Glassman 1991: 294–5.
[178] Constantin 1987: 85–9; Pouwels 1987: 198; Vikør 2000: 448.
[179] Constantin 1987: 87–8, 96.
[180] Fair 2001: 19–20, 29–30, 90–1, 152–3.

ing rebels were migrants from the mainland, rather than descendants of former plantation slaves.[181]

Holy wars have caught the imagination of many authors, and might appear to have been exhaustively investigated. However, some 'progressive' writers ignore the issue of slavery, whereas others use servitude as a stick with which to beat Muslims. Reality was more finely balanced. Many charismatic leaders initially displayed emancipatory tendencies, which need to be better understood. Conversely, the changing nature of enslavement illustrated the old adage that all power tends to corrupt. It would be helpful to identify religious factors in this process, such as the adoption of literalist or traditionalist interpretations of the sharia.

The experiences of quietist mystics and millenarians are much less well explored. These people would repay closer examination, for some continued earlier traditions of succouring the oppressed and the poor. To what extent this involved taking a position against slavery remains uncertain. The influence of millenarian sects is particularly hard to ascertain, especially as they were often treated as heretics by mainstream believers.

Revolutionary Mahdism is an intriguing topic, especially for an understanding of the religious beliefs of slaves themselves. Transcending the existing sharia, so that justice could fill the earth, made it possible to desert an owner while remaining a Muslim. Even though the end times failed to materialise, the legacy of religious revival may have perpetuated critiques of slavery. Apart from the Satiru case, other forms of Mahdism may have acted as ideologies of self-liberation.

Much work remains to be done on how mystics and millenarians shaped the Islam of ex-slaves and their descendants. Many authors have noted the lack of polarisation around former slave status in the Islamic world, which contrasts with the distressing legacy of servitude in the West. Sufi orders profoundly influenced this outcome in the Maghrib and Sub-Saharan Africa, but there is currently a complete lack of information for the rest of Islamdom.

[181] Bennett 1978: 265–8.

9

LITERALISM

There was a recurring tendency for Muslims to adopt a literalist reading of Quran and Hadith, rejecting schools of law, sects, mystics, millenarians, and all other dubious innovations. This meant minimising abrogation, analogy, and the consensus of the learned. Literalists were called 'people of the Hadith' from early times, as the traditions tended to loom larger than the Quran in their approach. The terms fundamentalist, Islamist, restorationist, or *salafi* (faithful to the pious ancestors), are less satisfactory, for rationalists, analysed in the following chapter, shared the urge to return to the founding texts.

It took the eighteenth-century Wahhabi movement in Arabia to make literalism the official ideology of a state. Wahhabi adherents sought to return to the social and political models of the Prophet's Medina. To the extent that they accepted schools of law, they followed the Hanbali line. The power of a sultan was tempered by consultation and social egalitarianism, and the restoration of a universal caliphate was their ultimate goal. Hatred for mystics and sects was intense, matched by intolerance of the West and its modern ways. Holy war was the way to cleanse Islam.[1]

More modernist interpretations emerged in the twentieth-century. The Muslim Brothers, created in Egypt in 1928 by Hasan al-Banna (1906–49), spread across the Arab world. Mawlana Sayyid Abul Al'a Mawdudi (1903–79) developed related doctrines in South Asia, culminating in the creation of the Jama'at-i Islami in 1941. Less nostalgic for the times of the Prophet, and less hostile to Sufism and sects, these groups selected what seemed best from the schools of law. Receptive to education and technology, they stressed political mobilisation. Elections were acceptable, although parlia-

---

[1] Ruthven 2000: 265–8.

ments should neither challenge the sharia nor confer high office on women, schismatics or unbelievers. Islamic states within national boundaries were acceptable as the building blocks for an Islamic confederation.[2]

Slavery was a conundrum for literalists, because it was both canonical and inegalitarian. A routinised representation of servitude permeated the Hadith literature, the Prophet had owned slaves, and they featured in the Medinan state. Embracing the sharia as the law of the land, the Wahhabi movement found it difficult to accept international pressure for abolition. For the disciples of al-Banna and Mawdudi, clinging to the embarrassing institution hampered mass mobilisation.

From the 1970s a greater number of Muslim statesmen began to contemplate making the sharia the law of the land, raising the problem of servitude. Ideologues argued that secular regimes had sold the pass by abolishing slavery, and scrutinised international treaties for compatibility with the sharia. However, leaders of Islamist regimes knew that reinstating slavery risked raising a storm of international condemnation. No government had yet dared do so at the time of writing.

To complicate matters, new forms of literalism erupted onto the world scene from the 1990s. Those associated with Usama b. Ladin called for global and continuing jihad against 'Crusaders and Jews', recalling earlier notions of permanent revolution. While influenced by the Muslim Brothers, their espousal of violence was in line with Wahhabi traditions.[3] This strand of Islam side-stepped the problem of slavery, despite the need to determine the fate of captives taken in holy war.

The first Wahhabi state and its wider impact

Muhammad b. 'Abd al-Wahhab (1703–92) preached a literalist form of Islam in central Arabia from 1736. Adepts called themselves Muwahhidun, or Unitarians, but the name Wahhabi stuck to them. The Saudi family adopted these beliefs in 1744, and imposed them over much of the Arabian peninsula by force of arms. Hostile to Sufi, Ibadi, and Shi'i Muslims, they conquered the holy places of Islam in 1802–4. They wrecked the installations around the Prophet's grave in Medina, in protest at 'idolatrous' practices of asking for intercession with God.[4]

[2] Roy 1994: 35–47; Ruthven 2000: 307–22, 327–34; Nasr 1996.
[3] Roy 1994.
[4] Peskes 1993; Sabini 1981.

Wahhabi forces sometimes enslaved the dependants of Muslim foes. When they turned on Oman in 1800–3, Abu Nabhan Ja'id b. Khamis al-Kharusi, a leading Ibadi scholar, complained: 'The Wahhabi religion calls for Muslims to kill each other and declares other Muslims who do not adhere to its doctrines as polytheists, allowing the plunder of their goods, the enslavement of their women and children, the taking of booty, and the imposition of poll tax and land tax'.[5] Wahhabi forces sacked the city of Karbala in 1801, smashing the sacred Shi'i tomb of Imam Husayn, and slaughtering men of fighting age.[6] They withdrew with many captives, although some were ransomed.[7] In 1817, 'Abdallah b. Sa'ud (r. 1814–18) said of his neighbours: 'All these people are our enemies, and by the Almighty aid, wherever we may find them or their people we will assuredly slay the one and seize the other'.[8]

Other strategies towards fellow Muslims were deployed. Qasimi raiders of the Trucial Coast, adherents of the Wahhabi creed, were notorious for killing every soul on board captured vessels in the Gulf.[9] In contrast, on taking the holy cities of Islam in the early 1800s, commanders guaranteed the safety of the urban population, aware that the eyes of the Muslim world were upon them.[10]

Enslaving infidels raised no concerns. Sa'ud b. 'Abd al-'Aziz himself owned several Abyssinian concubines, 'as was the custom of the great men of Najd'. A Christian woman was among those taken in a raid on Syria in 1810, although she was later released. Wahhabi leaders disrupted caravans bringing slaves to the holy cities during their campaigns, but made no systematic attempt to hinder the trade.[11] Qasimi shaykhs, negotiating with Britain in 1820, defended the purchase of Africans.[12] Wahhabi objections to Syrian Christians and Jews buying slaves from Muslims, or hiring slaves belonging to Muslims, reflected established literalist concerns.[13]

Nevertheless, aspects of slavery conflicted with Wahhabi beliefs. Disliking pompous titles, they 'call each other brothers: this is the name by which the master addresses the slave, and with which in

---

[5] Bhacker 1992: 40.
[6] Sabini 1981: 67; Corancez 1995: 21.
[7] Litvak 1998: 121–2.
[8] Rashid 1981: 54.
[9] Bhacker 1992: 40, 58.
[10] Sabini 1981: 68–9; Peskes 1993: 318; Corancez 1995: 53, 61.
[11] Sabini 1981: 80, 82.
[12] Nicholls 1971: 231; Adam 1840: 81.
[13] Corancez 1995: 97–101.

turn the servant replies'.[14] Wahhabi rulers rejected administrative and military slavery, non-existent under the Prophet but increasingly prominent in the Hijaz from the 1770s.[15] Salim b. Hilal al-Hariq, commanding their forces in eastern Arabia, was allegedly a Black slave, but he was probably a freedman.[16] Eunuchs were a further source of disquiet. On taking Medina in 1804, Sa'ud b. 'Abd al-'Aziz laid a heavy fine on the chief eunuch, and exiled many of those who looked after the Prophet's tomb, although a few were allowed to remain.[17] Homosexual practices, popularly associated with eunuchs, were repressed.[18]

Expelled from the holy places by an Egyptian army in 1812–13, and comprehensively defeated by 1818, Saudi forces regrouped in the Najd region of central Arabia, where Turki b. 'Abdallah b. Sa'ud (r. 1823–34) restored a smaller state. He 'gained economically from the flourishing slave trade', straining relations with Britain from the 1840s.[19] By 1870, it was estimated that up to a third of the population of parts of this state consisted of Blacks, although many were free and enjoyed complete social equality.[20]

The spectacular capture of the holy places, at the dawn of the nineteenth-century, made Neo-Sufis receptive to Wahhabi ideas, albeit rejecting the antipathy towards mysticism and saints' tombs. The leaders of West Sumatra's Padri Wars from 1803 were strongly influenced by returning pilgrims, who had witnessed the capture of Mecca.[21] Usuman dan Fodio, nemesis of the Hausa city-states of West Africa from 1804, was also susceptible to Wahhabi ideas.[22] As was shown in Chapter 8, such leaders protested against the enslavement of free Muslims, and yet themselves enslaved 'bad Muslims' and Animists on a grand scale.

Influenced by Wahhabi doctrines, the South Asian Ahl-i-Hadis (people of the Hadith) clung to the obligation to wage holy war against the infidel, and considered slavery to be legitimate.[23] Siddiq Hasan, prominent in this movement and prince consort of the autonomous state of Bhopal, attacked progressive South Asian views on

[14] *Ibid.*: 16.
[15] Burckhardt 1993: 223–6; Corancez 1995: 101–2.
[16] Bhacker 1992: 41.
[17] Burckhardt 1993: 344; Marmon 1995: 106; Sabini 1981: 69, 82.
[18] Corancez 1995: 97–8; Sabini 1981: 143.
[19] Winder 1965: 60, 89, 216, 218.
[20] Berlioux 1870: 311–13.
[21] Dobbin 1983: 129–41.
[22] Levtzion 1987: 33.
[23] Hunter 1964; Ahmad 1966: 17, 336–7; Metcalf 1982: 36–43, 47–52, 264–83.

slavery. He justified the institution by referring to Quran and Hadith, and himself manumitted a male slave in Mecca.[24] In 1885, a newspaper accused him of importing female slaves, contributing to his political downfall.[25] The Begum, ruler of Bhopal, declared that the slaves had been obtained to gain religious merit by freeing them.[26]

Saudi Arabia

The Saudi family temporarily lost power in 1880, but 'Abd al-'Aziz b. 'Abd al-Rahman al-Sa'ud (Ibn Saud, r. 1902–53) revived the dynasty's fortunes.[27] After conquering 'Asir and the Hijaz between 1924 and 1926, he made the sharia the law of the land.[28] Himself the owner of an estimated 3,000 people, he distributed slave girls to his close collaborators.[29] The Dutch consul in Jidda reported in 1923 that Hijazi people saw slavery as a 'sacrosanct institution of Allah'.[30]

British representatives pressed 'Abd al-'Aziz on the issue, arguing that slaves had not been captured in properly constituted jihads. He admitted that the institution was 'barbarous', but feared that ulama and the people would not countenance the ending of the slave trade, let alone slavery. By the Treaty of Jidda in 1927, he agreed to co-operate in repressing the infamous traffic, and yet continued to levy import duties on slaves. When informed in 1928 that slaves were sold by pilgrims, he replied that slaves 'lived like beasts' in their homelands, and were better off in servitude. The British retaliated by retaining the right to manumit slaves fleeing to their legation.[31]

Despite 'Abd al-'Aziz's attempts to hide behind the ulama, some Meccan scholars of the mid-1920s were prepared to limit enslavement narrowly to capture in holy war and descent from a servile mother.[32] The chief qadi of the Hijaz even said that the 'general consent of the Muhammadans' would be sufficient to abolish slavery.[33] The ulama of the Hijaz were still a cosmopolitan group at this stage, far from being entirely won over to Wahhabi ideas.

[24] Claudia Preckel, personal communication.
[25] Metcalf 1982: 268–9, 278–80.
[26] Leitner 1893: 17.
[27] Ruthven 2000: 4–6.
[28] Hodgson 1974: III, 280; Ruthven 2000: 5–6, 58, 267–8.
[29] Rihani 1928: 151–3; Miers 1989: 119.
[30] Schmidt 1992: 71.
[31] Miers 1989: 116–19; Miers 2003: 179–83; Piscatori 1986: 71.
[32] Rutter 1928: II, 90–4.
[33] Rutter 1933: 323–4.

British consular personnel in Jidda thus sought to influence delegates arriving for the 1926 Congress of the Muslim World in Mecca.[34] The task was not always easy, for one Yemeni delegate arrived 'with a large retinue of retainers and slaves'.[35] Arnold Toynbee claimed that the congress, affected by 'humanitarianism', passed an 'antislavery resolution'. This statement was later repeated without qualification, although Toynbee indicated that the resolution actually called for a commission of enquiry to report on whether slavery in the Hijaz contravened the sharia.[36] The preamble stressed that the Prophet cursed anybody who sold a free person, and that no free Muslim should be reduced to servitude. The importance of freedom in Islam was stressed, as well as the need to ensure that sharia rules were observed.[37] However, no commission appears ever to have sat or reported.

Pressure grew, for the League of Nations complained that the pilgrimage was a major source of slave trading.[38] Renaming his state Saudi Arabia in 1932, and seeking to join the League of Nations, 'Abd al-'Aziz promulgated new regulations in 1936. Imports of slaves by sea were prohibited, because the sharia banned enslaving or buying subjects of countries in treaty relations with Muslims. Slaves could still come overland, but only with proof of their servile status. All owners and slaves were to be registered. Liberation was promised to those enslaved in ways contrary to the sharia after the foundation of the kingdom in 1926. Slaves were to be well treated, and could insist on buying their freedom.[39]

This decree was patchily enforced, especially as oil wealth boosted demand.[40] Saudi Arabia sucked in Baluchi children from the Iran-Pakistan borderlands, Nusayri girls from the Syrian mountains 'sold like cattle', and even local Arabs.[41] Within Oman, slave raiding broke out to seize Blacks and Persians belonging to rival tribesmen.[42] Eunuchs were retained in the holy places.[43] Prominent

---

[34] Confidential Print, FO371/11446.
[35] Kramer 1986: 111.
[36] Toynbee 1927: 317; DeJong 1934: 141; Gordon 1989: 47.
[37] Sékaly 1926: 201; *Oriente Moderno*, 1926, 6/7: 358.
[38] DeJong 1934: 130.
[39] *Oriente Moderno*, 1936, 16/11: 633–6; Nallino 1939: 241–3; Lewis 1990: 167–8; Miers 2003: 254–60.
[40] Greenidge 1958: 50–4.
[41] Maugham 1961: 1–3; Laffin 1982: 61–3; Phillips 1966: 87–93; Miers 2003: 270, 305, 307, 343, 347–8.
[42] O'Shea 1947: 56–7, 171–2, 177; Wilkinson 1987: 282.
[43] Marmon 1995: 107–11.

exiles in Egypt, including a trade union leader and 20 dissident princes, vociferously criticised these abuses.[44]

The end came suddenly in late 1962, when Prince Faysal b. 'Abd al-'Aziz took effective power from his more conservative elder brother. Faysal already seems to have played a leading role in pushing through the 1936 regulations.[45] He expressed a marked distaste for slavery as early as 1935, and never bought any himself. He freed all his remaining dependants in 1956, even though Saudi Arabia failed to endorse the United Nations Supplementary Slavery Convention of that year.[46] He told a Western journalist that some two-thirds of slaves in the kingdom had probably lost their freedom in non-scriptural ways.[47]

Addressing the newly formed council of ministers in 1962, Faysal declared:

> The attitude of the Shari'a towards slavery and its keen interest in liberating slaves is well known. It is also known that any slavery existing at present fails to fulfil many of the Shari'a conditions laid down by Islam to allow slavery. ... The government now finds a favourable opportunity to announce the absolute abolition of slavery and the manumission of all slaves.

Compensation was promised to 'deserving' owners, and the prince's words were broadcast over the state radio.[48] No specific legislation followed, and the proclamation was not everywhere immediately enforced, but substantial indemnities were paid over the next few years.[49]

While Faysal appears to have been relying on the doctrine of doubtful provenance, widely utilised by Sunni ulama, Norman Anderson argues that this was a rare instance of public interest overriding the sharia in Saudi Arabia, for reasons of state.[50] Faysal may also have obtained a ruling from the ulama that slavery should be 'discouraged' in Islam's fivefold ethical scale, a tactic employed by the regime on other occasions.[51] Malise Ruthven calls the proclamation an 'innovation', but notes that 'this is sanctioned in the Quran'.[52]

[44] Laffin 1982: 69–72; Segal 2001: 201.
[45] *Oriente Moderno*, 1936, 16/11: 633.
[46] Miers 2003: 255, 349.
[47] Awad 1966: 121.
[48] Gaury 1966: 151, 155.
[49] Laffin 1982: 71–3; Awad 1966: 121–3; Miers 2003: 350.
[50] Anderson 1976: 186.
[51] Piscatori 1986: 124.
[52] Ruthven 2000: 268.

Freeing slaves was not universally accepted by Wahhabi believers in Arabia. There were those who complained that 'Abd al-'Aziz and his successors had crushed the Brothers who brought them to power, and progressively diluted literalist doctrines. These purists gained confidence in the 1990s, as aged princes seemed increasingly unsure of how to prop up the regime. In 2003, an opposition group in the United States cited a highly placed cleric stating that, 'slavery is part of Islam. Slavery is part of jihad, and jihad will remain as long as there is Islam'. Those who considered slavery to be illegitimate were simply 'infidels'.[53]

The Muslim Brothers

The Muslim Brothers generally rejected the embarrassing institution, finding it an obstacle to propaganda among educated urban youths. However, they were hesitant, and often put forward justifications of past slavery, notably stating that Muslims could retain slaves as long as their enemies did so. One writer on warfare vindicated this position by citing 2:194 in the Quran: 'Whoso commits aggression against you, do you commit aggression against him'.[54]

Hasan al-Banna, the founder, side-stepped the issue in an article originally published in 1948, and much reprinted thereafter. He elaborated at length on the conditions under which holy war could be waged, stressing defensive aspects, but leaving open the possibility for aggressive campaigns. When it came to slaves, he said that 'we will talk about them in detail on another occasion. For now it suffices to say that Islam replaced the historical sentence for a captive from capital punishment (death) to life imprisonment through enslavement. However, Islam has made it very easy for the slave to regain his freedom'.[55] As he died the following year, it seems that al-Banna never elaborated on this ambiguous formulation.

The most famous ideologue among the Muslim Brothers was Sayyid Qutb (1906–66), executed by the Egyptian government.[56] In the first volume of an Arabic commentary on the Quran, he declared Islam to be in principle opposed to slavery. Those already in bondage at the time of the Prophet had rapidly been freed, but enslaving of prisoners of war remained necessary if infidels refused

[53] <http://www.arabianews/english/article.cfm?qid=132&sid=2>
[54] <http://www.islamonline.net> Fatwa Bank, 1 June 2003.
[55] Banna 1997.
[56] Ruthven 2000: 307–22; Choueiri 1997: 135, 140–3.

to give up the institution. Muslims should not be apologetic about past forms of servitude, for they were not responsible for rulers abusing the harem system.[57] This account failed to address the legitimacy of enslaving conquered populations.

In *Social justice in Islam*, first published in 1945, Sayyid Qutb cited a Hadith of the Prophet that, 'people are all equal as the teeth of a comb', but failed to address slavery in a section entitled 'human equality'. He quoted Taha Husayn's criticism of 'idle aristocrats' for whom 'all the work was done by their imported slaves', but only to lambast élite corruption. Without citing any authority, he described raiding for plunder as a legitimate and routine aspect of Islamic economies. The Prophet's prohibition of castration was mentioned, but not imports of servile eunuchs. Apologetic snippets addressed the ban on enslaving free Muslims, manumission, good treatment, and the social integration of former slaves. Rather lamely, he declared slavery to be irrelevant, as 'this practice has now disappeared, owing to the circumstances of our time'.[58]

Sayyid's brother, Muhammad Qutb, tackled the issue more squarely, albeit equally ambiguously. He devoted a long and early chapter to slavery in *Islam the misunderstood religion*, published in Arabic in Cairo in 1964, and reprinted many times thereafter. English editions appeared in Delhi in 1964 and in Kuwayt in 1967, and later on the internet.[59] Although Muhammad Qutb eventually left the Muslim Brothers, siding with moderate elements after the assassination of Anwar Sadat in 1981, his views on slavery are still widely quoted.

Muhammad Qutb at first seemed to condemn slavery, attacking Communists for seducing Muslim youths by portraying Islam as reactionary and feudal because it sanctioned slavery. Indeed he stated that this is 'perhaps ... the most odious form of doubt exploited by the Communists'. He further denounced the 'vicious crimes' perpetrated 'by some Muslim rulers in the name of Islam', including enslaving Muslims and trading in slaves, contrary to 'perfect equality among men'. However, he went on to demonstrate the superiority of slavery in Islam over all other historical forms, and stated that Muslims were obliged to enslave captives taken in war against infidel nations. He noted 'in passing' that 47:4 in the Quran recommended the freeing of prisoners of war. As unbelievers took

---

[57] Youssef Choueiri, personal communication.
[58] Kotb 1970: 44, 47–9, 112–13, 136, 156–9, 214.
[59] Qutb 1967; Gunasekara n.d.: 27; Rawat 1985: 343; <http://www.islam4all.com/islamand.htm>

slaves, Muslims did likewise to prevent the maltreatment of captives in infidel hands. When non-Muslim nations decided to abolish slavery, 'Islam welcomed it'. He then appeared to double back, suggesting that Muslims were still slaves to capitalist bosses, Communist bureaucrats, and colonial officials.[60]

Most disturbing was a long passage on concubines. Muhammad Qutb claimed that sexuality in the West was reduced to adultery and prostitution. In contrast,

> Islam made it lawful for a master to have a number of slave women captured in wars, and enjoined that he alone may have sexual relations with them ... [and] that these slave women would belong to their masters only; they were to provide for their maintenance, feed and safeguard them from falling prey to such a depravation, gratifying their sexual needs, along with satisfying their own, in a clean respectable manner.

He concluded that 'there is nothing common in this filthy abominable trade in human bodies [in the West] and that clean and spiritual bond that ties a maid to her master in Islam'.[61] The transitions from 'slave' to 'maid' and from past to present tense are striking, although both may spring from faulty translation.

Moderates in this tradition, such as Tunisia's Rashid al-Ghannushi (born 1941), stressed liberty. Influenced for a time by the Muslim Brothers, he embraced democracy from 1981, and published a book on civil liberties in 1993. While failing to mention slavery explicitly, he endorsed personal freedom, and rejected violence. The book was dedicated to such literalist luminaries as Sayyid Qutb and Mawdudi, and yet it simultaneously paid homage to a curious medley of liberal and rationalist Islamic figures.[62] The papers of a conference held in Tunis in 1985 opposed slavery, but presented an apologetic portrait of its history in Islam.[63]

The Muslim Brothers gained great political influence in the Sudan, where Hasan 'Abdallah al-Turabi (born 1932) became the regime's *éminence grise* from 1989 to 2000. Even though the new Sudanese penal code of 1991 failed to recognise slavery as licit, Arab militia units took and sold slaves, during attempts to crush non-Muslim southern rebels. Accounts of de facto enslavement prolifer-

---

[60] Qutb 1967: 62–99, 101–5, 110.
[61] Qutb 1967: 105–7.
[62] Hamdi 1998: 101–3, 108, 120–1, 181–2, 187–9.
[63] Toledano 1998: 142–52.

ated, for productive, domestic, and sexual purposes. Public auctions of children were reported.[64] Quizzed on this in 1994, al-Turabi answered evasively that slavery had never been a 'substantial institution' in the Sudan before the Egyptian occupation, and that all men were equal in Islam.[65]

Al-Turabi's most famous disciple was Usama b. Ladin, a Saudi of Hadhrami origins, based in the Sudan from 1989 to 1996.[66] He then moved to Afghanistan, where the Taliban regime declared that it 'did not feel bound by UN human rights instruments, recognizing only the Shari'a'.[67] To be sure, Bin Ladin denounced slavery in an open letter to Pakistani Muslims in 2001, but only as part of a long list of evils attributed to the enemies of the faith.[68] In the aftermath of the Western destruction of the Taliban regime, there were reports of Afghan exports of slaves to Pakistan, with some boys allegedly sent on as camel jockeys to the United Arab Emirates.[69] Unverified reports in the Western media stated that a radical literalist preacher promised to present the womenfolk of defeated foes to holy warriors.[70]

Mawdudi and Hamidullah in South Asia

Abul Al'a Mawdudi [Maududi], the leading South Asian neo-literalist, was intransigent on the subject of slavery. In articles originally written around 1935, and published in English in 1972, he violently denounced Islamic timidity. 'The Europeans ... found fault with slavery, and the Muslims averred that it was absolutely unlawful in Islam'. He upbraided Muslims for being ashamed of slavery, holy war, polygyny and other fundamental aspects of their faith, unaware that to alter any part of Islam was to undermine the entire religious edifice. He censured exaggerated notions of liberty emanating from the Enlightenment and the French Revolution, causing licentiousness in the West.[71] Mawdudi also alleged that slavery in Islam was greatly superior to its counterpart in the West.[72]

[64] Burr and Collins 2003: 75, 276; Jok 2001: viii–ix, 2–3, 28–33, 126, 164; Segal 2001: 216–20; Collins 1992: 155–9.
[65] Miller 1996: 129, 160.
[66] Burr and Collins 2003: 69–73.
[67] Ruthven 2000: 395.
[68] <http://groups.yahoo.com.group.KashmirForum/message/1702>
[69] See Bushell 2002.
[70] Channel 4, 'Dispatches', 13 April 2003.
[71] Maududi 1972: 20–2, 28, 218–19.
[72] Nasr 1996: 168.

Al-Ash'ari, the editor and translator of the 1972 text, apparently
embarrassed by one of Mawdudi's outbursts on the subject, inserted a rare footnote. Without denying the legitimacy of the institution, he explained to the unwary reader that Islam strictly forbade
enslavement, except for prisoners of war, and then only as a 'necessary evil'. Moreover, Islam treated slaves humanely and encouraged
manumission.[73]

Mawdudi refused to retreat from this position. Through one of
his followers in the 1970s, he ridiculed the idea of setting infidel
captives free, as this would allow them to fight once more against
believers, and would prevent exchanges of prisoners.[74] In an undated talk, he held that not only war captives but also 'their womenfolk' were legitimately enslaved.[75] Two years before his death,
Mawdudi chided 'people who denounce Muslims day and night for
recognising the institution of slavery'. Slaves were humanely treated,
and could rise in society, in contrast to Muslims in Christian hands.
At best, Mawdudi nudged the debate in an emancipatory direction
by interpreting the Prophet's saying forbidding the enslavement of
a free man as applying to free people of any religion.[76]

As in so many Islamic debates about slavery, concubinage loomed
large. In one purple passage, Mawdudi proclaimed the harem to
be, 'the last place of refuge where Islam guards its civilisation and
culture, ... the strongest fortress of the Islamic civilisation, which
was built for the reason that, if it ever suffered a reverse, it may then
take refuge in it'.[77] He taught that the Prophet had owned at least
one concubine, and believed that male Muslims could own an un-
limited number.[78]

In a lecture first given in 1939 Mawdudi also reprimanded his
Muslim opponents for restricting jihad to defensive conflicts, in
their anxiety to rebut Western accusations. Holy war could legitimately be waged to spread the message of Islam across the world,
though political power was the goal, not the forcible conversion of
infidels.[79] He berated proponents of defensive jihad as defeatists,
betraying the principles of Islam. Peace treaties with polytheists
were void, and revolution might be necessary to establish God's sov-

[73] Maududi 1972: 21.
[74] Sarwar Qureshi 1983: 15–16.
[75] <http://www.jamaat.org/islam/HumanRightsPolitical.html>
[76] Maududi 1977: 17–19.
[77] Khan 1972: 38.
[78] Sarwar Qureshi 1983: 28–32.
[79] Choueiri 1997: 143–4.

ereignty and law. At one point he exclaimed that 'Islam wants the whole earth'.[80] Muhammad Hamidullah (1908–2002), born and raised in southern India, was more restrained. Educated at Osmania University in Hyderabad, he proceeded to study in Germany and France, and taught in the Osmania law department from 1936. He went into exile in France in 1948, following the forcible annexation of the princely state of Hyderabad by the Indian army, and wrote numerous books and articles. He maintained relations with Pakistan, but resigned from the commission writing a constitution for the new country.[81]

In his doctoral thesis on Islamic law, written in German in 1935 and published a decade later in a revised English version, Hamidullah admitted that 'there is no verse in the Qur'an directly permitting enslavement'. He also opined that 'the Prophet had the emancipation of slaves so much at heart'. However, Hamidullah took the existence of slavery for granted, cited the Prophet's example in enslaving Qurayza women and children, and mused that the duty to spread the faith might well be executed through slavery.[82]

Two more books followed in the late 1950s, both originally published in French, of which the introduction to Islam volume proved immensely popular. Frequently reissued, it has been translated into a wide variety of languages. Hamidullah continued to treat slavery as a regular aspect of Islamic law, and justified it as a kind of social service. Enslavement in holy war provided shelter for the destitute who could not be repatriated, offering them the chance of education in Islamic surroundings.[83] There was silence on the descendants of slaves.

In the new Islamic country of Pakistan after 1947, ulama of the 'absolutist' type called for slavery to be reinstated, together with the sharia. The report into the Punjab Disturbances of 1953 particularly mentioned the wish to enslave enemy soldiers and keep concubines.[84] In 1977, when General Zia ul-Haqq seized power and began to apply the sharia, some seized the opportunity to argue that the need for manumission 'means that slavery cannot be abolished, since to do so would be to deny future generations the opportunity to commit the virtuous deed of freeing slaves'.[85]

---

[80] Peters 1979: 130–3.
[81] <http://www.islamonline.net/english/news/2002-12/20/article16.shtml>
[82] Hamidullah 1945: 204–13, 277.
[83] Hamidullah 1959: II, 461–4; Hamidullah 1979: 70.
[84] Ahmed 1987: 88, 103, 133, 156, 168.
[85] Elias 1999: 108.

Other expressions of literalism

Literalists elsewhere in Islamdom oscillated between moderate and absolute positions. Indonesia's Persatuan Islam [Persis] was a small but combative West Javanese ginger group, led from 1926 by Ahmad Hasan. Acquainted with South Asian literalists in Singapore, where he was brought up by his Tamil father, Ahmad Hasan implicitly accepted slavery in 1941. He stated that no deviation was possible from what was permitted and forbidden in Quran and Hadith 'with regard to temporal matters'. He further quoted a famous Hadith of the Prophet, according to which the faithful must obey constituted authorities, even if a Black slave were to be placed over them.[86]

West African literalists, influenced by Saudi Wahhabi scholars, accepted socio-economic inequality but were uneasy about slavery. Some even argued that a 'non-complacent' reading of Quran and Hadith implied monogamy, implicitly criticising concubinage.[87] Established families criticised Wahhabi reformers in northern Côte d'Ivoire for undermining the social hierarchy, in which slaves and members of castes were at the bottom of the heap.[88] One author cited Muhammad Qutb in a discussion of slavery in Nigeria, but ultimately favoured abolition.[89]

Participants in the Iranian Revolution of 1979 displayed uncertainty over slavery. Sayyid Mahmud Taleqani, the 'red ayatollah' who died shortly after the fall of the Shah, argued that Islam's commitment to social equality was antithetical to slavery, and that modern Muslims should reject the institution. Reducing fellow Muslims to slavery was a Sunni abuse, as was the slave trade. Nevertheless, it would have been counter-productive for Muhammad to have abolished the institution, and Muslims treated slaves better than adherents of other faiths. Taleqani even condoned enslavement in a properly constituted jihad.[90]

Despite his sobriquet of 'champion of the oppressed', Ayatollah Ruhollah Khomeini expressed fewer qualms in accepting slavery. He originally gave his imprimatur to a 'question and answer' book written by somebody else, in a hackneyed genre popular among leading ayatollahs from the 1950s. The 1982 edition contained numerous details on the conditions for the sale and manumission of

---

[86] Federspiel 1977: 55–6, 70–1.
[87] Kaba 1974: 127–9; Kaba 2000: 190.
[88] Launay 1990: 187, 196.
[89] Jumare 1996.
[90] Taleqani 1983: xii–xiii, 186–200.

human beings. In effect, slavery figured as an integral part of holy law.[91] In the same year, an edition of the English version of Hamidullah's introduction to Islam was published in the clerical centre of Qom.

Slavery became a practical question in Shi'i areas of Iraq, following the American invasion of 2003. Responding to pictures of the abuse of prisoners by American interrogators in Abu Ghraib prison, Shaykh 'Abd al-Sattar al-Bahadli, of Basra, declared in a Friday sermon in May 2004 that anyone capturing a female soldier could keep her as a slave. As a senior aide of the radical leader Moqtada al-Sadr, he represented a militant strand in Iraq's Shi'i constellation.[92]

The West and the web

Literalists in the West reflected divisions over slavery, albeit with a tendency to take a moderate line. In 1955, the editor of the *Islamic Quarterly*, published in London, considered slavery to be licit, even if it was 'the greatest shame in the history of humanity'. The Quran regulated the institution and the Prophet and his companions had owned slaves. To resolve this conundrum, he turned to the well worn tactic of pinning the blame on infidels for maintaining the institution.[93]

The Islamic Council of Europe was promoted from 1973 by the Islamic Secretariat of Jidda, and thus strongly influenced by Saudi Arabia. The council sponsored two conferences in London, in 1975 and 1980, during which human rights were cautiously tackled. The first conference was organised by the Islamic Foundation of Leicester, UK, giving rise to a volume entitled, *Islam: its meaning and message*. The second conference volume, *Islam and contemporary society*, included a 'Universal Islamic Declaration', which upheld individual freedom.[94]

Muhammad Qutb of Egypt, by this stage Professor of Islamic Studies at the King Abdul Aziz University in Mecca, advanced some sibylline statements on slavery. Twentieth-century *jahiliyya*, ignorance of God, had the consequence that, 'people must, unavoidably, be divided into masters and slaves'. However, he then glossed this metaphorically, to repeat his 1967 statement that people were

---

[91] Khomeini 1984: xvi, 86, 220, 254, 274, 278, 353, 354, 429.
[92] *Independent on Sunday*, 9 May 2004; *Financial Times*, 13 May 2004.
[93] Ghoraba 1955.
[94] Ahmad 1976; Azzam 1982.

enslaved by feudal lords, capitalist bosses, and Communist bureau-crats. He concluded: 'True freedom will be enjoyed only when the individuals strictly follow God's revealed laws and all become equal in their servitude to God, the Almighty'.[95]

Allahbukhsh Brohi, Minister of Law and Religious Affairs in Paki-stan in the 1950s, confronted servitude more directly and in a more obviously liberal spirit. He declared that 'Islam came to terminate the age of slavery', arguing that man could only worship God prop-erly if he was free. He also affirmed that Islam always had an 'evolu-tionary programme for the progressive realisation of the ideal of human liberty and freedom'.[96]

Mawlana Mahmud Ahmad Mirpuri, a Kashmiri, propagated South Asia's Ahl-i-Hadis movement in Britain, where he died in 1988.[97] A volume of his fatwas in English was published in Saudi Arabia, but typeset in England, in Birmingham. It included a query emanating from Bradford, a city with a large Muslim population, as to whether reformers were right to argue that 47:4 in the Quran had abrogated all other texts relating to slavery. More specifically, was it still legiti-mate to hold concubines, even though the chances of acquiring slaves in a jihad were nowadays so small? Mirpuri answered robustly that 47:4 in the Quran did not invalidate other canonical texts on slavery, but he prudently added two qualifications. First, 'Islam has tried to reduce slavery and gradually remove the *jahiliyyah* thinking on this issue'. Secondly, 'it is then up to the Muslim Rulers to de-cide according to necessity and circumstances how they will deal with such situations'.[98]

In 1987, Fadel Abdallah, a doctoral candidate at the University of Minnesota, cited the Qutb brothers in a confused and contradic-tory article. He claimed that after the death of the Prophet, 'in Ara-bia itself within forty years, except for temporary prisoners of war, slavery had disappeared'. Western Orientalists denigrated 'gover-nance and justice in Islam' in 'sugar-coated language', since 'a reli-gion that calls for equality cannot at the same time encourage and give religious sanctions to slavery'. However, he then stressed the impracticality of rapidly abolishing slavery, and justified the institu-tion as a means of conversion. More lyrically than convincingly, he concluded that, 'the issue of slavery is one, among many others, in

[95] Qutb 1982: 7–8.
[96] Brohi 1976: 93; Brohi 1982: 251.
[97] Claudia Preckel, personal communication.
[98] Mirpuri 1998: 202–4.

which one can appreciate in Islam a delicate and miraculous ideal-
ism effectively in practice'.[99]

The web site 'IslamOnline' took an ambiguous position in a
series of fatwas from 1999 to 2003, disowning slavery in principle.
Dr Yusuf al-Qaradawi, an Egyptian former member of the Muslim
Brothers, presented a bland and brief gradualist position. Dr Taha
Jaber al-'Alwani cited Caliph 'Umar b. al-Khattab rejecting the
enslavement of free people, but failed to note that this was long applied only to free Muslims. He also referred to the 'custom' of enslaving conquered women. Unnamed muftis considered that slavery
protected women, and described it 'an inevitable side-product of
combating the enemies of Allah'. Overall, there was a pervasive
refusal to apologise, combined with the argument that Muslim abolition hinged on enemies of the faith abandoning servitude.[100]

'Islam Questions and Answers' returned to the intransigence of
Mawdudi in its fatwas, issued from 1997 to answer questions that
revealed a persistent interest in acquiring concubines. These fatwas
drew mainly on two muftis. One, Muhammad al-Amin Mahmud al-
Shinqiti (1872–1932/3), was an Iraqi scholar of Wahhabi orienta-
tion. The other, Nasir al-Din al-Albani (1914–99), was an Albanian
trained in Istanbul, who migrated to Damascus and moved in Ahl-i
Hadis circles. Slavery was not 'in principle' desirable, and manumission was encouraged. Nevertheless, servitude was allowed when
taking infidel captives. Authors remonstrated with Muslims for
being ashamed of this aspect of their faith. Rights to seize non-
combatants and traffic in slaves were affirmed without scriptural
justification, and with no mention that other Muslims rejected these
propositions.[101]

It remains unclear whether Wahhabi leaders ever pronounced sys-
tematically on the issue of servitude. Deeper examination is needed
of the tensions that may have arisen from conflicting approaches
espoused by early reformers. Keen to stress comradeship between
owner and slave, and repudiating administrative and military slavery, they nevertheless failed to contest the legitimacy of the institution itself. Indeed, they even enslaved 'bad Muslims'.

[99] Abdallah 1987: 31, 46–7.
[100] <http://www.islamonline.net>
[101] <http://www.islam-qa.com>; information on Shinqiti and Albani from Claudia
Preckel, personal communication.

The Saudi state from the mid-1920s was caught between the hammer of Western hostility and the anvil of adopting prohibited innovations. Religious reactions to the abolition of the slave trade in 1936, and of slavery itself in 1962, would thus repay closer investigation. The extent to which Wahhabi adherents have continued to believe in the legitimacy of slavery since 1962 is a crucial question today, as the Saudi regime faces ever more determined opposition from literalists.

The tortuous and confused approach to slavery taken by modernising literalists deserves to be tracked down more carefully. The extent to which the Muslim Brothers jettisoned servitude, if only as a tactical move, needs to be established. Conversely, it remains to be determined why Mawdudi adopted such a resolutely pro-slavery position, and whether the Jamaat-i Islami and other movements consistently backed him on this controversial point.

As for those currently engaged in global jihad against the West, their attitudes towards slavery require clarification. Muslim opinion around the world has increasingly swung against slavery, making a defence of servitude embarrassing, and unlikely to be publicly aired. However, it might be possible to track down debates and attitudes through web sites and internal documents.

Overall, literalist positions appear surprising, given slavery's weak scriptural foundations. Reluctance to embrace abolition more ardently may spring from an unwillingness to admit that Muslims of the golden age sinned grievously in this respect, for a famous Hadith affirms that, 'my community will not agree upon error'. The paradox is all the more cruel for originating in Islam's precocious concern with slavery. The very frequency of references to the institution in Quran and Hadith becomes an argument for stating that what God has established no human can abolish.

10

RATIONALISM

Rationalists are sometimes called modernists, but the appeal to reason went back to the Mu'tazili tradition considered in Chapter 3. Differing from literalists by relying on the faculty of reason to renovate Islam's social and political teachings, many rationalists believed the Quran to be a created artefact, of which the 'spirit' was more important than the literal text. They held social regulations in the Quran to be valid only for the time of the Prophet, questioned the authenticity of numerous Hadith, and limited holy war to self-defence. Rather than wishing to return to an idealised golden age of the pious ancestors, they wanted Muslims to raise their societies to ever higher planes of submission to God's will.

Rationalists quickly split into two camps on the issue of slavery. Radicals endorsed abolitionism enthusiastically and unreservedly. The Quran, correctly interpreted, required the immediate ending of slavery. Vast numbers of Muslims had therefore failed to obey their God and their Prophet for centuries. Abolition was an urgent and imperative moral necessity, unrelated to Western demands. Gradualists, in contrast, thought that Muhammad had not found conditions propitious for immediate abolition. Complete emancipation was to be achieved by believers when the time was ripe, which normally meant the 'modern age'.

Secularism nearly overwhelmed both types of rationalism after 1918. Attracted by a wide range of fashionable ideologies, including Communism and Fascism, many thinkers relegated Islam to the sphere of family and folklore. They thus fought servitude as a purely social and political evil. However, late-nineteenth-century rationalist arguments about slavery were resurrected from the 1970s, as a 'neo-modernist' resurgence battled the secularist appeal.

The South Asian shock-troops of abolition

South Asian radicals, led by Sayyid Ahmad Khan [Khan Bahador] (1817–98), were the first rationalists unequivocally opposed to slavery. Sayyid Ahmad Khan was in London in 1869–70, where he was shocked by the strength of Western popular opposition to 'Arab slaving'.[1] To counter this dismal portrait, he first wrote in English in 1870. He asserted that Islam treated slaves well, citing Western authors. The Quran, 47:4, only permitted enslaving a prisoner of war, who should be ransomed or freed, unless the owner was 'unwilling to grant him his liberty'.[2]

A more determined assault in Urdu followed, characterised by a passion rare in his usually unemotional prose. From 1871, he published a set of articles in his periodical, subtitled in English, *Mohammedan Social Reformer*. In 1877, he published further letters on the topic, originally sent to Istanbul to influence the new Ottoman sultan. His 1871 articles came out as a book in 1893, under the title *Ibtal-i ghulami*, or 'the refutation of slavery'.[3] A vitriolic British propaganda campaign against the Sudanese Mahdi from 1885 contributed to this republication.[4]

In his Urdu writings, Ahmad Khan rejected any form of slavery for war captives, as 47:4 in the Quran only specified ransom or immediate release. He now boldly declared that 'set them free' was an absolute command, and that these 'freedom verses' could never be abrogated. Moreover, the injunction applied to all prisoners of war at all times. Slavery was contrary to the will of God, and the institution should have rapidly disappeared soon after the revelation of the Quran. This iniquitous system risked plunging both owners and slaves into deep immorality.[5]

No Muslim of his generation was as categorical or as zealous in attacking slavery as Ahmad Khan, and this was one of the three really novel aspects of his voluminous writings.[6] He expressly rejected the idea that slavery did not need to be discussed, because it had been abolished by colonial legislation in 1843–4. Instead, he argued that 'we have to be certain in our hearts that this practice

---

[1] Powell forthcoming.
[2] Khan Bahador 1979: 422–7.
[3] See Powell forthcoming; Muhammad 1969: 215–17.
[4] Ahmad 1967: 52.
[5] Powell forthcoming; Ahmad 1967: 51–2; Baljon 1970: 43–4; Muhammad 1969: 217; Dar 1957: 236–9; 258–60; Mujeeb 1967: 450–1; Ruthven 2000: 298.
[6] Baljon 1970: 143.

was contrary to the Islamic religion, and was in essence bad and unworthy'.[7]

Chiragh 'Ali (1844–95), employed in the southern princely state of Hyderabad, was a stout supporter. He penned an initial defence of Ahmad Khan in 1874, after virulent criticism by Sayyid Muhammad 'Askari of Kanpur.[8] In a book published in English in 1883, Chiragh 'Ali returned to the attack.[9] Stressing that 47:4 in the Quran had not been abrogated by later revelations, he devoted a long section to censuring 'fanatical Moslems' who defended concubinage, a topic that Ahmad Khan had rather neglected.[10] Two years later, in a book dedicated to Ahmad Khan, Chiragh 'Ali propagated a narrowly defensive concept of jihad. Challenging the authenticity of numerous traditions, he declared that slaves appeared in the Quran *de facto* rather than *de jure*, and that the command to free captives applied to all Muhammad's battles. He also went into considerable exegetical detail to refute traditions that the Prophet had ever owned concubines.[11]

Another valiant partisan of Ahmad Khan was Dilawar Husayn [Delawarr Hosaen] (1840–1914), from a Shi'i background.[12] A distinguished civil servant in Bengal, he wrote mainly in English, and his ideas circulated widely. Enthusiastic for science and opposing 'improvident habits', he overtly harked back to Mu'tazili ideas. In publications from 1876, he attacked slavery as one of the factors retarding Islamic civilisation around the globe. He wrote that,

> slavery is gradually dying away, and the sanction given to it by Islaam [sic] will not now save it from annihilation. In the present day slavery amongst the Mohammedan nations exists for the sake of concubinage, so that when slavery should be completely put down, concubinage would cease and disappear of itself.[13]

Progressive South Asian Muslims agreed, some being 'aghast at the discovery that a clear injunction of the Qur'an had been overlooked, and a whole code of law relating to slavery built up in a manner that betrayed the intention of making worldly interest override

---

[7] Avril Powell, personal communication.
[8] Powell forthcoming; Ahmad 1967: 52, 57, 63.
[9] Hardy 1972: 112–13.
[10] Ali 1883: xxxii–iii, 144–83.
[11] Ali 1885: 193–215.
[12] Walter 1998: 66.
[13] Delawarr Hosaen 1980: iii–vii, x, 24, 59–60, 65.

the word of God'.[14] Abolition was frequently placed alongside temperance, sanitation, and female education on reformist agendas.[15] Fear that young Indian Muslims might drift into secularism, or even socialism, prompted scholars to search for authentically Islamic principles of social justice.[16]

The debate died down from the turn of the century, but flared up again in the 1930s, when Sayyid Muhammad Hasanain Zaidi, a Shi'a of some repute, wrote that the Prophet had been survived by two concubines. This was fiercely contested by one Barakatullah, for whom 'concubinage is against the clear teaching of the Qur'an and the Hadith, and it is a libel on the Prophet to say that he had Rahaina and Mary for concubines'. Reformers, notably in Bengal, re-interpreted passages from the Quran as injunctions to free and marry a bondmaid, revising Muhammad's biography accordingly.[17] A scandal also broke out at this time, as Omani Arabs were caught kidnapping boys from Calcutta to sell in Arabia.[18]

Ghulam Ahmad Parwez (1903–85) was the most significant figure to carry the radical torch after independence in 1947, when he opted for Pakistan. He adamantly opposed demands that slavery be reinstated in the new Islamic country.[19] Criticising literalist and obscurantist ulama, he preached the primacy of Quran over Hadith, emphasised social justice, called for monogamy, and taught that slavery had been banned from the dawn of the new faith. He argued that references to slaves in the Quran should actually read, 'those whom your right hand possessed', in the past tense, and thus referring only to people already enslaved at the time of the Prophet's revelations. As for 47:4, it meant that 'the door for future slavery was thus closed by the Qur'an for ever. Whatever happened in subsequent history was the responsibility of Muslims, and not of the Qur'an'.[20]

Parwez was part of a broader movement in the subcontinent, and the Tolu-e-Islam organisation continued his work after his death.[21] Islamic Socialists questioned private property and labour exploitation. Hanif Muhammad Ramey, former chief minister of the Punjab

---

[14] Mujeeb 1967: 450–1.
[15] Powell forthcoming.
[16] Hardy 1972: 218–19.
[17] Bevan Jones 1941: 207–10; Zaidi 1935: 85–6, 89–91.
[18] Stark 1946: 249.
[19] Ahmed 1987: 133.
[20] Parwez 1989: 345–6.
[21] <http:/www.tolueislam.com>

and editor of a weekly publication, *Nusrat*, explicitly rejected slavery. These thinkers were fond of citing 53:38–40 in the Quran, 'that no soul laden bears the load of another, and that a man shall have to his account only as he has laboured'.[22] Concubinage was denounced as a root cause of Islamic decadence, together with polygyny and female seclusion. These ills were blamed on ulama, Sufi shaykhs, and literalists.[23]

South Asian abolitionists combed the Quran minutely for injunctions against slavery, for example, Hafiz M. Sarwar Qureshi in his attack on concubinage.[24] Brigadier Nazir Ahmed apparently translated 3:79 as, 'It is not meet for a mortal that Allah should give him the Book and the wisdom and "Nabuwah" [prophethood], then he should say to men: be my slaves rather than Allah's'.[25] Others render 'slaves' as 'servants' or 'worshippers', but Riffat Hassan, a Pakistani living in the United States, interprets this excerpt as condemning slavery.[26]

South Asian gradualism

Sayyid Amir 'Ali [Syed Ameer Ali] (1849–1928), a Shi'i Muslim from Bengal who travelled frequently to Britain, launched a somewhat less radical attack on slavery.[27] *A critical examination of the life and teachings of Mohammed* came out in 1873, denouncing servitude. Slightly revised in 1891 as *The life and teachings of Mohammed, or the spirit of Islam*, it was reprinted countless times thereafter, under the catchy title, *The spirit of Islam*. Amir 'Ali further attacked slavery in an influential legal text of 1880, *Mahommedan Law*, which went into numerous editions.

In famous words, often cited by later generations, Amir 'Ali wrote that,

> the Moslems especially, for the honour of their noble Prophet, should try to efface that dark page from their history—a page which would never have been written but for their contravention of the spirit of his laws. … The day is come when the voice which proclaimed liberty, equality, and universal brotherhood

[22] Jawed 1999: 105–12.
[23] Khan 1972; Sarwar Qureshi 1983; Khan 1996: 64–70.
[24] Sarwar Qureshi 1983.
[25] <http://www.central-mosque.com/fiqh/slav4.htm>
[26] Hassan 1995.
[27] Aziz 1968.

among all mankind should be heard with the fresh vigour acquired from the spiritual existence and spiritual pervasion of thirteen centuries. It remains for the Moslems to show the falseness of the aspersions cast on the memory of the great and noble Prophet, by proclaiming in explicit terms that slavery is reprobated by their faith and discountenanced by their code'.[28]

Amir 'Ali was most radical on the question of concubines, interpreting 5:7 in the Quran as an unqualified ban on cohabiting with slave girls. Muslim men were only permitted sexual access to women, 'in wedlock, and not in licence, or as taking lovers'. He bolstered his position by asserting that the Prophet had freed all women who came into his hands.[29]

On other aspects of servitude, Amir 'Ali was more circumspect. The Quran clearly disapproved of slavery, but, as temporal ruler, Muhammad could not abolish the institution overnight. This would have disrupted both society and economy, and might have turned Arabs against Islam. The Prophet thus ordered an immediate amelioration in status and treatment, and encouraged manumission, trusting that slavery would soon die out. Reflecting his Shi'i background, Amir 'Ali blamed the Umayyad 'usurper' Mu'awiya for authorising the purchase of slaves and the employment of eunuchs. Conversely, Amir 'Ali praised the Shi'i law-giver Ja'far al-Sadiq, Qarmati dissenters and Mu'tazili rationalists for raising their voices against slavery. To fulfil the Prophet's expectations, Amir 'Ali declared that, 'it is earnestly to be hoped that before long a synod of Moslem doctors will authoritatively declare that polygamy, like slavery, is abhorrent to the laws of Islam'.[30]

In his later writings, Amir 'Ali's condemnation of slavery became increasingly perfunctory, with little or nothing of the earlier ardour. Indeed, unpleasant racist overtones crept into some texts. At one point, he even criticised servitude because it had led to a degeneration of Muslims of the core lands, through admixture with 'lower races, such as Ethiopians'.[31]

His stature grew after his death, as the *Spirit of Islam* was constantly re-published and translated into many languages, but Amir 'Ali was often dismissed as a collaborator in his own time. He married an Englishwoman, and in 1904, moved permanently to Eng-

[28] Ali 1891: 380.
[29] *Ibid.*: 331–9, 349–50.
[30] Ali 1891: 330–1, 366–80; Ali 1917: II, 31–2.
[31] Ali 1899: 205.

land, where he was buried. Moreover, he was marginalised by his Shi'i origins, and his lack of formal grounding in the intricacies of traditional jurisprudence.[32] He wrote exclusively in English, and disdained debate with the ulama.[33]

Some South Asian Muslims took a gradualist approach to slavery without overt reference to Amir 'Ali. Sayyid Ahmad Khan's son, Sayyid Mahmud, the first Muslim Chief Justice of British India, was more of a gradualist than his father. In *The Pioneer* of Allahabad in 1878 Sayyid Mahmud declared that polygyny, divorce and slavery were 'as abominable to us as to Sir William Muir himself'. However, he drifted off into censuring biblical slavery, praising the good treatment of slaves under Muslim rule, and noting their ability to become sultans. On another occasion, in a legal judgement, he noted that slavery was no longer allowed by the British in India, and yet he proceeded to explain how it would have affected the case in question.[34]

Muhammad Iqbal (1877–1938), celebrated poet and 'intellectual father of Pakistan', condemned slave purchases in 1909, and admitted that slavery posed problems for Islam as a religion of social equality. However, his solution was to depict slavery in Islam as an institution so benign as to have nothing in common with true servitude:

> The Prophet of Islam ... declared the principle of equality and though, like every wise reformer, he slightly conceded to the social conditions around him in retaining the name of slavery, he quietly took away the whole spirit of the institution. ... The truth is that the institution of slavery is a mere name in Islam.

Iqbal justified his conclusion by uncritical references to social mobility, manumission, and the lack of social stigma pertaining to servile origins.[35]

Gradualist positions were manifest in Pakistan after 1947 and later in Bangladesh. Authors declared verses on servitude in the Quran to be 'contextual, revealed at a time when Muslims owned slaves, moving them toward a time when they would no longer do so'. What really mattered was the Quran's 'ethical standard in favour of equality between human beings', which precluded any return to

[32] Aziz 1968; Snouck Hurgronje 1906: II, 345–6.
[33] Hardy 1972: 105–7.
[34] Alan Guenther, personal communications.
[35] Iqbal 2002: 304, 307–8.

the embarrassing institution.[36] Professor Muhammad Usman, a leading Muslim modernist, took this position in a book published in Lahore in 1969.[37] Abdun Noor, professor at the University of Chittagong in Bangladesh, argued that social freedom was a religious obligation, while studiously avoiding the dreaded word 'slavery'.[38] Moiz Amjad, a Pakistani from Lahore, founded and co-ordinated the 'Understanding Islam' web site affiliated to the al-Mawrid Institute of Islamic Sciences. In response to a question on whether captives can be enslaved, posed in 2000, he began with the usual gradualist statement. However, he added two riders that significantly strengthened his position. Islam 'would never approve any steps that may, in any way, contribute to the reestablishment of the institution'. Moreover, Muslim nations were bound to honour international treaties regulating the treatment of prisoners of war.[39]

The great caution of Egypt

Deliberations stimulated by Western ideas of liberty were precocious in the Middle East, especially in Egypt.[40] However, these debates were initially conducted almost exclusively at the political level. Only gradually, and incompletely, did discussions spill over into considerations of social unfreedom.

Shaykh Muhammad b. 'Umar al-Tunisi [el-Tounsy], an immigrant from Tunisia, resided in the Sudan from 1803 to about 1820, and wrote accounts, translated into French, of the sultanates of Darfur and Wadai. He took part in Egypt's Greek campaign in the 1820s as 'regimental chaplain', administered a medical school in Cairo, and supervised translations from Western languages. In terms of enslavement, he noted that 'the Muslim inhabitants of the Sudan, in their raids on idolaters, do not obey what is prescribed by God's word. They never summon these idolaters to adopt Islam before attacking them'. Raids were preceded neither by peaceful proselytism, nor by repeated warnings of the consequences of unbelief. However, this did not invalidate enslavement, as infidels thereby became Muslims. In terms of servile conditions, large harems condemned women to 'enforced chastity', or encouraged them to commit adultery. Making eunuchs was reprehensible, but

[36] Elias 1999: 108.
[37] See Ahmed 1987: 156.
[38] Noor 2000: 441–2.
[39] <http://www.understanding-islam.com/related/text.asp?type=question&qid=653>
[40] Hourani 1970; Delanoue 1982.

blame lay with infidels who mutilated them, for Muslims employed castrati out of charity.[41] More prudent and parsimonious in his opinions was Rifa'a al-Tahtawi (1801–73), a Sayyid from a family of Shafi'i ulama. He was among the first batch of Egyptians to study in France, from 1826 to 1831. Working as a translator, he lauded political freedom, and called for social reform in many spheres. However, he remained almost entirely mute on slavery, despite living for some years as a virtual exile in Khartoum. His silence was only breached in three asides. In 1869, defending a restrictive definition of holy war, he criticised those who declared jihads 'to seize booty, enslave people, gain a reputation for bravery and glory, or seek the goods of this world'. In publications of 1870 and 1872 he further stated that a ruler had the right to force owners to free their slaves in cases of 'public calamity'.[42]

Other authors publishing in Egypt were only slightly bolder, or were socially marginal. 'Ali Mubarak (1824–93), an educational reformer and civil servant, studied in France. He condemned polygyny and concubinage in his 1868 book, and added tantalisingly that 'there would be much to say concerning slavery in our time'.[43] Fransis Marrash wrote an outspoken denunciation of slavery in 1881. However, the impact among Muslims was limited, for he was a French-educated Christian secularist from Aleppo.[44]

Muhammad 'Abduh (1849–1905), the most famous Arab reformer of his time, trod carefully on this controversial issue. He came to terms with British colonialism, serving as Grand Mufti of Egypt from 1899, but differed from South Asian reformers in coming from a poor rural background, cherishing his hard won status as an Islamic scholar.[45] This may explain why he was so coy in his most influential work, *The theology of unity*. The only clear reference to slavery comes in a rhetorical question: 'If religion eagerly anticipates the liberation of slaves, why have Muslims spent centuries enslaving the free?' This could be read as referring only to seizing free Muslims. His disappointing answer is that a careful reading of the Quran supports his interpretation, and that he will confound his critics in another book.[46]

---

[41] Tounsy 1845: viii–xi, 269–70; Tounsy 1851: 404–5; 467–90.
[42] See Delanoue 1982: 384–7, 398, 441, 458–9, 478–81; Hourani 1970: 68–83.
[43] See Delanoue 1982: 546–50.
[44] Hourani 1970: 247.
[45] Badawi 1978; Ruthven 2000: 301–5; Hourani 1970: 143; Crecelius 1972: 192–3.
[46] See 'Abduh 1966: 125, 135, 140, 152–4.

Nevertheless, 'Abduh's reputation for opposing slavery was noted by many authors.[47] Commenting on 2:177 in the Quran, where ransoming a slave was numbered among actions of true piety, he trod a fine line between traditionalist exegesis and modernist interpretation. He argued that manumission was a form of charity obligatory for the faithful. From this he deduced that freedom was the norm, indeed a necessity for the perfection of humanity. Only in exceptional cases could liberty be breached, and only in a transitory manner. In effect, he transformed captives into modern prisoners of war.[48]

In a fatwa, found among his papers after his death, 'Abduh also attacked concubinage. Muslims had abused this custom abominably for centuries, corrupting the ethics of the faithful. He accepted that concubinage could be a legitimate by-product of war, but he called on political and religious authorities to stamp out the practice in the name of public interest.[49]

When participating in a government desperate to prevent a British assault in 1882, 'Abduh sent a letter to Wilfrid Blunt, who was attempting to mediate.[50] This missive smacked as much of al-Nasiri as of Ahmad Khan:

> The present Ministry is trying hard to suppress domestic slavery. The Mohammedan religion offers no obstacle at all to this; nay, according to Mohammedan dogma, Moslems are not allowed to have slaves except taken from infidels at war with them. In fact they are captives or prisoners taken in legal warfare, or who belonged to infidel peoples not in friendly alliance with Mohammedan princes, nor protected by treaties or covenants. But no Moslem is allowed to be taken as a slave. Moreover, if a person is an infidel, but belongs to a nation in peaceful treaty with a Mohammedan prince, he cannot be taken as a slave. Hence the Mohammedan religion not only does not oppose abolishing slavery as it is in modern times, but radically condemns its continuance. ... A fetwa will in a few days be issued by the Sheykh el Islam to prove that the aboli-

---

[47] Hourani 1970: 156; Elbashir 1983: 14–15; Fredriksen 1977: 145; Brunschvig 1960: 38; Blunt 2003: 149–50, 222.

[48] Riad Nourallah, personal communication, summarising IV, 433, in 'Abduh's *Complete works* [in Arabic], edited by M. 'Amarah.

[49] Riad Nourallah, personal communication, summarising a 1927 fatwa in *al-Manar*, Jomier 1954: 231–2.

[50] Blunt 1907: 244; Hourani 1970: 110–11, 143, 155–6.

tion of slavery is according to the spirit of the Koran, to Mohammedan tradition, and to Mohammedan dogma.[51]

Understanding 'Abduh's position is rendered more difficult by
the intervention of his forceful disciple, Muhammad Rashid Rida
(1865–1935). An immigrant from Tripoli in Lebanon, who had
studied under Husayn al-Jisr, he arrived in Egypt in 1897. Rida
edited the widely disseminated Cairo journal *al-Manar* and the
multi-volume commentary on the Quran of the same name.[52] The
problems involved in knowing who thought what are illustrated by
an issue of *al-Manar* in 1905, in which Rida summarised the views
on servitude of 'Abd al-Rahman al-Kawakibi (1854–1902), a Syrian
reformer established in Cairo since 1898 and inspired by 'Abduh.[53]

In response to questions from readers around the globe, Rida
published opinions on slavery in *al-Manar* over several decades.
Generalising from this medley of statements, Rida held that there
was no longer a caliph, necessary to declare a holy war and testify
that the enslavement of captives was in the public interest. Even led
by a caliph, holy wars should be defensive. It was wrong to enslave
women and children in war, kidnap children, buy slaves from the
infidel, or fail to seek proof of servile descent. Moreover, freeing
slaves was the greatest offering to God. Sudden liberation would
have been disruptive in Islamic lands, but gradual abolition accorded with the spirit of Islam, and was the final goal of the faith. If
Muslim rulers had obeyed Quran and Hadith, slavery should have
died out within a few centuries. Amelioration in conditions of servitude paved the way for abolition, which rulers were at liberty to
decree in the public interest.

For all that, Rida's views were ambivalent, and probably became
more conservative over time. He recalled 'Abduh saying that men
should free and marry concubines, but commented that respected
jurists rejected this interpretation. Rida clung to the notion that
taking slaves in holy wars against infidel aggressors was licit, as long
as captives were not Muslims, Arabs, or close relatives, the latter a
stipulation of Hanafi law. Children had to inherit servile status
from both parents, a feature of Shi'i law. In 1922, he took the line
that Muslims were obliged to retain slavery if their enemies did so,
to improve their bargaining position. This argument was to typify
the approach of the Muslim Brothers. Towards the end of his life,

[51] Blunt 1907: 253–4.
[52] Kurzman 2002: 31, 77.
[53] See Ghazal 2003; Kurzman 2002: 151.

Rida even opined that servitude could be a refuge for the poor and weak, notably women, and could give all women a chance to bear children.[54] An associate of Rida and the son of a Circassian concubine, Ahmad Shafiq (1860–1940) tackled the topic in a more focused manner, albeit revealing many contradictions.[55] He studied politics and law in Paris, where he attended Cardinal Lavigerie's famous harangue on Muslim slavery in 1888. Shocked by the experience, Shafiq addressed the Société Khédiviale de Géographie in November 1890 and January 1891, and published his two talks as a short French book, *L'Esclavage au point de vue musulman*, in Cairo in 1891. He took a gradualist line, defending the 'mildness' of slavery in Islam, while noting that 47:4 in the Quran included a command to free captives. He considered international law to have superseded the sharia in determining the treatment of prisoners of war. Nevertheless, he clung to jihads against unbelievers as a licit way of making slaves, as long as wars were 'in the interest of Islam', and were preceded by a summons to either convert or accept Muslim rule. He conceded that this meant that few, if any, of Egypt's slaves had been properly enslaved. However, he went on to suggest that the West should support Egypt's efforts to create a vast African empire and convert its inhabitants to Islam, given that free Muslims were not to be enslaved.[56]

This little work was widely discussed and disseminated. Extracts were rapidly published in English in the *Egyptian Gazette*, and the whole book was translated into Arabic in 1892. It then appeared in Turkish in 1896–7, causing quite a stir.[57] Indeed, an Ottoman diplomat presented a copy of the French version to his Portuguese counterpart, smarting at international criticism of covert colonial slavery.[58] South Asians gained wider access to the book in an Urdu version in 1907.[59] The French edition was reprinted in Cairo in 1938, with a regretful acknowledgement that the author had never written the more extensive treatise that he had once planned.[60]

---

[54] Ghazal 2003; Jomier 1954: 231–2; Siddiqi 1982: 182; Eccel 1984: 416–17; Peters 1979: 126–7; Badawi 1978: 114; Hourani 1970: 142, 239; *al-Manar* 1909.

[55] See Powell 2003: 137, 145, 170; Kramer 1986: 121.

[56] Chafik 1938.

[57] Powell 2003: 145–6; Sagaster 1997: 31; Toledano 1998: 45.

[58] Powell 2003: 146; Duffy 1967.

[59] Avril Powell, personal communication.

[60] Chafik 1938.

The radicalisation of the Arab world

Some Egyptian followers of 'Abduh focused on a critique of concubinage. The writer Qasim Amin (1865–1908) called for monogamy in two controversial books, *The liberation of women* (1899), and *The new woman* (1900). He thus rejected concubinage by implication.[61] He had attended Ahmad Shafiq's talks on slavery in 1890–1.[62] Dedicating his 1913 Paris thesis to Qasim Amin, The Egyptian Sociologist Mansour Fahmy (1886–1959) called for the abolition of slavery, which had corrupted Muslim women. He subsequently lost his job at the university, because he had dared to criticise the Prophet, and was not reinstated till 1919.[63]

Al-Tahir al-Haddad (1899–1935), disciple of 'Abduh and shaykh of the great Zaytuna *madrasa* in Tunis, remained in the gradualist mould. In a book that rocked the religious establishment in 1930, he differentiated between the 'founding principles of Islam', including 'equality among human beings', and 'the contextual givens, such as real human situations and mind-sets rooted in the pre-Islamic era'. As situations changed, he thought it necessary to drop pre-Islamic relics, citing 'the example of slaves, of concubines, of polygamy, which do not come from Islam'.[64]

Two historians took a cautious line. Taha Husayn (1889–1973), the blind doyen of this profession in Egypt, objected to the abuse of slavery after the time of the Prophet, but without directly calling for emancipation.[65] Ali 'Abd al-Wahid Wafi [Elwahed], probably Egyptian, wrote a scholarly thesis on slavery in 1931, in French. While overtly confining his analysis to early Islamic times, he implicitly reproduced the premises of Shafiq's work.[66]

Arab authors fell into line with Amir 'Ali's ideas about the 'spirit' of Islam after 1945. Subhi Mahmasani, a lawyer wrote that slavery,

> was widespread in the early days of Islam and remained so until it was gradually abolished. Nowadays it is rare. The abolition of slavery is consonant with the spirit of the Islamic sharia, which ordered that slaves be well treated and urged their liberation in many situations. Therefore, no useful point would be served by elaborating on this point.[67]

[61] Ahmad 1963: 103–8; Hourani 1970: 164–70.
[62] Powell 2003: 145.
[63] Fahmy 1990: 9–12, 93–113, 159–60.
[64] Chater 1994: 46–7.
[65] Siddiqi 1982: 183; Hourani 1970: 326–34; Kotb 1970: 214.
[66] See Elwahed 1931.
[67] Mahmasani 1955: 196.

Radical South Asian ideas took longer to filter into the Arab world, but a new Arabic edition of Ahmad Khan's *Ibtal-i ghulami* stirred interest in 1958.[68] Two books accepting 47:4 in the Quran as a command for the cessation of enslavement followed, one in Beirut in 1965, written by the respected Syrian scholar al-Zuhayli. The other appeared in Kuwayt in 1972, apparently a doctoral thesis.[69] In 1962, Dar al-Tali'a, a left-wing Beirut publishing house, translated Sean O'Callaghan's sensational journalistic account of modern slavery in the Middle East.[70]

A 'second renaissance' swept the writing of history in politically progressive Arab countries at this time. Often publishing in Beirut, these authors lambasted Muslim élites for slavery, despotism and the oppression of women, excoriating self-serving and misleading glorification of the Islamic past. Refreshingly, these authors showed a willingness to apologise to past generations of slaves. They blamed the ulama for much that had gone wrong, expressing horror that some scholars continued to vindicate slavery. Courageously broaching the topic of race, writers such as Ahmad 'Ulabi and Faysal al-Samir evoked the ninth-century Zanj rebellion.[71]

Maghribi authors took up the radical torch. Habib Boularès, former Tunisian Minister of Culture and Information, accepted that the Quran did not explicitly prohibit slavery, but concluded that 'there is no doubt that the faith opposed it, founded as it is on the equality of all men before God'. The gradualist position was untenable, and Muslims had erred from the outset in concluding that they could keep slaves. His greatest ire was vented on literalists who still asserted that slavery was legitimate.[72] Fatima Mernissi, teaching sociology in Morocco, considered that Quran and Hadith established equality among the faithful, making slavery unthinkable. She accused Muslim men of having deployed a variety of 'linguistic and juridical tricks' to disobey God for centuries, even if some tried to improve the treatment of slaves.[73] In contrast, the Moroccan historian Milouda Charouiti Hasnaoui propagated a rather conservative gradualist line.[74]

[68] Brunschvig 1960: 38; Jahanbakhsh 2001: 38.
[69] Peters 1979: 148–9, 200; Ruud Peters, personal communication.
[70] Sivan 1978: 300; O'Callaghan 1961.
[71] Sivan 1978: 283–300.
[72] Boularès 1983: 114.
[73] Mernissi 1987: 188–92.
[74] Charouiti Hasnaoui 2000.

Progress in the Turco-Iranian world

Ottoman debates on servitude were markedly secular in nature, but sometimes demonstrated 'a fascinating cultural translation of Western-phrased opposition to slavery into Ottoman, but indeed Islamic, terms'.[75] Newspapers played a significant early role, although journalists initially reported without comment on abolitionism around the world. With a freer press from 1860, *al-Jawa'ib* (*The Replies*) called on the authorities to intervene against slavery in 1868.[76] This Arabic-language paper, which lasted from 1860 till 1883, was widely read in Islamdom, including in Inner, South, and Southeast Asia. The editor was the Lebanese Faris al-Shidyaq, possibly involved in abolition in Tunisia in the 1840s, and by this time professing Islam.[77]

A Young Ottoman paper published in Paris under the name of *Hürriyet* (*Freedom*) agreed in principle with *al-Jawa'ib*. Indeed, Ali Suavi, a leading Young Ottoman, lamented his inability to persuade the Shaykh al-Islam to issued a fatwa 'which considers the purchase and sale of slaves as disapproved of by God'. In 1888 he again appealed to the Shaykh al-Islam for such a fatwa. However, Ali Suavi also noted that 'wild tribes' were civilised through servitude. Moreover, he suggested that the chief problem was the treatment of ordinary Ottoman citizens as slaves.[78]

Intellectuals in Istanbul attacked slavery in novels, plays, and poems from 1860. Although Islam tended to remain in the background, some authors suggested that slavery was a pre-Islamic institution, wrongly retained by Muslims.[79] Ahmet Midhat, Abdülhak Hamit, and Sami Pashazade Sezai were the staunchest critics of servitude. Their mothers were Circassian slaves, and their reproaches concentrated on the personal tragedies of White concubines. However, they also condemned the illegal splitting up of families by sale.[80]

Fatma Aliye (1862–1936), a woman novelist from a conservative religious background, objected to concubinage in books appearing between 1891 and 1897. Unlike male authors, she projected a realistic portrayal of the hard and menial work involved in domestic servitude. However, she accepted the institution as legitimate in

---

[75] Toledano 1993: 48.
[76] Sagaster 1997: 29.
[77] Hourani 1970: 98–9; Chater 1984: 552; Berg 1886: 174.
[78] Sagaster 1997: 29, 33, 36, 41–2, 45.
[79] *Ibid.*: 157.
[80] *Ibid.*: 27–8, 153–7; Toledano 1998: 122–3; Toledano 1993: 49–52; Kandiyoti 1988: 38–41.

sharia terms, leaving documentary evidence of her own purchases of slaves.[81]

Whereas South Asian radicals failed in attempts to sway Ottoman counterparts, Sayyid Ahmad Khan greatly influenced Tatar Muslims, at least by the 1900s.[82] The leading rationalist of the Russian empire was a Crimean Tatar, Ismail Gaspirali [Gasprinski] (1851–1914). From 1883, he dedicated much of his time to running *Tercüman* (*The Interpreter*), a reformist newspaper read across the Turkic-speaking world.[83] In 1909 this newspaper published a plea to Young Turk revolutionaries in Istanbul, begging them to abolish slavery and thereby make the empire a model for the Islamic world.[84]

It was a Volga Tatar scholar, Musa Jarullah Bigi [Bigiyev] (1875–1949), who attacked slavery most fiercely. Born in Rostov-on-the-Don of a family of ulama, Bigi was educated in a Russian elementary school. He pursued Islamic studies from Egypt to India, coming under the influence of Muhammad 'Abduh. Back in the Russian empire, he studied law in Saint Petersburg, and taught in a reformist Islamic school in Orenburg. In a stream of radical publications, he called for a 'Protestant Reformation' in Islam, to the point of offending fellow rationalists. He lost his teaching post, the Ottomans banned his writings, and traditionalists branded him a heretic.[85]

In 1910 Bigi published a book in Tatar, containing some of the most ringing denunciations of slavery ever penned by a Muslim author. He summarised his views on the topic in another book, published two years later. Slavery was quite simply the greatest evil in the history of humanity. The Quran had forbidden all further enslavement, and had commanded that all existing slaves should be freed.[86]

Other Muslims of the Russian empire did not confront slavery so bluntly. Jadid reformers of West Turkistan merely criticised 'the practices of polygyny'.[87] Tatar militants proclaimed the freedom of the individual at three Islamic congresses in the revolutionary years 1905–6, two held in Nizhny-Novgorod [Gorky] and the other in Saint Petersburg. An All-Russia Muslim Congress rejected polygyny in May 1917, and appointed the first known woman qadi in Islamic

[81] Sagaster 1997: 82, 85–6, 153–4; Toledano 1998: 131; Findley 1995.
[82] Kanlidere 1997: 92–3.
[83] Kurzman 2002: 223–6.
[84] Zambaco 1911: 60–1.
[85] Kanlidere 1997: 52–6; Bigi 2002: 254–6; Rorlich 1986: 59–61, 214.
[86] Ahmet Kanlidere, personal communication.
[87] Khalid 1998: 222–3.

history, but most radical Tatars then drifted into the Communist Party.[88] In contrast, Bigi left Russia for a life of exile.[89]

Rationalist critiques took time to evolve in Iran. Persian intellectuals became aware of Ahmad Khan's attack on slavery through the 1958 Arabic edition.[90] 'Ali Shari'ati (1933–77), the son of a progressive teacher, was a highly popular lecturer, propounding left-wing Islam in Tehran from 1967 to 1973. Indeed, his audience extended well beyond Iran. He denounced slavery as one of the 'evils of class society' that 'true Islam' would overthrow.[91]

Southeast Asian metamorphosis

Munshi Abdullah raised the issue of slavery as early as the 1820s in Southeast Asia, but this was a flash in the pan. Working as an interpreter for Europeans in Malaya, he was horrified by conditions witnessed aboard a slave ship in Singapore. For him 'the man who owned these slaves behaved like a beast, shameless and without fear of Allah'. He continued: 'Had I been someone in authority, I would most certainly have punished the wicked man'.[92]

Al-Manar, widely read in Southeast Asia, revealed an incipient debate a century or so later. In 1930–1 Abdallah b. Nabitan, an Arab resident in Java, wrote that many slaves in his native Hadhramaut were of doubtful provenance, and not captives from among the unbelievers as required by holy law. He added, 'I do not believe that you are ignorant of the way in which they are enslaved'.[93] However, another reader declared in 1911 that 'years are spent abroad to study...the issue of slavery and other matters, which is completely in vain because none of these are practised in the Archipelago'.[94] A letter from Singapore in 1922, asking whether it was legitimate to buy Chinese girls as concubines from their families, showed how misleading the earlier letter was.[95]

Indian rationalism percolated into Indonesia in the interwar years, notably through the leader of Sarekat Islam from 1912, Omar Said Tjokroaminoto ['Umar Sa'id Cokroaminoto] (1882–1934).

[88] Kanlidere 1997: 74, 92–3, 136, 149, 155; Rorlich 1986: 63.
[89] Rorlich 1986: 214.
[90] Jahanbakhsh 2001: 38.
[91] Shari'ati 1979: 103–9.
[92] Abdullah 1970: 183.
[93] *al-Manar* 1909; Mona Abaza personal communication.
[94] Abaza 1998: 98.
[95] Ghazal 2003.

The scion of an aristocratic East Javanese family, he worked as an engineer in a sugar factory, and read English rather than Arabic.[96] His *Tarikh Agama Islam* (*History of the Islamic religion*) relied heavily on Amir 'Ali's *The spirit of Islam*, albeit omitting the section expressly condemning slavery. Tjokroaminoto also collaborated with Lahori Ahmadi missionaries, considered here in Chapter 8, on translating Muhammad 'Ali's commentary on the Quran, which was strongly critical of slavery. However, it is not clear how much of this project was completed.[97]

In a pamphlet first published in 1924, and often reprinted thereafter, Tjokroaminoto declared that the Prophet had desired to abolish slavery. There followed an apologetic description of the good treatment and upward social mobility that Islam provided for slaves, curiously containing no examples from Southeast Asia.[98] In newspaper articles of 1921 and 1929, however, Tjokroaminoto denounced Javanese nobles for their traditional practice of kidnapping 'good-looking women of common stock'. Sarekat Islam's 'Basic Principles' of 1921 and 1933 also included a commitment to release the people 'from any kind of slavery'.[99]

Muhammad Misbach, the 'Red Haji,' left Sarekat Islam in the early 1920s, to forge a short-lived synthesis between Islam and Communism. He attacked Muslim élites for shamefully exploiting their fellow believers since the death of the Prophet, and drew up a long indictment of their transgressions against the lower orders.[100] Takashi Shiraishi, the historian of Sarekat Islam, does not include slavery among these manifold forms of exploitation, but it would be surprising if Misbach had not included it.

Rationalists, often with higher education in the West, brought attention back to the topic of freedom after 1965, in the context of General Suharto's authoritarian rule in Indonesia.[101] Ali Yafie argued that the Islamic concept of 'public interest' made the United Nations' 1948 Universal Declaration of Human Rights acceptable to Muslims, including its strictures against slavery. Harun Nasution, the modernist intellectual known for his Mu'tazili views, referred to 'freedom from slavery' in 1987.[102] He used slavery as an example of

[96] Shiraishi 1990: 48–54; Noer 1973: 107–8.
[97] Noer 1973: 150–1.
[98] Tjokroaminoto c. 1950: 32–3.
[99] Noer 1973: 103, 130, 141–2.
[100] Shiraishi 1990: 262, 292.
[101] Riddell 2001: 230–60; Abdillah 1997.
[102] Abdillah 1997: 84–5.

legal rules in the Quran that were no longer relevant to contemporary society.[103]

Gradualist arguments were probably more common. Ahmad Azhar Basyir [Ba Ashir] (born 1928) at one time chaired the national board of Indonesia's Muhammadiyah. Of Arab extraction, he was partly educated in Cairo. In 1988, he stated that the Quran did not explicitly forbid slavery, due to 'the conditions of the social structure at that time'. Purchases of slaves from the infidel were unlawful, but Muslim captives in enemy hands would have suffered more had Muslims not taken slaves themselves. The abolition of slavery in secular law could never abrogate Quran and Hadith, but since these holy texts did not actually prohibit abolition, the faithful could relinquish slavery under present conditions.[104]

Ahmad Syafi Maarif, also from Muhammadiyah, stressed in 1985 that the 'right to life implies the right to life as a free man'. He cited the second rightly guided Caliph, 'Umar b. al-Khattab, 'Why did you treat the people as slaves, whereas they were born free from their mothers?' Maarif implied that this famous question applied to free persons in general, rather than just to free Muslims.[105]

Among Indonesian gradualists, Munawir Sjadzali [Syadzali] paid the most detailed attention to slavery. He obtained higher education in Britain and the United States, and, as Minister of Religious Affairs from 1983 to 1993, had texts used in sharia courts codified and published in 1991. Keen to 'reactualise' Islam for the modern world, Sjadzali rejected traditional views of slavery. Stressing that the social prescriptions of the Quran and the Prophet were only for their time, he singled out the second rightly guided caliph as a courageous example of adapting to change, albeit citing the rather unfortunate example of apportioning the spoils of war.[106] Overall, Sjadzali maintained that the Prophet encouraged manumission and good treatment, at a time when conditions were not yet ripe for abolition. In the modern age, with human beings in general agreement about condemning slavery, Islam should do likewise.[107]

Africa and the 'second message' of the Quran

Many African rationalists also chose the gradualist path. 'Abbas Ibrahim Muhammad 'Ali simply cited Amir 'Ali verbatim, and at

---

[103] Johan Meuleman, personal communication.
[104] Abdillah 1997: 86.
[105] Maarif 1985: 168–70.
[106] Effendy *et al.* 1998: 408–11.
[107] Abdillah 1997: 86; Muslimin 1998: 4.

considerable length, in his historical study of Sudanese slavery.[108] Ibrahima Kake, from West Africa, stated that Muhammad wished to alleviate slave conditions, and possibly to prepare the way for its disappearance.[109] Writing in Senegal, Amar Samb refused to interpret 47:4 in the Quran as an absolute and immediate prohibition on any further taking of slaves, while accepting that the institution was destined to disappear over time.[110]

The rationalist line was inflected in an original manner by an engineer and Sudanese nationalist, Mahmud Muhammad Taha (c. 1909–85). He developed his teachings after release from a British prison in 1951, publishing the first edition of his controversial work *The second message of Islam*, in 1967. The 'second message' referred to the radical social programme outlined in the early Meccan phase of the Prophet's revelations. Once in political control of Medina, Muhammad's revelations had become more apposite to ruling a community steeped in ancient traditions. However, Taha insisted that the Medinan verses had only postponed the implementation of the original Meccan teachings, without abrogating them permanently. Strongly influenced by Sufism, he saw the victory of the 'second message' as the achievement of a higher plane of consciousness, when mere believers would truly submit to God's will. President Ja'far Muhammad Numayri's regime reacted by sentencing him to death for apostasy in 1985, burying him in an unmarked grave.[111]

Despite the new twist that he imparted to rationalist arguments, Taha was no radical on slavery. On gradualist lines, he argued that the Prophet had been forced to compromise with a situation in which slavery was integral to social order. Taha also opined that the 'circumstances and human capacities of the time necessitated the propagation of Islam via methods including enslavement'. The disappearance of the need for slavery only arose with the triumph of 'second message'. Even then, Taha was surprisingly reticent when discussing this new phase, at best noting that 'slavery is not an original precept in Islam'.[112]

'Abdullahi al-Na'im, a disciple of Taha obliged to leave the Sudan in 1985 for the United States, was only slightly less cautious regarding the 'first message'. He attacked radicals for interpreting

[108] Ali 1972: 68–9.
[109] Kake 1979: 164.
[110] Samb 1980: 93–7.
[111] Taha 1987: 2–23; 31, 47.
[112] *Ibid.*: 137–8, 161–4.

47:4 in the Quran as a command for immediate abolition, given that numerous other verses regulated slavery, the Prophet and his companions possessed slaves, and the founders of the schools of law all accepted the institution. In terms of the 'first message', he concluded, 'slavery is lawful under sharia to the present day'.

However, al-Na'im developed the 'second message' more than his master in relation to servitude. This allowed 'modern Islamic law to implement the fundamental Islamic legislative intent to prohibit slavery forever'. It thus became abhorrent, and morally indefensible, for the sharia to continue to sanction slavery. Al-Na'im further pointed out that a persistent assertion of the legitimacy of slavery in holy law perpetuates derogatory stereotypes about former slaves and their descendants, legitimises 'secret practices akin to slavery', enhances discrimination against women, and complicates adherence by Muslim governments to international agreements for the eradication of servitude.[113]

Muhammad Khalil adopted an even more radical stance. He deplored Taha's unnecessary concession that the Meccan verses had ever been abrogated at all, even temporarily. Khalil cited the teachings of Najm al-Din al-Tufi, a thirteenth-century Hanbali jurist resurrected by *al-Manar* in 1906, for whom verses exhorting justice and mercy could never be abrogated. According to Khalil, public interest should always be the guiding principle, and slavery had thus not been legitimate since the time of the Prophet.[114]

Developments in the West

Rationalists found an early home in Europe, mainly in Britain. Gottlieb Leitner, a Hungarian who contributed to educational reform in the Punjab, founded the Oriental Nobility Institute at Woking, incorporating England's first mosque. Leitner echoed the gradualist line on slavery in a letter first published in a British newspaper in 1884, and republished in Woking in 1889. A second edition of this pamphlet came out in Lahore in 1893. Leitner added further examples to those of Amir 'Ali, citing the Prophet's saying that the seller of men was the worst of men.[115] Abdullah Quilliam, a leading British convert to Islam, took an anti-slavery position at about the same time.[116]

[113] Na'im 1998: 228–31, 234, 237.
[114] Khalil 2002.
[115] Leitner 1893: 16–19.
[116] [Quilliam] 1895.

The *Islamic Quarterly* of London adopted a gradualist line in the
1960s, breaking with earlier literalism discussed in Chapter 9.
W. 'Arafat, possibly the noted writer on Islamic mathematics of that
name, criticised jurists in 1966 for an obsession with detail that
made them miss the wider picture. He considered pro-slavery views
carefully, but praised Tunisia's pioneer abolitionists, and concluded that 'the complete liberation of all slaves is more in accordance with the spirit of Islam'.[117] A year later, Ali 'Abd al-Wahid
Wafi, returning to the topic of his thesis (see Elwahed 1931), argued
that slavery was an 'anachronistic remnant of an archaic past, and is
considered as a flagrant violation of human rights. ... These practices are absolutely contrary to the principles of the very spirit of
Islam'. His bibliography included an Arabic translation of Amir
'Ali's writings on slavery, edited by Mustafa al-Shak'a and apparently published in Beirut.[118]

Marcel Boisard (born 1939) a Swiss academic and diplomat sympathetic to Islamic reform, specifically proposed Amir 'Ali as the
voice of consensus on servitude. Stressing equality as the cornerstone of Islam, Boisard argued that the Prophet had personally
wished to abolish slavery. Muslims had only been able to achieve
this meritorious goal gradually, but Islam now rejected the institution.[119] Fernando Monteiro, who served in the Portuguese army in
northern Mozambique, called for the 'emancipation of man from
servitude', citing the injunction in 53:38–40 of the Quran 'that no
soul laden bears the load of another'.[120]

North America became the major focus for rationalist debates on
servitude. Many Muslim intellectuals headed for the continent,
often forced out of their own countries, as in the case of 'Abdullahi
al-Na'im discussed above. An earlier migrant was Majid Khadduri
(born 1908), from Mosul in Iraq. Coming to the United States in
the 1940s, he explored the evolution of the doctrine of holy war,
taking a gradualist line on its implications for enslavement.[121]

Gradualism generally dominated, as in the case of Fazlur Rahman (1919–88), perhaps the single most influential Islamic rationalist of modern times. He directed the Islamic Research Institute
of Pakistan from 1962 to 1968, but conservative elements obliged

[117] 'Arafat 1966.
[118] Wafi 1967: 74.
[119] Boisard 1979: 111–17;
[120] Monteiro 1993: 265.
[121] Khadduri 1984: 233–4; <http://www.washington-report.org/backissues/0796/
9607023.htm>

him to leave. Achieving international fame as Professor of Islamic Thought at the University of Chicago, he regarded slavery and the social position of women as examples of 'contingent' legal regulations in scripture, valid for their age only. The Prophet could not abolish slavery in his time, and the institution might even have provided protection for the weak. Nevertheless, both Quran and Hadith clearly exhibited the intention that abolition should be achieved when conditions were propitious.[122] Asserting that no 'intelligent and morally sensitive Muslim' could possibly argue in favour of slavery today, Rahman exclaimed, 'surely the whole tenor of the teaching of the Qur'an is that there should be no slavery at all'.[123]

African–American and feminist Muslims began to probe slavery in Islam from the 1960s. Amina Wadud, of African–American background, made waves for her radical opinions on women and other issues, including in South Africa and Malaysia. Wadud asserted that 'no Qur'anic precedent existed for the right of all human beings to live free from slavery'. The spirit of the Quran was opposed to slavery, but she considered that, as far as abolition was concerned, Muslims simply went along with Western decisions.[124]

Riffat Hassan, of Pakistani origins and teaching in the United States, maintained that 'the Qur'an does not state explicitly that slavery is abolished', despite citing Ghulam Parwez and 47:4 in the Quran.[125] In an earlier work she stated that the Quran merely fails to command that the institution should be continued.[126] However, one of her students adopted a more radical line, portraying the Quran as a 'one of the greatest anti-slavery books' and Muhammad as 'one of the greatest abolitionists'.[127]

An item in an internet discussion, citing one Nasiruddin to refute literalists, sums up the popular view:

Prophet Muhammad [...] stated that releasing a slave is an excellently good deed, hence it must be also a very good and valuable deed to liberate all slaves and to prohibit all slavery. I do not change *deen* [religion], because this is no subject of belief itself; it is a subject of politics, society structure and

---

[122] Rahman 1979: 38–9; Rippin 1993: 110–11.
[123] Rahman 1982: 19.
[124] Wadud 2000: 15.
[125] Hassan 2000: 244.
[126] Hassan 1995.
[127] Watson 2002.

Islamic law, and we Muslims are ordered by Allah [...] to enforce justice, hence we must seek to clear our society of injus-
tices, and slavery is an injustice.[128]

The broad lines of division between radical and gradualist approaches to abolition are easily perceptible, even if occasionally
blurred at the edges. However, the degree of support for each wing
is much less evident, in terms of geography, class and period. There
is a particular need to establish how the audience of the two camps
fluctuated over time.

Gradualist dominance of the debate was probably the rule in
most places and at most times, and the implications of this need to
be explored. Gradualism may have made anti-slavery ideas more
palatable to a wider stratum of Muslims, but such views denied
Islam a pioneering role in the unfolding of a global idea of social
freedom. Leaving infidels to determine the timing of abolition also
allowed for the theoretical possibility of a return to slavery.

Regional variations need to be probed further. What caused
South Asia to assume the lead is hazy. Sayyid Ahmad Khan, the
Islamic William Wilberforce, had an ardent commitment to ending
slavery, but the roots of his passion remain to be uncovered. Conversely, Muhammad 'Abduh and Rashid Rida did not contribute as
much to the rationalist cause as might have been expected. The *al-
Manar* project may have been less radical than has been alleged, or
slavery may have been a stumbling-block for particular reasons.
The poor showing by Turkey and Iran in the debate probably
reflected precocious secularism, but this needs to be demonstrated. Although distinctive critiques of slavery emerged in Africa,
Southeast Asia, and the West, their impact on the heartlands of
Islam remains uncertain.

---

[128] <http://www.jihadwatch.org/dhimmiwatch/archives/2004/06/002354print.
html>

11

TIMING AND COMPARISONS

Since the processes whereby most Muslims have come to recognise slavery as illegitimate have been so diverse, a final challenge is to determine whether these strands can be woven together into a coherent chronological sequence. The synthesis presented here is highly provisional. It is intended as a clarion call to stimulate further research on this neglected historical transformation.

Timing raises the further issue of comparison with other world religions. It is customary to draw a distinction between Christian sensitivity to slavery, and the ingrained conservatism of other faiths. In reality, acceptance of slavery lasted for centuries in all religions, and yet went hand in hand with doubts, criticisms, and occasional outright condemnations. The similarities between Islam and other creeds stand out as much as the differences. Every major community of believers was internally divided over the issue, with the possible exception of Hindus, for whom disagreements over Dalits played much the same role. At most, it can be suggested that Islam was quite precocious in questioning servitude, and yet something of a laggard in embracing abolition.

The dogged refusal by some Muslims to accept the modern consensus about the sinfulness of slavery is not unique, although surprisingly little is known about such strands in other faiths. Islamic minorities refusing to let go of slavery have perhaps been larger, or at least more vocal, than in other religions. At one level, this merely reflects the entrenched position of Islam across the great arid zone of the Old World, where environmental conditions have impeded the penetration of new ideas. However, a certain reluctance to let go of slavery also stems from a broader salience of traditionalism and literalism, in a faith which often perceives itself as singled out for persecution by a triumphant West.

The course of Islamic abolitionism

The first critics of slavery were sectarians, usually millenarians in the Isma'ili tradition. The only unambiguous process of abolition was that enacted by the Druzes in the eleventh-century. This had no obvious consequences for emancipation among the wider Muslim community, but sectarian views of slavery remain a somewhat obscure subject, and further research may hold surprises.

A second phase of Islamic unhappiness with slavery emerged from the sixteenth-century in 'gunpowder empires', this time emanating from enlightened despots and their religious advisers. Many reformers simply concentrated on clipping the wings of élite slaves. The usual explanation is that such slaves constituted an obstacle to political and military efficiency. However, royal collaboration with sharia-minded ulama has probably been underestimated. More work needs to be done on attitudes to élite slavery in the context of the wider desire to conform with holy law.

Some rulers went further, questioning the legitimacy of modes of enslavement. It is perfectly plausible to argue that this was intended to head off damaging rebellions, as reforms emerged mainly in areas where numerous subjects stubbornly refused to convert to Islam, as in the Balkans, India, West Africa, and Southeast Asia. Nevertheless, the possible religious wellsprings of these measures need to be scrutinised, especially as a deeper unease about servitude surfaced here and there, hard to explain purely in terms of social and political tensions.

Western diplomatic and military intervention, from the late eighteenth-century, was partly justified by a desire to suppress the slave trade and slavery. Writers desiring to portray anti-imperialist leaders as spotless heroes have thus tended to downplay violent Muslim reactions, or even deny them altogether. As the lustre of nationalism fades, examples of strong-armed defence of slavery need to be recognised more openly, and dissected more dispassionately.

Much less research has been undertaken on Muslims who took the opposite tack, believing slavery to be a deviation from the path of God, and therefore contributing to the community's weakness. From the 1870s, radical and gradual rationalists, together with moderate literalists and progressive ulama, could all be placed in the broad category of opponents of slavery, despite their manifold disagreements. In the present state of research, it is difficult to tell what audience they had among the bulk of the faithful. The greatest uncertainty concerns the beliefs of slaves themselves, especially when they imbibed millenarian ideas of justice filling the earth.

The majority of the faithful eventually accepted abolition as religiously legitimate, but pinpointing this crucial moment is difficult. Khaled Abou el-Fadl, writing at the dawn of the third millennium, is vague: 'Muslims of previous generations reached the awareness that slavery is immoral and unlawful, as a matter of conscience'.[1] Reuben Levy is probably overly optimistic in thinking that victory had been achieved by the 1950s, for examples of slave holding, and belief in the legitimacy of slavery, abounded in that decade.[2] The 1960s probably constituted the true watershed, when an Islamic accord against slavery triumphed, hastened by secularist agitation, and mainly informed by the cautious gradualism of Amir 'Ali.

The Organisation of the Islamic Conference (OIC) emerged in 1969, as an association of Muslim governments. The OIC financed a conference on human rights in Belgrade in 1980, co-sponsored by the United Nations Educational Scientific and Cultural Organization (UNESCO). The published proceedings asserted the right to freedom, and rejected the enslavement of prisoners and conquered peoples.[3] Representing 54 countries by 1990, the OIC published the 'Cairo Declaration on Human Rights in Islam'. Article 11a stated that 'human beings are born free, and no one has the right to enslave, humiliate, oppress or exploit them'. The authors hedged their bets, however, stressing that all human rights were subject to the authority of the sharia.[4]

There remains the tricky problem of estimating the size and influence of Muslim groups who refuse to accept the new consensus. Persistent manifestations of bondage in remote deserts could be dismissed as antediluvian relics of scant significance, but urban literalists are also calling for the restoration of slavery, considering the legitimacy of the institution to be engraved in God's law. Internet web sites defending such views show that this position is no mere archaic remnant in Islam.

Judaic approaches to slavery

Judaism is of special interest among world religions, because it probably exercised the greatest influence on early Islam. Slavery was as old as the Torah, and posed few problems as long as outsiders

---

[1] Abou El Fadl 2001: 269.
[2] Levy 1957: 88–9.
[3] Boisard 1985: 4, 107, 124.
[4] <http://www.humanrights.harvard.edu/documents/regionaldocs/Cairo_dec.htm>

were the victims.[5] Deuteronomy, 20:13–14, taught that 'when the Lord your God delivers [the city] into your hand, put to the sword all the men in it. As for the women, the children, the livestock and everything else in the city, you may take these as plunder for yourselves'. Leviticus 25:44 further allowed purchases of gentiles: 'Your male and female slaves are to come from the nations around you; from them you may buy slaves'.

Although holding Hebrew slaves grated with the founding story of liberation from bondage in Egypt, exceptions were made and safeguards were ignored.[6] Exodus 21:2–16 allowed the purchase of Hebrew children, but commanded the release of males in the seventh year of their bondage, and forbade kidnapping on pain of death. Deuteronomy 15:1–18 allowed self-enslavement, but called for the release of female as well as male slaves in the seventh year, together with the cancellation of debts. Leviticus, 25:10, further commanded that slaves be freed after seven times seven years, in the year of the jubilee.

The prophetic books criticised slavery. Isaiah, 61:1–2, trumpeted that God 'has sent me ... to proclaim freedom for the captives' and to 'proclaim the year of the lord's favour [the jubilee]'. Ezekiel, 46:17, also referred to freedom in the year of the jubilee. Jeremiah, 4:8–22, identified disobedience in releasing Hebrew slaves in the seventh year as causing the wrath of God to fall upon his people. Joel, 3:6, fulminated against the sale of Jewish slaves to Greeks, while Amos, 1:6 and 1:9–10, condemned the sale of 'whole communities of captives'.

Sects, flourishing around the beginning of the Common Era, took this a step further. The austere and pacifist Essenes, centred in Palestine, declared enslavement to be against God's will. Through John the Baptist, they may have influenced early Christianity. The Therapeutae, in Egypt, pronounced slavery to be contrary to nature. They probably reflected the ideas of Stoics and other Ancient authors, who opposed Aristotle's views on 'natural slavery'.[7]

Despite this sectarian ferment, rabbinical Judaism clung to slavery after the destruction of the Jerusalem temple. At best, rabbis were uncertain whether uncircumcised gentiles broke purity rules by residing in the household, whether efforts should be made to convert slaves, and what impact this might have on their servile status. At the same time, they tightened rules on manumitting Jewish

---

[5] Maxwell 1975: 23–5.
[6] Davis 1984: 85.
[7] Meltzer 1993: I, 44–5, 93–6; Quenum 1993: 16–18, 39–40.

slaves, to keep the community united. The twelfth-century Maimonides code recognised both Jewish and non-Jewish slaves, and the Genizah records of tenth- to thirteenth-century Egypt depict slavery as part of everyday life.[8] Early Modern rabbis debated whether it was right to hold 'Canaanite' gentiles as slaves, but Jews participated in Atlantic slave trading and slave production.[9]

The onset of Judaic repudiation of slavery came in the nineteenth-century, when some Jews were affected by Western abolitionist fervour. Moses Mielziner's closely argued German dissertation, written in 1859, circulated in abolitionist circles, but his views were hotly contested. The United States Jewish community split over the issue on broadly North–South lines, like their Christian compatriots. Even after legal emancipation in the United States, a minority of Jewish scholars 'continued to insist on the abstract lawfulness of human bondage as an ordinance of God'.[10] Jews in Islamic lands may have been particularly slow to take up the cause.[11]

Catholicism and servitude

Christianity, another model for early Islam, also accepted slavery. It was hard to draw social lessons from the allegorical parables of Jesus, even if Matthew 18:25 could be read as accepting enslavement for debt. In contrast, in Luke 4:18–19, Jesus cited Isaiah 61:1–2 in the synagogue at Nazareth, proclaiming the year of the jubilee and freedom for 'captives', the Greek word having the specific connotation of 'prisoners of war'. The teachings of the Gospels generally valued the poor and humble, but with no specific references to servitude.

Saint Paul exhorted masters to treat slaves kindly, for all were equal before God, but commanded slaves to obey their masters. Paul's letter to Philemon, returning a fugitive slave to his master as a convert, has often been taken as the most detailed example of this attitude. Although Paul placed slave traders among the wicked in 1 Timothy 1:10, the lack of any formal encouragement of manumission contrasted forcefully with Quran and Hadith.

The early church fathers took opposing positions. Origen (c. 185–254) approved of the Jewish freeing of slaves in their seventh year.

---

[8] Davis 1984: 88–92.
[9] Davis 1984: 94–101; Faber 1998; Schorsch 2000; Jonathan Schorsch, personal communication.
[10] Davis 1984: 82–4, 112; Korn (1971–2).
[11] Schroeter 1992: 203.

Saint Gregory of Nyssa (c. 335–94) condemned the ownership of human beings as contrary to divine and natural law. However, Christians listened more to the views of Saint Augustine of Hippo (354–430), who held that servitude was 'the just sentence of God upon the sinner', the fruit of both original and personal sin. Slaves taken in war were saved from death. Moreover, servitude accorded with civil law, was a guarantee of social order, and profited both slave and owner.[12] However Augustine recommended manumission, in the context of a strong tradition of people marking their conversion to Christianity by freeing their slaves.[13]

Controversy surrounds the role of Catholicism in the transition from slavery to serfdom, almost universal in northwestern Europe by the twelfth-century. The Church promoted the transformation, giving the example on its own extensive properties. Enslaving fellow Catholics was prohibited in 992, manumission was declared to be a pious act, and there was much contractual freeing after a fixed period, especially at the death of an owner. However, it remained licit to enslave heretics, Muslims, Jews, heathens, rebels against papal authority, clerics breaking their vows of celibacy, and those aiding the infidel. Popes themselves owned slaves, as did priests and clerical corporations. Canon law anathemised those who encouraged slaves to leave their owners, and incorporated aspects of the Roman law of servitude.[14]

There was even a certain revival of Catholic slavery from the thirteenth-century, with the revitalised study of Aristotle and Roman law. Saint Thomas Aquinas (1225–72), the great Dominican theologian, held the view that slavery was contrary to the 'first intention' of nature, but not to its 'second intention'. He relegated slavery to the family, outside the sphere of public law, and reiterated Augustine's points about the social utility of slavery and its origins in sin.[15] Saint Bonaventure (c. 1217–74), a weighty Franciscan contemporary, admitted slavery's validity in civil law and as a punishment for sin, and yet denounced it as 'infamous' and 'perverting virtue'.[16]

Catholic slavery thus went in curiously contradictory directions after the Black Death of the fourteenth-century. Northwestern Cath-

[12] Quenum 1993: 41–5, 49; Meltzer 1993: I, 206.
[13] Lengellé 1976: 14, 47.
[14] Meltzer 1993: I, 207, 211–12, 218; Lengellé 1976: 59, 74–6; Quenum 1993: 44–51; Maxwell 1975: 18–19; Heers 1981: 247–61; Heers 2003: 43; Stark 2003: 290–1, 329; Davis 1984: 51–60; Hernando 2000: 226–43.
[15] Quenum 1993: 47–9; Meltzer 1993: I, 211; Lengellé 1976: 14–15.
[16] Quenum 1993: 48.

2

olics replaced serfdom with wage work, tenancy, and sharecropping. Indeed, the soil of France gained the reputation of conferring freedom.[17] Northeastern Catholics eliminated the last vestiges of slavery, but participated in the rise of Eastern Europe's repressive 'second serfdom'.[18] Southwestern Catholics obtained fresh levies of Muslim, heretic, and Animist slaves, coming from the Black Sea, the Canary Islands, and Sub-Saharan Africa.[19] Only gradually, from the seventeenth-century, was this Mediterranean slavery restricted.[20]

It was southwestern Europeans who took over the New World, developing an even more flourishing variety of Catholic slavery, with helots from the Americas and Africa. Papal bulls sought to end Amerindian bondage from 1435, culminating in Paul III's three pronouncements in 1537 on protecting the subjects of Iberian kings. In passing, these texts also mentioned the rights of 'all other peoples'.[21] However, the same pope authorised the purchase and possession of Muslim slaves in the Papal States in 1548, 'for the public good'.[22] Jacques Bénigne Bossuet, Bishop of Meaux, fell back on Paul and Augustine in the 1680s to justify the monstrous new slavery of the Americas.[23]

The Holy Office of Inquisition pinpointed a central loophole in canon law in 1686, ruling that the right to freedom applied only to those who 'have harmed no one'.[24] Rodney Stark strangely fails to realise that this not only allowed the purchase of Africans and Asians taken in 'just wars', but even permitted the continuing enslavement of unsubdued Amerindians. Serious crimes, slave descent and the benefits of conversion were further adduced to authorise buying unbelievers. Baptism, which entailed freedom in Europe, mysteriously ceased to have the same effect overseas. A number of clerics spoke out against this cynicism, but they were ruthlessly silenced.[25]

The eighteenth-century Philosophes are usually portrayed as secularists, but they were mainly Catholics, who cited Christian texts in opposing servitude.[26] Charles de Secondat, Baron de Montesquieu

[17] Quenum 1993: 127; Stark 2003: 305–7.
[18] Hellie 1982: 696.
[19] Furió 2000; Renault and Daget 1985: 35.
[20] Davis 2003: 8–9.
[21] Stark 2003: 305–7, 329–32; Quenum 1993: 72, 79, 82, 98.
[22] Prud'homme 2002: 76.
[23] Lengellé 1976: 15–16.
[24] Stark 2003: 333.
[25] Quenum 1993: 86–90, 99–126, 139–42, 147–50, 162–4, 168–9; Prud'homme 2002: 76; Vila Vilar 1990; Pimentel 1995: 239–50; Marques 1999: 71–3.
[26] Quenum 1993: 159–60, 164–8, 185–6.

(1689–1755), saw no contradiction between his Catholic faith and his attack on slavery.[27] He launched his celebrated offensive chiefly on grounds of incompatibility with natural law.[28] In 1721, he put in the mouths of imaginary Muslim Persian visitors a satirical attack on Christian contradictions between growing freedom in Europe and spreading servitude in the Americas, associated with appalling mortality in the slave trade.[29] Among later major critics of servitude were two priests, Guillaume-Thomas Raynal (1713–96) and Henri Grégoire (1750–1831), who both fell foul of the Church for their political views.[30]

The trauma of the French Revolution made the Church intensely suspicious of liberty. However, Pope Pius VII, needing British backing for the return of the Papal States, condemned the slave trade in letters to the kings of France and Portugal, in 1814 and 1823 respectively. His delegates also signed the Congress of Vienna declaration of 1815. However, he quickly stifled incipient critiques of slavery in Swiss and German Catholic circles.[31] The employment of Muslim slaves in the Papal States lingered on, even if converts were automatically freed.[32]

Pope Gregory VI's landmark ruling in 1839, that methods of enslavement in Africa were unjust, was the first public Catholic rejection of the slave trade. It owed something to continuing British pressure, but Gregory VI had been head of Propaganda Fide from 1826, and had gained an insight into how the trade hampered evangelisation. The pope's failure to condemn slavery itself pleased pro-slavery Catholics, notably in the United States, which no longer relied on imports of fresh slaves.[33]

Papal condemnation of the trade did not cause Monseigneur Jean-Baptiste Bouvier, Bishop of Le Mans, to alter his treatise on moral theology, first published in 1834. Employed in Catholic seminaries around the world up to the 1880s, this textbook followed Aquinas in teaching that owning people was underpinned by scripture, canon law, civil law, and natural law. Self-enslavement was acceptable, and servitude was preferable to execution after defeat or for a crime. Slaves should be treated humanely, and emancipation

---

[27] Jean Ehrard, personal communication.
[28] Wirz 1984: 187.
[29] Montesquieu 1960: 159–60, 249.
[30] Quenum 1993: 190–6.
[31] Quenum 1993: 222–7, 232–6; Stark 2003: 343.
[32] Prud'homme 2002: 75–6.
[33] Quenum 1993: 48, 236–40; Marques 1999: 263; Vila Vilar 1990: 26.

was the ideal, but only through moral persuasion. Both slavery and the slave trade remained legitimate in theory, even if the latter might be rejected in practice for not conforming to the Church's rules.[34] Even progressive Catholics remained cautious gradualists, warning of social cataclysm if slaves were to be suddenly emancipated.[35] Radical French priests of the 1840s denounced inhumane conditions, rather than the institution itself.[36] Some abolitionist writings were relegated to the index of prohibited books, and Pope Pius IX referred to the curse of Ham afflicting Africans as late as 1873.[37] Catholic objections to Muslim eunuchs were undermined by the Vatican's own employment of castrated singers till 1878, even if they were free.[38] Alexis de Tocqueville noted acutely in 1831–2 that racism resolved the contradiction between freedom at home and slavery overseas, but only by 'inflicting a wound on humanity which was less extensive, but infinitely harder to heal'.[39]

The Catholic turning point of 1888 was not exempt from ambiguity. In that year, Brazil became the last Catholic country to end slavery in law, Cardinal Charles Lavigerie launched his crusade against slavery in Islam, and Pope Leo XIII addressed an encyclical letter, *In plurimis*, to Brazilian bishops. The latter opened with a reference to Luke 4:18–19, with captives interpreted to mean 'slaves' rather than 'prisoners'. However, the pope presented no reasoned refutation of traditional Catholic justifications for slavery.[40] Moreover, he called on missionaries to increase the practice of ransoming slaves, which risked intensifying the trade and corrupting clerical morals.[41]

Orthodox and Protestant dispositions

The views of Eastern Orthodox Christians have been little studied. Byzantine law codes from the sixth to the ninth-century modified the Roman inheritance by stressing the humanity of slaves, and by providing increased protection for them.[42] Saint Nilus of southern Italy (d. 1005), taught that Genesis 9:5–6 allowed for the enslave-

---

[34] Prud'homme 2002: 77–86.
[35] Davis 1984: 114.
[36] Prud'homme 2002: 85.
[37] Maxwell 1975: 14–17, 20.
[38] Croutier 1989: 129.
[39] Lengellé 1976: 54.
[40] Prud'homme 2002: 86–7; Quenum 1993: 240.
[41] Lazzarotto 1982: 46; Clarence-Smith forthcoming.
[42] Hellie 1993: 293–5.

ment of fellow Christians who committed murder, but his may have been an isolated voice.[43] Obdurate Muslims, as the descendants of Hagar, were natural slaves, and servile tribute may have been taken from Balkan Animists.[44] Individual clergymen could own slaves, but not clerical organisations.[45] However, the Byzantine Church recommended freeing converts.[46] From the eleventh-century, 'semi-feudal relations' largely replaced slavery, seen as 'an evil contrary to nature, created by man's selfishness', even if permissible in law.[47]

A few Russian priests and monks voiced opposition to slavery prior to the transformation of slaves into serfs in 1723, but the Church as such took longer to embrace freedom.[48] The clergy began to murmur against servitude as clerical serfs were being 'secularised' between 1701 and 1764, and as serfs came to be increasingly, if illicitly, sold independently from the land.[49] Old Believers, schismatics with millenarian and mystical inclinations, were even more hostile.[50] Some Russians, including serfs themselves, drew on the biblical story of release from Egyptian bondage.[51] From timidly opposing the abuses of owners, 'leading churchmen evinced growing disenchantment with serfdom' because it disrupted family and spiritual life.[52] Symbolically, the Archbishop of Moscow drafted the decree of liberation in 1861.[53]

The Eastern Orthodox church of Egypt appears to have hesitated for a long time before rejecting slavery.[54] A British official declared in 1881 that not a single indigenous Egyptian Coptic Christian opposed slavery. However, *al-Fayum*, a Christian newspaper edited by Ibrahim Ramzi, condemned buyers of slaves as 'barbarians' during a famous trial in 1894. Indeed, the paper stood alone in doing so.[55]

The allied Ethiopian Orthodox church adopted Judaic and Byzantine prescriptions of bondage, reflected in the thirteenth-century Fetha Nagast code. Clerics even gave credence to the Curse of Ham,

[43] Kazhdan 1985: 215.
[44] Kazhdan 1985: 218–19; Cahen 1970: 215–16.
[45] Hellie 1982: 75.
[46] Hellie 1982: 73–4; Kazhdan 1985: 218–19.
[47] Kazhdan 1985: 215, 219, 222–4.
[48] Hellie 1982: 585–6.
[49] Kolchin 1987: 38–9, 41–6, 225, 374–5.
[50] Nolte 2004.
[51] Moon 2001: 31–2.
[52] See Freeze 1989.
[53] Seton-Watson 1952: 43.
[54] Elbashir 1983: 70, 140; Baer 1969: 167.
[55] Powell 2003: 143, 154.

applied to 'real' Blacks.[56] Nevertheless, the Ethiopian church expressed occasional doubts about servitude.[57] Emperor Tewodros (r. 1855–68), a deeply religious monarch, banned the slave trade and tried to root out the enslavement of Christians. Repeated by his successors, the prohibition on slave trading remained a dead letter.[58] Measures against slavery proper, culminating in a 1942 decree under British military occupation, were patchily enforced.[59]

Protestants, emerging from the early sixteenth century, were initially preoccupied with assuring their own uncertain future. Trusting in faith rather than works, and often believing that only a finite number of humans would be saved, they merely reaffirmed the unacceptability of slavery on European soil. They tended to duck the question overseas, although a few early Spanish converts condemned the trade.[60] Protestant owners avoided the moral dilemma of possessing fellow Christians by delaying baptism till slaves were at death's door.[61] However, Pierre Jurieu (1637–1713), an exiled French Calvinist, wrote in the 1680s that an implicit pact between masters and slaves should govern the treatment of the latter.[62]

The millenarian and mystical Quakers initiated a radical attack in Pennsylvania in 1688. Valuing works and intuition as much as faith, they believed that the 'internal light' of Jesus overrode the letter of scripture, and that all wars were illegitimate. John Woolman (1720–72), an early environmentalist and evangelist of Native Americans, launched an uncompromising onslaught from the 1750s.[63] The Quakers proclaimed that owning slaves was sinful, citing Matthew 25:40, 'whatever you did for one of the least of these brothers of mine, you did for me'. From this they deduced that 'to enslave a "Negro" was to enslave Christ'.[64]

Shamed by Quaker activism, most Protestants shifted their perception from sin as slavery to slavery as sin, and preached this new gospel with fervour.[65] To back their campaign, they scoured the Bible, and interpreted both Isaiah 61:1–2 and Luke 4:18 as rejecting slavery. Their world was largely cleansed of servitude by the

---

[56] Hellie 1993: 294; Derrick 1975: 152; Greenidge 1958: 46.
[57] Moore-Harell 1999: 409.
[58] Trimingham 1965: 118–19; Renault and Daget 1985: 221.
[59] Greenidge 1958: 46–7; Derrick 1975: 152–4; Renault and Daget 1985: 221–6.
[60] Hellie 1993: 293; Schorsch 2000: 125.
[61] Quenum 1993: 104.
[62] Lengellé 1976: 15.
[63] Punshon 1984: 69, 115–19, 162–4, 167–8, 179–81.
[64] Stark 2003: 340–52.
[65] Hellie 1993: 292.

Union's victory in the American civil war of 1861–5, although a few theologians continued to maintain the legitimacy of servitude.[66]

From Hinduism to Confucianism

The roots of slavery stretched back to the earliest Hindu texts, and belief in reincarnation led to the interpretation of slavery as retribution for bad deeds in an earlier life. Servile status originated chiefly from capture in war, birth to a bondwoman, sale of self and children, debt, or judicial procedures. Caste and slavery overlapped considerably, but were far from being identical. In practice, slaves came from any caste, although priestly Brahmins tried to have themselves exempted. It was also believed that no slave should belong to someone from a lower caste.[67]

Although Hindu opposition to slavery is seemingly not documented, Bhakti movements, spreading from the early centuries CE, stressed personal devotion to one divine being. They welcomed followers from all caste backgrounds, and thus criticised slavery by implication.[68] Faced with the British colonial challenge, a new generation reinvented Hinduism as a reformed world religion, but emphasised caste over slavery.[69] Ambiguous views of bondage were nicely illustrated by Mahatma Jotirao Phule of Maharashtra (1827–90). In *Slavery*, a popular and much reprinted book of 1873, he praised the Western abolition of 'Negro slavery' but wrote only of caste struggles against Brahmins in South Asia.[70]

Buddhism inherited slavery from Hinduism, while marginalising or rejecting caste. The canonical texts mentioned servitude without criticising it, and excluded slaves from becoming monks, although practice diverged from this norm.[71] The Buddha forbade his followers from making a living out of dealing in slaves, and showed compassion for their lot. Ashoka (r. 269–32 BCE), the archetypal Buddhist ruler, inscribed in stone his injunctions to cease slave trading and treat slaves decently, but without eliminating servitude.[72]

Merciful Buddhist precepts may have hastened a transition from slavery to serfdom, similar to that of mediaeval western Europe.

[66] Davis 1984: 107–8, 112–13, 136–53; Pétré-Grenouilleau 2004, ch. 4; Quenum 1993: 206–16.
[67] Chanana 1960; Bongert 1963; Ramachandran Nair 1986.
[68] Kumar 1993: 114.
[69] Kusuman 1973: 133–4, 163–5.
[70] Phule 2002: 2–99.
[71] Mabbett 1998: 27, 29.
[72] Moosvi 2003; Chakravarti 1985: 67–8; See also Chanana 1960.

Restricted to Sri Lanka and Mainland Southeast Asia by the thirteenth-century, Theravada Buddhist kingdoms contained many more serfs than slaves. The main goal of frequent military campaigns was to seize people and settle them as whole communities attached to the soil, sometimes on monastic estates. Unredeemed debtors, who were numerous, blended into this wider serf population.[73]

Serfdom, slavery, debt bondage and corvée labour were abolished in stages in the Theravada Buddhist world from the nineteenth-century. Western imperialism was significant, together with rising population, commercialisation of the economy, belief in the superiority of free labour, and royal strategies to restrict noble powers.[74] However, a Buddhist revival, premised on a return to original texts and the exemplary life of the Buddha, also played a part. The initial Thai abolition decree of 1873 was couched in terms of Buddhist ethics, and the private correspondence of King Chulalongkorn (r. 1868–1910) indicates that he was sincere in these beliefs.[75]

East Asia's Mahayana Buddhism and Daoism were generally subordinate to Confucianism, which initially only sanctioned forced labour for the state, inflicted on captives and criminals. However, private, commercial and hereditary forms of slavery and serfdom soon became rampant.[76] As Neo-Confucian reform movements spread from the twelfth-century, some Korean scholars criticised private slavery as uncanonical and inhumane, for slaves are 'still Heaven's people'. Servitude engendered endless lawsuits, brutalised both owner and chattel, and undermined the family, the cornerstone of Confucian ethics. However, other sages argued that patrimonial property should be protected at all costs.[77]

Ming and Qing Chinese rulers cited Neo-Confucian norms to improve the lot of 'mean people', including slaves. A wave of servile uprisings prompted noted reforms in the 1720s. The authorities prohibited raiding, kidnapping, and trading in people, while tolerating servitude by birth, self-enslavement, and the sale of children in cases of dire necessity. Forced labour for life persisted as a punishment, and officials allocated such people to private individuals, but these 'state slaves' could be neither transferred nor manumitted without official permission. Moreover, the worst offenders were more rarely castrated than in earlier centuries.[78]

---

[73] See Turton 1980; Feeny 1993: 88–90.
[74] Feeny 1993.
[75] Wyatt 1982: 175–8, 188, 192.
[76] Palais 1996: 232, 235; Jenner 1998: 70–1.
[77] Palais 1996: 217–19, 232–7.
[78] See Meijer 1980; Rowe 2002: 497–8, 500–1; Huang 1974: 228–31; Tsai 1996: 17–19, 27–8; Jenner 1998: 71–2; Hellie 1993: 299.

Confucianism was weaker in Japan, and Mahayana Buddhism may have played a greater role in the transition from slavery to serfdom, more or less complete by the tenth-century. Serfs in turn slowly evolved into a free peasantry in early modern times.[79] Prisoners of war ceased to be legally enslaved from the early seventeenth-century, although descendants of former captives might still be traded, and destitute parents continued to sell their children into bondage.[80] The modernising Meiji regime, faced with an upsurge in exports of girls to Southeast Asian brothels after 1868, passed a law forbidding all buying and selling of females in 1872.[81] A 'Japanese-sponsored cabinet' then imposed complete emancipation on Korea in 1894.[82]

Chinese abolition became more secular in tone, in response to Western pressure. The sale of girls, in part for export to Southeast Asia, provoked an international scandal from the mid-nineteenth-century.[83] The Qing thus took the ultimate step of abolishing slavery in 1906, to take effect in 1910.[84] The prohibition was repeated by the Republicans after they took power in 1911, and again by the Communists after 1949.[85] Even the latter found it hard to stamp out sales of abducted women and children, however. In the 1980s and 1990s it was necessary to 'make propaganda to persuade rural people that buying women and children is wrong'.[86]

---

[79] Sansom 1978: 220–2.
[80] Livingston 1976: I, 11–12.
[81] Hane 2003: 208.
[82] Palais 1996: 266.
[83] Lasker 1950: 52–3.
[84] Hellie 1993: 293.
[85] Watson 1980: 240.
[86] Jenner 1998: 72.

ENVOI

Deeper studies of religious attitudes towards servitude and abolition are urgently needed, because the subject has generated so much vulgar polemic. Serious scholarship is often the first casualty of the heated exchanges that sizzle along the internet, filtering into a varied range of publications. Participants in such controversies rarely heed Jacques Jomier's wise words that no religion is in a position to cast the first stone in the matter of slavery.[1]

To achieve the eradication of slavery throughout the world and avoid the danger of its resurgence, people of all beliefs should begin by uniting in humble apology for the pain and sorrow inflicted on generations of coerced and humiliated human beings. Every world faith has condoned some version of servitude in its time, including the atheistic creed of Communism. However, there were always courageous people, prepared to row against the current by denouncing evils that those of their own persuasion accepted.

Above all, there is a need for a better understanding of why adherents of different belief systems accepted slavery for so long, and why and how they ceased to do so. Replacing partisan diatribes by sober and self-critical assessments is a priority, which could do much to heal current rifts between religious communities. Re-emerging in the late twentieth-century, to the surprise of many scholars, these tensions threaten to tear our world apart.

[1] Jomier 1988: 102.

233

REFERENCES

Abaza, Mona (1998) 'Southeast Asia and the Middle East: *al-Manar* and Islamic modernity,' in Claude Guillot *et al.*, eds, *From the Mediterranean to the China Sea*, Wiesbaden: Otto Harrassowitz, 93–111.

Abd el-Schafi (2000) *Behind the veil: unmasking Islam*, [n.p.; n. pub.], 2nd edn.

Abdallah, Fadel (1987) 'Islam, slavery, and racism: the use of strategy in the pursuit of human rights,' *American Journal of Islamic Social Sciences*, 4/1: 31–50.

Abdillah, Masykuri (1997) *Responses of Indonesian Muslim intellectuals to the concept of democracy, 1966–1993*, Hamburg: Abera.

'Abduh, Muhammad (1966) *The theology of unity*, London: George Allen and Unwin.

Abdullah bin Abdul Kadir (1970) *The hikayat Abdullah*, ed. and tr. A. H. Hill, Kuala Lumpur: Oxford University Press.

Abou El Fadl, Khaled (2001) *Speaking in God's name: Islamic law, authority and women*, Oxford: Oneworld.

Abu-Izzedin, Nejla M. (1984) *The Druzes: a new study of their history, faith and society*, Leiden: E. J. Brill.

Abul Fazl, 'Allami (1972) *The Akbar Nama of Abul Fazl*, ed. and tr. Henry Beveridge, Delhi: Rare Books.

Adam, William (1840) *The law and custom of slavery in British India*, Boston, MA: Weeks, Jordan and Co.

Addoun, Yacine D., and Lovejoy, Paul E. (2004) 'Muhammad Kaba Saghanughu and the Muslim community of Jamaica,' in Paul E. Lovejoy, ed., *Slavery on the frontiers of Islam*, Princeton, NJ: Markus Wiener, 199–218.

Afroz, Sultana (1999) 'From Moors to marronage: the Islamic heritage of the maroons of Jamaica,' *Journal of Muslim Minority Affairs*, 19/2: 161–79.

Aga Khan III (1998) *Aga Khan III: selected speeches and writings of Sir Sultan Muhammad Shah*, ed. K. K. Aziz, London: Kegan Paul International.

Ahmad, 'Abdelhamid M. (1963) *Die Auseinandersetzung zwischen al-Azhar und der modernistischen Bewegung in Ägypten*, Universität Hamburg.

Ahmad, Aziz (1967) *Islamic modernism in India and Pakistan, 1857–1964*, London: Oxford University Press.

Ahmad, Jamal-ud-Din (1934) *Afghanistan, a brief survey*, Kabul: Dar-ut-Talif.

Ahmad, Khurshid, ed. (1976) *Islam: its meaning and message*, London: Islamic Council of Europe.

Ahmad, Qeyamuddin (1966) *The Wahabi movement in India,* Calcutta: K. L. Mukhopadhyay.

Ahmad, Safi (1971) *Two kings of Awadh, Muhammad Ali Shah and Amjad Ali Shah, 1837–1847,* Aligarh: P. C. Dwadash Shreni and Co.

Ahmed, Ishtiaq (1987) *The concept of an Islamic state: an analysis of the ideological controversy in Pakistan,* London: Frances Pinter.

Ahmed, Leila (1992) *Women and gender in Islam: historical roots of a modern debate,* New Haven, CT: Yale University Press.

Ali, A. Mukti (1969) *Alam pikiran Islam modern di Indonesia: modern Islamic thought in Indonesia,* Jogjakarta: Jajasan Nida.

Ali, Abbas I. M. (1972) *The British, the slave trade and slavery in the Sudan, 1820–1881,* Khartoum University Press.

Ali, Ameer [Amir 'Ali] (1873) *A critical examination of the life and teachings of Mohammed,* London: Williams and Norgate.

────── (1891) *The life and teachings of Mohammed, or the spirit of Islam,* London: W. H. Allen.

────── (1899) *A short history of the Saracens,* London: Macmillan.

────── (1917) *Mohammedan law,* Calcutta: Thacker, Spink & Co., 4th edn.

────── (1922) *The spirit of Islam, a history of the evolution and ideals of Islam, with a life of the Prophet,* London: Christophers.

Ali, Cherágh [Chiragh] (1883) *The proposed political, legal and social reforms in the Ottoman empire and other Mohammadan states,* Bombay: Education Society's Press.

────── (1885) *A critical exposition of the popular jihad,* Calcutta: Thacker, Spink & Co.

'Ali, Muhammad (1920) *The Holy Qur-an, containing the Arabic text with an English translation and commentary,* Lahore: Ahmadiyya Anjuman-i-Ishaat-i-Islam, 2nd edn.

────── (1936) *The religion of Islam, a comprehensive discussion of the sources, principles and practices of Islam,* Lahore: Ahmadiyya Anjuman Isha'at Islam.

Allen, Calvin (1987) *Oman, the modernization of the sultanate,* Boulder, CO: Westview.

Allworth, Edward, ed. (1994) *Central Asia; 130 years of Russian dominance, a historical overview,* Durham, NC: Duke University Press.

Andaya, Barbara W. (1993) *To live as brothers; Southeast Sumatra in the seventeenth and eighteenth centuries,* Honolulu: University of Hawaii Press.

Andaya, Barbara W., and Andaya, Leonard Y. (1982) *A History of Malaysia,* London: Macmillan.

Andaya, Leonard Y. (1993) *The world of Maluku, eastern Indonesia in the early modern period,* Honolulu: University of Hawaii Press.

Anderson, John (1876) *Mandalay to Momien: a narrative of two expeditions to western China, of 1868 and 1875,* London: Macmillan.

Anderson, John (1971) *Mission to the East Coast of Sumatra in 1823,* Kuala Lumpur: Oxford University Press, reprint of 1826 edn.

Anderson, Norman (1976) *Law reform in the Muslim world,* London: Athlone.

ANRI [Arsip Nasional Republik Indonesia] (1836–9) 29: 580, Algemeen verslag, Gouvernement Amboina.
———— (1859) 29: 1538, Memorie van overgave, Ternate.
———— (1876–9) 30: 162a, Algemeen verslag, Ternate.
Anti-Slavery Reporter (1903) 23/2.
'Arafat, W. (1966) 'The attitude of Islam to slavery,' *Islamic Quarterly*, 10/1–2: 12–18.
Arberry, A. J. (1969) *The Koran interpreted*, Toronto: Macmillan.
Arnold, T. W. (1913) *The preaching of Islam: a history of the propagation of the Muslim faith*, London: Constable.
Ashkenazi, Tovia (1938) *Tribus semi-nomades de la Palestine du nord*, Paris: Paul Geuthner.
Aubin, Eugène (1908) *La Perse d'aujourd'hui: Iran, Mesopotamie*, Paris: Librairie Armand Colin.
Austen, Ralph A. (1987) *African economic history, internal development and external dependency*, London: James Currey.
———— (1989) 'The nineteenth-century Islamic slave trade from East Africa (Swahili and Red Sea coasts): a tentative census,' in William G. Clarence-Smith, ed., *The economics of the Indian Ocean slave trade in the nineteenth-century*, London: Frank Cass, 21–44.
———— (1992) 'The Mediterranean Islamic slave trade out of Africa: a tentative census,' in Elizabeth Savage, ed., *The human commodity: perspectives on the trans-Saharan slave trade*, London: Frank Cass, 214–48.
Austin, Allan D. (1997) *African Muslims in antebellum America*, London: Routledge.
Austin, R. W. J. (1971) *Sufis of Andalusia: the 'Ruh al-quds' and 'al-Durrat al-fakhirah' of Ibn 'Arabi*, Berkeley, CA: University of California Press.
Awad, Mohamed (1966) *Report on slavery*, New York: United Nations.
Awde, Nicholas (2000) *Women in Islam: an anthology from the Quran and Hadiths*, New York: St Martin's Press.
Ayalon, David (1951) *L'esclavage du mamelouk*, Jerusalem: Israel Oriental Society.
———— (1999) *Eunuchs, caliphs and sultans: a study in power relationships*, Jerusalem: Magnes Press.
Azarya, Victor (1978) *Aristocrats facing change: the Fulbe in Guinea, Nigeria and Cameroon*, Chicago, IL: University of Chicago Press.
Aziz, K. K. (1968) *Ameer Ali, his life and work*, Lahore: Publishers United.
Azra, Azyumardi (1992) 'The transmission of Islamic reformism to Indonesia: networks of Middle Eastern and Malay–Indonesian "ulama" in the seventeenth and eighteenth centuries,' PhD thesis, Columbia University, New York.
———— (1995) 'Hadhrami scholars in the Malay–Indonesian diaspora: a preliminary study of Sayyid 'Uthman,' *Studia Islamika*, 2/2: 1–33.
Azumah, John A. (2001) *The legacy of Arab-Islam in Africa: a quest for inter-religious dialogue*, Oxford: Oneworld.
Azzam, Salem, ed. (1982) *Islam and contemporary society*, London: Longman.

Ba, Amadou, and Daget, Jacques (1962) *L'empire peul du Macina*, Paris and The Hague: Mouton, Vol. 1.

Babaie, Susan *et al.* (2004) *Slaves of the Shah: new élites of Safavid Iran*, London: I. B. Tauris.

Bacharach, Jere L. (1981) 'African military slaves in the medieval Middle East: the cases of Iraq (869–955) and Egypt (868–1171),' *International Journal of Middle East Studies*, 13: 471–95.

Bacon, Elizabeth E. (1980) *Central Asians under Russian rule: a study in culture change*, Ithaca, NY: Cornell University.

Badawi, M. A. Zaki (1978) *The reformers of Egypt*, London: Croom Helm.

Baddeley, John F. (1999) *The Russian conquest of the Caucasus*, Richmond, Surrey: Curzon, reprint of 1908 edn.

Baer, Gabriel (1969) 'Slavery and its abolition,' in Gabriel Baer, ed., *Studies in the social history of modern Egypt*, University of Chicago Press, 161–89.

Baghdiantz McCabe, Ina (1999) *The Shah's silk for Europe's silver: the Eurasian trade of the Julfa Armenians in Safavid Iran and India, 1530–1750*, Atlanta, GA: Scholars Press.

Baha'u'llah and 'Abdu'l-Baha (1956) *Baha'i world faith: selected writings of Baha'u'llah and 'Abdu'l-Baha*, Wilmette, IL: Baha'i Publishing Trust.

Baillie, N. B. E. (1957) *A digest of Moohummudan law*, Lahore: n. pub., reprint of 1869–75 edn.

Baldé, Mamadou S. (1975) 'L'esclavage et la guerre sainte au Fuuta-Jalon,' in Claude Meillassoux, ed., *L'esclavage en Afrique précoloniale*, Paris: François Maspéro, 183–220.

Baldus, Bernd (1977) 'Responses to dependence in a servile group: the Machube of northern Benin,' in Suzanne Miers and Igor Kopytoff, eds, *Slavery in Africa: historical and anthropological perspectives*, Madison, WI: University of Wisconsin Press, 435–58.

Balfour, Edward (1885) *The cyclopaedia of India and of eastern and southern Asia, commercial, industrial and scientific*, London: Bernard Quaritch, 3rd edn.

Baljon, J. M. S. (1970) *The reforms and religious ideas of Sir Ahmad Khan*, Lahore: Sh. Muhammad Ashraf.

Balogun, Ismail A. B. (c. 1975) *Islam versus Ahmadiyya in Nigeria*, Beirut: Dar al-Arabia.

Banaji, D. R. (1933) *Slavery in British India*, Bombay: D. B. Taraporevala.

al-Banna, Hasan (1997) 'Peace in Islam,' <http://www.youngmuslims.ca/online_library/books/peace_in_islam/>

Barbour, Bernard, and Jacobs, Michelle (1985) 'The Mi'raj: a legal treatise on slavery by Ahmad Baba,' in John R. Willis, ed., *Slaves and slavery in Muslim Africa*, London: Frank Cass, Vol. I, 125–59.

Barrett, Thomas M. (1999) *At the edge of empire: the Terek cossacks and the North Caucasus frontier, 1700–1860*, Boulder, CO: Westview.

Barry, Boubacar (1998) *Senegambia and the Atlantic slave trade*, Cambridge: Cambridge University Press.

References

Barry, Ismaël (1997) *Le Fuuta-Jaloo face à la colonisation: conquête et mise en place de l'administration en Guinée, 1880–1920*, Paris: L'Harmattan.

Batran, Aziz A. (1985) 'The 'ulama of Fas, M. Isma'il and the issue of the Haratin of Fas,' in John R. Willis, ed., *Slaves and slavery in Muslim Africa*, London: Frank Cass, Vol. II, 1–15.

Battuta, Muhammad b. 'Abdallah ibn [Ibn Battuta] (1983) *Travels in Asia and Africa, 1325–1354: selections*, London: Routledge and Kegan Paul.

Beachey, R. W. (1976a) *The slave trade of Eastern Africa*, London: Rex Collings.

—— (1976b) *A collection of documents on the slave trade of Eastern Africa*, London: Rex Collings.

—— (1990) *The warrior mullah: the Horn aflame, 1892–1920*, London: Bellew.

Becker, Seymour (1968) *Russia's protectorates in Central Asia: Bukhara and Khiva 1865–1924*, Cambridge, MA: Harvard University Press.

Beg, Muhammad A. J. (1975) 'The "serfs" of Islamic society under the 'Abbasid regime,' *Islamic Culture*, 49/2: 107–18.

Bel, Alfred (1938) *La religion musulmane en Berbérie, tome I: Établissement et développement de l'Islam en Berbérie, du VIIe au XXe siècle*, Paris: Paul Geuthner.

Bemath, Abdul S. (1992) 'The Sayyid and Saalihiya tariqa: reformist anticolonial hero in Somalia,' in Said S. Samatar, ed. *In the shadow of conquest: Islam in colonial Northeast Africa*, Trenton, NJ: Red Sea Press, 33–47.

Bennett, Norman R. (1960) 'Christian and Negro slavery in eighteenth-century North Africa,' *Journal of African History*, 1/1: 65–82.

—— (1978) *A history of the Arab state of Zanzibar*, London: Methuen.

Berg, L. W. C. van den (1882–84) *Minhadj at-talibin, le guide des zélés croyants: manuel de jurisprudence musulmane selon le rite de Chafi'i*, Batavia: Imprimerie du Gouvernement.

—— (1886) *Le Hadhramout et les colonies arabes dans l'archipel indien*, Batavia: Imprimerie du Gouvernement.

Berlioux, Étienne F. (1870) *La traite orientale: histoire des chasses à l'homme organisées en Afrique depuis quinze ans pour les marchés de l'Orient*, Paris: Guillaumin et Cie.

Bernus, Edmond and Suzanne (1975) 'L'évolution de la condition servile chez les Touaregs sahéliens,' in Claude Meillassoux, ed., *L'esclavage en Afrique précoloniale*, Paris: François Maspéro, 27–47.

Berque, Jacques (1978) *L'intérieur du Maghreb, XVe–XIXe siècle*, Paris: Gallimard.

Bevan Jones, V. R. and L. B. (1941) *Women in Islam: a manual with special reference to conditions in India*, Lucknow Publishing House.

Bhacker, M. Reda (1992) *Trade and empire in Muscat and Zanzibar: the roots of British domination*, London: Routledge.

Bidwell, Robin (1983) *The two Yemens*, London: Longman.

Bigalke, T. (1983) 'Dynamics of the Torajan slave trade in South Sulawesi,' in Anthony Reid, ed. *Slavery, bondage and dependency in Southeast Asia*, Saint Lucia: University of Queensland Press, 341–63.

Bigi, Musa Jarullah [Bigiyev] (2002) 'Why did the Muslim world decline while the civilised world advanced?,' in Charles Kurzman, ed., *Modernist Islam, 1840–1940: a sourcebook*, Oxford University Press, 254–6.

Binger [Louis G.] (1891) *Esclavage, islamisme et christianisme*, Paris: Société d'Éditions Scientifiques.

Bird, Isabella L. (1883) *The Golden Chersonese and the way thither*, London: John Murray.

Bivar, A. D. H. (1961) 'The Wathiqat ahl al-Sudan, a manifesto of the Fulani jihad,' *Journal of African History*, 2/2: 235–43.

Blank, Jonah (2001) *Mullahs on the mainframe: Islam and modernity among the Daudi Bohras*, University of Chicago Press.

Blunt, Wilfrid S. (1907) *Secret history of the English occupation of Egypt*, London: T. Fisher Unwin.

—— (2002) *The future of Islam*, London: RoutledgeCurzon, 2nd edn.

Boahen, A. Adu (1964) *Britain, the Sahara and the Western Sudan, 1788–1861*, Oxford: Clarendon Press.

Bohdanowicz, L. (1942) 'The Muslims in Poland: their origin, history and cultural life,' *Journal of the Royal Asiatic Society*, 163–80.

Boisard, Marcel A. (1979) *L'humanisme de l'Islam*, Paris: Albin Michel.

—— (1985) *L'Islam aujourd'hui*, Paris: UNESCO.

Bongert, Yvonne (1963) 'Réflexions sur le problème de l'esclavage dans l'Inde ancienne, à propos de quelques ouvrages récents,' *Bulletin de l'École Française d'Extrême Orient*, 51/1: 143–94.

Bonin, Charles-Eudes (1910) 'Les mahométans du Kansu et leur dernière révolte,' *Revue du Monde Musulman*, 10/2: 211–33.

Bonné, Alfred (1948) *State and economics in the Middle East, a society in transition*, London: Kegan Paul.

Bono, Salvatore (1964) *I corsari barbareschi*, Turin: RAI.

Botte, Roger (1994) 'Stigmates sociaux et discrimination religieuse: l'ancienne classe servile au Fuuta Jaloo,' *Cahiers d'Études Africaines*, 34/1–3: 109–36.

—— (1999) 'Riimaybe, Haratin, Iklan: les damnés de la terre, le développement et la démocratie,' in André Bourgeot, ed., *Horizons nomades en Afrique sahélienne: sociétés, développement et démocratie*, Paris: Karthala, 55–78.

Boularès, Habib (1983) *L'Islam, la peur et l'espérance*, Paris: J.-C. Lattès.

Bourgeot, André (1975) 'Rapports esclavagistes et conditions d'affranchissement chez les Imuhag, Twarg Kel Ahaggar,' in Claude Meillassoux, ed., *L'esclavage en Afrique précoloniale*, Paris: François Maspéro, 77–97.

Bousquet, Georges H. (1938) *La politique musulmane et coloniale des Pays-Bas*, Paris: Paul Hartmann.

Braude, Benjamin (2002) 'Cham et Noé. Race, esclavage et exégèse entre Islam, Judaïsme et Christianisme,' *Annales. Histoire, Sciences Sociales*, 57/1: 93–125.

Bret, René-Joseph (1987) *Vie du sultan Mohamed Bakhit, 1856–1916: la pénétration française au Dar Sila, Tchad*, Paris: Éditions du CNRS.

240 *References*

Brett, Michael (1982) 'Modernisation in 19th century North Africa,' *Maghreb Review*, 7/1–2: 16–22.

—— (2000) 'Le mahdi dans le Maghreb mediéval,' *Revue des Mondes Musulmans et de la Méditerranée*, 91/4: 93–106.

—— (2001) *The rise of the Fatimids: the world of the Mediterranean and the Middle East in the fourth-century of the hijra, tenth-century CE*, Leiden: E. J. Brill.

Broersma, R. (1916) *De Lampongsche districten*, Batavia: Javasche Boekhandel en Drukkerij.

Brohi, Allahbuksh K. (1976) 'The Qur'an and its impact on human history,' in Khurshid Ahmad, ed. *Islam: its meaning and message*, London: Islamic Council of Europe, 81–97.

—— (1982) 'Human rights and duties in Islam: a philosophic approach,' in Salem Azzam, ed., *Islam and contemporary society*, London: Longman, 231–52.

Broomhall, Marshall (1987) *Islam in China, a neglected problem*, London: Darf, reprint of 1910 edn.

Brown, L. Carl (1972) 'The religious establishment in Husaynid Tunisia,' in Nikki Keddie, ed., *Scholars, saints and Sufis: Muslim religious institutions in the Middle East since 1500*, Berkeley: University of California Press, 47–91.

—— (1974) *The Tunisia of Ahmad Bey, 1837–1855*, Princeton University Press.

Brummett, Palmira (2000) *Images of imperialism in the Ottoman revolutionary press, 1908–1911*, Albany, NY: State University of New York Press.

Brunschvig, R. (1960) "Abd,' *Encyclopaedia of Islam*, vol. I, 24–40, Leiden: E. J. Brill.

Burckhardt, John L. (1992) *Notes on the Bedouins and Wahabys*, Reading: Garnet Publishing, reprint of 1830 edn.

—— (1993) *Travels in Arabia*, London: Darf, reprint of 1829 edn.

Burger, D. H. (1975) *Sociologisch-economische geschiedenis van Indonesia*, Amsterdam: Koninklijk Instituut voor de Tropen.

Burr, J. Millard, and Collins, Robert O. (2003) *Revolutionary Sudan: Hasan al-Turabi and the Islamist state, 1989–2000*, Leiden: E. J. Brill.

Burton, Audrey (1998) 'Russian slaves in seventeenth-century Bukhara,' in Touraj Atabaki and John O'Kane, eds, *Post-Soviet Central Asia*, London: I. B. Tauris, 345–65.

Burton, Richard F. (1973) *Sindh and the races that inhabit the valley of the Indus*, Karachi: Oxford University Press, reprint of 1851 edn.

Bushell, Andrew (2002) 'Pakistan's slave trade,' <http://www.bostonphoenix.com/boston/news_features/top/features/documents/02161802.htm>

Cable, Mildred, and French, Francesca (1942) *The Gobi Desert*, London: Hodder and Stoughton.

Cahen, Claude (1970) 'Note sur l'esclavage musulman et le devshirme ottoman, à propos de travaux récents,' *Journal of the Economic and Social History of the Orient*, 13/2: 211–18.

Canot, Theodore (1940) *Memoirs of a slave-trader*, London: Jonathan Cape.

Caro Baroja, Julio (1955) *Estudios saharianos*, Madrid: Instituto de Estudios Africanos.

Caroselli, Francesco S. (1931) *Ferro e fuoco in Somalia, venti anni di lotte contro mullah e dervisc*, Rome: Sindicato Italiano Arti Grafiche.

Carrère d'Encausse, Hélène (1966) *Réforme et révolution chez les musulmans de l'empire russe: Bukhara 1867–1924*, Paris: Armand Colin.

Cassanelli, Lee V. (1988) 'The ending of slavery in Italian Somalia: liberty and the control of labor, 1890–1935,' in Suzanne Miers and Richard Roberts, eds, *The end of slavery in Africa*, Madison, WI: University of Wisconsin Press, 308–31.

Cattelani, G. (1897) *L'avvenire coloniale d'Italia nel Benadir*, Naples: F. Giannini e Figli.

Cave, Basil S. (1909–10) 'The end of slavery in Zanzibar and British East Africa,' *Journal of the African Society*, 9/1: 20–33.

Cehajic, Dzemal (1990) 'Socio-political aspects of the Naqshbandi Dervish order in Bosnia and Herzegovina, and Yugoslavia generally,' in Marc Gaborieau *et al.*, eds, *Naqshbandis: cheminement et situation actuelle d'un ordre mystique musulman*, Istanbul: Isis, 663–8.

Cerulli, Enrico (1957–64) *Somalia, scritti vari editi ed inediti*, Rome: Istituto Poligrafico dello Stato.

Ceulemans, P. (1959) *La question arabe et le Congo, 1883–1892*, Brussels: Académie Royale des Sciences Coloniales.

Chabot, H. T. (1996) *Kinship, status and gender in South Celebes*, Leiden: KITLV Press.

Chafik, Ahmed [Ahmad Shafiq] (1938) *L'esclavage au point de vue musulman*, Cairo: Imprimerie Nationale, 2nd edn.

Chakravarti, Uma (1985) 'Of dasas and karmakaras: servile labour in ancient India,' in Utsa Patnaik and Manjari Dingwaney, eds, *Chains of servitude: bondage and slavery in India*, Madras: Sangam, 35–75.

Chanana, Dev R. (1960) *Slavery in ancient India, as depicted in Pali and Sanskrit texts*, New Delhi: People's Publishing House.

Charouiti Hasnaoui, Milouda (2000) 'Esclavos y cautivos según la ley islámica: condiciones y consecuencias,' in Maria Teresa Ferrer i Mallol and Josefina Mutgé i Vives, eds, *De l'esclavitud a la llibertat: esclaus i lliberts a l'edat mitjana*, Barcelona: Consell Superior d'Investigacions Científiques, 1–18.

Chater, Khalifa (1984) *Dépendance et mutations précoloniales; la régence de Tunis de 1815 à 1857*, Université de Tunis.

—— (1994) 'A rereading of Islamic texts in the Maghrib in the nineteenth and early twentieth centuries: secular theories or religious reformism?,' in John Ruedy, ed., *Islamism and secularism in North Africa*, Basingstoke: Macmillan, 37–51.

Chatterjee, Indrani (1999) *Gender, slavery and law in colonial India*, New Delhi: Oxford University Press.

Chattopadhyay, Amal K. (1977) *Slavery in the Bengal presidency, 1772–1843*, London: Golden Eagle Publishing House.

Chittick, William C. (1983) *The Sufi path of love: the spiritual teachings of Rumi*, Albany: State University of New York Press.

Choueiri, Youssef M. (1997) *Islamic fundamentalism*, London: Pinter, 2nd edn.

Christelow, Allan (1985a) *Muslim law courts and the French colonial state in Algeria*, Princeton University Press.

———— (1985b) 'Slavery in Kano, 1913–1914: evidence from the judicial records,' *African Economic History*, 14: 57–74.

———— (1994) *Thus ruled Emir Abbas: selected cases from the records of the Emir of Kano's judicial council*, East Lansing: Michigan State University.

Churchill, C. H. (1994) *Mount Lebanon, a ten years' residence, from 1842 to 1852*, Reading: Garnet, reprint of 1853 edn.

Clancy-Smith, Julia A. (1994) *Rebel and saint: Muslim notables, populist protest, colonial encounters; Algeria and Tunisia, 1800–1904*, Berkeley: University of California Press.

Clarence-Smith, William G., ed. (1989) *The economics of the Indian Ocean slave trade in the nineteenth century*, London: Frank Cass.

———— (forthcoming) 'L'Église catholique face à l'abolition de l'esclavage dans les colonies portugaises, 1878–1913,' in Olivier Pétré-Grenouilleau, ed. *Abolitionnisme et société, France, Suisse et Portugal, XVIII–XIXᵉ siècles*.

Clarke, Peter B. (1982) *West Africa and Islam, a study of religious development*, London: Edward Arnold.

———— (1995) *Mahdism in West Africa; the Ijebu Mahdiyya movement*, London: Luzac.

Clayer, Nathalie (1994) *Mystiques, état, société: les Halvetis dans l'aire balkanique de la fin du XVᵉ siècle à nos jours*, Leiden: E. J. Brill.

Cleveland, William L. (1994) *A history of the modern Middle East*, Boulder, CO: Westview.

Clifford, Sir Hugh C. (1913) *Malayan monochromes*, London: John Murray.

Clissold, Stephen (1977) *The Barbary slaves*, London: Elek.

Collet, Octave J. A. (1925) *Terres et peuples de Sumatra*, Amsterdam: Elsevier.

Colley, Linda (2002) *Captives: Britain, empire and the world, 1600–1850*, London: Jonathan Cape.

Collins, Robert O. (1992) 'The Nilotic slave trade, past and present,' in Elizabeth Savage, ed., *The human commodity: perspectives on the trans-Saharan slave trade*, London: Frank Cass, 140–61.

Constable, Olivia R. (1994) *Trade and traders in Muslim Spain: the commercial realignment of the Iberian peninsula, 900–1500*, Cambridge University Press.

Constantin, François (1987) 'Le saint et le prince: sur les fondements de la dynamique confrérique en Afrique orientale,' in François Constantin, ed., *Les voies de l'Islam en Afrique orientale*, Paris: Karthala, 85–109.

Coon, Carleton S. (1968) 'Southern Arabia, a problem for the future,' in Carleton S. Coon and James M. Andrews IV, eds, *Studies in the anthropology of Oceania and Asia*, New York: Kraus, reprint of 1943 edn., 187–220.

Cooper, Frederick (1977) *Plantation slavery on the East coast of Africa*, New Haven, CT: Yale University Press.

—— (1980) *From slaves to squatters: plantation labour and agriculture in Zanzibar and coastal Kenya 1890–1925*, New Haven, CT: Yale University Press.

—— (1981) 'Islam and cultural hegemony: the ideology of slave-owners on the East African coast,' in Paul Lovejoy, ed., *The ideology of slavery in Africa*, Beverley Hills, CA: Sage, 271–307.

Cooper, Joseph (1968) *The lost continent, or slavery and the slave-trade in Africa 1875, with observations on the Asiatic slave-trade carried on under the name of labour traffic*, London: Frank Cass, reprint of 1875 edn.

Corancez, Louis A. O. de (1995) *The history of the Wahhabis from their origin until the end of 1809*, Reading: Garnet, tr. from the 1810 edn.

Cordell, Dennis D. (1985) *Dar al-Kuti and the last years of the trans-Saharan slave trade*, Madison: University of Wisconsin Press.

—— (1999) 'No liberty, not much equality, and very little fraternity: the mirage of manumission in the Algerian Sahara in the second half of the nineteenth-century,' in Suzanne Miers and Martin Klein, eds, *Slavery and colonial rule in Africa*, London: Frank Cass, 38–56.

Crecelius, Daniel (1972) 'Non-ideological responses of the Egyptian ulama to modernization,' in Nikki Keddie, ed., *Scholars, saints and Sufis: Muslim religious institutions in the Middle East since 1500*, Berkeley, CA: University of California Press, 167–209.

Crone, Patricia (1980) *Slaves on horses: the evolution of the Islamic polity*, Cambridge University Press.

Crone, Patricia, and Cook, Michael (1977) *Hagarism: the making of the Islamic world*, Cambridge University Press.

Croutier, Alev L. (1989) *Harem, the world behind the veil*, London: Bloomsbury.

Cruise O'Brien, Donal B. (1971) *The Mourides of Senegal: the political and economic organization of an Islamic brotherhood*, Oxford: Clarendon Press.

Cumming, Duncan, ed. (1977) *The country of the Turkomans: an anthology of exploration for the Royal Geographical Society*, London: Oguz Press.

Daly, M. W. (1986) *Empire on the Nile: the Anglo-Egyptian Sudan, 1898–1934*, Cambridge University Press.

Damsté, H. T. (1928) 'Hikajat perang sabi,' *Bijdragen tot de Taal- Land- en Volkenkunde*, 84: 545–608.

Daniel, Norman (1966) *Islam, Europe and empire*, Edinburgh University Press.

Danziger, Raphael (1977) *'Abd al-Qadir and the Algerians: resistance to the French and internal consolidation*, New York: Holmes and Meier.

Dar, Bashir A. (1957) *Religious thought of Sayyid Ahmad Khan*, Lahore: Dr. Khalifa Abdul Hakim.

Davids, Achmat (1980) *The mosques of Bo-Kaap: a social history of Islam at the Cape*, Athlone, Cape Town: South African Institute of Arabic and Islamic Research.

Davis, David B. (1984) *Slavery and human progress*, New York: Oxford University Press.

Davis, Robert C. (2003) *Christian slaves, Muslim masters: White slavery in the Mediterranean, the Barbary Coast and Italy, 1500–1800,* Basingstoke: Palgrave Macmillan.

Day, Francis (1863) *The land of the Permauls, or Cochin, its past and its present,* Madras: Gantz Brothers.

Deardon, Seton (1976) *A nest of corsairs: the fighting Karamanlis of the Barbary Coast,* London: John Murray.

Defarge, Claude, and Troeller, Gordian (1969) *Yemen 62–69, de la révolution 'sauvage' à la trêve des guerriers,* Paris: Robert Laffont.

Deherme, Georges (1994) 'L'esclavage en Afrique Occidentale Française: étude historique, critique et positive,' in Paul E. Lovejoy and A. S. Kanya-Forstner, eds, *Slavery and its abolition in French West Africa,* Madison: University of Wisconsin, 11–206.

DeJong, Garrett E. (1934) 'Slavery in Arabia,' *The Moslem World,* 24/2: 126–44.

Delanoue, Gilbert (1982) *Moralistes et politiques musulmans dans l'Égypte du XIXᵉ siècle,* Cairo: Institut Français d'Archéologie Orientale.

Delawarr Hosaen [Dilawar Husayn], Ahamed Meerza (1980) *Muslim Modernism in Bengal; selected writings of Delawarr Hosaen Ahamed Meerza, 1840–1913,* ed. Sultan Jahan Salik, Dacca: Dacca University, Vol. 1.

Derman, William, and Derman, Louise (1973) *Serfs, peasants and socialists: a former serf village in the Republic of Guinea,* Berkeley: University of California Press.

Dermenghem, Émile (1954) *Le culte des saints dans l'Islam maghrébin,* Paris: Gallimard.

Derrick, Jonathan (1975) *Africa's slaves today,* London: George Allen and Unwin.

Dharma, Po (1987) *Le Pànduranga (Campâ), 1802–1835: ses rapports avec le Vietnam,* Paris: École Française d'Extrême-Orient.

Digby, Simon (1984) 'The *Tuhfa i nasa'ih* of Yusuf Gada: an ethical treaty in verse from the late-fourteenth-century Delhi sultanate,' in Barbara D. Metcalf, ed., *Moral conduct and authority: the place of adab in South Asian Islam,* Berkeley, University of California Press, 91–123.

Dillon, Michael (1999) *China's Muslim Hui community: migration, settlement and sects,* Richmond, Surrey: Curzon.

Dingwaney, Manjari (1985) 'Unredeemed promises: the law and servitude,' in Utsa Patnaik and Manjari Dingwaney, eds, *Chains of servitude: bondage and slavery in India,* Madras: Sangam, 283–347.

Djajadiningrat, Hoesein (1929) 'Toepassing van het Mohammedaanischen slavenrecht in de Lampoengs,' in *Feestbundel uitgegeven door het Koninklijk Bataviaasch Genootschap van Kunsten en Wetenschappen,* Weltevreden: G. Kolff, Vol. 1, 87–92.

Dobbin, Christine (1972) 'Tuanku Imam Bondjol, 1772–1864,' *Indonesia,* 13: 5–35.

—— (1983) *Islamic revivalism in a changing peasant economy: Central Sumatra 1784–1847,* London: Curzon.

Dodge, Bayard (1961) *Al-Azhar, a millennium of Muslim learning*, Washington, DC: Middle East Institute.

Douin, Georges (1936–41). *Histoire du règne du Khédive Ismail*, Rome and Cairo: Société Royale de Géographie d'Égypte.

Dozy, Reinhart P. A. (1913) *Spanish Islam: a history of the Moslems in Spain*, London: Chatto and Windus.

Dresch, Paul (2000) *A history of modern Yemen*, Cambridge University Press.

Duffy, James (1967) *A question of slavery: labour policies in Portuguese Africa and the British protest, 1850–1920*, Cambridge, MA: Harvard University Press.

Durham, M. E. (1909) *High Albania*, London: Edward Arnold.

Dutta, Abhijit (1987) *Muslim society in transition: Titu Meer's revolt, 1831, a study*, Calcutta: Minerva Associates.

Dymond, Maud M. (1929) *Yunnan*, London: Marshall Brothers.

Eccel, A. Chris (1984) *Egypt, Islam and social change: al-Azhar in conflict and accommodation*, Berlin: Klaus Schwarz.

Effendy, Bahtiar, Prasetyo, Hendro, and Subhan, Arief (1998) 'Munawir Sjadzali, MA, pencairan ketegangan ideologis,' in Azyumardi Azra and Saiful Uman, eds. *Menteri-menteri agama RI: biografi sosial-politik*, Jakarta: Pusat Pengkajian Islam dan Masarakat, 367–412.

Elbashir, Ahmed E. (1983) *The United States, slavery and the slave trade in the Nile valley*, Lanham, MD: University Press of America.

Elias, Jamal J. (1999) *Islam*, London: Routledge.

Elwahed, Ali Abd (1931) *Contribution à une théorie sociologique de l'esclavage*, Paris: Éditions Albert Mechelinck. [See also Wafi.]

Emerit, Marcel (1949) 'L'abolition de l'esclavage,' in Marcel Emerit, ed., *La révolution de 1848 en Algérie*, Paris: Éditions Larose, 29–42.

—— (1951) *L'Algérie à l'époque d'Abd-el-Kader*, Paris: Éditions Larose.

Encyclopaedie van Nederlandsch-Indië (1917–21), The Hague: Martinus Nijhoff.

Endicott, K. (1983) 'The effects of slave raiding on the aborigines of the Malay peninsula,' in Anthony Reid, ed. *Slavery, bondage and dependency in Southeast Asia*, Saint Lucia: University of Queensland Press, 216–45.

Ennaji, Mohammed (1999) *Serving the master: slavery and society in nineteenth-century Morocco*, Basingstoke: Macmillan.

Erdem, Y. Hakan (1996) *Slavery in the Ottoman empire and its demise, 1800–1909*, London: Macmillan.

Ewald, Janet J., and Clarence-Smith, William G. (1997) 'The economic role of the Hadhrami diaspora in the Red Sea and Gulf of Aden, 1820s to 1930s,' in Ulrike Freitag and William G. Clarence-Smith, eds, *Hadhrami traders, scholars and statesmen in the Indian Ocean, 1750s–1960s*, Leiden: E. J. Brill, 281–96.

Faber, Eli (1998) *Jews, slaves and the slave trade: setting the record straight*, New York University Press.

Fahmy, Mansour (1990) *La condition de la femme dans l'Islam*, Paris: Éditions Allia.

Fahri, Findikoglu Ziyaeddin (1936) *Essai sur la transformation du code famil-ial en Turquie*, Paris: Berger-Levrault.

Fair, Laura J. (2001) *Pastimes and politics: culture, community and identity in post-abolition urban Zanzibar, 1890–1945*, Oxford: James Currey.

Federspiel, Howard M. (1977) 'Islam and nationalism in Indonesia,' *Indonesia*, 24: 39–85.

——— (1998) 'Islam and Muslims in the southern territories of the Philippine Islands during the American colonial period, 1898–1946,' *Journal of Southeast Asian Studies*, 29/2: 340–56.

Feeny, David (1993) 'The demise of corvée and slavery in Thailand, 1782–1913,' in Martin Klein, ed., *Breaking the chains: slavery, bondage and emancipation in modern Africa and Asia*, Madison: University of Wisconsin Press, 83–111.

Fields, Lanny B. (1978) *Tso Tsung-T'ang and the Muslims: statecraft in Northwest China, 1868–1880*, Kingston, Ont.: Limestone Press.

Fika, Adamu M. (1978) *The Kano civil war and British overrule, 1882–1940*, Ibadan: Oxford University Press.

Findley, Carter V. (1995) 'La soumise, la subversive: Fatma Aliye, romancière et féministe,' *Turcica*, 27: 153–76.

Firestone, Reuven (1999) *Jihad, the origins of holy war in Islam*, Oxford University Press.

Firro, K. M. (1992) *A history of the Druzes*, Leiden: E. J. Brill.

Fisher, Alan W. (1972) 'Muscovy and the Black Sea slave trade,' in *Canadian-American Slavic Studies*, 6/4: 575–94.

——— (1980a) 'Chattel slavery in the Ottoman empire,' *Slavery and Abolition*, 1/1: 25–45.

——— (1980b) 'Studies in Ottoman slavery and slave trade, 2: Manumission,' *Journal of Turkish Studies*, 4: 49–56.

Fisher, Humphrey J. (2001) *Slavery in the history of Muslim Black Africa*, London: Hurst.

Florentino, Manolo (2002) 'Alforrias e etnicidade no Rio de Janeiro oitocentista, notas de pesquisa,' *Topoi*, 5: 9–40.

Fontrier, Marc (2003) *Abou-Bakr Ibrahim, pacha de Zeyla, marchand d'esclaves: commerce et diplomatie dans le Golfe de Tadjoura, 1840–1885*, Paris: L'Harmattan.

Forand, Paul G. (1971) 'The relation of the slave and the client to the master or patron in medieval Islam,' *International Journal of Middle Eastern Studies*, 2/1: 59–66.

Forget, D.-A. (1900) *L'Islam et le christianisme dans l'Afrique centrale*, Paris: Librairie Fischbacher.

Fredriksen, Børge (1977) 'Slavery and its abolition in nineteenth-century Egypt,' Hovedoppgave thesis, University of Bergen.

Freeze, Gregory L. (1989) 'The Orthodox Church and serfdom in pre-reform Russia,' *Slavic Review*, 48/3: 361–87.

Frere, Bartle (1873) 'Correspondence respecting Sir Bartle Frere's mission to the East Coast of Africa, 1872–73,' *Parliamentary Papers*, Vol. 61, C-820.

Friedmann, Yohanan (1989) *Prophecy continuous: aspects of Ahmadi religious thought and its medieval background,* Berkeley: University of California Press.

Furió, Antoni (2000) 'Esclaus i assalariats: la funció econòmica de l'esclavitud en la península Ibèrica a la baixa etat mitjana,' in Maria Teresa Ferrer i Mallol and Josefina Mutgé i Vives, eds, *De l'esclavitud a la llibertat: esclaus i lliberts a l'edat mitjana,* Barcelona: Consell Superior d'Investigacions Científiques, 19–38.

Furneaux, Rupert (1967) *Abdel Krim, emir of the Rif,* London: Secker and Warburg.

Fyzee, Asaf A. A. (1969) *Compendium of Fatimid law,* Simla: Indian Institute of Advanced Study.

Gaborieau, Marc (2000) 'Le mahdi oublié de l'Inde britannique: Sayyid Ahmad Barelwi, 1786–1831, ses disciples, ses adversaires,' *Revue des Mondes Musulmans et de la Méditerranée,* 91/4: 257–73.

Gabriel, Theodore P. C. (1996) *Hindu-Muslim relations in North Malabar, 1498–1947,* Lewiston, NY: Edwin Mellen Press.

Gammer, Moshe (1994) *Muslim resistance to the tsar: Shamil and the conquest of Chechenia and Daghestan,* London: Frank Cass.

García-Arenal, Mercedes (2000) 'Mahdisme et millénarisme en Islam,' *Revue des Mondes Musulmans et de la Méditerranée,* 91/4, special issue.

Garcia, Sylvianne (1997) 'Al-Hajj Seydou Nourou Tall "grand marabout" tijani: l'histoire d'une carrière, c. 1880–1980,' in David Robinson and Jean-Louis Triaud, eds. *Le temps des marabouts: itinéraires et stratégies islamiques en Afrique Occidentale Française, v. 1880–1960,* Paris: Karthala, 247–75.

Gardell, Matias (1999) 'North America,' in David Westerlund and Ingvar Svanberg, eds. *Islam outside the Arab world,* Richmond, Surrey: Curzon, 420–42.

Gardner, Alexander H. C. (1898) *Soldier and traveller: memoirs of Alexander Gardner,* Edinburgh: William Blackwood.

Garnier, Francis (1996) *Further travels in Laos and in Yunnan: the Mekong Exploration Commission Report (1866–68),* Bangkok: White Lotus, Vol. 2.

Garnett, Lucy M. J. (1891) *The women of Turkey and their folklore,* London: David Nutt.

——— (1909) *The Turkish people: their social life, religious beliefs and institutions, and domestic life,* London: Methuen.

Gaury, Gerald de (1966) *Faisal, king of Saudi Arabia,* London: Arthur Barker.

Gavin, R. J. (1975) *Aden under British rule, 1839–1967,* London: Hurst.

Geertz, Clifford (1960) *The religion of Java,* Glencoe, IL: Free Press.

Gervaise, Nicolas (1971) *An historical description of the kingdom of Macasar in the East Indies,* Farnborough, Hants Gregg International, reprint of 1701 edn.

Ghazal, Amal (2001) 'Sufism, ijtihad and modernity: Yusuf al-Nabhani in the age of 'Abd al-Hamid II,' *Archivum Ottomanicum,* 19: 239–71.

——— (2003) 'Debating slavery in the Arab Middle East: abolition between Muslim reformers and conservatives,' paper for the Slavery,

Islam and Diaspora conference, Harriet Tubman Center, Toronto, 24–6 October, forthcoming in the edited volume of papers.

Ghoraba, Hammouda (1955) 'Islam and slavery,' *Islamic Quarterly*, 2/3: 153–9.

Glassman, Jonathon (1991) 'The bondsman's new clothes: the contradictory consciousness of slave resistance on the Swahili coast,' *Journal of African History*, 32/2: 277–312.

Goeje, M. J. de (1886) *Mémoire sur les Carmathes du Bahraïn et les Fatimides*, Leiden: E. J. Brill.

Goichon, A.-M. (1927) *La vie féminine au Mzab: étude de sociologie musulmane*, Paris: Paul Geuthner.

Golden, Peter B. (1992) *An introduction to the history of the Turkic peoples: ethnogenesis and state formation in medieval and early modern Eurasia and the Middle East*, Wiesbaden: Otto Harrassowitz.

Goldziher, Ignaz (1967) *Muslim studies*, Chicago: Aldine.

Gordon, Matthew S. (2001) *The breaking of a thousand swords: a history of the Turkish military of Samarra (A.H. 200–275/815–889 C.E.)*, Albany, NY: State University of New York Press.

Gordon, Murray (1989) *Slavery in the Arab world*, New York: New Amsterdam Books.

Gowing, Peter G. (1983) *Mandate in Moroland: the American government of Muslim Filipinos, 1898–1920*, Quezon City: New Day Publishers.

Grandin, Nicole (1987) 'Sayyid Muhammad 'Uthman al-Mirghani, 1793–1853: une double lecture des ses hagiographies,' in François Constantin, ed., *Les voies de l'Islam en Afrique orientale*, Paris: Karthala, 35–58.

Graves, Elizabeth E. (1981) *The Minangkabau response to Dutch colonial rule in the nineteenth-century*, Ithaca, NY: Cornell University.

Gray, Richard (1961) *A history of the Southern Sudan, 1839–1889*, London: Oxford University Press.

Green, Arnold H. (1978) *The Tunisian ulama, 1873–1915*, Leiden: E. J. Brill.

Greenidge, C. W. W. (1958) *Slavery*, London: George Allen and Unwin.

Gregorian, Vartan (1969) *The emergence of modern Afghanistan: politics of reform and modernisation, 1880–1946*, Stanford University Press.

Guillaume, Alfred (1955) *The life of Muhammad: a translation of Ibn Ishaq's Sirat Rasul Allah*, London: Oxford University Press.

Gullick, J. M. (1958) *Indigenous political systems of Western Malaya*, London: Athlone.

Gunasekara, Victor A. (n.d.) 'Slavery and the infidel in Islam: essays on Islamic theory and practice considered in a Humanist perspective' <www.uq.net.au/slsoc/manussa/tr05manu.htm>

Habib, Irfan (1988–89) 'Slavery in the Delhi Sultanate, thirteenth and fourteenth centuries: evidence from the Sufi literature,' *Indian Historical Review*, 15/1–2: 248–56.

Haeri, Shaykh Fadhlalla (1993) *The elements of Islam*: Shaftesbury, Dorset: Element Books.

Halm, Heinz (1967) *Die Traditionen über der Aufstand 'Ali ibn Muhammads, des 'Herrn der Zang': eine quellenkritische Untersuchung*, Bonn: Rheinische Friedrich-Wilhelms-Universität.

—— (1985) 'Courants et mouvements antinomistes dans l'Islam mediéval,' in George Makdisi *et al.*, eds, *La notion de liberté au Moyen Age: Islam, Byzance, Occident*, Paris: Les Belles Lettres, 135–41.

—— (1991) *Shiism*, Edinburgh University Press.

—— (1996) *The empire of the Mahdi: the rise of the Fatimids*, Leiden: Brill.

Hamada, Masami (1990) 'De l'autorité religieuse au pouvoir politique: la révolte de Kuca et Khwaja Rashidin,' in Marc Gaborieau *et al.*, eds, *Naqshbandis: cheminement et situation actuelle d'un ordre mystique musulman*, Istanbul: Isis, 455–89.

Hambly, Gavin (1974) 'A note on the trade in eunuchs in Mughul Bengal,' *Journal of the American Oriental Society*, 94: 125–30.

—— (1991a) 'Iran during the reigns of Fath 'Ali Shah and Muhammad Shah,' in *The Cambridge History of Iran*, Cambridge University Press, Vol. VII, 144–73.

—— (1991b) 'The traditional Iranian city in the Qajar period,' in The *Cambridge history of Iran*, Cambridge University Press, Vol. VII, 542–89.

Hamdi, Mohamed E. (1998) *The politicization of Islam: a case study of Tunisia*, Boulder, CO: Westview.

el-Hamel, Choukri (2002) '"Race", slavery and Islam in Maghribi Mediterranean thought: the question of the Haratin in Morocco,' *Journal of North African Studies*, 7/3: 29–52.

Hamès, Constant, and Ould Cheikh, Abdel Wedoud (1991) *Al-Ansâb, la quête des origines: anthropologie historique de la société tribale arabe*, Paris: Éditions de la Maison des Sciences de l'Homme.

Hamidullah, Muhammad (1945) *Muslim conduct of state*, Lahore: Sh. Muhammad Ashraf, 4th edn.

—— (1959) *Le prophète de l'Islam*, Paris: Librairie Philosophique J. Vrin.

—— (1979) *Introduction to Islam* (originally published in French), London: MWH London Publishers.

Hamilton, Charles, and Grady, Standish G. (1870) *The Hedaya, or guide: a commentary on the Mussulman laws*, London: W. H. Allen and Co.

Hane, Mikiso (2003) *Peasants, women and outcasts: the underside of modern Japan*, Lanham, MD: Rowman and Littlefield, 2nd edn.

Hanimefendi, Leyla (1994) *The imperial harem of the sultans: daily life at the Çiragar palace during the nineteenth-century*, Istanbul: Peva.

Hardinge, Arthur H. (1928) *A diplomatist in the East*, London: Jonathan Cape.

Hardy, P. (1972) *The Muslims of British India*, Cambridge University Press.

Hargey, Taj (1981) 'The suppression of slavery in the Sudan, 1898–1939,' DPhil thesis, University of Oxford.

Harlan, Josiah (1939) *Central Asia; personal narrative of General Josiah Harlan, 1823–1841*, ed. Frank E. Ross, London: Luzac.

250   *References*

Harries, Lyndon (1965) *Swahili prose texts: a selection from the material collected by Carl Velten from 1893 to 1896*, London: Oxford University Press.

Harrison, Paul W. (1924) *The Arab at home*, New York: T. Y. Crowell.

Harrison, Paul W. (1939) 'Slavery in Arabia,' *The Moslem World*, 29/2: 207–9.

Hartmann, Martin (1921) *Zur Geschichte des Islams in China*, Leipzig: Wilhelm Heims.

Hassan, Riffat (1995) 'Are human rights compatible with Islam?' <http://www.religiousconsultation.org/hassan2.htm>

—— (2000) 'Human rights in the Qur'anic perspective,' in Gisela Webb, ed., *Windows of faith: Muslim women scholar-activists in North America*, Syracuse University Press, 241–8.

Hasselt, A. L. van (1882) *Voksbeschrijving van Midden-Sumatra*, Leiden: E. J. Brill.

Hawkins, Joye Bowman (1980) 'Conflict, interaction and change in Guinea-Bissau: Fulbe expansion and its impact, 1850–1900,' PhD thesis, University of California at Los Angeles.

Heers, Jacques (1981) *Esclaves et domestiques au moyen âge dans le monde méditerranéen*, Paris: Fayard.

—— (2003) *Les négriers de l'Islam: la première traite des Noirs, VIIᵉ–XVIᵉ siècle*, Paris: Perrin.

Hellie, Richard (1982) *Slavery in Russia, 1450–1725*, University of Chicago Press.

—— (1993) 'Slavery,' *The New Encyclopaedia Britannica*, Chicago, IL: Encyclopaedia Britannica Inc., Vol. XXVII, 288–300.

Hernando, Josep (2000) 'Els esclaus sarraïns: de l'esclavitud a la llibertat, Blancs, Negres, Llors i Turcs,' in Maria Teresa Ferrer i Mallol and Josefina Mutgé i Vives, eds, *De l'esclavitud a la llibertat: esclaus i lliberts a l'edat mitjana*, Barcelona: Consell Superior d'Investigacions Científiques, 213–44.

Heyd, Uriel (1961) 'The Ottoman 'ulema and westernization in the time of Selim III and Mahmud II,' in Uriel Heyd, ed., *Studies in Islamic history and civilization*, Jerusalem: Magnes Press, 63–96.

Heyworth-Dunne, Gamal-Eddine (1952) *Al-Yemen, a general social, political and economic survey*, Cairo: Renaissance Bookshop.

Hill, Polly (1976) 'From slavery to freedom: the case of farm slavery in Nigerian Hausaland,' *Comparative Studies in Society and History*, 18/3: 395–426.

Hilliard, Constance (1985) 'Zuhur al-Basatin and Ta'rikh al-Turubbe: some legal and ethical aspects of slavery in the Sudan, as seen in the works of Shaykh Musa Kamara,' in John R. Willis, ed., *Slaves and slavery in Muslim Africa*, London: Frank Cass, Vol. I, 160–81.

Hiskett, Mervyn (1985) 'Enslavement, slavery and attitudes towards the legally enslavable in Hausa Islamic literature,' in John R. Willis, ed., *Slaves and slavery in Muslim Africa*, London: Frank Cass, Vol. I, 106–24.

—— (1994) *The sword of truth: the life and times of the Shehu Usuman dan Fodio*, Evanston, IL: Northwestern University Press, 2nd edn.

Hjejle, Benedicte (1967) *Slavery and agricultural bondage in South India in the nineteenth-century,* Copenhagen: Scandinavian Institute of Asian Studies.

Hoadley, Mason (1983) 'Slavery, bondage and dependency in pre-colonial Java: the Cirebon-Priangan region, 1700,' in Anthony Reid, ed., *Slavery, bondage and dependency in Southeast Asia,* Saint Lucia: University of Queensland Press, 90–117.

Hodgson, Marshall G. S. (1955) *The order of the Assassins: the struggle of the early Nizari Isma'ilis against the Islamic world,* The Hague: Mouton.

—— (1974) *The venture of Islam: conscience and history in a world civilization,* University of Chicago Press.

Hogendorn, Jan S. (2000) 'The location of the "manufacture" of eunuchs,' in Toru Miura and John E. Philips, eds, *Slave élites in the Middle East and Africa, a comparative study,* London: Kegan Paul International, 41–68.

Hollingsworth, L. W. (1953) *Zanzibar under the Foreign Office, 1890–1913,* London: Macmillan.

Holsinger, Donald C. (1994) 'Islam and state expansion in Algeria: nineteenth-century Saharan frontiers,' in John Ruedy, ed., *Islamism and secularism in North Africa,* Basingstoke: Macmillan, 3–21.

Holy Bible, New International Version (1991), London: Hodder and Stoughton.

Hooker, M. B. (1988) 'Muhammadan law and Islamic law,' in M. B. Hooker, ed. *Islam in South-East Asia,* Leiden: E. J. Brill.

Hopkirk, Peter (2001) *The great game: on secret service in high Asia,* Oxford: Oxford University Press. 3rd edn.

Hourani, Albert (1970) *Arabic thought in the liberal age, 1798–1939,* London: Oxford University Press.

Hourani, Albert, and Shehadi, Nadim, eds (1992) *The Lebanese in the world: a century of emigration,* London: I. B. Tauris.

Huang, Pei (1974) *Autocracy at work: a study of the Yun-cheng period, 1723–1735,* Bloomington: Indiana University Press.

Hughes, Thomas P. (1885) *A dictionary of Islam,* London: W. H. Allen.

Huici Miranda, Ambrosio (2000) *Historia política del imperio Almohade,* Granada: Archivum, reprint of 1957 edn.

Hunter, W. W. (1964) *The Indian Musalmans,* Lahore: Premier Book House, reprint of 1872 edn.

Hunwick, John (1985) *Shari'a in Songhay: the replies of al-Maghili to the questions of al-Hajj Muhammad,* Oxford University Press.

—— (1992) 'Black Africans in the Mediterranean world: introduction to a neglected aspect of the African diaspora,' in Elizabeth Savage, ed., *The human commodity: perspectives on the trans-Saharan slave trade,* London: Frank Cass, 5–38.

—— (1999) 'Islamic law and polemics over race and slavery in North and West Africa, sixteenth to nineteenth-century,' *Princeton Papers, Interdisciplinary Journal of Middle Eastern Studies,* 7: 43–68.

—— (2003) '"I wish to be seen in our land called Afrika," 'Umar b. Sayyid's appeal to be released from slavery, 1819,' *Journal of Arabic and Islamic Studies,* 5: 62–77 <http://www.uib.no/jais/v005/Hunwick1WMd.pdf>

—— and Harrak, Fatima (2000) *Mi'raj al Su'ud, Ahmad Baba's replies on slavery*, Rabat: Institute of African Studies.

Hunwick, John, and Powell, Eve Troutt (2002) *The African diaspora in the Mediterranean lands of Islam*, Princeton, NJ: Markus Wiener.

Ileto, Reynaldo C. (1971) *Magindanao 1860–1888: the career of Datu Uto of Buayan*, Ithaca, NY: Cornell University Press.

Iliffe, John (1979) *A modern history of Tanganyika*. Cambridge University Press.

Imber, Colin (1997) *Ebu's-Su'ud; the Islamic legal tradition*, Edinburgh University Press.

—— (2002) *The Ottoman empire, 1300–1650*, Basingstoke: Palgrave Macmillan.

Inalcik, Halil (1979) 'Servile labour in the Ottoman empire,' in Abraham Ascher *et al.*, eds, *The mutual effects of the Islamic and Judeo-Christian worlds: the East European pattern*, New York: Brooklyn College, 25–52.

—— (1997) *An economic and social history of the Ottoman empire*, Vol. 1: *1300–1600*, Cambridge University Press.

Ingrams, Doreen (1970) *A time in Arabia*, London: John Murray.

Ingrams, Harold (1942) *Arabia and the isles*, London: John Murray.

Iqbal, Muhammad (2002) 'Islam as a moral and political ideal,' in Charles Kurzman, ed., *Modernist Islam, 1840–1940: a sourcebook*, Oxford University Press, 304–13.

Israeli, Raphael (1980) *Muslims in China, a study in cultural confrontation*, London: Curzon.

Iwabuchi Akifumi (1994) *The people of the Alas valley, a study of an ethnic group of northern Sumatra*, Oxford: Clarendon Press.

Jackson, Peter (1999) *The Delhi sultanate: a political and military history*, Cambridge University Press.

Jacobs, J. 1894. *Het familie- en kampongsleven op Groot-Atjeh: eene bijdrage tot de ethnographie van Noord-Sumatra*. Leiden: E. J. Brill.

Jahanbakhsh, Forough (2001) *Islam, democracy and religious modernism in Iran, 1953–2000, from Bazargan to Soroush*, Leiden: E. J. Brill.

al-Jahiz, 'Amr b. Bahr (1980) *The epistle on singing-girls of Jahiz*, ed. and tr. A. F. L. Beeston, Warminster: Aris and Phillips.

Jaimoukha, Amjad (2001) *The Circassians: a handbook*, New York: Palgrave.

Jambet, Christian (1990) *La grande resurrection d'Alamût: les formes de la liberté dans le shi'isme ismaélien*, Lagrasse: Verdier.

Jaussen, Antonin (1927) *Coutumes palestiniennes, I: Naplouse et son district*, Paris: Paul Geuthner.

—— (1948) *Coutumes des Arabes au pays de Moab*, Paris: Librairie d'Amérique et d'Orient.

Jawed, Nasim A. (1999) *Islam's political culture: religion and politics in predivided Pakistan*, Austin: University of Texas Press.

Jennings, Lawrence C. (2000) *French anti-slavery: the movement for the abolition of slavery in France, 1802–1848*, Cambridge University Press.

Jenner, W. J. F. (1998) 'China and freedom,' in David Kelly and Anthony Reid, eds, *Asian freedoms: the idea of freedom in East and Southeast Asia*, Cambridge University Press, 65–92.

Jok, Jok M. (2001) *War and slavery in Sudan*, Philadelphia: University of Pennsylvania Press.

Jomier, Jacques (1954) *Le commentaire coranique du Manâr: tendances modernes de l'exégèse coranique en Égypte*, Paris: Maisonneuve.

—— (1988) *Pour connaître l'Islam*, Paris: Éditions du Cerf.

Judy, Ronald A. T. (1993) *(Dis)forming the American canon: African-Arabic slave narratives and the vernacular*, Minneapolis: University of Minnesota Press.

Julien, Charles-André (1964) *Histoire de l'Algérie contemporaine: la conquête et les débuts de la colonisation*, Paris: Presses Universitaires de France.

Jumare, Ibrahim M. (1996) 'The ideology of slavery in the context of Islam and the Sokoto jihad,' *The Islamic Quarterly*, 40/1: 31–8.

Juynboll, T. W. (1912) 'Eunuch, Muslim,' *Encyclopaedia of Religion and Ethics*, Edinburgh: T. & T. Clark, Vol. V, 584–5.

—— and Piekaar, A. J. (1960) 'Atjeh,' *Encyclopaedia of Islam*, Leiden: E. J. Brill, Vol. I, 739–47.

Jwaideh, Albertine, and Cox, J. W. (1989) 'The black slaves of Turkish Arabia during the nineteenth-century,' in William G. Clarence-Smith, ed., *The economics of the Indian Ocean slave trade in the nineteenth-century*, London: Frank Cass, 45–59.

Kaba, Lansiné (1974) *The Wahhabiyya, Islamic reform and politics in French West Africa*, Evanston, IL: Northwestern University Press.

—— (2000) 'Islam in West Africa: radicalism and the new ethic of disagreement, 1960–1990,' in Nehemia Levtzion and Randall L. Pouwels, eds, *The history of Islam in Africa*, Athens: Ohio University Press, 189–208.

Kafadar, Cemal (1995) *Between two worlds: the construction of the Ottoman state*, Berkeley: University of California Press.

Kake, Ibrahima B. (1979) 'The slave trade and the population drain from Black Africa to North Africa and the Middle East,' in *The African slave trade from the fifteenth to the nineteenth-century*, Paris: UNESCO, 164–74.

Kamal-ud-Din, Khawaja (1925) *The ideal Prophet*, Woking, Surrey: Basheer Muslim Library.

Kamara, Ousmane (2000) 'Les divisions statutaires des descendants d'esclaves au Fuuta Tooro mauritanien,' *Journal des Africanistes*, 70/1–2: 265–89.

Kandiyoti, Deniz (1988) 'Slave girls, temptresses and comrades: images of women in the Turkish novel,' *Feminist Issues*, 8/1: 35–50.

—— (1991) 'End of empire: Islam, nationalism and women in Turkey,' in Deniz Kandiyoti, ed., *Women, Islam and the state*, Philadelphia: Temple University Press, 22–47.

Kanlidere, Ahmet (1997) *Reform within Islam: the Tajdid and Jadid movement among the Kazan Tatars, 1809–1917; conciliation or conflict?* Istanbul: Eren.

Kaptein, Nico, ed. (1997) *The Muhimmat al-Nafa'is, a bilingual Meccan fatwa collection for Indonesian Muslims from the end of the nineteenth-century*, Jakarta: Indonesian-Netherlands Co-operation in Islamic Studies.

Karim, Abdul (1936) *Prophet of Islam and his teachings*, Calcutta: A. Rasul.

Karrar, Ali Salih (1985) 'The Sufi brotherhoods in the Sudan until 1900, with special reference to the Shayqiyya region,' PhD thesis, University of Bergen.

Kazhdan, Alexandre (1985) 'The concept of freedom (*eleutheria*) and slavery (*duleia*) in Byzantium,' in George Makdisi *et al.*, eds, *La notion de liberté au Moyen Age: Islam, Byzance, Occident*, Paris: Les Belles Lettres, 215–26.

Kelly, John B. (1968) *Britain and the Persian Gulf, 1795–1880*, Oxford: Clarendon Press.

Kelsay, John (1993) *Islam and war: a study in comparative ethics*, Louisville, KY: Westminster/John Knox.

Khadduri, Majid (1955) *War and peace in the law of Islam*, Baltimore, MD: Johns Hopkins University Press.

—— (1984) *The Islamic conception of justice*, Baltimore, MD: Johns Hopkins University Press.

Khalid, Adeeb (1998) *The politics of Muslim cultural reform: Jadidism in Central Asia*, Berkeley, CA: University of California Press.

Khalil, Mohamed I. (2002) 'Human rights and Islamization of the Sudan legal system,' in Yusuf Fadl Hasan and Richard Gray, eds, *Religion and conflict in Sudan*, Nairobi: Paulines Publications Africa.

Khan, In'amullah (1965) 'The Mo'tamar al-'Alam al-Islami (the World Muslim Congress): a brief description of its sixth conference held at Mogadishu,' *The Islamic Review*, 53/6: 27–9.

Khan, Mazhar ul-Haq (1972) *Purdah and polygamy; a study in the social pathology of the Muslim society*, Peshawar: Nashiran-e-Ilm-o-Taraqiyet.

Khan, Mohammad S. (1996) *Status of women in Islam*, New Delhi: APH Publishing.

Khan, Muhammad Z. (1976) *Islam and human rights*, London: London Mosque.

Khan, Sarfraz (1998) 'The development of Muslim reformist (Jadid) political thought in the emirate of Bukhara, 1870–1924, with particular reference to the writings of Ahmad Donish and Abdal Rauf Fitrat,' PhD thesis, University of London.

Khan Bahador, Ahmed [Sayyid Ahmad Khan] (1979) *Life of Mohammed and subjects subsidiary thereto*, Lahore: Sh. Mubarak Ali, reprint of 1870 edn.

Khayr ed-Din (1987) *Essai sur les réformes nécessaires aux états musulmans*, ed. Magali Morsy, La Calade: Édisud.

Khomeini, Ruhollah M. (1984) *A clarification of questions*, Boulder, CO: Westview.

Khuri, Ra'if (1983) *Modern Arab thought: channels of the French Revolution to the Arab East*, Princeton, NJ: Kingston Press.

Kidwai, Salim (1985) 'Sultans, eunuchs and domestics: new forms of bondage in medieval India,' in Utsa Patnaik and Manjari Dingwaney, eds, *Chains of servitude: bondage and slavery in India*, Madras: Sangam, 76–96.

Kiefer, Thomas M. (1972) *The Tausug: violence and law in a Philippine Moslem society*, New York: Holt, Rinehart and Winston.

Kinenge, Kimena K. (1979) *Tippo Tip, traitant et sultan du Manyema*, Kinshasa: Centre de Recherches Pédagogiques.

Klein, Martin A. (1968) *Islam and imperialism in Senegal: Sine-Saloum, 1847–1914*, Edinburgh University Press.

Klein, Martin A., ed. (1993) *Breaking the chains: slavery, bondage and emancipation in modern Africa and Asia*, Madison, WI: University of Wisconsin Press.

Klein, Martin A., (1998) *Slavery and colonial rule in French West Africa*, Cambridge University Press.

Knappert, Jan (1979) 'The theme of conversion in Swahili literature,' in Nehemia Levtzion, ed., *Conversion to Islam*, New York: Holmes and Meier, 177–88.

Knighton, William (1921) *The private life of an eastern king, together with Elihu Jan's story, or the life of an eastern queen*, ed. S. B. Smith, London: Oxford University Press.

Knysh, Alexander (2000) *Islamic mysticism, a short history*, Leiden: E. J. Brill.

Kohlberg, E. (1976) 'The development of the Imami Shi'i doctrine of jihad,' *Zeitschrift der Deutschen Morgenländischen Gesellschaft*, 126: 64–86.

Kolchin, Peter (1987) *Unfree labor: American slavery and Russian serfdom*, Cambridge, MA: Belknap Press.

Kolff, Dirk H. A. (1990) *Naukar, Rajput and sepoy: the ethnohistory of the military labour market in Hindustan, 1450–1850*, Cambridge University Press.

Koningsveld, P. S. van (1995) 'Muslim slaves and captives in western Europe during the late Middle Ages,' *Islam and Christian-Muslim Relations*, 6/1: 5–23.

Korn, Bertram W. (1971–2) 'Slave trade,' *Encyclopaedia Judaica*, Jerusalem and New York: Macmillan, XIV, 1660–4.

Kotb, Sayed [Sayyid Qutb] (1970) *Social justice in Islam*, New York: Octagon Books.

Kramer, Martin (1986) *Islam assembled: the advent of the Muslim congresses*, New York: Columbia University Press.

Kraus, Werner (1984) *Zwischen Reform und Rebellion: über die Entwicklung des Islams in Minangkabau (Westsumatra) zwischen den beiden Reformbewegungen der Padri (1837) und der Modernisten (1908)*, Wiesbaden: Franz Steiner.

Kreemer, J. (1922–3) *Atjèh: algemeen samenvattend overzicht van land en volk van Atjèh en onderhoorigheden*, Leiden: E. J. Brill.

Kumar, Ann (1997) *Java and modern Europe: ambiguous encounters*, Richmond, Surrey: Curzon.

Kumar, Dharma (1993) 'Colonialism, bondage and caste in British India,' in Martin A. Klein, ed. *Breaking the chains: slavery, bondage and emancipation in modern Africa and Asia*, Madison: University of Wisconsin Press, 112–30.

Kunt, I. Metin (1982) 'Transformation of *zimmi* into *askeri*,' in Benjamin Braude and Bernard Lewis, eds, *Christians and Jews in the Ottoman empire:*

the foundations of a plural society, New York: Holmes and Meier, Vol. I, 55–67.

Kuropatkin, A. N. (1882) *Kashgaria: eastern or Chinese Turkistan*, Calcutta: Thacker, Spink and Co.

Kurzman, Charles, ed. (2002) *Modernist Islam, 1840–1940: a sourcebook*, Oxford University Press.

Kusuman, K. K. (1973) *Slavery in Travancore*, Trivandrum: Kerala Historical Society.

Laffin, John (1982) *The Arabs as master slavers*, Englewood, NJ: SBS Publishing Co.

Lal, K. S. (1994) *Muslim slave system in medieval India*, New Delhi: Aditya Prakashan.

Lambton, Ann K. S. (1970) 'A nineteenth-century view of jihad,' *Studia Islamica*, 32: 180–92.

Lane, Edward W. (1895) *An account of the manners and customs of the modern Egyptians*, London: Alexander Gardner, 2nd edn.

Lang, David M. (1957) *The last years of the Georgian monarchy, 1658–1832*, New York: Columbia University Press.

Lapanne-Joinville, J. (1952) 'La reconnaissance de paternité de l'enfant issu du concubinat légal,' *Revue Marocaine de Droit*, 4/4: 153–68.

Larguèche, Abdelhamid (2003) 'The abolition of slavery in Tunisia: towards a history of the Black community,' in Marcel Dorigny, ed., *The abolitions of slavery, from Léger Félicité Sonthonax to Victor Schoelcher*, New York: Berghahn Books, 330–9.

Lasker, Bruno (1950) *Human bondage in Southeast Asia*, Chapel Hill: University of North Carolina Press.

Launay, Robert (1990) 'Pedigrees and paradigms: scholarly credentials among the Dyula of the northern Ivory Coast,' in Dale F. Eickelman and James Piscatori, eds, *Muslim travellers: pilgrimage, migration, and the religious imagination*, Berkeley: University of California Press, 175–99.

Law, Narendra N. (1916) *Promotion of learning in India during Muhammadan rule, by Muhammadans*, London: Longmans, Green.

Layish, Aharon (2000) 'The Mahdi's legal methodology as a mechanism for adapting the shari'a in the Sudan to political and social purposes,' *Revue des Mondes Musulmans et de la Méditerranée*, 91–4, 221–37.

Lazzarotto, Angelo S. (1982) *Nasce la chiesa nello Zaïre: prime tappe di evangelizzazione nel'ex-Congo Belga, 1880–1933*, Roma: Pontificia Universitas Urbaniana.

Lee, Anthony A. (1999), 'Editor's notes,' for the second and third editions of Abu'l-Qasim Afnan (1988 and 1999) *Black Pearls: servants in the household of the Bab and Baha'u'llah*, Los Angeles, CA: Kalimat Press. <http://bahai-library.com/articles/black.pearls.html>

Leitner, Gottlieb W. (1893) *Muhammadanism*, Lahore: Muhammadan Tract and Book Depot, 2nd edn.

Lenci, Mario (1990) *Eritrea e Yemen: tensioni italo-turche nel Mar Rosso, 1885–1911*, Milan: Franco Angeli.

Lengellé, Maurice (1976) *L'esclavage*, Paris: Presses Universitaires de France, 4th edn.

Leone, Enrico de (1973) *Riformatori musulmani del XIX secolo nell'Africa e nell'Asia mediterranee*, Milano: Giuffrè Editore.

Letourneau, Ch. (1897) *L'évolution de l'esclavage dans les diverses races humaines*, Paris: L. Battaille.

Levi, Scott C. (2002) 'Hindus beyond the Hindu Kush: Indians in the Central Asian slave trade,' *Journal of the Royal Asiatic Society*, 12/3: 277–88.

Lévi-Provençal E. (1960) 'Ahmad b. Khalid b. Hammad al-Nasiri,' *Encyclopaedia of Islam*, Leiden: E. J. Brill, Vol. I, 290–1.

Levtzion, Nehemiah (1987) 'The eighteenth-century background to the Islamic revolutions in West Africa,' in Nehemiah Levtzion and John Voll, eds, *Eighteenth-century renewal and reform in Islam*, Syracuse, NY: Syracuse University Press, 21–38.

Levy, Reuben (1957) *The social structure of Islam*, Cambridge University Press.

Lewis, Bernard (1990) *Race and slavery in the Middle East, an historical enquiry*, New York: Oxford University Press.

Lewis, Herbert S. (1965) *A Galla monarchy: Jimma Abba Jifar, Ethiopia, 1830–1932*, Madison: University of Wisconsin Press.

Linehan, W. (1973) *A history of Pahang*, Kuala Lumpur: Malaysian Branch of the Royal Asiatic Society.

Lipman, Jonathan N. (1997) *Familiar strangers: a history of Muslims in Northwest China*, Seattle: University of Washington Press.

Litvak, Meir (1998) *Shi'i scholars of nineteenth-century Iraq: the 'ulama' of Najaf and Karbala*, Cambridge University Press.

Livingston, Jon, *et al.* (1976) *The Japan reader*, Harmondsworth: Penguin.

Loeb, Edwin M. (1972) *Sumatra, its history and people*, Kuala Lumpur: Oxford University Press, 2nd edn.

Loh, Philip F. S. (1969) *The Malay States, 1877–1895, political change and social policy*, Kuala Lumpur: Oxford University Press.

Lohdi, Abdulaziz Y. (1973) *The institution of slavery in Zanzibar and Pemba*, Uppsala: Scandinavian Institute of African Studies.

Lombard, Denys (1967) *Le sultanat d'Atjéh au temps d'Iskandar Muda, 1607–1636*, Paris: École Française d'Extrême-Orient.

—— (1990) *Le carrefour javanais: essai d'histoire globale*, Paris: École des Hautes Études en Sciences Sociales.

Lovejoy, Paul E. (1981) 'Slavery in the Sokoto caliphate,' in Paul E. Lovejoy, ed., *The ideology of slavery in Africa*, Beverley Hills, CA: Sage, 201–43.

—— (1983) *Transformations in slavery, a history of slavery in Africa*, Cambridge University Press.

—— (2000) *Transformations in slavery: a history of slavery in Africa*, Cambridge University Press, 2nd edn.

—— (2004) 'Slavery, the Bilad al-Sudan and the frontiers of the African diaspora,' in Paul E. Lovejoy, ed., *Slavery on the frontiers of Islam*, Princeton, NJ: Markus Wiener, 1–30.

Lovejoy, Paul E., and Hogendorn, Jan S. (1990) 'Revolutionary Mahdism and resistance to colonial rule in Sokoto,' *Journal of African History*, 31/2: 217–44.

———— (1993) *Slow death for slavery: the course of abolition in northern Nigeria, 1897–1936*, Cambridge University Press.

Low, Hugh (1968) *Sarawak: its inhabitants and products*, London: Frank Cass, reprint of 1848 edn.

Loyré-de-Hauteclocque, Ghislaine (1989) *À la recherche de l'Islam philippin: la communauté maranao*, Paris: L'Harmattan.

Maarif, Ahmad Syafi (1985) *Islam dan masalah kenegaraan; studi tentang percaturan dalam Konstituante*, Jakarta: LP3ES.

Mabbett, Ian (1998) 'Buddhism and freedom,' in David Kelly and Anthony Reid, eds, *Asian freedoms: the idea of freedom in East and Southeast Asia*, Cambridge University Press, 19–36.

Machado, A. J. de Mello (1970) *Entre os Macuas de Angoche: historiando Moçambique*, Lisbon: Prelo.

Mack, Beverley B. (1992) 'Women and slavery in nineteenth-century Hausaland,' in Elizabeth Savage, ed., *The human commodity: perspectives on the trans-Saharan slave trade*, London: Frank Cass, 89–110.

McDougall, E. Ann (1988) 'A topsy-turvy world: slaves and freed labour in the Mauritanian Adrar, 1910–1950,' in Suzanne Miers and Richard Roberts, eds, *The end of slavery in Africa*, Madison: University of Wisconsin Press, 362–88.

———— (1992) 'Salt, Saharans and the trans-Saharan slave trade: nineteenth-century developments,' in Elizabeth Savage, ed., *The human commodity: perspectives on the trans-Saharan slave trade*, London: Frank Cass, 61–88.

MacLean, Derryl N. (2000) 'La sociologie de l'engagement politique: le Mahdawiya indien et l'état,' *Revue des Mondes Musulmans et de la Méditerranée*, 91/4: 239–56.

Madariaga, María Rosa de (1987) 'L'Espagne et le Rif: pénétration coloniale et résistances locales, 1909–1926,' PhD thesis, Paris-I.

Madden, R. R. (1835) *A twelvemonth's residence in the West Indies during the transition from slavery to apprenticeship*, London: James Cochrane and Co.

Madelung, Wilferd (1988) *Religious trends in early Islamic Iran*, Albany, NY: State University of New York Press.

Mahadi, Abdullahi (1992) 'The aftermath of the jihad in the central Sudan as a major factor in the volume of the trans-Saharan slave trade in the nineteenth-century,' in Elizabeth Savage, ed., *The human commodity: perspectives on the trans-Saharan slave trade*, London: Frank Cass, 111–28.

Mahmasani, Subhi (1955) 'Transactions in the Shari'a,' in Majid Khadduri and Herbert J. Liebesny, eds, *Law in the Middle East*, Vol. 1: *Origin and development of Islamic law*, Washington, DC: Middle Eastern Institute, 179–202.

Mahmud Ahmad, Hazrat Mirza Bashir-ud-Din (1924) *Ahmadiyyat, or the true Islam*, Qadian: Book Depot.

Mahmud bin Mat (1954) 'The passing of slavery in East Pahang,' *Malayan Historical Journal*, 1/1: 8–10.

Majerczak, R. (1912) 'Le mouridisme au Caucase,' *Revue du Monde Musulman*, 20: 162–241.

Malcolm, Noel (1994) *Bosnia, a short history*, London: Macmillan.

—— (1998) *Kosovo, a short history*, London: Macmillan.

al-Manar (1909) Cairo, 31 [pp. 189–91 only].

Mangat, J. S. (1969) *A history of the Asians of East Africa, c. 1886–1945*, Oxford: Clarendon Press.

Manning, Patrick (1990) *Slavery and African life: Occidental, Oriental and African slave trades*, Cambridge University Press.

el-Mansour, Mohamed, and Harrak, Fatima, eds, (2000) *A Fulani jihadist in the Maghrib: admonition of Ahmad ibn al-Qadi at-Timbukti to the rulers of Tunisia and Morocco*, Rabat: Institute of African Studies.

Manzoni, Renzo (1884) *El Yèmen, tre anni nell'Arabia Felice, escursioni fatte dal settembre 1877 al marzo 1880*, Rome: Eredi Botta.

Margoliouth, D. S. (1905) *Mohammed and the rise of Islam*, New York: G. P. Putnam's Sons, 3rd edn.

Margoliouth, D. S. (1915) *On Mahdis and Mahdism*, London: British Academy.

Marmon, Shaun (1995) *Eunuchs and sacred boundaries in Islamic society*, New York: Oxford University Press.

Marques, João P. (1999) *Os sons do silêncio: o Portugal de oitocentos e a abolição do tráfico de escravos*, Lisbon: Imprensa das Ciências Sociais.

Martin, Bradford G. (1976) *Muslim brotherhoods in nineteenth-century Africa*, Cambridge University Press.

—— (1985) 'Ahmad Rasim Pasha and the suppression of the Fazzan slave trade, 1881–1896,' in John R. Willis, ed., *Slaves and slavery in Muslim Africa*, London: Frank Cass, Vol. II, 51–82.

Martin, Vanessa (1989) *Islam and modernism; the Iranian revolution of 1906*, Syracuse University Press.

Marty, Paul (1921) *Islam en Guinée: Fouta-Diallon*, Paris: Ernest Leroux.

—— (1926) *Études sur l'Islam au Dahomey*, Paris: Ernest Leroux.

[*The*] *Martyr of Sumatra: a memoir of Henry Lyman* (anon., 1861), New York: Robert Carter & Bros.

Mason, John E. (2003) *Social death and resurrection: slavery and emancipation in South Africa*, Charlottesville: University of Virginia Press.

Matheson, V., and Hooker, M. B. (1983) 'Slavery in the Malay texts: categories of dependency and compensation,' in Anthony Reid, ed., *Slavery, bondage and dependency in Southeast Asia*, Saint Lucia: University of Queensland Press, 182–208.

Maududi, Abul A'la (1972) *Purdah and the status of woman in Islam*, Lahore: Islamic Publications Ltd.

—— (1977) *Human rights in Islam*, Lahore: Islamic Publications Ltd.

Maugham, Robin (1961) *The slaves of Timbuktu*, London: Longmans.

Maxwell, John F. (1975) *Slavery and the Catholic Church: the history of Catholic teaching concerning the moral legitimacy of the institution of slavery*, Chichester, Sussex: Barry Rose.

Maxwell, W. E. (1879), 'The aboriginal tribes of Perak,' *Journal of the Straits Branch of the Royal Asiatic Society*, 4: 46–50.

—— (1890) 'The law relating to slavery among the Malays,' *Journal of the Straits Branch of the Royal Asiatic Society*, 22: 247–98.

Mazumdar, Sucheta (1998) *Sugar and society in China: peasants, technology and the world market*, Cambridge, MA: Harvard University Press.

Mednick, Melvin (1965) 'Encampment of the lake: the social organization of a Moslem-Philippine (Moro) people,' PhD thesis, University of Chicago.

Meijer, Marinus J. (1980) 'Slavery at the end of the Ch'ing dynasty,' in Jerome A. Cohen *et al.*, eds, *Essays on China's legal tradition*, Princeton University Press, 327–58.

Meillassoux, Claude (1991) *The anthropology of slavery: the womb of iron and gold*, London: Athlone.

Meinardus, Otto (1969) 'The Upper Egyptian practice of the making of eunuchs in the eighteenth and nineteenth-century,' *Zeitschrift für Ethnologie*, 94/1–2: 47–58.

Meltzer, Milton (1993) *Slavery: a world history*, New York: Da Capo Press, 2nd edn.

Ménage V. L., (1956) 'Sidelights on the *devshirme* from Idris and Sa'duddin,' *Bulletin of the School of Oriental and African Studies*, 18/1: 181–3.

—— (1965) 'Devshirme,' *Encyclopaedia of Islam*, Leiden: E. J. Brill, Vol. II, 210–13.

Mercer, John (1976) *Spanish Sahara*, London: George Allen and Unwin.

Mernissi, Fatima (1987) *Le harem politique: le Prophète et les femmes*, Paris: Albin Michel.

Messaoud, Boubacar (2000) 'L'esclavage en Mauritanie: de l'idéologie du silence à la mise en question,' *Journal des Africanistes*, 70/1–2: 291–337.

Metcalf, Barbara D. (1982) *Islamic revival in British India: Deoband 1860–1900*, Princeton University Press.

Michaux-Bellaire, E., (1907) 'L'esclavage au Maroc,' *Revue du Monde Musulman*, 11/7–8: 422–7.

Miers, Suzanne (1989) 'Diplomacy versus humanitarianism: Britain and consular manumission in Hijaz, 1921–1936,' *Slavery and Abolition*, 10/3: 102–28.

—— (2003) *Slavery in the twentieth-century; the evolution of a global problem*, Walnut Creek, CA: AltaMira.

Miers, Suzanne, and Roberts, Richard L., eds. (1988) *The end of slavery in Africa*, Madison: University of Wisconsin Press.

Migeod, Heinz-Georg (1990) *Die persische Gesellschaft unter Nasiru'd-Din Sah, 1848–1896*, Berlin: Klaus Schwarz.

Millant, Richard (1908) *Les eunuques à travers les ages*, Paris: Vigot Frères.

Miller, Donald E. and Miller Lorna T. (1993) *Survivors: an oral history of the Armenian genocide*, Berkeley: University of California Press.

Miller, Joseph C. (1992) 'Muslim slavery and slaving, a bibliography,' in Elizabeth Savage, ed., *The human commodity: perspectives on the trans-Saharan slave trade*, London: Frank Cass, 249–71.

Miller, Judith (1996) *God has ninety-nine names: reporting from a militant Middle East*, New York: Simon and Schuster.

Miran, Jonathan (2004) 'Facing the land, facing the sea: commercial transformation and urban dynamics in the Red Sea port of Massawa, 1840s–1900s,' PhD thesis, Michigan State University.

Mirpuri, Mahmood A. (1998) *Fatawa Sirat-e-Mustaqeem*, Riyadh: Darussalam [in English].

Mirza, Sarah, and Strobel, Margaret (1989) *Three Swahili women: life histories from Mombasa, Kenya*, Bloomington: Indiana University Press.

Mirzai, Behnaz (2000) 'The sharia and the anti-slave trade *farman* of 1848 in Iran,' paper for Workshop on Slave Systems in Asia and the Indian Ocean, Université d'Avignon, forthcoming in selected papers.

Mitter, Ulrike (2001) 'Unconditional manumission of slaves in early Islamic law: a hadith analysis,' *Der Islam*, 78/1: 35–72.

Miura, Toru, and Philips, John E., eds. (2000) *Slave élites in the Middle East and Africa: a comparative study*, London: Kegan Paul International.

Moitt, Bernard (1989) 'Slavery and emancipation in Senegal's peanut basin: the nineteenth and twentieth centuries,' *International Journal of African Historical Studies*, 22/1: 27–50.

Monlaü, Jean (1964) *Les états barbaresques*, Paris: Presses Universitaires de France.

Montana, Ismael M. (2001) 'Islamic law, the religious establishment and abolition of slavery in the Regency of Tunis,' unpublished paper, 44th Annual Meeting of the African Studies Association, Houston, Texas, 15–18 November.

—— (2004) 'Ahmad ibn al-Qadi al-Timbuktawi on the *bori* ceremonies of Tunis,' in Paul E. Lovejoy, ed., *Slavery on the frontiers of Islam*, Princeton, NJ: Markus Wiener, 173–98.

Monteiro, Fernando Amaro (1993) *O Islão, o poder, e a guerra: Moçambique 1964–1974*, Oporto: Universidade Portucalense.

Montesquieu, Charles de Secondat, Baron de (1960) *Lettres persanes*, Paris: Garnier.

Moon, David (2001) *The abolition of serfdom in Russia, 1762–1907*, Harlow, Essex: Pearson Education.

Moor, J. H., ed. (1968) *Notices of the Indian Archipelago and adjacent countries*, London: Frank Cass, reprint of 1837 edn.

Moore-Harell, Alice (1999) 'Economic and political aspects of the slave trade in Ethiopia and the Sudan in the second half of the nineteenth-century,' *International Journal of African Historical Studies*, 32/2–3: 407–21.

Moosvi, Shireen (1998) *Episodes in the life of Akbar: contemporary records and reminiscences*, New Delhi: National Book Trust.

—— (2003) 'Domestic service in precolonial India: bondage, caste and market,' paper for Models of Domestic Service conference, Munich 11–14 September 2003, forthcoming in the conference volume, ed. Antoinette Fauve-Chamoux.

Morell, John R. (1984) *Algeria, the topography and history, political, social and natural, of French Algeria*, London: Darf, reprint of 1854 edn.

Morgenthau, Henry (1918) *Ambassador Morgenthau's story*, New York: Doubleday, Page & Co.

Moroney, Michael G., ed. (2003) *Manufacturing and labour*, The Formation of the Classical Islamic World Series, Vol. 12, Aldershot: Ashgate.

Morton, Fred (1990) *Children of Ham: freed slaves and fugitive slaves on the Kenya coast, 1873–1907*, Boulder, CO: Westview.

Moszkowski, Max (1909) *Auf neuen Wegen durch Sumatra: Forschungsreisen in Ost- und Zentral-Sumatra, 1907*, Berlin: Dietrich Reimer.

Mowafi, Reda (1981) *Slavery, slave trade and abolition attempts in Egypt and the Sudan, 1820–1882*, Malmö: Scandinavian University Books.

Muhaiyaddeen, M. R. Bawa (2002) *Islam and world peace*, Philadelphia, PA: Bawa Muhaiyaddeen Fellowship.

Muhammad, Sha'ban H. (1999) *The role of Islam in Indonesian politics*, Delhi: Ajanta.

Muhammad, Shan (1969) *Sir Syed Ahmad Khan, a political biography*, Begum Bridge, Meerut: Meenakshi Prakashan.

Muir, William (1877) *The life of Mahomet from original sources*, London: Smith, Elder, abridged edn.

────── (1891) *The caliphate, its rise, decline and fall, from original sources*, London: Religious Tract Society.

Mujeeb, M. (1967) *The Indian Muslims*, London: George Allen and Unwin.

Müller, Hans (1980) *Die Kunst des Sklavenkaufs, nach arabischen, persischen, und türkischen Ratgebern vom 10. bis 18. Jahrhundert*, Freiburg: Klaus Schwarz.

Munson Jr., Henry (1993) *Religion and power in Morocco*, New Haven, CT: Yale University Press.

al-Muqaddasi, (1950) *Description de l'occident musulman au IVe/IXe siècle*, ed. and tr. Charles Pellat, Algiers: Éditions Carbonel.

el-Murjebi, Hamed ben Mohammed (1974) *L'autobiographie de Hamed ben Mohammed el-Murjebi, Tippo Tip, ca. 1840–1905*, ed. François Bontinck, Brussels: Académie Royale des Sciences d'Outre-Mer.

Musca, Giosuè, and Colafemmina, Cesare (1989) 'Tra Longobardi e Saraceni: l'emirato,' in Francesco Tateo, ed., *Storia di Bari, dalla preistoria al mille*, Rome: Editori Laterza, 285–313.

Muslimin, J. M. (1998) 'The reactualization of Islamic law: a study of trends and methods of Islamic legal reform in Indonesia, 1945–1995,' MA thesis, University of Leiden.

Nadir, Ahmad (1972) 'Les ordres religieux et la conquête française, 1830–1851,' *Revue Algérienne des Sciences Juridiques, Économiques et Politiques*, 9/4: 819–72.

an-Na'im, 'Abdullahi A. (1998) 'Shari'a and basic human rights concerns,' in Charles Kurzman, ed., *Liberal Islam: a sourcebook*, New York: Oxford University Press, 222–38.

Na'ini, Muhammad Husayn (2002) 'Government in the Islamic perspective,' in Charles Kurzman, ed., *Modernist Islam, 1840–1940, a sourcebook*, Oxford University Press, 116–25.

Nallino, Carlo A. (1939) *Raccolta di scritti editi e inediti*, Vol. 1: *L'Arabia Sa'udiana*, Rome: Istituto per l'Oriente.

Nasr, Vali Reza (1996) *Mawdudi and the making of Islamic revivalism*, New York: Oxford University Press.

Nerval, Gérard de (1958) *Oeuvres*, Paris: Garnier.

Netton, Ian R. (1992) *A popular dictionary of Islam*, London: Curzon.

Nicholls, C. S. (1971) *The Swahili coast: politics, diplomacy and trade on the East African littoral, 1798–1856*, London: George Allen and Unwin.

Nicolini, Beatrice (2002) *Il sultanato di Zanzibar nel XIX secolo: traffici commerciali e relazioni internazionali*, Turin: L'Harmattan Italia.

Nieuwenhuis, Tom (1981) *Politics and society in early modern Iraq: mamluk pashas, tribal shaykhs and local rule between 1802 and 1831*, The Hague: Martinus Nijhoff.

Nizami, Khaliq Ahmad (1989) *Akbar and religion*, Delhi: Idarah-i-Adabiyat-i-Delli.

Noelle, Christine (1997) *State and tribe in nineteenth-century Afghanistan: the reign of Amir Dost Muhammad Khan, 1826–1863*, Richmond, Surrey: Curzon.

Noer, Deliar (1973) *The modernist Muslim movement in Indonesia, 1900–1941*, Singapore: Oxford University Press.

Nolte, Hans-Heinrich (2004) 'Religion and industrial development in 19th century Russia: the Raskolniki,' unpublished paper, GEHN conference, University of Konstanz, 3–6 June.

Noor, Abdun (2000) 'Outlining social justice from an Islamic perspective: an exploration,' *Islamic Quarterly*, 44/2: 435–50.

Norris, H. T. (1969) 'Znaga Islam during the seventeenth and eighteenth centuries,' *Bulletin of the School of Oriental and African Studies*, 32/3: 496–526.

―――― (1975) *The Tuaregs, their Islamic legacy, and its diffusion in the Sahel*, Warminster: Aris and Phillips.

―――― (1978) 'The Himyaritic Tihama: evidence for a multi-racial society in pre-Islamic and early Islamic Arabia,' *Abbay*, 9: 101–19.

―――― (1980) *The adventures of Antar*, Warminster: Aris and Phillips.

Northrup. David (1988) 'The ending of slavery in the eastern Belgian Congo,' in Suzanne Miers and Richard Roberts, eds, *The end of slavery in Africa*, Madison: University of Wisconsin Press, 462–82.

Nurbakhsh, Javad (1980) *Masters of the Path: a history of the masters of the Nimatullahi Sufi order*, New York: Khaniqahi Nimatullahi Publications.

O'Callaghan, Sean (1961) *The slave trade today*, New York: Crown Publishers.

O'Fahey, R. S., and Radtke, Bernd (1993) 'Neo-Sufism reconsidered,' *Der Islam*, 70: 52–87.

Olcott, Martha B. (1987) *The Kazakhs*, Stanford University Press.

Olivier de Sardan, J.-P. (1975) 'Captifs ruraux et esclaves impériaux du Songhay,' in Claude Meillassoux, ed., *L'esclavage en Afrique précoloniale*, Paris: François Maspéro, 99–134.

Olufsen, O. (1911) *The emir of Bokhara and his country: journeys and studies in Bokhara*, London: William Heinemann.

Oriente Moderno, rivista mensile d'informazioni e di studi per la diffusione e la conoscenza dell'oriente, sopratutto musulmano, Rome: Istituto per l'Oriente, 1921–.

O'Shea, Raymond (1947) *The sand kings of Oman, being the experiences of an RAF officer in the little known region of Trucial Oman, Arabia*, London: Methuen.

Ould Ahmed Salem, Zekeria (2003) 'Droit du statut personnel et équivalence citoyenne en République Islamique de Mauritanie: le cas du mariage à travers deux affaires récentes de procès en kefa'a, équivalence,' to be published in *La Pensée*, 336: 37–53.

Özbay, Ferhunde (1999a) *Turkish female child domestic workers: Project report submitted to ILO/IPC*, Istanbul: Bogaziçi University Press.

——— (1999b) 'Gendered space: a new look at Turkish modernisation,' *Gender and History*, 11/3: 555–68.

Palais, James B. (1996) *Confucian statecraft and Korean institutions*, Seattle: University of Washington Press.

Panikkar K. N. (1989) *Against lord and state: religion and peasant uprisings in Malabar, 1836–1921*, Delhi: Oxford University Press.

Papoulia, Basilike D. (1963) *Ursprung und Wesen der 'Knabenlese' im osmanischen Reich*, Munich: R. Oldenbourg.

Parla, Taha (1985) *The social and political thought of Ziya Gökalp, 1876–1924*, Leiden: E. J. Brill.

Parwez, Ghulam A. (1989) *Islam, a challenge to religion*, New Delhi: Islamic Book Service.

Patterson, Orlando (1982) *Slavery and social death: a comparative study*, Cambridge, MA: Harvard University Press.

Peirce, Leslie P. (1993) *The imperial harem: women and sovereignty in the Ottoman empire*, New York: Oxford University Press.

Pellat, Ch., Lambton, A. K. S., and Orhonlu, Cengis (1978) 'Khasi,' *Encyclopaedia of Islam*, Leiden: E. J. Brill, Vol. IV, 1087–93.

Pelras, Christian (2001) 'Religion, tradition and the dynamics of Islamization in South Sulawesi,' in Alijah Gordon, ed., *The propagation of Islam in the Indonesian-Malay archipelago*, Kuala Lumpur: Malaysian Sociological Research Institute, 209–49.

Pennell, C. R. (1986) *A country with a government and a flag: the Rif War in Morocco, 1921–1926*, Wisbech, Cambridgeshire: Middle East and North African Studies Press.

——— (1989) *Piracy and diplomacy in seventeenth-century North Africa; the journal of Thomas Baker, English consul in Tripoli, 1677–1685*, Rutherford, NJ: Fairleigh Dickinson University Press.

Person, Yves (1968–75) *Samori, une révolution Dyula*, Dakar: IFAN.

Peskes, Esther (1993) *Muhammad b. 'Abdalwahhab (1703–1792) in Widerstreit: Untersuchungen zur Rekonstruktion der Frühgeschichte der Wahhabiya*, Beirut: Franz Steiner Verlag.

Peters, Rudolph (1979) *Islam and colonialism: the doctrine of jihad in modern history*, The Hague: Mouton.

Pétré-Grenouilleau, Olivier (2004) *Les traites négrières: essai d'histoire globale*, Paris: Gallimard.

Petrushevsky, I. P. (1985) *Islam in Iran*, London: Athlone.

Philips, John E. (2000) 'The persistence of slave officials in the Sokoto caliphate,' in Miura, Toru, and Philips, John E. eds, *Slave élites in the Middle East and Africa, a comparative study*, London: Kegan Paul International, 215–34.

Phillips, Wendell (1966) *Unknown Oman*, New York: McKay & Co.

Phule, Jotirao (2002) *Selected writings of Jotirao Phule*, ed. G. P. Deshpande, New Delhi: LeftWord Books.

Pimentel, Maria do Rosário (1995) *Viagem ao fundo das consciências: a escravatura na época moderna*, Lisbon: Colibri.

Pipes, Daniel (1981) *Slave soldiers and Islam: the genesis of a military system*, New Haven, CT: Yale University Press.

Piscatori, James P. (1986) *Islam in a world of nation-states*, Cambridge University Press.

Polak, Jakob E. (1865) *Persien, das Land und seine Bewohner*, Leipzig: F. A. Brockhaus.

Popovic, Alexandre (1976) *La révolte des esclaves en Iraq au IIIe/IXe siècle*, Paris: Paul Geuthner.

—— (1978) 'Les Cerkesses dans les territoires yougoslaves,' *Bulletin d'Études Orientales*, 30: 159–71.

Poulet, Georges (1994) 'Enquête sur la captivité en Afrique Occidentale Française,' in Paul E. Lovejoy and A. S. Kanya-Forstner, eds, *Slavery and its abolition in French West Africa*, Madison: University of Wisconsin, 19–92.

Poullada, Leon B. (1973) *Reform and rebellion in Afghanistan, 1919–1929: King Amanullah's failure to modernize a traditional society*, Ithaca, NY: Cornell University Press.

Pourjavady, Nasrollah, and Wilson, Peter Lamborn (1978) *Kings of love: the poetry and history of the Ni'matullahi Sufi order*, Tehran: Imperial Iranian Academy of Philosophy.

Pouwels, Randall L. (1987) *Horn and crescent: cultural change and traditional Islam on the East African coast, 800–1900*, Cambridge University Press.

Powell, Avril (forthcoming) 'Indian Muslim modernists and the issue of slavery in Islam', in Richard Eaton and Indrani Chatterjee, eds, *Slavery in India*, Indiana University Press.

Powell, Eve M. Troutt (2003) *A different shade of colonialism: Egypt, Great Britain and the mastery of the Sudan*, Berkeley: University of California Press.

Prakash, Gyan (1990) *Bonded histories: genealogies of labor servitude in colonial India*, Cambridge University Press.

Pringle, Robert (1970) *Rajahs and rebels: the Ibans of Sarawak under Brooke rule, 1841–1941,* London: Macmillan.

Prud'homme, Claude (2002) 'L'Église catholique et l'esclavage: une aussi longue attente,' in Edmond Maestri, ed., *Esclavage et abolitions dans l'Océan Indien,* Paris: L'Harmattan, 75–88.

Punshon, John (1984) *Portrait in grey: a short history of the Quakers,* London: Quaker Home Service.

Putra, Heddy Shri Ahimsa (1988) *Minawang: hubungan patron-klien di Sulawesi Selatan,* Yogyakarta: Gadjah Mada University Press.

al-Qaddafi, Muammar (1987) *The green book,* Tripoli: World Center for Studies and Research of the Green Book.

Quenum, Alphonse (1993) *Les Églises chrétiennes et la traite atlantique du XVe au XIXe siècle,* Paris: Karthala.

[Quilliam, Abdullah] (1895) 'Islam and slavery,' *The Islamic World,* 3/26: 54–6 [authorship suggested by Eric Germain].

Qutb, Muhammad (1967) *Islam, the misunderstood religion,* Kuwait: al-Assriya.

—— (1982) 'Islam as a supreme doctrine,' in Salem Azzam ed., *Islam and contemporary society,* London: Longman, 1–35.

Raffles, Thomas S. (1978). *The history of Java,* Kuala Lumpur: Oxford University Press, reprint of 1817 edn.

Rahal, Ahmed (2000) *La communauté noire de Tunis: thérapie initiatique et rite de possession,* Paris: L'Harmattan.

Rahman, Fazlur (1979) *Islam,* University of Chicago Press, 2nd edn.

—— (1982) *Islam and modernity: transformation of an intellectual tradition,* University of Chicago Press.

Ramachandran Nair, Adoor K. K. (1986) *Slavery in Kerala,* Delhi: Mittal Publications.

al-Rashid, Zamil Muhammad (1981) *Su'udi relations with eastern Arabia and 'Uman, 1800–1871,* London: Luzac.

Rawat, Hasan M. (1985) *Slave trade in Africa: a historical perspective,* Karachi: Motamar al-Alam al-Islami.

Reclus, Élisée (1883) *Nouvelle géographie universelle, la terre et les hommes,* I: *l'Europe méridionale,* Paris: Librairie Hachette.

Reid, Anthony (1969) 'Indonesian diplomacy: a documentary study of Atjehnese foreign policy in the reign of sultan Mahmud, 1870–4,' *Journal of the Malaysian Branch of the Royal Asiatic Society,* 42/2: 74–114.

—— (1983a) 'Introduction: slavery and bondage in Southeast Asian history,' in Anthony Reid, ed. *Slavery, bondage and dependency in Southeast Asia,* Saint Lucia: University of Queensland Press, 1–43.

—— (1983b) '"Closed" and "open" slave systems in pre-colonial Southeast Asia,' in Anthony Reid, ed. *Slavery, bondage and dependency in Southeast Asia,* Saint Lucia: University of Queensland Press, 156–81.

—— (1993) 'The decline of slavery in nineteenth-century Indonesia,' in Martin A. Klein, ed., *Breaking the chains: slavery, bondage and emancipation in modern Africa and Asia,* Madison: University of Wisconsin Press, 64–82.

Reis, João J., ed. (1988) *Rebelião escrava no Brasil: a história do levante dos malês*, São Paulo: Editora Brasiliense.

Renault, François (1971) *Lavigerie: l'esclavage africain et l'Europe, 1868–1892*, Paris: F. de Boccard.

—— (1987) *Tippo Tip: un potentat arabe en Afrique centrale au XIXe siècle*, Paris: Société Française d'Histoire d'Outre-Mer.

—— (1989) *La traite des noirs au Proche-Orient mediéval, VIIe–XIVe siècles*, Paris: Paul Geuthner.

—— (1992) *Le cardinal Lavigerie, 1825–1892: l'Église, l'Afrique, et la France*, Paris: Fayard.

Renault, François, and Daget, Serge (1985) *Les traites négrières en Afrique*, Paris: Karthala.

Repp, R. C. (1968) 'A further note on the devshirme,' *Bulletin of the School of Oriental and African Studies*, 31/1: 137–9.

Richards, John F. (1993) *The Mughal empire*, Cambridge University Press.

Richardson, James (1853) *Narrative of a mission to Central Africa*, London: Chapman and Hall.

Richardson, Kristina L. (2004) 'Negotiating slavery through sexuality and motherhood: singing slave-girls of the Abbasid court,' paper for 'Children in Slavery' conference, Avignon, 19–21 May.

Ricklefs, M. C. (1993) *A history of modern Indonesia since c. 1300*, London: Macmillan, 2nd edn.

Riddell, Peter (2001) *Islam and the Malay-Indonesian world*. London: Hurst.

Rihani, Ameen (1928) *Ibn Sa'oud of Arabia: his people and his land*, London: Constable.

Rinn, Louis (1884) *Marabouts et khouans: étude sur l'Islam en Algérie*, Algiers: Adolphe Jourdan.

Rippin, Andrew (1993) *Muslims: their religious beliefs and practices*, Vol. 2: *The contemporary period*, London: Routledge.

Risso, Patricia (1986) *Oman and Muscat: an early modern history*, London: Croom Helm.

—— (1995) *Merchants and faith: Muslim commerce and culture in the Indian Ocean*, Boulder, CO: Westview.

Rizvi, Athar A. (1978–83) *A history of Sufism in India*, New Delhi: Munshiram Manoharlal.

Rizvi, Sa'eed Akhtar (1987) *Slavery from Islamic and Christian perspectives*, 2nd edn. <http://www.al-islam.org/slavery>

Roberts, Robert (1925) *The social laws of the Qoran, considered and compared with those of the Hebrew and other ancient codes*, London: Williams and Norgate.

Rodinson, Maxime (1966) *Islam et capitalisme*, Paris: Éditions du Seuil.

Rodney, Walter (1968) 'Jihad and social revolution in Futa Djalon in the eighteenth-century, *Journal of the Historical Society of Nigeria*, 4/2: 269–84.

Roemer, H. R. (1986) 'The Safavid period,' *The Cambridge History of Iran*, Cambridge University Press, Vol. VI: 189–350.

Romero, Patricia W. (1997) *Lamu: history, society, and family in an East African port city*, Princeton, NJ: Markus Wiener.

Rorlich, Azade-Ayse (1986) *The Volga Tatars: a profile in national resilience*, Stanford, CA: Hoover Institution Press.

Rosenthal, Franz (1960) *The Muslim conception of freedom prior to the nineteenth-century*, Leiden: E. J. Brill.

Rotter, Gernot (1967) *Die Stellung des Negers in der islamisch-arabischen Gesellschaft bis zum XVI. Jahrhundert*, Bonn: Rheinische Friedrich-Wilhelms-Universität.

Rouaud, Alain (1979) *Les Yemen et leurs populations*, Brussels: Éditions Complexe.

Rowe, William T. (2002) 'Social stability and social change,' in *The Cambridge History of China*, Cambridge University Press, Vol. 9, Part 1: 473–562.

Roy, Olivier (1994) *The failure of political Islam*, London: I. B. Tauris.

Ruf, Urs P. (1999) *Ending slavery: hierarchy, dependency and gender in central Mauritania*, Bielefeld: Transcript Verlag.

Ruibing, A. H. (1937) *Ethnologische studie betreffende de Indonesische slavernij als maatschappelijk verschijnsel*, Zutphen: W. J. Thieme.

Ruiz de Cuevas, Teodoro (1973) *Apuntes para la historia de Tetuán*, Madrid: IMNASA.

Ruthven, Malise (2000) *Islam in the world*, London: Penguin, 2nd edn.

Rutter, Eldon (1928) *The holy cities of Arabia*, London: G. P. Putnam's Sons.

——— (1933) 'Slavery in Arabia,' *Journal of the Royal Central Asian Society*, 20/3: 315–32.

Rutter, Owen (1986) *The pirate wind: tales of the sea-robbers of Malaya*, Singapore: Oxford University Press, reprint of 1930 edn.

Sabini, John (1981) *Armies in the sand: the struggle for Mecca and Medina*, London: Thames and Hudson.

Sagaster, Börte (1997) *'Herren' und 'Sklaven': der Wandel im Sklavenbild türkischer Literaten in der Spätzeit des Osmanischen Reiches*, Wiesbaden: Harrassowitz.

Said, Edward W. (1991) *Orientalism: Western conceptions of the Orient*, London: Penguin.

Saifi, Naseem (1956) *Women in Islam*, Lagos: Ahmadiyya Bookshop.

el-Sakkakini, Widad (1982) *First among Sufis: the life and thought of Rabi'a al-'Adawiyya, the woman saint of Basra*, London: Octagon Press.

Salim, Ahmed I. (1973) *Swahili-speaking peoples of Kenya's coast, 1895–1965*, Nairobi: East African Publishing House.

Salman, Michael (2001) *The embarrassment of slavery: controversies over bondage and nationalism in the American colonial Philippines*, Manila: Ateneo de Manila Press.

Salme, Sayyida [Emily Ruete] (1993) *An Arab princess between two worlds: memoirs; letters home; sequels to the memoirs; Syrian customs and usages*, ed. E. van Donzel, Leiden: E. J. Brill.

al-Saltana, Taj (1993) *Crowning anguish: memoirs of a Persian princess from the harem to modernity*, ed. Abbas Amanat, Washington, DC: Mage.

Salvadei, G. P. (1927) 'Il tramonto della schiavitù nelle colonie italiane di diretto dominio,' in *Atti del quarto congresso nazionale della Società Antischiavista d'Italia*, Rome: Anonima Romana Editoriale, 164–8.

Samatar, Said S. (1992) 'Sheikh Uways Muhammad of Baraawe, 1847–1909, mystic and reformer in East Africa,' in Said S. Samatar, ed. *In the shadow of conquest: Islam in colonial Northeast Africa*, 48–74, Trenton, NJ: Red Sea Press.

Samb, Amar (1980) 'L'Islam et l'esclavage,' *Notes Africaines*, 168: 93–7.

Sanneh, Lamin (1989) *The Jakhanke Muslim clerics: a religious and historical study of Islam in Senegambia*, Lanham, MD: University Press of America.

——— (1997) *The crown and the turban: Muslims and West African pluralism*, Boulder, CO: Westview Press.

Sansom, G. B. (1978) *Japan, a short cultural history*, Stanford University Press.

Sarkar, Tanika (1985) 'Bondage in the colonial context,' in Utsa Patnaik and Manjari Dingwaney, eds, *Chains of servitude: bondage and slavery in India*, Madras: Sangam, 97–126.

Sarwar Qureshi, Hafiz M. (1983) *The Qur'an and slavery: a critique of Maudoodi's commentary on Sura Ahzab*, London: published by the author.

Savage, Elizabeth, ed. (1992) *The human commodity: perspectives on the trans-Saharan slave trade*, London: Frank Cass.

Schleifer, S. Abdullah (1983) 'Jihad and traditional Islamic consciousness,' *Islamic Quarterly*, 27/4: 173–203.

Schmidt, Jan (1992) *Through the legation window: four essays on Dutch, Dutch-Indian, and Ottoman history*, Istanbul: Nederlands Historisch-Archaeologisch Instituut.

Schneider, Irene (1999) *Kinderverkauf und Schuldknechtschaft: Untersuchungen zur frühen Phase des islamischen Rechts*, Stuttgart: Deutsche Morgenländische Gesellschaft.

Schorsch, Jonathan (2000) 'American Jewish historians, colonial Jews and Blacks, and the limits of *Wissenschaft*: a critical review,' *Jewish Social Studies*, 6/2: 102–32.

Schroeter, Daniel (1992) 'Slave markets and slavery in Moroccan urban society,' in Elizabeth Savage, ed., *The human commodity: perspectives on the trans-Saharan slave trade*, London: Frank Cass, 185–213.

Schwartz, Werner (1983) *Die Anfänge der Ibaditen in Nordafrika: der Beitrag einer islamischen Minderheit zur Ausbreitung des Islams*, Wiesbaden: Harrassowitz.

Searing, James F. (2002) *'God alone is king': Islam and emancipation in Senegal; the Wolof kingdoms of Kajoor and Bawol, 1859–1914*, Portsmouth, NH: Heinemann.

Segal, Ronald (2001) *Islam's Black slaves: the other Black diaspora*, New York: Farrar, Straus and Giroux.

Sékaly, Achille (1926) *Le Congrès du Khalifat (Le Caire 13–19 mai 1926) et le Congrès du Monde Musulman (La Mekke, 7 juin–5 juillet 1926)*, Paris: E. Leroux.

Seton-Watson, Hugh (1952) *The decline of imperial Russia, 1855–1914,* New York: Praeger.

Shar'iati, Ali (1979) *On the sociology of Islam,* Berkeley, CA: Mizan Press.

Shaw, Stanford J. and Shaw, Ezel. K. (1976–7) *History of the Ottoman empire and modern Turkey,* Cambridge University Press.

Sheean, Vincent (1926) *Adventures among the Riffi,* London: George Allen and Unwin.

Sheik-'Abdi, 'Abdi (1993) *Divine madness; Mohammed 'Abdulle Hassan, 1856–1920,* London: Zed Books.

Shemmassian, Vahram L. (2003) 'The League of Nations and the reclamation of Armenian genocide survivors,' in Richard G. Hovannisian, ed., *Looking backward, moving forward: confronting the Armenian genocide,* New Brunswick, NJ: Transaction Publishers, 81–112.

Shepherd, Gill (1980) 'The Comorians and the East African slave trade,' in James L. Watson, ed., *Asian and African systems of slavery,* 73–99, Oxford: Basil Blackwell.

Sheriff, Abdul (1987) *Slaves, spices and ivory in Zanzibar: integration of an East African commercial Empire into the world economy, 1770–1873,* London: James Currey.

Shinar, Pessah (1961) 'Ibadiyya and orthodox reformism in modern Algeria,' in Uriel Heyd, ed., *Studies in Islamic history and civilization,* Jerusalem: Magnes Press, 97–120.

Shiraishi, Takashi (1990) *An age in motion: popular radicalism in Java, 1912–1926,* Ithaca, NY: Cornell University Press.

Shourie, Arun (1995) *The world of fatwas, or the shariah in action,* New Delhi: ASA Publications.

Siddiqi, Mazheruddin (1982) *Modernist reformist thought in the Muslim world,* Islamabad: Islamic Research Institute.

Sikainga, Ahmad A. (1996) *Slaves into workers: emancipation and labor in colonial Sudan,* Austin: University of Texas Press.

—— (1999) 'Slavery and Muslim jurisprudence in Morocco,' in Suzanne Miers and Martin Klein, eds, *Slavery and colonial rule in Africa,* London: Frank Cass, 57–72.

Sivan, Emmanuel (1978) 'Arab revisionist historians,' *Asian and African Studies,* 12/3: 283–311.

Sirriyeh, Elizabeth (1999) *Sufis and anti-Sufis: the defence, rethinking and rejection of Sufism in the modern world,* Richmond, Surrey: Curzon.

Skrine, C. P., and Nightingale, Pamela (1973) *Macartney at Kashgar: new light on British, Chinese and Russian activities in Sinkiang, 1890–1918,* London: Methuen.

Slama, B. (1967) *L'insurrection de 1864 en Tunisie,* Tunis: Maison Tunisienne de l'Édition.

Smith, Margaret (1994) *Rabi'a: the life and work of Rabi'a and other women mystics in Islam,* Oxford: Oneworld.

Snouck Hurgronje, C. (1903) *Het Gajoland en zijne bewoners.* Batavia: Landsdrukkerij.

———— (1906) *The Achehnese*, Leiden: E. J. Brill.

———— (1916) *Mohammedanism: lectures on its origin, its religious and political growth, and its present state*, New York: G. P. Putnam's Sons.

———— (1923–4) *Verspreide geschriften*, The Hague: Martinus Nijhoff.

———— (1931) *Mekka in the latter part of the nineteenth-century; daily life, customs and learning: the Muslims of the East Indian archipelago*, Leiden: E. J. Brill.

———— (1957) *Selected works*, Leiden: E. J. Brill.

———— (1957–65) *Ambtelijke adviezen van C. Snouck Hurgronje*, The Hague: Martinus Nijhoff.

Sourdel D. *et al.* (1965) 'Ghulam,' *Encyclopaedia of Islam*, Leiden: E. J. Brill, II, 1079–91.

Sourdel Dominique (1985) 'Peut-on parler de liberté dans la société de l'Islam mediéval?,' in George Makdisi *et al.*, eds, *La notion de liberté au Moyen Age: Islam, Byzance, Occident*, Paris: Les Belles Lettres, 119–33.

Spaulding, Jay (1982) 'Slavery, land tenure and social class in the northern Turkish Sudan,' *International Journal of African Historical Studies*, 15/1: 1–20.

———— (2000) 'Precolonial Islam in the eastern Sudan,' in Nehemia Levtzion and Randall L. Pouwels, eds, *The history of Islam in Africa*, Athens: Ohio University Press, 117–29.

Stark, Freya (1945) *A winter in Arabia*, London: John Murray, 3rd edn.

———— (1946) *The southern gates of Arabia: a journey in the Hadhramaut*, London: John Murray, 8th edn.

Stark, Rodney (2003) *For the glory of God: how monotheism led to the reformation, science, witch-hunts, and the end of slavery*, Princeton University Press.

Stauth, Georg (1992) 'Slave trade, multiculturalism and Islam in colonial Singapore: a sociological note on Christian Snouck Hurgronje's 1891 article on slave trade in Singapore,' *Southeast Asian Journal of Social Science*, 20/1: 67–79.

Steenbrink, Karel (1993) *Dutch colonialism and Indonesian Islam, contacts and conflicts 1596–1950*, Amsterdam: Rodopi.

Stilwell, Sean (1999) '"*Amana*" and "*asiri*": royal slave culture and the colonial regime in Kano, 1903–1926,' in Suzanne Miers and Martin Klein, eds, *Slavery and colonial rule in Africa*, London: Frank Cass, 167–88.

———— (2004) 'The development of "mamluk" slavery in the Sokoto caliphate,' in Paul E. Lovejoy, ed., *Slavery on the frontiers of Islam*, Princeton, NJ: Markus Wiener, 87–110.

Strobel, Margaret (1979) *Muslim women in Mombasa, 1890–1975*, New Haven, CT: Yale University Press.

Sugar, Peter F. (1977) *Southeastern Europe under Ottoman rule, 1354–1804*, Seattle: University of Washington Press.

Sullivan, Patrick (1982) *Social relations of dependence in a Malay state: nineteenth-century Perak*, Kuala Lumpur: Malaysian Branch of the Royal Asiatic Society.

Sutherland, Heather (1983) 'Slavery and slave trade in South Sulawesi, 1660s–1800s,' in Anthony Reid, ed., *Slavery, bondage and dependency in Southeast Asia,* Saint Lucia: University of Queensland Press, 263–85.

Sy, Yaya (2000) 'L'esclavage chez les Soninkés: du village à Paris,' *Journal des Africanistes,* 70/1–2: 43–69.

Tabandeh, Sultanhussein (1970) *A Muslim commentary on the Universal Declaration of Human Rights,* London: F. T. Goulding.

Taha, Mahmoud M. (1987) *The second message of Islam,* Syracuse University Press.

Talbi, Mohamed (1981) 'Law and economy in Ifriqiya (Tunisia) in the third Islamic century: agriculture and the role of slaves in the country's economy,' in A. L. Udovitch, ed. *The Islamic Middle East, 700–1900: studies in economic and social history,* Princeton, NJ: Darwin Press, 209–49.

Taleqani, Seyyed Mahmood (1983) *Islam and ownership,* Lexington, KY: Mazda Publishers.

Talhami, Ghada H. (1977) 'The Zanj Rebellion reconsidered,' *International Journal of African Historical Studies,* 10/3: 443–61.

Taylor, Jean G. (1983) *The social world of Batavia: European and Eurasian in Dutch Asia,* Madison: University of Wisconsin Press.

Temimi, Abdeljelil (1971) *Recherches et documents d'histoire maghrébine: la Tunisie, l'Algérie et la Tripolitaine, de 1816 à 1871,* Université de Tunis.

—— (1985) 'L'affranchissement des esclaves et leurs recensements au milieu du XIXe siècle,' *Revue d'Histoire Maghrébine,* 39–40: 213–18.

Theobald, Alan B. (1951) *The Mahdiyya: a history of the Anglo-Egyptian Sudan, 1881–1899,* London: Longmans.

Thomas, Bertram (1937) *The Arabs,* London: Thornton Butterworth.

—— (1938) *Arabia Felix: across the empty quarter of Arabia,* London: Readers' Union.

Thomaz, Luís Filipe F. R. (1994) 'A escravatura em Malaca no século XVI,' *Studia,* 53: 253–316.

Thosibo, Anwar (2002) *Historiografi perbudakan: sejarah perbudakan di Sulawesi Selatan abad XIX,* Magelang: Indonesiatera.

Tjokroaminoto [Cokroaminoto], H. O. S. (c. 1950) *Islam dan socialisme, tertulis di Mataram dalam bulan November 1924,* Jakarta: Bulan Bintang.

Toledano, Ehud R. (1982) *The Ottoman slave trade and its suppression,* Princeton University Press.

—— (1984) 'The imperial eunuchs of Istanbul: from Africa to the heart of Islam,' *Middle Eastern Studies,* 3: 379–90.

—— (1993) 'Ottoman conceptions of slavery in the period of reform, 1830s–1880s,' in Martin A. Klein, ed., *Breaking the chains: slavery, bondage and emancipation in modern Africa and Asia,* Madison: University of Wisconsin Press, 37–63.

—— (1998) *Slavery and abolition in the Ottoman Middle East,* Seattle: University of Washington Press.

el-Tounsy, Mohammed ibn-Omar (1845) *Voyage au Darfour,* ed. and tr. S. Perron, Paris: Benjamin Duprat.

—— (1851) *Voyage au Ouadây*, ed. and tr. S. Perron, Paris: Benjamin Duprat.

Townsend, John (1977) *Oman: the making of the modern state*, London: Croom Helm.

Toynbee, Arnold J. (1927) *Survey of international affairs, 1925*, Vol. 1: *The Islamic world since the peace settlement*, London: Oxford University Press.

Triaud, Jean-Louis (1995) *La légende noire de la Sanussiya: une confrérie musulmane saharienne sous le regard français, 1840–1930*, Paris: Maison des Sciences de l'Homme.

Trimingham, J. Spencer (1959) *Islam in West Africa*, Oxford: Clarendon Press.

—— (1964) *Islam in East Africa*, Oxford: Clarendon Press.

—— (1965) *Islam in Ethiopia*, London: Frank Cass, reprint of 1952 edn.

Trocki, Carl A. (1979) *Prince of pirates: the Temenggongs and the development of Johor and Singapore, 1784–1885*, Singapore University Press.

Trotman, David V., and Lovejoy, Paul E. (2004) 'Community of believers: Trinidad Muslims and the return to Africa, 1810–1850,' in Paul E. Lovejoy, ed., *Slavery on the frontiers of Islam*, Princeton, NJ: Markus Wiener, 219–32.

Tsai, Shih-shan H. (1996) *The eunuchs in the Ming dynasty*, Albany, NY: State University of New York Press.

et-Tsouli, 'Aly (1907–09) 'Traduction de la fetoua du Faqih Sidi 'Aly et Tsouli, contenant le "soual" du Hadji Abdelqader ben Mahdi ed Din et la réponse,' tr. E. Michaux-Bellaire, *Archives Marocaines*, 11: 116–28, 394–45, and 15: 157–84.

Tucker, Judith E. (1985) *Women in nineteenth-century Egypt*, Cambridge University Press.

Turton, Andrew (1980) 'Thai institutions of slavery,' in James L. Watson, ed., *Asian and African systems of slavery*, Oxford: Basil Blackwell, 251–92.

al-Tusi, Nadir al-Din (1964) *The Nasirean ethics*, tr. and ed. G. M. Wickens, London: George Allen and Unwin.

[Ufford, H. Quarles van] (1856) *Aantekeningen betreffende eene reis door de Molukken van Z. E. den Gouverneur-Generaal Mr. A. J. Duymaer van Twist*, The Hague: Martinus Nijhoff.

Valensi, Lucette (1969) *Le Maghreb avant la prise d'Alger, 1790–1830*, Paris: Flammarion.

—— (1977) *Fellahs tunisiens: l'économie rurale et la vie des campagnes aux 18e et 19e siècles*, Paris: Mouton.

Vecchi di Val Cismon, Cesare M. de (1935) *Orizzonti d'impero: cinque anni in Somalia*, Milan: A. Mondadori.

Velthoen, Esther J. (1997) 'Wanderers, robbers, and bad folk: the politics of violence, protection and trade in eastern Sulawesi, 1750–1850,' in Anthony Reid, ed., *The last stand of Asian autonomies: responses to modernity in the diverse states of Southeast Asia and Korea, 1750–1900*, Basingstoke: Macmillan, 367–88.

Verger, Pierre (1968) *Flux et reflux de la traite des nègres entre le Golfe de Bénin et Bahia de Todos os Santos, du XVIIe au XIXe siècle*, Paris and The Hague: Mouton.

Verkerk Pistorius, A. W. P. (1868) 'Iets over de slaven en de afstammelingen van slaven in de Padangsche Bovenlanden,' *Tijdschrift voor Nederlansch-Indië*, 2/1: 434–43.

Verlinden, Charles (1955) *L'esclavage dans l'Europe mediévale*, Tome premier: *Péninsule ibérique, France*, Bruges: De Tempel.

Veth, P. J. (1873) *Atjin en zijn betrekkingen tot Nederland; topographisch-historisch beschrijving*, Leiden: Gualth Kolff.

Vikør, Knut S. (1995) *Sufi and scholar on the desert edge: Muhammad b. 'Ali al-Sanusi and his brotherhood*, London: Hurst.

―――― (2000) 'Sufi Brotherhoods in Africa,' in Nehemia Levtzion and Randall L. Pouwels, eds, *The history of Islam in Africa*, Athens: Ohio University Press, 441–76.

Vila Vilar, Enriqueta (1990) 'La postura de la iglesia frente a la esclavitud, siglos XVI y XVII,' in Francisco de Solano and Agustín Guimerá, eds, *Esclavitud y derechos humanos, la lucha por la libertad del negro en el siglo XIX*, Madrid: Consejo Superior de Investigaciones Científicas, 25–31.

Vilhena, Ernesto Jardim de (1906) 'A influencia Islámica na costa oriental d'Africa,' *Boletim da Sociedade de Geografia de Lisboa*, 24/5–7: 133–46, 166–80 and 197–218.

Vlora, Ekrem Bey (1911) *Aus Berat und vom Tomor*, Sarajevo: Daniel a Kajon.

―――― (1968) *Lebenserinnerungen*, Munich: R. Oldenbourg.

Wadud, Amina (2000) 'Alternative Qur'anic interpretation and the status of Muslim women,' in Gisela Webb, ed., *Windows of faith: Muslim women scholar-activists in North America*, Syracuse University Press, 3–21.

Wafi, 'Ali 'Abd el-Wahid (1967) 'Human rights in Islam,' *Islamic Quarterly*, 11/1–2: 64–75. [See also Elwahed.]

Waines, David (1995) *An introduction to Islam*, Cambridge University Press.

Walker, Benjamin (1998) *Foundations of Islam: the making of a world faith*, London: Peter Owen.

Walter, H. A. (1998) *The Ahmadiyya movement*, New Delhi: Manohar, reprint of 1918 edn.

Walz, Terence (1985) 'Black slavery in Egypt during the nineteenth-century, as reflected in the Mahkama archives of Cairo,' in John R. Willis, ed., *Slaves and slavery in Muslim Africa*, London: Frank Cass, Vol. II, 137–60.

al-Wanscharisi [Wansharisi], Ahmad (1908–9) 'La pierre de touche des fétwas,' tr. E. Amar, *Archives Marocaines*, 12–13.

Warburg, Gabriel R. (1981) 'Ideological and practical considerations regarding slavery in the Mahdist state and the Anglo-Egyptian Sudan, 1881–1918,' in Paul E. Lovejoy, ed., *The ideology of slavery in Africa*, Beverley Hills, CA: Sage, 245–70.

Warren, James F. (1981) *The Sulu zone, 1768–1898: the dynamics of external trade, slavery and ethnicity in the transformation of a Southeast Asian maritime state*, Singapore: Singapore University Press.

Watson, Adam (2002) 'Muhammad the abolitionist: slavery in the Qur'an' <http://home.insight.com/~adamwatson/showcase/quranslavery.html>

Watson, James L. (1980) 'Transactions in people: the Chinese market in slaves, servants, and heirs,' in James L. Watson, ed., *Asian and African systems of slavery*, Oxford: Basil Blackwell, 223–50.

Watson, R. L. (1990) *The slave question: liberty and property in South Africa*, Hanover, NH: Wesleyan University Press.

Wei, Alice B. G. (1974) 'The Moslem rebellion in Yunnan, 1855–1873,' PhD thesis, University of Chicago.

Wertheim, W. F. (1959) *Indonesian society in transition: a study of social change*, Brussels and The Hague: A. Manteau and W. van Hoeve.

Wilkinson, John C. (1987) *The Imamate tradition of Oman*, Cambridge University Press.

Williams, Brian G. (2001) *The Crimean Tatars: the diaspora experience, and the forging of a nation*, Leiden: E. J. Brill.

Willis, John R. (1967) 'Jihad fi sabil Allah: its doctrinal basis in Islam, and some aspects of its evolution in nineteenth-century West Africa, *Journal of African History*, 8/3: 395–415.

—— (1979) *Studies in West African Islam*, Vol. 1: *The cultivators of Islam*, London: F. Cass.

—— (1980) 'Islamic Africa: reflections on the servile estate,' *Studia Islamica*, 52: 183–97.

Willis, John R. (1989) *In the path of Allah: the passion of al-Hajj 'Umar, an essay into the nature of charisma in Islam*, London: Frank Cass.

—— ed. (1985) *Slaves and slavery in Muslim Africa*, London: Frank Cass.

Willis, C. J. (1891) *In the land of the lion and the sun, or modern Persia*, London: Ward, Lock, 2nd edn.

Winder, R. Bayly (1965) *Saudi Arabia in the nineteenth-century*, London: Macmillan.

Wink, André (1999) *Al-Hind: the making of the Indo-Islamic world*, Vol. 1 and 2, New Delhi: Oxford University Press.

Winstedt, Richard (1981) *The Malays: a cultural history*, ed. Tham Seong Chee, Singapore: Graham Brash.

Winter, Michael (1992) *Egyptian society under Ottoman rule, 1517–1798*, London: Routledge.

Wirz, Albert (1984) *Sklaverei und kapitalistisches Weltsystem*, Frankfurt-am-Main: Suhrkamp.

Wittek, Paul (1955) 'Devshirme and shari'a,' *Bulletin of the School of Oriental and African Studies*, 17/2: 271–8.

Wolf, John B. (1979) *The Barbary coast: Algiers under the Turks, 1500–1830*, New York: Norton.

Worcester, Dean C. (1913) *Slavery and peonage in the Philippine Islands*, Manila: Bureau of Printing.

Wright, John (1989) *Libya, Chad and the central Sahara*, London: Hurst.

Wuld al-Bara, Yahya (1997) 'Les théologiens mauritaniens face au colonialisme français: étude de *fatwa*-s de jurisprudence musulmane,' in

David Robinson and Jean-Louis Triaud, eds, *Le temps des marabouts: itinéraires et stratégies islamiques en Afrique Occidentale Française, v. 1880–1960*, Paris: Karthala, 85–117.

Wyatt, David K. (1982) *Thailand, a short history*, New Haven, CT: Yale University Press.

Yamba, C. Bawa (1995) *Permanent pilgrims: the role of the pilgrimage in the lives of West African Muslims in the Sudan*, Washington, DC: Smithsonian Institution Press.

Yarikkaya, Gulay (2004) 'Becoming a *devsirme*,' paper for 'Children in Slavery' conference, Avignon, 19–21 May, under consideration for publication.

Yegar, Moshe (1975) 'The abolition of servitude in British Malaya: an historical analysis,' *Israel Yearbook on Human Rights*, 5: 202–13.

Yemelianova, Galina M. (2002) *Russia and Islam: a historical survey*, Basingstoke: Palgrave.

Young, George (1905–6) *Corps de droit ottoman: recueil des codes, lois, règlements, ordonnances et actes les plus importants du droit intérieur, et études sur le droit coutumier de l'empire ottoman*, Oxford: Clarendon Press.

Young, Ken (1994) *Islamic peasants and the state: the 1908 anti-tax rebellion in West Sumatra*, New Haven, CT: Yale University.

Zaidi, M. H. (1935) *Mothers of the faithful: being a discourse on polygamy, with a biographical sketch of the wives of Muhammad*, Calcutta: the author.

Zambaco, Demetrius A. (1911) *Les eunuques d'aujourd'hui et ceux de jadis*, Paris: Masson et Cie.

el-Zein, A. H. M. (1974) *The sacred meadows: a structural analysis of religious symbolism in an East African town*, Evanston, IL: Northwestern University Press.

Zelkina, Anna (2000) *In quest for God and freedom: Islam, society and politics in the nineteenth century in the northern Caucasus*, London: Hurst.

Zeys, E. (1886) *Législation mozabite: son origine, ses sources, son présent, son avenir*, Algiers: Adolphe Jourdan.

Zouber, Mahmoud A. (1977) *Ahmad Baba de Tombouctou, 1556–1627: sa vie et son oeuvre*, Paris: Maisonneuve et Larose.

Zwemer, Samuel M., (1965) *Islam, a challenge to faith*, London: Darf, reprint of 1907 edn.

INDEX